LEONARDO

Supplemental Issue 1988

JOURNAL OF THE INTERNATIONAL SOCIETY FOR THE ARTS, SCIENCES AND TECHNOLOGY

ELECTRONIC ART

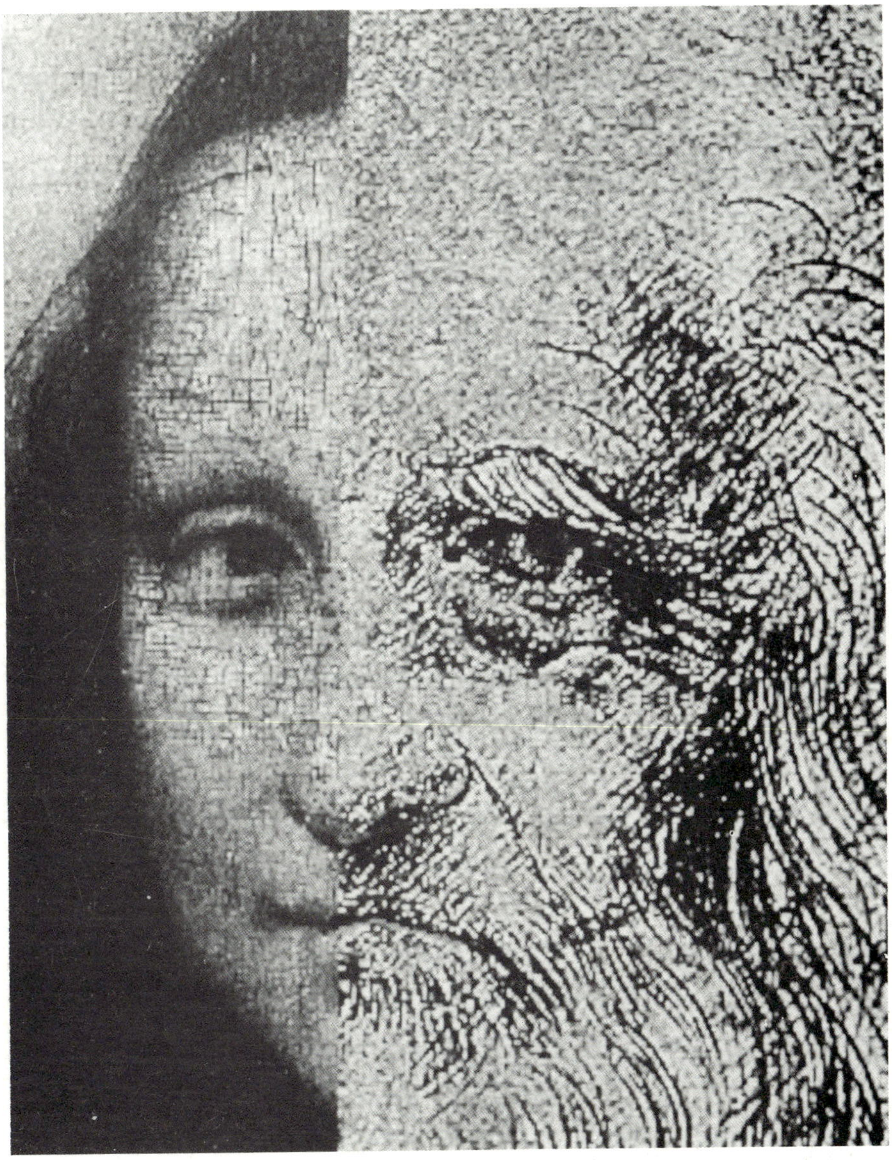

Pergamon Press

OXFORD · NEW YORK · BEIJING · FRANKFURT · SÃO PAULO · SYDNEY · TOKYO · TORONTO

First International Symposium on Electronic Art

September 27–30, 1988

Presented by the Foundation for Creative Computer Applications (SCCA) and the Center for Art, Media and Technology of the Utrecht Academy of Arts

Acknowledgments
The members of the Organizing Committee wish to express their gratitude to the following for their cooperation and support:
Ministry of Economic Affairs
Ministry of Welfare, Health and Culture Affairs
Gemeente Utrecht
Provincie Utrecht
A. Fentener van Vlissingenfonds
Anjerfonds Utrecht
Computer Music Association
I.S.A.S.T./*Leonardo*
KLM
Netherlands Universities Foundation for International Cooperation (NUFFIC)
Royal Dutch Jaarbeurs
Stichting Post Kunstvakonderwijs
Stichting voor Publieksvoorlichting over Wetenschap en Techniek (PWT)

Secretariat
SCCA/FISEA
P. O. Box 23330
3001 KJ Rotterdam
The Netherlands
Telephone: 31-10-4 36 0371
Fax: 31-10-4 36 0346
E-mail: movax!hku!fisea

Leonardo Supplementary Issue—Electronic Art

Published in conjunction with the First International Symposium on Electronic Art

Coordinating Editor
Pamela Grant-Ryan

Main Editorial Office
Leonardo
2020 Milvia Street
Berkeley, CA 94704, U.S.A.

European Editorial Office
Leonardo
8 rue Émile Dunois
92100 Boulogne sur Seine, France

Executive Editor
Roger F. Malina

Managing Editor
Pamela Grant-Ryan

Associate Editors
Lisa Bornstein
Elizabeth Crumley
Marjorie Malina
Christine Maxwell
Susannah Gardiner

Electronic Composition
Richard A. Wilson/Intelligent Tool & Eye

Design
Thomas Ingalls + Associates, San Francisco

Publisher's Offices

Pergamon Press plc, Headington Hill Hall, Oxford OX3 0BW, U.K. Tel. 0865 64881

Pergamon Press Inc., Maxwell House, Fairview Park, Elmsford, NY 10523, U.S.A. Tel 914–592 7700

ISBN 0–08–036978–2

Indexed/Abstracted in
Current Contents, RILM Abstracts

The Item-Fee Code for this publication is:
0024-094X/88 $3.00 + 0.00
ISBN 0-08-036978-2 ISSN 0024-094X
LEONDP SUPP 1–123 (1988)

CONTENTS

ELECTRONIC ART

Front cover: Lillian F. Schwartz, *Mona Leo*, computer-generated image, 1987. Side-by-side juxtapositioned halves of the *Mona Lisa* and reversed *Self-Portrait* by Leonardo da Vinci. The striking unity of these two 'different' subjects led Lillian Schwartz to identify Leonardo as the primary model for the *Mona Lisa*, thereby bringing the 500-year-old riddle of the identity of the celebrated surface *Mona Lisa* to a remarkable conclusion.

LEONARDO

Supplemental Issue 1988

JOURNAL OF THE INTERNATIONAL SOCIETY FOR THE ARTS, SCIENCES AND TECHNOLOGY

£16.50

EDITORIAL

The First International Symposium on Electronic Art (FISEA)

Computers are more and more becoming creative tools in music as well as visual arts and design. In the last few years, it has become clear that digital technology provides a platform for multimedia productions as well as a medium for new art forms. Computer Music and Computer Graphics & Animation have their own international forums. The need was felt, however, to bring together in one international event the diverse disciplines within art and technology.

The initial announcement of the First International Symposium on Electronic Art (FISEA) by the Foundation for Creative Computer Applications (SCCA) in 1986 attracted great interest and support for the idea. A joint Call for Proposals and Participation was distributed by the SCCA and the new Centre for Art, Media and Technology of the Utrecht Academy of Arts in 1987. This resulted in several hundreds of papers, contributions to the competitions, proposals for the exhibition, music performances and so on. Unfortunately, only a relatively small number of the papers and other proposals could be accepted for inclusion in the symposium program due to limitations in time and space.

The selection, done by the International Program Committee and the Organizing Committee, was not an easy job because of the high quality of most of the contributions. A number of the selected papers appear in this special issue of *Leonardo*, journal of the International Society for the Arts, Sciences and Technology.

FISEA was meant to bring together experts (artists, scientists and engineers) in the field of electronic art. The enormous international interest in this event shows the importance of continued research and development in this interdisciplinary field. The availability of the new headquarters of the Centre for Art, Media and Technology will further stimulate the international interest in applications of new technology in music, visual arts and design. The centre offers students as well as artists and faculty the opportunity to work and study in an international environment.

TON HOKKEN

Director, Research and Development, Utrecht Academy of Arts

Conference Chairman, Member of the Board, SCCA

JOHAN DEN BIGGELAAR

Coordinator, Centre for Art, Media and Technology, Utrecht Academy of Arts

Conference Chairman

WIM VAN DER PLAS

Director, SCCA

Advisor, FISEA

Pergamon Press plc. Printed in Great Britain.
0024-094X/88 $3.00+0.00

Perceptual Correspondences of Abstract Animation and Synthetic Sound

Adriano Abbado

ABSTRACT

Composing with timbres involves an approach that is very different from the usual way of conceiving traditional Western music. In fact, it is problematic to attempt to organize timbres according to traditional principles. The author believes that if it is possible to establish links between audio and video events, then it is both possible to use the visual language to organize a music composition and possible to create abstract visual objects that correspond to synthetic sounds, consequently having a bi-univocal link between audio and video events. The relationships between abstract animation and synthetic sounds are investigated in light of the correspondences between sound timbres and visual shapes, between perceived audio and video spatial locations and between perceived audio and video intensities. An audiovisual work called *Dynamics* was based on these correspondences.

In order better to explain why I am interested in such a project, I would like to review the steps that in the past have led me to this current research.

I started to be interested in 'musique concrète' and electronic music in 1974. In 1975, I began to study electronic music at the Conservatory of Milan. My music compositions since then have been conceived together with images. At first, in order to have a visual counterpart, I used simple tools such as slides and lights, but soon realized that a dynamic medium would be necessary to match the time-based structure of music. Therefore, I decided to paint a Super8-mm film by hand: I exposed a blank film to light without a camera and painted the transparent result with different inks. The final film was a very fast sequence of spots changing colors and shapes. The film was then coupled with a soundtrack containing a similar sequence of events. Even though there was not a one-to-one correlation between the audio and visual events, the effect was striking and successful. However, at that time I was not aware of the abstract films that many artists produced in the 1920s and 1930s using many different techniques, such as hand painting, optical filters and colored papers, to create dynamic synthetic shapes [B2, B19, B24, B32, V9, V10, V13–V22, V26, V29–V35]. The first abstract film ever produced was probably *Diagonal Symphony* by Viking Eggeling (1921), while the first abstract film with a synthetic soundtrack (i.e. not recorded) was *Tonende Handschrift* by Rudolf Pfenninger (1929). In *Tonende Handschrift,* Pfenninger painted the area of the film normally used for the soundtrack, thereby controlling the sound with a synthetic tool. It was particularly important and encouraging for me to realize that the way I was following was not new and, on the contrary, that many artists had been on the same track in the past.

The first decades of this century were very active in terms of experimentation with mixed media. Artists such as Scriabin, Kandinsky and Klee were interested in combining music and visual arts [B17]. Even more important, the Soviet director Eisenstein was the first artist to create a movie based on a contemporary composition, *Alexander Nevsky* by Prokofiev [V11]. Eisenstein also introduced many important ideas for organizing the visual and the musical aspects of film when creating the work and when editing. He wrote several books in which he explained his montage technique in detail and stated the possibility of having an *audiovisual counterpoint,* a fundamental concept for this kind of art [B7]. However, although he introduced new ideas about audiovisual language, his movies were narrative, and in this sense traditional, while the other filmmakers I have mentioned created non-narrative films, the kind that I have always been interested in. It is interesting to note, however, that towards the end of the 1920s music visualization using abstract animation was quite popular in Europe, and it was regularly shown in public theatres. The most famous of these filmmakers, O. Fishinger, was even hired by the Disney studios to direct part of the film *Fantasia.*

I saw many of those films and other films made in the 1940s and 1950s [V23, V25–V28, V37, V38] and realized that the electronic media would be suited for me to create audiovisual works. I subsequently came across other artists' work. I found that John Whitney Sr.'s concepts were ideally connected to the works of the early filmmakers, since Whitney has always created abstract films and videos. Also, Whitney began in the 1940s using the film as physical support, but subsequently ended up with videotape and eventually computers as image generators [B40, V38–V44]. I, too, began to use computers, an Apple II Plus specifically, in order to create images and music with a digital medium. The main advantage of such a medium is the great control of each event in the audio and video domains. My ideal has always been to have a common software controlling the audio and video devices.

I started creating several works with digital media in 1981. These included *Orbital City,* which used a common structure for the music and the images. Produced with a Yamaha CX5M, a small computer with low-resolution graphics and FM capabilities, *Orbital City* took into account many interesting ideas about the meaning of sacred shapes and their correlation with ancient music [B3, B4, B18, B33, B34, V1].

In the last few years I have met with other artists involved in this particular art field, and I have seen many other videos and works related to this idea [B8, B10, B11, B13, B14, V4–V8, V12, V36, V45, V46]. Even though some of the works and ideas were not interesting to me, they all contributed to a better understanding of how to continue this fascinating research. For example, in Milan I met painter called Luigi

Adriano Abbado, M.I.T. Media Lab., 20 Ames Street, Cambridge, MA 02139, U.S.A.
Received 25 April 1988.

Pergamon Press plc. Printed in Great Britain.
0024-094X/88 $3.00+0.00

Veronesi, who wrote an interesting paper *Proposta per una ricerca sui rapporti suono/colore* (Proposal for research about the relationships sound/color) [B38]. I then composed several pieces based on Veronesi's ideas and variations and displayed them at the Venice Biennale under the title *Isomorfismi Suono Luce* (Isomorphisms Sound Light) [V2].

DYNAMICS

Dynamics, which has received support from the Council for the Arts at M.I.T., is based on correspondences between aural and visual objects. The correspondences are extended across several perceived parameters of the audio and video objects. In *Dynamics* there are three fundamental correspondences between the audio and video events: timbre-shape, perceived location and perceived intensity.

Timbre-Shape

I have decided to establish this correspondence because I think that timbre and shape are the features that best define what we hear and see, respectively. Arnold Schoenberg more precisely states in his *Harmonielehre,* "I think that sound reveals itself by means of the timbre and that pitch is a dimension of the timbre. The timbre is therefore the whole, the pitch is part of this whole, or better, pitch is nothing more than timbre measured in just one dimension" [B35]. However, one of the original goals of this project was to create a composition using complex timbres. My musical interest is in fact highly concentrated on timbres. I think that timbre has become one of the areas of major interest in contemporary music [B35, B37]. One of the great innovations that computers have brought to music has been the possibility of synthesizing new sounds, immensely increasing the number of instruments a composer can deal with. Jean-Claude Risset and David Wessel also stated, "With the control of timbre now made possible through analysis and synthesis, composers . . . can articulate musical compositions on the basis of timbral rather than pitch variations. . . . It is conceivable that proper timbral control might lead to quite new musical architectures" [B28]. In the visual domain, I believe that shape is the element that defines an object. However, I think that the actual physical phenomena of sound and light have very different properties and behavior than hearing and vision. Nevertheless, I think that in our minds there are similar 'categories' (qualities) common to vision, hearing and other senses [B12]. This is why I believe it makes sense to speak, in everyday language, about 'cold color' or 'harsh sound' and so forth [B6, B16, B20, B21, B26–B28, B34, B39].

Perceived Spatial Location

This correspondence is established between the positions of the audio and video sources in a space. For instance, a visual object located in a certain position in space emits its sound from the same location. One way to achieve this result is to use a video projector, a big screen and four speakers located at corners of the screen. The speakers then create not only the usual stereo image (right-left), but also the top-bottom image, filling the area of the screen. However, the perception of the localization of sounds is not as precise as that of visual elements and is a function of the spectral content of the sound [B15, B36]. This fact influences the way I imagine the size of the shapes to be matched with the sounds. In other words, the original size of a certain shape is a function of the spatial extension of the corresponding sound, which is in turn a function of the spectral content of the sound itself.

Perceived Intensity

Another precise correspondence is between the perceived intensities of the audio and video events (loudness and brightness). As loudness changes, following an envelope, so does the brightness of the corresponding shape change. Eventually, the visual object can fade out while the loudness becomes zero [B15]. This correspondence has a side effect: since the attack of sounds influences the perception of timbres, the envelope of sounds can modify not only the brightness of the visual object, but also its shape.

When creating the correspondence, my approach is:

- I create a sound I am interested in. It is usually easier to model shapes on sounds than vice versa.
- I sketch an outline of the temporal behavior of the main components of the timbre.
- I imagine a shape that changes over time and matches the behavior of sound and I write down a description of the shape.
- When creating the 3-D model I listen again to the sound and if necessary modify the model so that it matches the sound. Since often the timbre changes over time, so does the shape. In order to produce this effect, I use three different methods:
    1. I create two 3-D models (initial and final) that are then interpolated when animated (in some cases I use more than two models).
    2. I rotate the object along one (or more) axes. Since the shape is irregular, it reveals other aspects that have not been seen yet.
    3. I use two (or more) different objects. At the beginning, object one is hidden by object two. Then object two arises, creating a more complex shape. This process can be reversed (two objects initially) and is particularly useful when I am dealing with processes of spectral fusion [B22, B23].

The way I decide how much to match timbres with shapes is clearly very important. I associate low-energy spectra with smooth shapes and high-energy spectra with edged shapes. I use textures and colors to enhance the idea already provided by the shape. Harmonic sounds become non-reflectant objects, while inharmonic sounds are associated with shiny and metallic objects. For example, white noise is represented with a highly irregular, bumpy and shiny object. Or, I have described an inharmonic sound with high energy content as rotary blades. Also, a sound that is present (i.e with components around 2000 Hz) is represented as close to the viewer.

Bibliography

B1. Adriano Abbado, Claudio Mordá and Gianluigi Rocca, *Immagini con il Computer* (Milan: Mondadori, 1985).

B2. Alfio Bastiancich, *L'opera di Norman McLaren* (Turin: Giappichelli, 1981).

B3. Louis Charpentier, *Les Mystères de la Cathédrale de Chartres* (Robert Laffont).

B4. Jules Combarieu, *La Musica e la Magia* (Milan: Mondadori, 1982).

B5. Charles Dodge and Thomas A. Jerse, *Computer Music* (New York: Macmillan, 1984).

B6. David Ehresman and David Wessel, *Perception of Timbral Analogies* (Paris: IRCAM, 1978).

B7. Sergei M. Eisenstein, *La natura non indifferente* (Venezia: Marsilio Editori, 1981).

B8. Brian Evans, "Integration of Music and Graphics through Algorithmic Congruence", *Proceedings of the 1987 International Computer Music*

Conference (Urbana, IL: University of Illinois at Urbana–Champaign, 1987).

B9. James D. Foley and Andries Van Dam, *Fundamentals of Interactive Computer Graphics* (Reading, MA: Addison–Wesley, 1984).

B10. Herbert W. Franke, *Computer-Grafik Galerie* (Cologne: DuMont Buchverlag, 1984).

B11. Herbert W. Franke, *Computer Graphics–Computer Art* (Berlin: Springer-Verlag, 1985).

B12. Howard Gardner, *Frames of Mind* (New York: Basic Books, 1983).

B13. Theo Goldberg, "The Prefiguration of a Musical Composition: Model of a Computer Graphics Program", unpublished paper (University of British Columbia).

B14. Theo Goldberg, "Frequency Modulation and Illumination of Colored Surfaces: An Analogy", unpublished paper (University of British Columbia).

B15. David Green, *An Introduction to Hearing* (Hillsdale, NJ: Lawrence Erlbaum Associates, 1976).

B16. John M. Grey, "An Exploration of Musical Timbre", Doctoral diss. (Stanford University, 1975).

B17. Wassily Kandinsky, *Concerning the Spiritual in Art* (New York: Dover, 1977).

B18. Robert Lawlor, *Sacred Geometry* (London: Thames and Hudson, 1982).

B19. Malcolm Le Grice, *Abstract Film and Beyond* (Cambridge, MA: MIT Press, 1977).

B20. Fred Lerdahl, "Timbral Hierarchies", in S. McAdams, ed., *Contemporary Music Review* **2**, No. 1 (London: Harwood Press, 1987).

B21. Fred Lerdahl, "Cognitive Constraints on Compositional Systems", in J. Sloboda, ed., *Generative Processes of Music* (London: Oxford University Press, 1985).

B22. Steven McAdams, *L'image auditive* (Paris: IRCAM, 1985).

B23. Steven McAdams, *Fusion spectrale et la création d'images auditives* (Paris: IRCAM, 1986).

B24. Jean Mitry, *Storia del cinema sperimentale* (Milan: Mazzotta, 1971).

B25. Michael E. Mortenson, *Geometric Modeling* (New York: John Wiley, 1985).

B26. Jean-Claude Risset, *Musical Acoustics* (Paris: IRCAM, 1978).

B27. Jean-Claude Risset, *Hauteur et timbre des sons* (Paris: IRCAM, 1978).

B28. Jean-Claude Risset and David Wessel, *Indagine sul timbro mediante analisi e sintesi* (Venice: Limb/La Biennale, 1982).

B29. Curtis Roads, *Composers and the Computer* (Los Altos: CA: William Kaufmann, 1985).

B30. David F. Rogers and J. Alan Adams, *Mathematical Elements for Computer Graphics* (New York: McGraw Hill, 1976).

B31. David F. Rogers, *Procedural Elements for Computer Graphics* (New York: McGraw Hill, 1985).

B32. Gianni Rondolino, *Storia del cinema d'animazione* (Turin: Einaudi, 1974).

B33. Marius Schneider, *Il significato della musica* (Milan: Rusconi, 1979).

B34. Marius Schneider, *Pietre che cantano* (Milan: Guanda, 1980).

B35. Arnold Schoenberg, *Harmonielehre* (Vienna: Universal Edition, 1911).

B36. John P. Stautner, "A Flexible Acoustic Ambience Simulator", *Proceedings of the 1982 International Computer Music Conference* (Venice, 1982).

B37. Marco Stroppa, *L'esplorazione e la manipolazione del timbro* (Venice: Limb/La Biennale, 1985).

B38. Luigi Veronesi, *Proposta per una ricerca sui rapporti suono/colore* (Milan: Siemens Data, 1977).

B39. David Wessel, *Low Dimensional Control of Musical Timbre* (Paris: IRCAM, 1978).

B40. John Whitney, *Digital Harmony* (New York: McGraw Hill, 1980).

B41. Iannis Xenakis, *Musique. Architecture* (Paris: Casterman, 1976).

Videography

V1. Adriano Abbado, *Orbital City* (Milan: 1984).

V2. Adriano Abbado, *Isomorfismi Suono Luce* (Milan: Commodore Italiana, 1986).

V3. Adriano Abbado, *Dynamics* (Cambridge, MA: MIT Media Lab., 1988).

V4. Mario Canali, *Minima* (Milan, 1985).

V5. Mario Canali, *Urbana* (Milan, 1986).

V6. Larry Cuba, *3/78* (Champaign, IL: Picture Start, 1978).

V7. Larry Cuba, *Two Space* (Champaign, IL: Picture Start, 1979).

V8. Larry Cuba, *Calculated Movements* (San Francisco: ACM SIGGRAPH Film & Video Show, 1985).

V9. Marcel Duchamp, *Anemic Cinema* (1926).

V10. Viking Eggeling, *Diagonal Symphony* (Berlin: 1925).

V11. Sergei M. Eisenstein, *Alexander Nevsky* (Moscow, 1938).

V12. Brian Evans, *Marie Duet* (Urbana, IL: School of Music, University of Illinois at Urbana–Champaign, 1987).

V13. Oskar Fishinger, *Studies 1–14* (1926–1933).

V14. Oskar Fishinger, *Kreise* (Berlin, 1933).

V15. Oskar Fishinger, *Quadrate* (Berlin, 1933).

V16. Oskar Fishinger, *Komposition in Blau* (Berlin, 1935).

V17. Oskar Fishinger, *Allegretto* (Hollywood, 1936).

V18. Oskar Fishinger, *An Optical Poem* (Hollywood, 1937).

V19. Oskar Fishinger, *Radio Days* (Hollywood, 1941).

V20. Fernand Léger, *Ballet Mécanique* (1924).

V21. Len Lye, *Colour Box* (Glasgow: GPO Film Unit, 1934).

V22. Len Lye, *Kaleidoscope* (Glasgow: GPO Film Unit, 1935).

V23. Jean Mitry, *Images pour Debussy* (1952).

V24. Norman McLaren, *Colour Cocktail* (Glasgow, 1935).

V25. Norman McLaren, *Begone Dull Care* (Ottawa: National Film Board of Canada, 1948).

V26. Norman McLaren, *Workshop Experiment in Animated Sound* (Ottawa: National Film Board of Canada, 1948).

V27. Norman McLaren, *Fiddle de Dee* (Ottawa: National Film Board of Canada, 1948).

V28. Norman McLaren, *Around is Around* (Ottawa: National Film Board of Canada, 1951).

V29. Rudolf Pfenninger, *Tonende Handschrift* (Geiselgasteig, 1929).

V30. Hans Richter, *Rhytmus 21* (Berlin, 1921).

V31. Hans Richter, *Rhytmus 23* (Berlin, 1923)

V32. Hans Richter, *Film Study* (Berlin, 1926).

V33. Walter Ruttmann, *Lichtspiel Opus II* (Berlin, 1921).

V34. Walter Ruttmann, *Lichtspiel Opus III* (Berlin, 1925).

V35. Walter Ruttmann, *Lichtspiel Opus IV* (Berlin, 1927).

V36. Lillian Schwartz, *Pixillation* (1970).

V37. Harry Smith, *Film Number 1–7* (pre-1950).

V38. James Whitney and John Whitney Sr., *Five Film Exercises* (Los Angeles, 1944).

V39. James Whitney, *Lapis* (Los Angeles, 1966).

V40. John Whitney, Sr., *Experiments in Motion Graphics* (Santa Monica, CA: Pyramid, 1968).

V41. John Whitney Sr., *Permutations* (Santa Monica, CA: Pyramid, 1968).

V42. John Whitney Sr., *Matrix* (Santa Monica, CA: Pyramid, 1971).

V43. John Whitney Sr., *Arabesque* (Santa Monica, CA: Pyramid, 1975).

V44. John Whitney Sr., *Victory Sausage* (Pacific Palisades, CA: 1987).

V45. Edward Zajec, *A Pair of Paradoxes.*

V46. Edward Zajec, *Chroma* (Syracuse, NY: Syracuse University, 1986).

Art and Education in the Telematic Culture

Roy Ascott

It was Simon Nora who coined the term *telematics* to describe the new electronic technology derived from the convergence of computers and telecommunications systems. His report to the President of France, *L'Informatisation de la Société*, published in 1978, is perhaps one of the most influential documents in this field to have been published in Europe—influential in that it led to the swift establishment by the French government of the *Programme Télématique*, which has resulted in the transformation of many aspects of French culture. This process of telematisation is most dramatically seen in the ubiquitous and rapid spread of Minitel, the public videotex system that enables widespread interaction between users and databases across an enormous range of services. Nowadays on the Paris Metro, for example, it is enough to see a poster of an island in the sun, a new household appliance, or racehorses pounding the turf, inscribed with a seven-figure sequence of numbers, to know that another Minitel service is being advertised. At home, at one's Minitel terminal (distributed by the PTT in place of volumes of telephone directories previously provided) one can interact in electronic space with friends, colleagues, institutions and organisations of all kinds. Artists, too, have not been slow to assimilate the medium.

Interactivity is the essence of the videotex system, as it is of all telematic systems, giving us the ability to interact in electronic space, via computer memory and beyond the normal constraints of time and space that apply to face-to-face communication. The concept of interactivity also has an important place in recent theories of communication, in contrast to the one-way linearity of older models. The new approach is found, for example, in the network analysis of Rogers and Kinkaid and in research into biology and cognition by Maturana and Varela. Neither of these studies is centrally concerned with electronic systems or telematic technologies. Both, however, deal with human interaction, language, meaning and memory, which is of value in our understanding of the potential of telematic systems to enrich visual culture.

Let me quote from both of these studies:

> Communication research in the past has almost always followed a linear 'components' model of the human communication act. Such research mainly investigated the effects of communication messages from a source to a receiver, in a one-way, persuasive type paradigm that is not consistent with our basic conception of the communication process as mutual information exchange, as sharing means, as convergence. [The new approach] is guided by a convergence model of communication based on a cybernetic explanation of human behaviour from a systems perspective [1].

> According to the metaphor of the tube, communication is something generated at a certain point. It is carried by a conduit (or tube) and is delivered to the receiver at the other end. Hence there is *something* that is communicated, and what is communicated is an integral part of that which travels in the tube. Thus, we speak of the 'information' contained in a picture, an object, or, more evidently, the printed word. According to our analysis, this metaphor is basically false. It presupposes a unity that is not determined structurally, where interactions are instructive, as though what happens to a system in an interaction is determined by the perturbing agent and not by its structural dynamics. It is evident, however, even in daily life, that such is not the case with communication: each person says what he says or hears what he hears according to his own structural determination . . . communication depends on not what is transmitted, but what happens to the person who receives it. And this is a very different matter from 'transmitting information' [2].

In both cases we see that meaning is created out of interaction between people rather than being 'something' that is sent from one to another. If there is an author of this 'meaning' then it may be the system of interaction itself, in all its particulars, that should be described as the author, or, we might want to refer to a 'dispersed authorship' covering all those involved in negotiating for meaning in a given context. Where the context includes artificial memory in a telematic system, the potential for the creation of meaning is greatly enlarged. And when such systems are activated globally, in an art context, we can expect to see quite richly layered fields of 'meaning' being created.

We can see art as a whole, regardless of what media may be employed, as constituting such a system; and where, in any given practice, art objects are involved, for example paintings or sculptures, we can recognise them as parts of a system in which a flux of meanings can be generated dependent upon the variety of interactions that arise within it. Art does not reside in the object alone, nor is meaning fixed or stable within the physical limits of the artist's work. Art is all process, all system. If, in the past, we have thought otherwise—for example, that art is an object, or that the artwork 'carries' a definitive meaning 'created' by the artist and received by the viewer—this can perhaps be understood in the light of our Renaissance heritage. The ordering of space in Renaissance painting, with its absolute rules of representation and of viewing, a space subject to the authority of the vanishing point, which also positioned the viewer in relation to the 'world' and established control of a reality consisting in separate and discrete parts (everything in its place and a place for everything), can be seen as the perfect metaphor of the ordering of parts in the societies to which it gave expression. Renaissance space is authorised as 'real' space by many of those societies in which information flows one way, from the apex of the social pyramid to the base, where it informs the thinking, the orthodoxies, the rules of conduct of

Roy Ascott, 64 Upper Cheltenham Place, Montpelier, Bristol, BS6 5HR, England.

This paper was prepared for the UNESCO Regional Experimental Training Workshop on the Use of audio-visual techniques as instruments of creativity, Ofenbach (F.R.G.) 6–11 December 1987.

Received 29 December 1987.

Pergamon Press plc. Printed in Great Britain.
0024-094X/88 $3.00+0.00

a culture. This one-way despatch fashions consciousness and enforces a dominant scientific paradigm just as the vanishing point and rules of representation determine, within the pyramid of space based at the picture plane, a coherent view of a world presented as 'reality'. Under these circumstances, the art object could well be understood as embodying not only unambiguous meaning and beauty but also absolute truth. This form of representation and this status of the object as art continues today, of course, in some quarters and has to some extent been automated by the photographic process. Its persistence is well understood given the seductive nature of the apparent certainty and coherence it claimed to depict.

But the art of our time is one of system, process, behaviour, interaction. As artists we deal in uncertainty and ambiguity, discontinuity, flux and flow. Our values are relativistic, our culture is pluralistic, and our images and forms are evanescent. If it is processes of interaction between human beings that create meaning and consequently cultures, then those systems and processes that facilitate and amplify interaction are the ones that we shall employ in order for more richly differentiated cultures and meanings to emerge. This is precisely the potential of telematic systems. Rather than limiting the individual to a narrow, parochial level of exchange, computer-mediated cable and satellite links spanning the whole planet open up a whole world community, in all its diversity, within which we can interact. Telematic networks are ubiquitous and can be accessed from virtually any location—the home, public institutions, libraries, hospitals, prisons, bars, beaches and mountain tops, as well as studios, museums, galleries, academies and colleges—anywhere in fact that is reached by telephone, including mobile telephones in cars, trains, ships and planes. The primary effect of creative interaction within such networks is to render obsolete the distinction in absolute terms between the artist and viewer as producer and consumer, respectively. The new composite role becomes that simply of *participant* in a system creating meaning seen as art. This contrasts forcibly with the Renaissance paradigm of the artist standing apart from the world and depicting it and the observer standing outside of the artwork and receiving this depiction. It was a paradigm which placed the scientist, also, outside the world looking in, and in turn led to all kinds of alienation and separateness in society.

Our assertion of *network* as the metaphor for the emerging culture appears to find support in fields beyond art. Quantum physicists, for example, speak of an 'undivided wholeness' at the quantum level of reality, of indeterminate behaviour, of non-local connectivity in the sub-atomic field, of the laboratory experiment being a part of the field of consciousness of the observer as participant. In literary theory and criticism, the status and identity of the 'author' is under scrutiny; the text is seen as a space within which the reader actively generates meanings, rather than as a container of messages and stable form. And in art it was not Duchamp alone who brought the power of context and new position of the observer as participant to our attention. The mobile viewpoint, montage and performance work all have contributed in various ways to breaking down the barriers, towards creating whole systems.

One effect of these holistic strategies in art and science, perhaps most evident in telematic systems, is to give credence to the idea of *mind at large*. In their various contributions to a science of wholeness, the new generalists—Gregory Bateson, with his idea of *an ecology of mind*, and Bertallanfy, with his *general system theory*—perhaps have done most in recent decades to reject the idea of the individual as an isolated entity, separate from his environment and other individuals. And it is the holistic view we must surely take when we consider art in relation to a telematic culture. Bateson argued that human plus computer system plus environment constitutes a thinking system. Just as he challenged the idea of separate, isolated mind that could be differentiated from body and from the individual's environment, so he showed that the lines between human, computer and environment are purely artificial and fictitious. They are the lines *across* the pathways along which information passes and within which meaning is created; they are not boundaries of the thinking system. With the convergence of computers and telecommunications the 'thinking system' becomes planetary.

Isolation and *convergence* are terms that encapsulate what could be seen as the problem and the remedy in our considerations of visual art in the electronic culture. The current problem is one of isolation through a rather crude differentiation between centres of operation in visual culture, inherited largely from the previous century. Despite some notable exceptions, we find for the most part a rather clear separation between atelier, museum, library, concert hall and academy. They are, by and large, autonomous entities, independent systems housed in distinctly separate physical structures. In many museums, as in academies, the flow of communication is usually one-way. Art is identified with objects; architecture is designed to support the consumption of culture rather than actively to participate in its creation. With electronic media, its flow of images and texts, and the ubiquitous connectivity of telematic systems, this isolation and separateness must eventually disappear, and new architectural structures and forms of cultural association will emerge. And in this emergence we can expect to see, as we are beginning to see, new orders of art practice, with new strategies and theories, new forms of public accessibility, new methods of presentation and display, new learning networks—in short whole new cultural configurations.

Within the planetary scope of these new configurations, however, we will want to do everything to avoid a homogenisation of culture. Telematic systems, through the massive memory of computers involved in their articulation, support great diversity and variety of input such that all the differences of individual experience, local culture and regional attributes can be preserved. The aim of a telematic culture cannot be to homogenise experience and unify ideas or conventionalise images but to generate *difference* in that multiplicity of viewpoints, preferences, dreams and concerns—spiritual, political, intellectual—that a whole planetary community can be expected to provide. At the same time, the richness of input that might be expected as creative collaboration around the world increases, and the profusion of images and meanings that could be generated to flow across the planet, will probably lead to a greater awareness of the world as a 'whole'.

It is as if the planet is at the 'stage du miroir', that point in its development when the infant sees in its newly reflected image its own unique identity and gains a sense of self (in this case provided by astronauts and remote sensors in space beaming back to us images of the whole earth). Is it too fanciful to suppose that we are approaching the next stage of planetary awareness—global consciousness? As Peter Russell has pointed out, although it is far from equaling the trillions of synapses through which human nerve cells interact, our global interaction through telecommunication networks, mediated by the hugely increased capability of parallel processing in the next generation of computers, seemingly is reaching a level of complexity and interconnectedness in which we can no longer perceive ourselves as isolated individuals or cultures.

Given the accelerated telematisation of culture, not only can we expect institutions to converge, but we are probably in the position of having to revise all our assumptions about our field of enquiry—that is to say, a complete revision of art in all its roles, institutions, behaviours, codes, protocols, methods, funding and so on. Our inherited conventions of, for example, practice, display, conservation and education in art may soon come to be seen as progressively irrelevant and redundant.

Even a cursory examination of the art academy will show that, while here and there significant changes are taking place, the curricula for the most part contain curious anomalies. Let us take, for example, the case of Life Drawing. While computer systems and other electronic media are moved in, and new paradigms of design and analysis are presented to students, the Life Drawing class in many cases remains not as an historical curiosity but as central—sometimes the anchor—to the practical curriculum. And yet, this is not where the living processes of the body are examined; it is often merely where archaic codes of representation are rehearsed and, in fact, assimilated into the students' consciousness. There we find the body immobilised, without mind; is that not the ideal of all repressive cultures? The practice of life drawing, sometimes called 'objective drawing', is defended as offering a complex structure against which hand-to-eye coordination can be perfected. But is it not hand-to-mind coordination we should seek? Students are frequently misled into thinking that the Life Drawing class is where they will confront 'reality' and that they can acquire a skill to master its representation. The human eye is insufficient to reveal the whole complexity of the living person. The mind, not the eye alone, knows it to be a complex organism, made up of systems within systems, a subtle and continuous transformation of energy and matter. If visual observation in the Life Drawing class is to reach maturity, it requires technological extensions of the senses to give access to the microscopic processes and macroscopic environments by which the 'life model' is maintained. There are many other strategies, in science and in mysticism, for example, that offer us ways into a more holistic understanding of ourselves. It is no longer enough, one might think, to rely on a stub of charcoal and specious historical precedent. For, despite recent marketing of a nostalgic classicism, presented in the guise of a (misunderstood) post-modernism, the project of the art of our century has been essentially to make the invisible visible. Art has progressively sought to be in touch with unseen forces and fields, systems, relationships, connections, and transformations and to make them visible.

And it is the computer that is the matrix through which the abundance of data in all its modes can pass, from remote sensors, scanners, metering devices and difference machines of all kinds. Digitisation can be the 'lingua franca' of an enormous range of visual and notational systems reporting on, recording and analyzing the world, as well as a device through which our dreams, fantasies, speculations and assertions can find expression. The computer is simply a universal machine that can facilitate new modes of communication of desire and of anxiety.

As a matrix it is much more than a stand-alone generator of images, for it extends enormously the capability of the artist to integrate and work between diverse media—film, video, photography, graphics, paint, print and text as well as plotting performance in 'virtual' space and 'virtual' time. This universal machine similarly is spawning output media of considerable variety: electronic image and synthesised sound coexist with print media, cybernetic structures and complex interactive environments. Computer-aided manufacture (CAM) is also open to investigation by the artist.

On the screen we have the power to summon up colour, to draw, erase, recall, mix, split, overlay, reverse images and texts; we can digitise, juxtapose, enlarge, shrink, stack, cut, fuse, file and retrieve material of our own making or made by collaborators—or even made by others unknown to us whose work may be available in a variety of archival sources. The digital mode can lead to endless metamorphosis, realignments, new associations, conjunctions and assimilations of ideas and images.

And let us not forget that this is just the beginning of a technology, despite its exponential growth in the past few decades. Unless we are unusually privileged, we have yet as artists to play with touch-sensitive, high-definition, wall-size computer screens. We are for the most part still tapping keyboards, scratching with light pens and playing with mice. We are at the 'horseless carriage' stage in the development of the artist-friendly interface.

Apart from telematic networks and the computer as matrix of creative work, we also have to consider the environment. As artists, we inhabit, of course, physical as well as electronic space. In this regard, electronic architecture, the information city, is part of our concern. As the Japanese 'Fifth Generation' becomes our generation, it is conceivable that Technopolis City could become a town planning standard. While it is doubtful that 'the city' will become an export commodity on the Tokyo stock exchange, it is clear that many ideas currently being developed through the agency of MITI concerning the design of living environments to support innovation and creativity will find their way to the West. The design brief and supporting portfolio for the 1986 International Concept Design Competition for an Advanced Information City at Kawasaki were breathtaking in the scope of their concerns and the issues they raised. No less comprehensive and visionary is the national Technopolis strategy for the planning of a series of high technology research cities. In all of this the artist and the creative participant in telematic systems will find a place, but that place can be defined properly only with the active involvement of the artist at the outset of the planning process. And this seems to me to be the case whether we are discussing such advanced concepts as MITI is proposing or more discrete projects such as academies or museums. To start with, we probably need to find new terminology to avoid the cultural baggage that the old vocabulary carries. Our first questions should probably be, in every case, what creativity and contact, what creative interaction, can the new institution *as system* be expected to generate and support? And then, as a sub-system of a larger whole, what other sub-systems must we plan to interact with? These are obvious questions to be sure, and yet how often today in our culture do we see new buildings put up ostensibly to serve art while actually they stand alone, physically alienated and alienating in their indifference to the larger processes and systems with which we expect them to integrate? The problem is even greater if we take the view that they are institutions that will increasingly need to serve an emerging culture radically unlike the culture from which they are derived.

The popular conception of high technology, we are told, is that of a sterile, inhuman and emotionless environment. And yet those of us who know of the sheer conviviality of communication in electronic networks, and have come to realise the sensitivity and receptivity towards the generating of images of which the computer is capable, will seek to change this perception. 'Garbage in, garbage out' is I suppose the phrase to invoke here. That is to say, the universal machine—which the computer is—can contain as much creative thought and express as much emotion as we put into it. There is no doubt though that telematic networks and computer systems, used merely as tools of production, will certainly and very effectively promote sterility and alienation in the culture. If we seek wisdom from the past, I imagine it should be to Socrates rather than to Cato we should turn, particularly insofar as the education of the artist is concerned. The principles of Socrates—critical reflection, personal development and sustained enquiry—must not be undermined in this new technological environment by the principles of Cato, which estimated everything by what it produced.

In my view, we might anticipate the dematerialisation of academies, galleries and museums or at least their fusion into pervasive and wide-reaching networks. While the physical presence of material artworks will always be valued in experience, electronic storage and distribution of these works, apart from the purposes of archival research, will come to be enjoyed also as electronic 'traces'. In addition, the ability for students, quite apart from artists themselves, to communicate through telematic networks with skill banks, data banks, artists, experts and professionals in all fields, to participate in world-wide electronic seminars, and to so engage from any location at any time of night or day would add considerably to their current face-to-face contact with a meager handful of professors (however well informed and dedicated as teachers), not to mention technicians, with depleted resources and an inadequate physical plant, housed in buildings designed to support a Beaux Arts culture scarcely attended to since their construction.

In conclusion, I am sure we all recognise that our cultural participation in intelligent telematic networks has long-term implications that we can scarcely imagine. The symbiosis of computers and human beings and the integration of natural and artificial intelligence will be realised in forms and behaviours the understanding of which is beyond our present conceptual horizon.

I would like to affirm what I hope may be confirmed as an outcome of this conference—that there is a need for artists, designers, architects, museum directors, educators, philosophers, scientists, technologists and politicians throughout the world to work together to create telematic networks and nodes of digital hardware and cybernetic systems that will support new forms of art practice, new means of public access and the involvement of a wider range of participants in the emerging global culture and to develop new strategies for creative learning and visual research.

APPENDIX

My professional activities are in two fields: art practice and art education. Below I describe briefly a number of projects in both these fields to illustrate a variety of strategies employing telematic media and interactive behaviour.

In the domain of art practice there are three projects in which I have been closely involved either as instigator, collaborator or participant. First, I was invited by Frank Popper to create a project for his exhibition ELECTRA at the Musée d'Art Moderne de la Ville de Paris in 1983. For this I conceived the idea of *La Plissure du Texte: A Planetary Fairy Tale* (in homage to Roland Barthes' "Le Plaisir du Texte"). This was to involve the creation of a text by 'dispersed authorship' by groups of artists located in 11 cities around the world: Honolulu, Vancouver, San Francisco, Pittsburgh, Toronto, Alma Quebec, Bristol, Paris, Amsterdam, Vienna and Sydney. Each group represented an archetypal fairy tale role or character: trickster, wicked witch, Princess, Wise Old Man, etc. From computer terminals at each location (usually in a public museum, art centre or artist studio) each group participated through an electronic network in the production of a text from the point of view of their assigned role. Thus the story developed and unfolded as each day a piece of text was logged in from each terminal, taking up the theme as it had developed from previous entries. Most terminals were linked to data projectors, enabling the generated text to become a publicly accessible feature of the museum or public place occupied by each group. Many layers of meaning from such diverse sources became embedded in the text; a feast of cultural allusions, puns, flights of imagination and political criticism in an unpredictably meandering and branching story line were pleated together for this 'plissure du texte'. Often the text was ingeniously manipulated to create simple visual images as well. The public too was able to contribute to the fairy tale, interacting within the worldwide dispersal of authorship through keyboards made available to them at most locations.

Second, at the Biennale de Venezia in 1985 I was involved in a planetary network of more ambitious dimensions, which combined electronic text exchange, slow scan TV and telefacsimile with an Apple Macintosh network. This was part of a larger digital laboratory, UBIQUA, which included interactive video disc works, personal computers, paint systems and cybernetically controlled interactive electronic structures and environments of various kinds. This *Art, Technology and Informatics* section of the Biennale was curated by Don Foresta, Tom Sherman, Tomaso Trini and myself as International Commissioners appointed by Maurizio Calvesi. Over 100 artists were involved from three continents. Planet Gaia had begun to beat the digital pulse. I should also explain that the entire exhibition, involving much coordination and planning of both equipment and artists—some to be present in Venice, others dispersed around the planet—was organised by the four commissioners *remotely,* that is, through an electronic mail network that connected our various working locations in Paris, Ottawa, Milan, Venice, Wales, Bristol and Vienna. Since I was regularly commuting at that time between Gwent, Bristol, Lille, Paris and Vienna, I carried a portable terminal with me at all times, a practice that now is habitual.

A third project was a small interactive videotex piece I created at the invitation of the group Art Access for Jean-François Lyotard's exhibition *Les Immatériaux* at the Centre Pompidou in 1985. My contribution was a treatment of two interwoven texts, one from Henri Bue's translation of *Alice in Wonderland* and the other a treatise, *Organe et Fonction,* by two scientists in Montreal. The pleating of the texts created new meanings, as did the selection of pages by users of the system. The piece was dispersed through the Minitel system to thousands of subscribers throughout France. Thus it broke through the physical barrier of the museum just as the exhibition itself sought to break through the barriers of art and science to a new immateriality.

In the domain of art education, I would like to cite three quite different but related projects in which I am or have been centrally involved.

In Austria, where I hold the Chair of Kommunikationstheorie in the Hochschule für angewante Kunst in Wien, on the instigation of Rektor Oswald Oberhuber I have developed, in close cooperation with my assistant Zelko Wiener, a Lehrkanzel devoted to the development of theory and practice of telematic systems and interactivity in the digital mode. This involves students in a electronic space that is planetary in its dimensions, linking them in interaction with students in other countries. Students can come to the Lehrkanzel from all departments of the university, though at present they come principally from the areas of media, graphics and painting. Initially we used a commercial electronic mailbox system accessing artists and art schools in a user group of 26 locations in North America, Europe and Australia. This was purely text exchange, although additionally at the time digital work on disc was exchanged through the postal system. We now use the European Academic Research Network (EARN) with free access and free computer time-sharing. Through EARN we now routinely exchange and collaborate on the production of digital images with students at the Carnegie-Mellon University in Pittsburgh (Pennsylvania), Gwent College in Wales and the City Art Institute in Sydney. Other colleges are set to join the network in the near future. These electronic seminars and collaborations bring my students in Vienna into regular contact with my students at Gwent College, where I am head of the Fine Art course.

The Fine Art course is housed in a new building, designed specifically to support its philosophy. It is wired for complete interactivity: data, video and audio lines link all the spaces, enabling all activities to interact. Monitors throughout the building allow for the flow of electronic images, videotex and digital/video work in progress. A comprehensive switching system allows for a flexible distribution of material and a varied interconnection of media. Just as there is no separation or alienation of diverse media in student practice, electronic media are integrated with the more traditional forms of art practice. The curriculum supports the relativism proper to a post-structuralist, post-modernist endeavour. Much emphasis is placed on the integration of theory and practice. The course is relatively small (120 students) and the provision in terms of personal computers, paint systems, digitising pads, video effects machines, sound synthesisers, video equipment and post production facilities, modems and printers is fairly comprehensive but modest. There is as yet no satellite tracking dish and no large-screen data projection. Essentially the course and its building are a small model of what could be, a testing ground circumscribed economically and by the constraints of a more conventional academic accreditation system. But it is a living model and it shows that an academy can be planned as a network and can network regularly in the wider context of an international electronic space. Well-advanced plans will integrate into a larger interactive network embracing three-dimensional design studies, graphic design and fashion. In my involvement with the development of this strategy at Gwent I have had the close collaboration of Michael Punt, and with recent forays into the extended EARN network, the assistance of Robert Pepperell.

The third, and quite different, telematic project with which I have been involved has been with the French Ministry of Culture as Chargé de Mission of a project for the creation of a centre for teaching and visual research in the Nord Pas-de-Calais region. This was to consider the possible transformation of an existing École des Beaux Arts and a College of Design in two adjacent cities into a telematic, networked entity that could assist in new ways in the release and development of creativity amongst both young people and the newly unemployed in that region. My colleague in the design of this project was Pierre Guislaine. Our basic approach in acquiring resources was to identify and solicit 'partners' in the network who could provide capital equipment, a plant and expertise from amongst the many industrial, scientific, commercial and university institutions in the area. All student learning would be through practical projects located in the real world. Project teams would include teachers drawn from a mixture of disciplines and professions. The entire structure would be decentralised, dispersed and highly interactive and would also constitute an arena in which visual research both in art and in science and technology would combine. The project has been designed but awaits implementation.

References

1. E.M. Rogers and D.L. Kincaid, *Communication Networks: Towards a New Paradigm for Research,* 1981.

2. H.R. Maturana and F.J. Varela, *The Tree of Knowledge: The Biological Roots of Human Understanding,* 1987.

The Electronic Bauhaus: Gestalt Technologies and the Electronic Challenge to Visual Art

Jürgen Claus

ABSTRACT

In linking the historical term 'Bauhaus' with the contemporary term 'electronics' and speaking of the 'Electronic Bauhaus', the author wishes to emphasize the continuity of the new and challenge it to discussion.

Walter Gropius's guiding conception of the Bauhaus as a pioneering school, founded on the idea that the urge to create is "an integral part of the substance of life in a civilized society", included the *grammar of creation*. Today immense efforts are still required to arrive at a grammar of creation pertinent to our own time, efforts that include knowledge of media technology.

This paper focuses on three main topics: the ISDN for art: towards an architecture of communication; ecotechnology: design with ecology; and the expert system artist: fifth-generation computer culture.

The historic Bauhaus belongs to the time of the Weimar Republic, from 1919 to 1933. It was in the 1920s that the school became, as Sibyl Moholy-Nagy points out, "the catalyst of the visual revolution for the 20. century": it provided a new vision for a new society that had to be shaped after the end of World War I [1]. Creation was, for Gropius, neither an intellectual nor a material concept, but an integral part of the life substance of civilized society. It brought together a consciously planned environment, a new scale of visual values, new forms of education and social changes. Technology in this context, at least from 1923 on (and certainly for Laszlo Moholy-Nagy and some others), emerged as the medium "by which a union was made possible between creative intuition and the severe discipline of design: *techne, logos*—the art of knowing how something is made, integrates ancient knowledge with the most futuristic research of the environment" [2].

We begin by taking the concept of an 'electronic Bauhaus' as our model, pointing out critical questions and suggesting the shape of some answers. These answers for the time being must remain provisional. And yet they provide the beginning of a new vision for a new society. It is essential to put art into the context of this new vision. And the challenge is that the participants of the cultural community must define it. To do this we must call upon three fundamental aspects of our artistic heritage: the traditions of art, the imaginary museum of Malraux and the energy phenomenon gleaned over the centuries that art is. However, not only must we familiarize ourselves again with our artistic heritage, we must also become aware of the foundations and standards of our own electronic age. This is an immense task for all of us, and we have not been trained for it. But it is only by using those standards that we can insert art into the living context of the communication society—art and what I call 'Gestalt technology' [3].

Gestalt technology combines *techne* and *logos* with the Gestalt that is created and perceived by humanity as a whole. The term *Gestalt* is a thoroughly German and untranslatable expression. It grew out of German poetry, philosophy and art, and I use the term precisely because of this tradition. Gestalt is related to *Gestaltung*, an emphatic reference to the never-definite, ever-emerging creation. In contrast to the machine-oriented approach of information technology, Gestalt technology embraces human perception and creation. (Art is perception and creation of Gestalt by Gestalt.) To clarify and elaborate on this theme, I focus on three topics: communication, design with ecology, and fifth-generation computer culture.

Fig. 1. Jürgen Claus, *SOLART Expert System*, videotex graphic, 1987. (Photo: H.-J. Hermann)

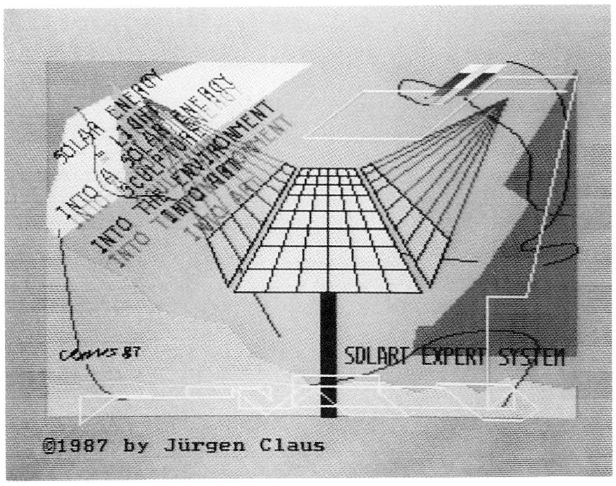

THE ISDN FOR ART: TOWARDS AN ARCHITECTURE OF COMMUNICATION

In evaluating our contemporary systems of networks and telecommunications we must consider their historical roots. In the 1880s Seurat, in his pointillist canvases, had discovered a visual code that might be called a precursor of the digital, pixel-oriented code [4]. The artist had become aware of the single elements of visual articulation—and their significance in establishing the proper meaning of image-communication. From the turn of the century on, art, in the process of becoming increasingly abstract, explored the fundamental meaning of signs, of symbols and of visual metaphors. The Bauhaus books *Point and Line to Plane* (1926) by Kandinsky and *from material to architecture* (1929) by Moholy-Nagy focused on the meaning of individual pri-

Jürgen Claus, Viktoriastrasse 3, D-8000 München 40, Federal Republic of Germany.

Received 5 May 1988.

0024-094X/88 $3.00+0.00

mary visual elements and at the same time their interconnection, or, as we might say, networking. On another level, they focused on the carriers of visual form: the proper technologies and media of creation. In the beginning this revolved around photography, film, light sculptures, sound sculptures and similar media, and again their interrelation. Together these two levels, abstraction and carriers, established the early foundations of an *architecture of communication.*

A third concern of the Bauhaus artists has to do with the social implications of this new synthesis, a concern that has been largely neglected by art historians. In *Vision in Motion* (1947) Moholy-Nagy gives a perceptive insight into the failures of the technological revolution. Although the industrial revolution started with an enthusiastic emphasis on human values, its great metamorphosis as it ushered in the technological revolution served mainly the accumulation of profits, an asocial ethic based on goals of economic superiority rather than on the principles of justice.

> These ills, with their resultant monopolistic and fascist tendencies, finally led to repeated world wars which were cruel attempts to win capitalistic competition. . . . By concentrating insight, passion and stamina, we may recover the neglected fundamentals. . . . By integrating this newly gained knowledge with the existing social dynamics, we could direct our steps toward a harmony of individuals and social needs [5].

Moholy conceived of a "Parliament of social design", made up of culturally active agencies working to restore the basic unity of all human experiences. These form the nuclei of "new, collective forms of cultural and social life" whose goal is "the development of all creative capacities for individual and social fulfillment" [6]. It would be extremely shortsighted not to take into account these historical roots of artistic networking, telecommunication and what I call an 'ISDN' (Integrated Services Digital Network) for art. The Bauhaus aims lead, as we will see, to our present and future fight for a human-oriented approach in expert systems and artificial intelligence.

The architecture of communication found a new structure and quality with the binary digital code, the new primary element of production, storage and transmission. A new alphabet was invented, in which the same characters served for acoustic, verbal and visual communication. "Thinking in relations" (Gropius) was now, at the advent of the 'electronic Bauhaus', implicit in the inner code of the digital age. Because production, transmission and receiving were all based on a single code, it was natural for artists to adopt the code as well as electronic networks. This led to an intercommunication of culture, a culture intercom that was formulated and practiced from the early 1960s on by Stan VanDerBeek. At the time of the first satellite transmissions ("Telstar", 23 July 1962) he proposed Image Libraries as a means for a nonverbal international language. He believed that via satellites and equipped with a code that probes for the "emotional denominator", we could reach any age, any culture. "There are (in 1970) an estimated 700 million people in the world who are unlettered; we have no time to lose or miscalculate" [7]. When telecommunication began being used in the arts community in the second half of the 1970s, satellite technology was part of it. The virtual image of an object, the body or a landscape could be beamed instantaneously to any location on earth. This was realized during the *Satellite Project* in 1977 by Sherrie Rabinowitz and Kit Galloway, with the support of NASA, via U.S.-Canadian Hermes CTS satellite. Four dancers, two in California and two in Maryland, joined for a dance in virtual space. "We see communication and information systems as environments people live in", explains Rabinowitz. "So we look at the aesthetics of that environment, the shaping of the space." Gene Youngblood adds that Rabinowitz

> invokes architecture: information environments can be exalting and inspirational like cathedrals (computer networks) or squalid and dehumanizing like ghettos (the mass media). As buildings are said to be democratic or oppressive, so the architecture of electronic space determines possible relations among people, establishes the contours of desire [8].

I introduced the model "ISDN for art" in 1984–1985 as a system for universal telecommunication for art and Gestalt technologies for the 1990s. The following year, I elaborated on some of its aspects in the *Terminal Art* exhibition for "ars electronica" in Linz, Austria [9]. I want to emphasize at this point that ISDN supports the coexistence of the different modes of communication such as speech, text, data and still pictures on one terminal with a standard 64 kilobits per sec. But with light as the medium, with optical waveguides as conductors, with chips performing the digitizing functions at a comparable speed, this will all change in the early 1990s [10]. Certain aspects of this emerging universal art network have been evident in the work of artists all over the world since the 1970s. One example is The Living Museum, which grew out of the Canadian ANNPAC organization and had its first colloquium in the summer of 1979. Using inexpensive computer terminals and one or more time-sharing computer data services, a number

Fig. 2. Jürgen Claus, *Solar Energy Sculpture* (model), 1987. (Photo: J. Claus)

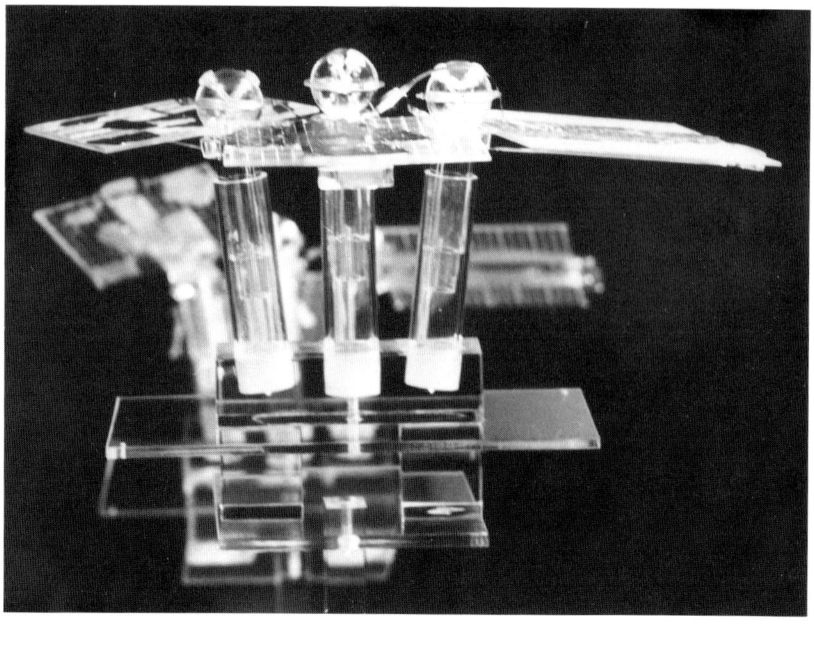

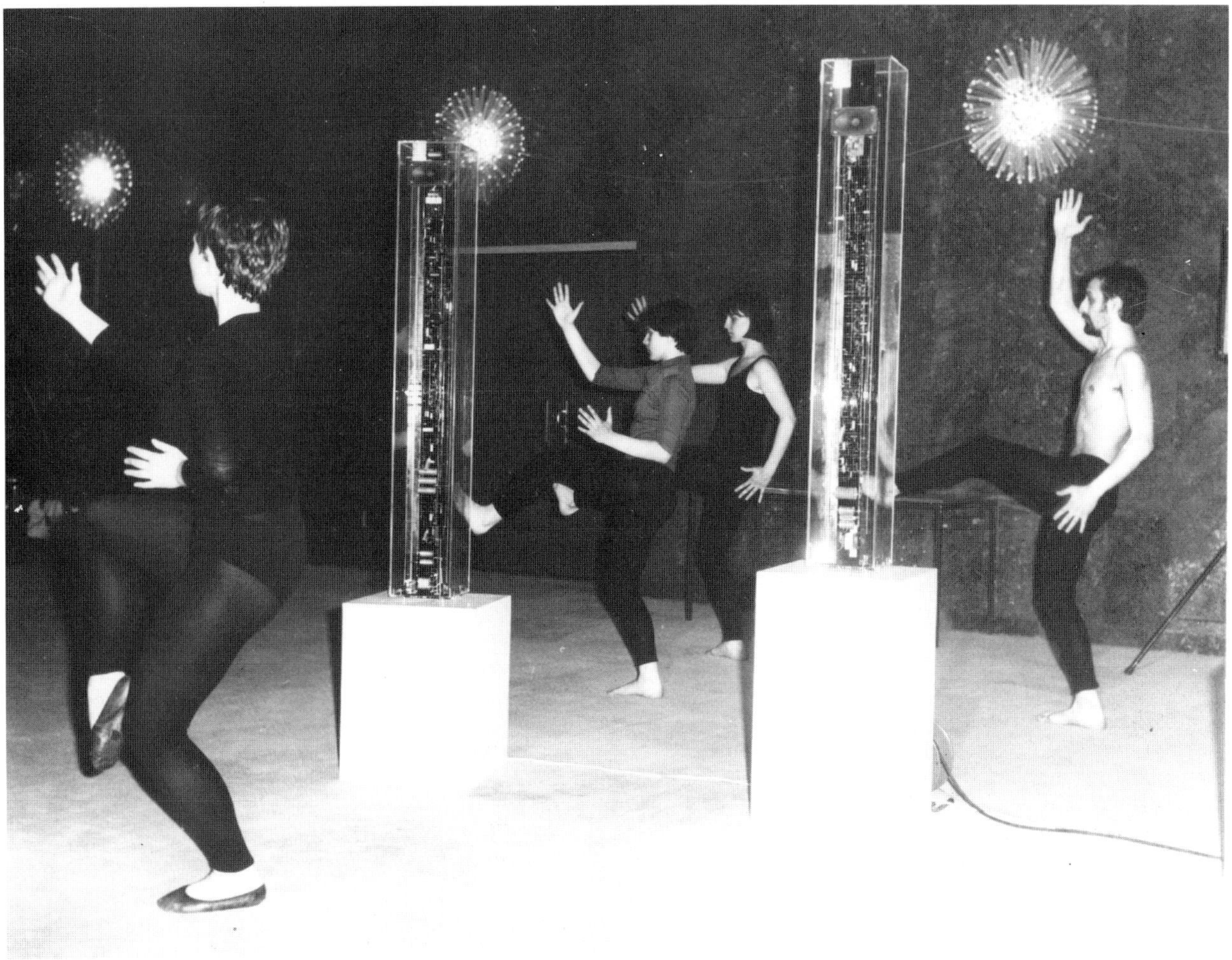

Fig. 3. Peter Vogel, *Musical-Cybernetical Environment*, Zagreb, 1977. (Photo: P. Vogel)

of artist-run organizations initiated an art-based, interactive data network [11]. Another example auguring an "ISDN for art" is the Videotex-Art-Network (V.A.N.). Headed by Manfred Eisenbeis, the group for media development/media research at the Academy of Design in Offenbach/Main has been concerned with videotex as a graphic system for some years. The V.A.N. project was the result: an international forum for the cultural and artistic utilization of the medium, facilitating the exchange of messages, images, text and notations between nations and continents via telephone [12].

The forthcoming "ISDN for art" is, on one hand, a data network, an image library, a research mailbox. On the other hand, it is a sort of echo chamber for associative thinking and creation—a fluid creativity. As Roy Ascott puts it, "Computer-mediated networks offer the possibility of a kind of planetary conviviality and creativity which no other means of communication has been able to achieve. One reason may be that networking puts you, in a sense, out of body, linking your mind into a kind of timeless sea" [13]. To summarize: It is important for the art community to develop pilot projects in the field of networking. Whether they are called Telematics, Telecommunications, The Living Museum, or "ISDN for art" is not important. What is important is that the art community itself articulates the foundations of visual image communication in the framework of information technology.

Ecotechnology: Design with Ecology

In the 1950s, dialectic relations between technology and energy forces of the widest spaces—heaven, sea, desert—started to develop on a new level. The age of the first satellites engendered a new awareness: the need for a new expression of our appreciation of nature.

For the 1986 "ars electronica" and within the *Terminal Art* exhibition my contribution focused on the topic of "Artificial Intelligence—Fluid Thinking": manipulative intelligence confronted with fluid intelligence. My metaphor for this was four glass containers filled with water dyed different shades of blue, a symbol of the fluid. The lesson of artificial intelligence is a despairing one—the confrontation with the natural—water, sand and light. This laboratory was entitled "Stake of Artificial Intelligence", an unfinished, even chaotic map between knowing and not-knowing. "The real is not rational, it is intelligent", said Michel Serres. Five years earlier, for the first SKY ART Conference at the Massachusetts Institute of Technology I contributed some thoughts about sky and ocean. They read, "Both the inner and the outer spaces of the earth are mirrors of our contemporary experience. They release us spiritually as well as physically. The inner and outer spaces have changed our visual con-

same time an immense system of energies of inconceivable abundance. We are not lost within this cosmic supply of energies as long as our mental and spiritual energies remain active" [16].

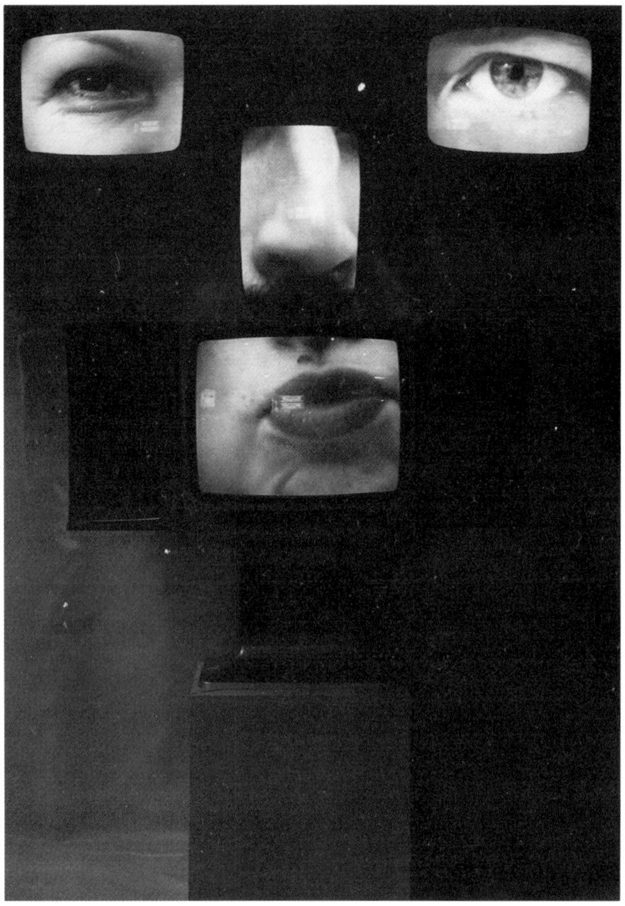

Fig. 4. Bernd Kracke, *Video Faces* (installation), 1982. (Photo: B. Kracke)

ception of this planet and the planet system as a whole" [14].

From the fourth and last SKY ART Conference in 1986 a manifesto emerged and was slow-scan-telecommunicated to artists at the University of São Paulo, Brazil. Written by sky artist Otto Piene, who inspired and shaped sky art, it reads like a manifesto for design with ecology: "Our reach into space constitutes an infinite extension of human life, imagination and creativity. The ascent into the sky is mirrored by the descent into inner space as it reflects the cosmos." And: "The artist as frontier poet with the artist's sensory instrumentarium goes into space to widen human perspective on the 'new world'—sky and space." This manifesto shows the expansion of the new vision for a new society.

The frightening consequences of high technology and the threat to our environment force me to raise the issues of ecotechnology, or design with ecology. Implicit is an intentional reference to the notion of "comprehensive design" (Buckminster Fuller), to design as "the conscious and intuitive effort to impose meaningful order" (Victor Papanek) [15]. Ecotechnology means the application of tools, materials, and technological processes in such a way as truly to harmonize them with nature: with the habitat of plant, animal and man; with the wider zones of our ecological home; indeed, with the entire globe and the cosmic space beyond. A good example of ecotechnology is photovoltaics, the use of sunlight as a source of energy. To use light as a creative medium came more naturally to earlier civilizations. But if we strip such conceptions of their mythical and religious content, we find them absolutely up-to-date. They portend the feasible, and perhaps the inevitable, solar age.

All energy events are closely related to each other because we do not have sources of energy, we have transformations of energy. In early Italian and Russian futurism, for instance, energy became the carrier in the continuum of space and time that entered pictorial art in the beginning of this century. Energy is probably the link between the spheres of natural and artistic phenomena. Heinz Mack, the former "Zero"–artist, notes, "The inner, cosmic constellation of our existence, of which the artistic existence appears to be a bright star, is at the

The Expert System Artist: Fifth-Generation Computer Culture

In a recent paper about the interface with the machine, René Berger invited intellectuals to regain a spirit of initiative by intervening in the processes of daily decisions. "This would be the real innovation" [17]. It is in exactly this sense that I understand this last topic, and it is here that I want to define some opportunities for art and *Gestaltung* within the framework of expert systems and artificial intelligence (AI).

Basically, I am aiming at a new definition of the image that takes into consideration the rich tradition of art as well as today's complex cultural, social and art network. So far we have many experts on art, but there exist expert systems (XPS) founded on concepts of knowledge that no visual art expert can agree on. Sometimes I feel as if I am living in the legendary Jewish town of Chelm with its amiable fools. When the rabbi of Chelm visited the prison, he heard all but one of the inmates insisting on their innocence. When he returned to the village he held a council of the wise men and recommended that there be two prisons in Chelm, one for the guilty and another for the innocent. The Chelm of today's experts would also like two systems: one for the experts, and another for the expert system community.

To make our way through this jungle of definitions, let me first talk about the expert system artist. Figuratively, the system is a living, not a machine-oriented, one; the artist is an expert of sensuous perception, visual pattern creation and recognition; he gives Gestalt to the known and unknown, be it with or without electronic media, processes and results; he creates the visual, intelligible and intelligent coordinates with which we perceive *Wirklichkeit als Gestalt,* reality as Gestalt.

As opposed to the synthetic electronic image, the intelligent image created by the expert system artist promotes our perception and knowledge and articulates them. Only the genuine intelligence of the artist-created image can be a product of the seen and the felt, with forms as well as colors, being objective and subjective at the same time. This intelligence is distinct from verbal, text-based knowledge. Yet if we acknowledge that this kind of knowledge includes that fundamental visual perception which the German language calls *Schauen* (the state of experience that precedes the recognition of visual pattern by 'looking at'), we must also admit that it is unlikely that we ever can store this knowledge. We can store and retrieve 'pattern', items that might be important to the data archives of art history. But that is not the point of intelligent art and the expert system artist [18].

In his contribution to the 1987 "ars electronica" symposium on the arts in the age of AI, Mihai Nadin wanted the intelligent machine to have ("contain") some sense of history and to display an awareness of it. The established AI techniques are actually, as he put it, "ill suited to handling such problems of the visual because, without exception, they are based on paradigms originating in language use and on logic along a synchronic axis. Consequently, we have to either establish new paradigms or to develop techniques which will also allow for the handling of qualitative properties of images and of dynamics (diachronic axis) implicit in an image" [19]. As an example, Nadin compared the CAD representation of a future product with the ability to identify the relevant elements of a problem (a computer graphics problem) to the designer's present task of generating solutions (which are issues of AI) using rules embodied in a program. What we call today an image machine can claim to have this kind of intelligence only if it takes into account human perception as well as the creation of Gestalt. As this is inseparably bound to more than just a machine approach, a basic notion of such an image machine must include the interaction of the human-oriented and the machine-oriented. This indeed is the new paradigm of the responsive environment where reality is not purely fabricated but where—once again according to René Berger—"the machine, the whole technology and therefore the computer join with us to elaborate a new vital environment".

As a practitioner of media and environmental art, I see this possible interaction lying within the process of creating or, more precisely, 'cutting' preselected realities (film, video, sound, dance, space) into the digital processor, or simply allowing reality to interfere with interactive technologies in real time and in real life. Yet, neither reality itself nor the tools are deemed intelligent. It is the interference of a *human creator* that establishes the image as intelligent, because it is her/his knowledge that gives rise to the never-final, ever-changing Gestalt. Yes, this is common sense! Or at least it should be.

As I have said, I am weaving through the jungle of experts, expertise, and expert systems as constrained by an image based on fifth-generation computer culture—but a sixth-generation optical neural computer is already on the way [20].

A king, old and eccentric, called the chief rabbi and told him, "Before I die I want you to teach my pet monkey how to talk. And do it within one year, or your head will be chopped off!" "But your majesty", said the rabbi, "to do this I need more than a year—I need at least ten." "I'll allow you five and not a day more", said the king. The rabbi went home, related the king's demand to the people and all asked him what he would do. "Well", said he, "in five years, many things can happen. The king could die. Or, I could die. Or—maybe I can teach that monkey how to talk." This might well be the case as we move from expert graphic systems to the far more difficult intelligent image producer.

For the 1985 Third Annual Conference on "AI for Society" organized by the SEAKE Centre at Brighton Polytechnic, Graham J. Howard presented a paper on art and design towards AI; it was concerned with the nature of image understanding, image use and the social and political implications of images. Whereas expert graphic systems only will enhance the ability of the visual expert to manipulate visual elements within a configurational and sequential format, an intelligent image producer will have to be an intelligent image consumer as well. "It would have to be capable of understanding images in order to intelligently produce images. Image understanding", continued Howard, "would involve the location of the image in the context of knowledge and belief structures; it would require the specific elaboration of its context and at least some of its potential contexts" [21].

If fifth-generation knowledge information processing systems are specifically designed to handle symbols and not just numbers, and if the actual expert systems are made the pilot projects for them, then art and design may contribute their rich heritage in visual languages. But a greater opportunity lies ahead in the development of optical neural computers, where optical elements will be arranged in the same way as neurons are arranged in the brain, either electronically or with holograms.

The 'electronic Bauhaus' will participate in developing art-and-design-specific software. As with its famous predecessor, this should happen in the context of the tradition of our social and cultural demands, the Moholy-Nagy "Parliament of social de-

Fig. 5. Exhibition sponsored by Siemens, *Youth and Chips*, Munich, 1985. (Photo: J. Claus)

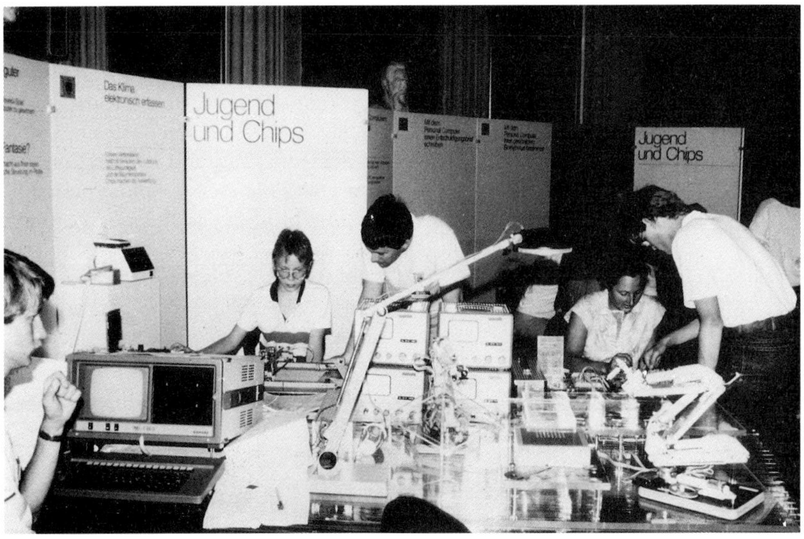

sign". It reinforces my own beliefs to know that I am standing on the shoulders of many practitioners of a new vision for a new society, some of them gathered around the Bauhaus, first in its German context and later, after emigration, in its American context. History here validates the practical experiment of today.

References and Notes

1. Sibyl Moholy-Nagy, *Laszlo Moholy-Nagy: Ein Totalexperiment* (Mainz, Berlin: Florian Kupferberg, 1972) p. 41. First published as *Moholy-Nagy. Experiment in Totality* (Cambridge, MA: MIT Press, 1969).

2. Moholy-Nagy [1] p. 13.

3. Jürgen Claus, "Gestalt-Technologie. Die Expansion der Medienkunst in den achtziger Jahren", *Kunst und Technologie* (Bonn: BMFT, 1984) pp. 9–13. English version: "Expansion of media art", in *ars electronica* (Linz: 1984) pp. 177–179. Gestalt technology has been incorrectly translated here as design technology. In a broader context, the idea of organic forms was especially well suited to Gestalt psychology, "whose cardinal precept was that perception of the whole preceded apprehension of the parts" (Phillip C. Ritterbush, *The Art of Organic Forms* [Washington, DC: Smithsonian, 1968] p. 87).

4. "McLuhan and Harley W. Parker note in their extremely interesting 'Beyond the Vanishing Point' (1968) that 'Seurat, by divisionism, anticipates quadricolor reproduction and color TV', but this echoes Moholy's perception that 'Seurat, for example, with his pointillist art, intuitively anticipates the science of color photography'" (Richard Kostelanetz, "A Mine of Perceptions and Prophecies", in his *Moholy-Nagy* [New York: Praeger, 1970] p. 214).

5. Laszlo Moholy-Nagy, *Vision in Motion* (Chicago: Theobald, 1947) pp. 13–16.

6. Moholy-Nagy [5].

7. Stan VanDerBeek, in *Science & Technology in the Arts*, Stewart Kranz, ed. (New York: Van Nostrand Reinhold, 1974) p. 240.

8. Gene Youngblood, "Virtual Space. The electronic environments of mobile image", in *Computer Culture* (Linz: 1986) pp. 351–352.

9. Jürgen Claus, *ChippppKunst* (Berlin: Ullstein Materialien, 1985) p. 123, and "The electronic screen", in *ars electronica* (Linz: 1986) pp. 353–370.

10. An optical waveguide can have a transmission capacity of about 100 times that of a copper line. Compared with the 64 kilobits per sec. one would need 144 megabits per sec. to transmit moving color pictures. 64 kilobits per sec. = 65,536-bit storage capacity. It is built with 150,000 elements on a silicium crystal of 25 mm^2 chip space. Kilobits are a measure of how many electric pulses (bits) a computer 'reads'. One kilobit is 1,024 pulses. It would take about one kilobit to put this definition into the computer. One megabit is a million bits.

11. "The Living Museum", in *Spaces by artists*, Tanya Rosenberg, ed. (Toronto: ANNPAC, 1979) pp. 107–154.

12. *Programm Mosaik. Handbuch für die Gestaltung von Bildschirmtext*, Manfred Eisenbeis, ed. (Nuremberg: Verlag Müller, 1985); and Manfred Eisenbeis, "Videotex Art Network", in *ars electronica* (Linz: 1986) pp. 354–356.

13. Roy Ascott, "Art and Telematics", in *Art-Telecommunication*, Heidi Grundmann, ed. (Vienna, Vancouver: 1984) pp. 29–30.

14. "SKY ART Conference '81", M.I.T., Cambridge, MA, 1981, p. 50.

15. Victor Papanek, *Design for the Real World* (London: Thames and Hudson, 1984) p. 4.

16. Heinz Mack, "Kunst als Ausdruck von Energie" (Art as an expression of energy), a talk with the author in *kunstreport* (Berlin: 1, 1981) p. 11.

17. René Berger, "Changements technologiques et nouvelle dimension esthétique: l'interface avec la machine", working paper for the international seminar and workshop "Visual Arts and the New Media", Offenbach/Main, 1987.

18. Jürgen Claus, *Das Elektronische Bauhaus. Gestaltung mit Umwelt* (Zurich, Osnabrück: Edition Interfrom, 1987).

19. Mihai Nadin, "Image Machine and Artificial Intelligence", working paper for "ars electronica", 1987.

20. The first public conference about neural computers was held in San Diego, 21–24 June 1987. I want to quote here from "Optical Neural Computers" by Yaser S. Abu-Mostafa and Demetri Psaltis, both members of the faculty at Caltech, Pasadena, Calif. "Is there another technology from which computers could be built that does not suffer from this limitation in data communication? The operation of the eye's lens suggests one. The lens takes light from each of millions of points in the entrance pupil of the lens and redistributes it to millions of sensors in the retina. It is in this sense that the lens can be thought of as a highly capable interconnection device: light from every point in the image focused in the retina. Moreover, multiple beams of light can pass though lenses or prisms and still remain separate. Indeed, two beams of light, unlike a pair of current-carrying wires, can cross without affecting each other. It is the ability to establish an extensive communication network among processing elements that primarily distinguishes optical technology from semiconductor technology in its application to computation" (*Scientific American*, March 1987, pp. 66–73).

21. Graham J. Howard, "Art and Design: AI and its consequences", in *AI for Society*, K.S. Gill, ed. (Chichester: John Wiley & Sons, 1986) pp. 125–139.

Logic and Time-Based Art Practice

Ernest Edmonds

ABSTRACT

This paper is concerned with art practice in the tradition of systematic construction. In particular, the underlying structures of work are seen to be logical, although no particular logic is emphasized. The problems of time-based work are discussed in relation to computer-generated video. It is argued that, in this context, logic programming is important and that images may be generated by such systems in an interesting way. Of particular significance is the fact that the inference system in a logic programming implementation can be seen to define the underlying structure of the time base of a work. An example is described and the implications discussed.

SYSTEMATIC CONSTRUCTION

The work described in this paper falls within a tradition that focuses on the underlying structure of the artwork, often referred to as the "underlying mathematical structure" [1]. Mathematics is a broad term applying to many different activities, but in this context it is formal systems, rather than all mathematical studies, that are of interest. They are covered within specific domains of mathematics. For the purposes of this paper we will consider the structure to be an underlying *logical* structure. We refer to mathematical logic but not to any particular logical formulation, any of which might be appropriate.

Of particular interest are time-based works, which certainly can be treated within the framework of systematic construction. Formal descriptions of time-based processes can be considered in different ways and using different logics [2]. The author has shown a fragment of a computer-generated video work which explores some of these issues [3]. This paper discusses the formal considerations relating to such art practice and illustrates a new video work.

LOGIC PROGRAMMING AND IMAGE HANDLING

As we have suggested, logics play a significant role in the domain of formal systems and, hence, in art practice involving systematic construction. In the context of electronic art, therefore, we are bound to consider the branch of computer science known as logic programming particularly carefully [4]. In effect, logic programming provides an executable, problem-solving interpretation of mathematical logic. We are able to define an underlying structure in a logic programming language and then ask the computer to find solutions to set goals automatically that conform to that structure. The details of this need not detain us here. Rather, we should simply note that underlying logical structures may be specified to computers in this way and that instances, or realizations, may be constructed as a result.

It has been shown that an image on a computer screen can be treated as an object within a logic programming system [5]. It is important to note that as a logical statement concerning the image object is applied, the image may be changed. In this way it is possible to define underlying logical structures for images in a computer and to use those structures to produce specific realizations in the class of images implicitly defined.

Ernest Edmonds, LUTCHI Research Centre, Loughborough University of Technology, Loughborough, Leicestershire, U.K.

Received 15 April 1988.

THE INFERENCE SYSTEM AND STRUCTURES IN TIME

At the heart of a logic programming language implementation lies what is known as an inference system. This is a piece of software that interprets the logic in order to attempt to achieve whatever goal has been set. Its particular organization determines the way in which the logic is applied to the problem at hand. Put simply, it determines the order in which the logical assertions provided are applied.

An important consequence of this is that the time-based structure of a work may be determined by the definition of the inference system's strategy. By setting forth a particular goal to a computer system that has specified within it both a defined underlying logical structure for the image and the particular inference system to be used, one is systematically constructing a time-based work. The pace of the work will be determined, of course, by the processing method used rather than by the inferencing strategy as such. However, it is quite simple to annotate either the description of the underlying logical structure of the image or the definition of the inference system's strategy, or both, with specifications of the pace at which particular acts should take place.

JASPER: A SAMPLE WORK

A computer-generated video work, *Jasper,* can be taken as an example of the ideas described above put into practice [6]. Some illustrations of stills from this video are shown in Fig. 1. The images of the work may be thought of as being constructed on a grid in which locations may be specified in normal rectangular coordinates. They are in shades of grey which can be identified by a number between 0 and 255, where 0 is black and 255 is white.

The structure of the image, in this work, was defined by the following simple rules (expressed here in English):

1. Square X is at position (X,X), has sides of length X and is of tone X *or* tone 255 – X.

2. Picture X is satisfied when square X is drawn *and* X is less than 250 *and* picture Y is satisfied, where Y = X + 10.

Pergamon Press plc. Printed in Great Britain.
0024-094X/88 $3.00+0.00

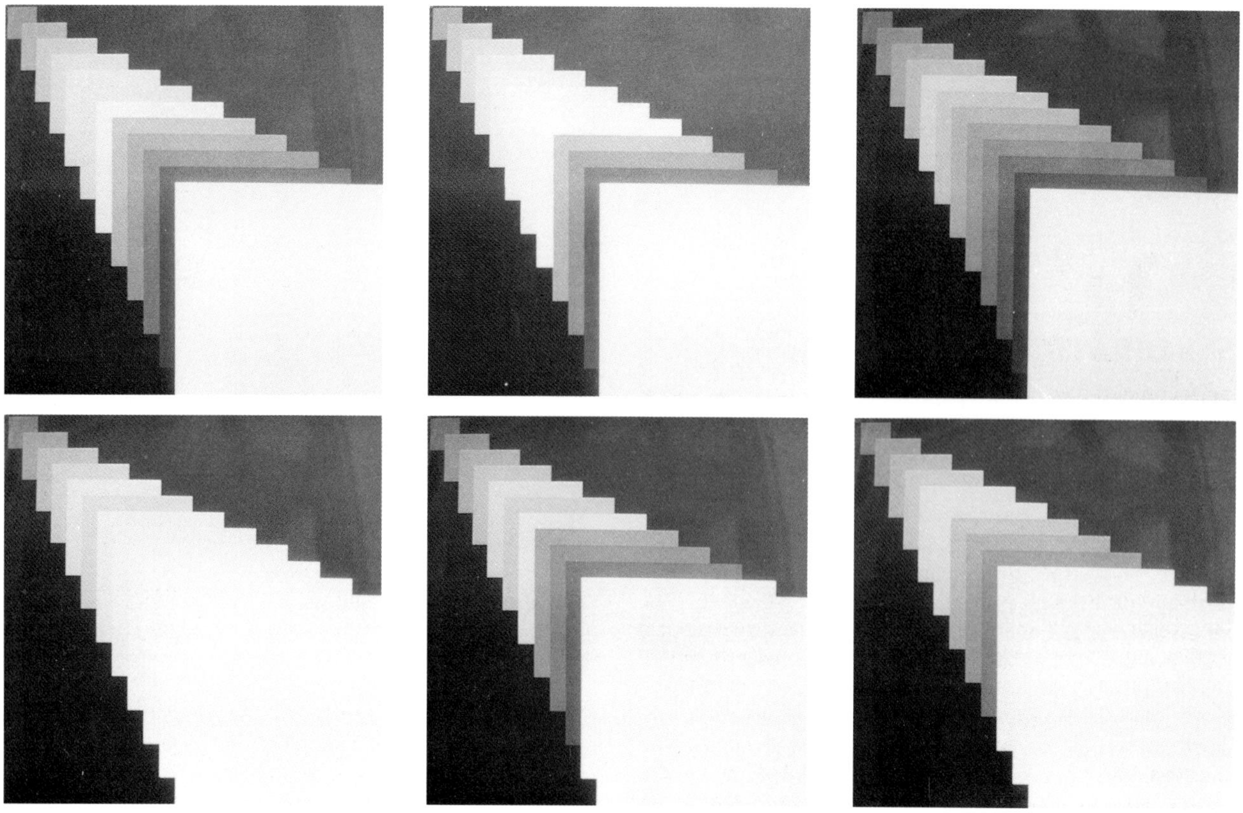

Fig. 1. Stills from *Jasper*, computer-generated video, 1988.

The image is generated by setting for the system the goal of producing picture 10.

Note that the second rule activates itself and hence produces a sequence of actions on the image. Such rules are known as 'recursive' and are very important in logic programming as well as in many other branches of computing and mathematics.

There are, clearly, many ways in which attempts may be made to satisfy these rules. The key point is in the choice of inference system to be used. In the case of *Jasper*, the rules were expressed in the logic programming language PROLOG and its standard inferencing system was applied to them [7]. As part of this strategy the system tries different ways of satisfying its prime goal whenever an attempt fails.

In our example, all attempts fail because satisfying picture 10 will always, in the end, rely upon satisfying picture 250, which is not possible. Thus, the standard inferencing system of PROLOG is used to generate a time-based work that can perhaps be thought of as a relentless attempt to satisfy these very simple, but, in fact, unsatisfiable rules. It might be noted, as an aside, that the negative aspect of this view, the inevitable failure, can be avoided if one sees the moment when X = 250 not as a failure of rule 2, but as the state at which the next alternative solution should be sought.

FURTHER OPPORTUNITIES

No annotation was used in *Jasper* in relation to pace and so the work has a regular driving rhythm. A different, related work, *Jasper Sighs* [8], has also been produced. In this work, rule 1 is annotated in order to specify the time it should take to draw the square, and that time changes in a fixed rhythm of its own.

I am currently exploring different inferencing strategies, ones that involve interaction with a human [9]. This last possibility is clearly addressing the central issue identified for electronic art by Cornock and Edmonds [10] and elaborated by Edmonds [11]: the exploration of the possibilities of art systems with which participants interact.

References

1. S. Bann, "Introduction", *Systems* (U.K.: Arts Council catalogue, 1972) pp. 4–14.

2. E.A. Edmonds, "Discussion 2: Time and Formal Systems", *Exhibiting Space 1985 Autumn Programme* (London: Conspectus, 1985) pp. 142–153.

3. E.A. Edmonds, "Exhibition 4: Duality and Co-Existence", *Exhibiting Space 1985 Autumn Programme* (London: Conspectus, 1985) pp. 23–25.

4. R. Kowalski, *Logic for Problem Solving* (North-Holland, 1979).

5. A. Schappo and E.A. Edmonds, "Support for Tentative Design: Incorporating the Screen Image, as an Object, into PROLOG", *IJMMS* **24** (1986) pp. 601–610.

6. E.A. Edmonds, *Jasper* (computer generated video) (Loughborough, U.K.: LUTCHI Research Centre, 1988).

7. W.F. Clocksin and C.S. Mellish, *Programming in Prolog* (Springer-Verlag, 1981).

8. E.A. Edmonds, *Jasper Sighs* (computer generated video) (Loughborough, U.K.: LUTCHI Research Centre, 1988).

9. E.A. Edmonds, "Negative Knowledge Towards a Strategy for Asking in Logic Programming", *IJMMS* **24** (1986) pp. 597–600.

10. S. Cornock and E.A. Edmonds, "The Creative Process Where the Artist is Amplified or Superseded by the Computer", *Proc. CG70*, Brunel University, U.K. Reprinted in *Leonardo* **6** (1973) pp. 11–15.

11. E. A. Edmonds, *Beyond Computable Numbers* (Loughborough, U. K.: Loughborough University of Technology, 1987).

Computational Art

A. Eliëns

ABSTRACT

The author conducts a simple thought experiment investigating the existence and scope of 'computational art': the utilization of the computer in the visual arts and music. In the experiment he sets the task of constructing an artifact that is capable of producing works of art. Since it appears that the artifact needs at least the capability of imagination, he queries the nature of images and imagery and argues that imagination is strongly intentional. Next he introduces the concept of notational systems, since they seem to govern the artistic activity of (not exclusively) machines. Confronted with the question of whether we are able to develop a computational analogue for taste, he finds that notational systems prove to be necessary for mediating the method of production of an artwork and the appraisal of its artistic value. Furthermore, the author shows that there are certain epistemological limits to the creativity of an imaginative device. Although the outcome of this hypothetical construction task clearly denies the possibility of an autonomously creative artifact, there seems to be no reason to worry about the opportunities for computational art: the computer appears to be a unique tool in exploring the possibilities of artistic production, guided by artists.

What value has the use of a computer for the visual arts and music? The ultimate answer to this question must come from those practicing the arts. For each form of art the answer might be different. Although I feel inclined to state my opinion right away, based upon my experience with electronic music, I would rather tackle this query by taking a step back, reflecting on the possible uses of the computer in the arts.

Evidently, in many branches of scientific endeavor the use of the computer has known significant growth. Can a similar growth be expected for the use of computers in the arts? At first sight there are many differences between the use of the computer in science and the use of the computer in art. Art or artistic experiments are not as likely to be put into numbers as, for instance, the experiments of the exact sciences. Moreover, whereas the goal or specification of the problem is usually clear in a scientific enterprise, one might not always be able to state a goal or criterion that must be met for an artistic enterprise.

I will not consider all possible uses of the computer in science, but will concentrate on a specific branch of Computer Science: Artificial Intelligence. Artificial Intelligence is relevant to our question since it is concerned with modelling and implementing functions that are thought to be intelligent. With this preference I state my first presupposition: artistic behavior is intelligent behavior. Although some of the results of Artificial Intelligence are controversial, this discipline of science has known some generally recognized successes, for instance in the field of computer chess.

Artificial Intelligence differs from other branches of Computer Science in that it is expressly concerned with 'symbolic computing'. This is exemplified in the research dealing with automated reasoning or computational logic, which involves investigating to what extent and how proof procedures can be effectively mechanized. The example of computational logic is of interest since, although it never attained its goal of providing procedures for discovering theorems, it has resulted in effective proof-verification programs and logic-based programming languages. Another well-known and significant application of automated reasoning techniques can be found in expert systems, which are increasingly becoming of interest in real-life situations.

Returning to our question, "What value has the use of the computer in the visual arts and music?", I note that there are several ways to phrase this question. For instance, it can be understood as "What possible uses does the computer have in the arts?" But an inventory is not what I am primarily interested in. Rather, I would like to take it as querying the possibility of *computational art,* stressing the analogy with computational logic: *to what extent can artistic behavior be automated?* Answering this question in its full depth is almost impossible. Therefore, I have chosen to follow a very particular method—constructing a creative artifact, a machine that is autonomously capable of producing art. This hypothetical engineering task is not of a practical nature, though. I will not deal with the pragmatics of constructing an artistic device, but rather with the philosophical issues involved: those concerning *imagination* and *taste.* In other words, this thought experiment will function as a vehicle for developing the argument concerning the possibility and scope of computational art: the approaches to the visual arts and music that involve the use of a computer in some essential way.

The plan of this essay is as follows: I investigate the possibility of mechanizing the process of imagination by using techniques from Artificial Intelligence. Then I introduce notational systems as a means to formalize the production of art. I will here raise the question whether notational systems are appropriate for the visual arts. Finally, I will assess whether our device is creative. To this end I will consider the possibility of implementing taste, since I regard the task of mechanizing creativity to be dependent on the mechanization of taste.

No knowledge of Artificial Intelligence or the philosophy of art is presupposed, although it would certainly aid in appreciating the argument.

THE CONSTRUCTION OF AN IMAGINATIVE ARTIFACT

I have set the task of constructing an artifact that has the ability to imagine things, people or perhaps other artifacts and is also capable, as an artist, of producing images that can be appreciated by other people or artifacts. More specifically, I ask the question "How do we program a computer to behave like an artist?"

The reason for choosing a computer for our engineering task instead of any other mechanical device is that the computer is a device with universal computational power. If art can be automated, then it can be automated by using a computer. The physical nature of the device we intend to pro-

A. Eliëns, Centre for Mathematics and Computer Science, P.O. Box 4079, 1009 AB Amsterdam, The Netherlands

Received 19 April 1988.

0024-094X/88 $3.00+0.00

gram as an artist is not of interest. What is of importance, however, is the kind of function we are trying to implement: artistic behavior. It is obvious that a simple picture-processor is not what we are looking for.

Intentionality

The class of programs we are interested in is, because of the nature of our problem, the class of programs that show 'intentionality'. Intentional behavior in this context means goal-directed behavior; more specifically, behavior that is somehow driven by the goal to produce images. We must implement a *behavioral function:* a function that allows the machine to react to feedback and to enter into a dialogue about its images and representations [1].

Artificial Intelligence has provided a computational model of human cognitive functioning. The strength of the model lies in the fact that it has enabled the development of a variety of intelligent programs, ranging from chess-playing programs to language-understanding systems. The working hypothesis underlying the model is that mental functioning can be mimicked by symbolic computation. Symbolic computation must be understood as the manipulation of symbols. Regarding computation as symbol manipulation has the advantage of separating the interpretation of the symbols from their representation. It enables us to manipulate formally the representations according to some formal rules without having to worry about the semantic content of the representations, provided that the rules are well chosen.

The success of the computational model of the human mind indicates that the image—the product of imagining—need not resemble the intermediary representations which led to it. Imagery, for instance as occurring in dreams or delusions, is more likely to be the result of a chain of symbol manipulations [2]. To quote Cohen: ". . . representation of the visual world is certainly not exclusively in visual terms. . . . actually [representations] might better be regarded as transcripts . . ." [3].

Learning

Assume that we are able to construct a machine that is capable of performing 'ordinary' intelligent functions such as perceiving and solving simple problems. Moreover, we assume that the machine is equipped with the hardware to display images. The device we have in mind, however, must be able not only to perform these functions, but also to improve on its skills. To this end, the machine must be endowed with the capability to learn, whether from brute experience, from intentionally experimenting with its environment or by being given the right examples.

Learning by Doing. The oldest example of a machine that is able to form concepts of perceptual regularities is based on a 'constructive' view of perception. Perception is regarded as a process of analysis-by-synthesis. This view is of particular relevance to our task because of the assumption of an image-generating process: the incoming information is matched with the generated information. By randomly varying the generated image, one can find the right concept without prior instruction [4]. Imagery, in this view, is simply constructive activity without any input to be matched. As an explanation of the adaptive power of the imagination, the notion of randomness as an information-generating principle is somewhat unsatisfactory. Obviously, some mechanism is needed to attune the preference of the mechanism for finding regularities and structure.

Learning by Discovery. AM, a program that discovers concepts of number-theory, is an example of how heuristics can guide the process of learning. Starting with some primitive built-in concepts, each concept that is discovered is evaluated in terms of its *interestingness* by means of heuristic rules. The measure of interestingness determines where the concept will be placed on the agenda for further exploration. For example, the likeliness of discovering the concept *prime* is enhanced by raising the interestingness of numbers having only two factors [5]. At the time this program was developed, this 'induction'-principle meant a significant step forward in constructing learning programs. A possible objection to this approach, however, is that the range of discovery is limited by the built-in heuristics. The generalization of this approach, applying heuristics to improve on heuristics, has currently not been achieved. Clearly, though, this use of heuristics demonstrates that it is possible, in principle, to endow our device with the intention to learn and to improve on its imaginative skills.

Learning By Example. In reality, the intention to learn is not always sufficient. Significant advances, also among students of art, are often achieved by presenting the right examples—in other words by teaching. Winston [6] describes a learning program that adapts its conceptual representation of a class of objects by reacting to examples presented by its teacher. When presenting the object, the teacher tells whether the object is typical for the class of objects or how it deviates. The assumption here is that the program has the intention to learn a specific concept. The process of learning is governed by the presentation of paradigmatic examples and counter-examples.

Motivation

The prospects for our hypothetical engineering task look good. We are able to build a machine that can form abstract perceptual categories, that can find interesting concepts, that can identify objects and, moreover, that is capable of constructive image-generating activity. What is still lacking, however, is a motivational or emotional component.

A motivational system can be computationally realized as an amplification mechanism of innate, built-in drives, such as the drive for self-preservation, a cognitive information-seeking drive, etc. [7]. Moreover, we may grant the device the pleasure of inspecting its inner life by allowing it to take its own state as a symbol of itself [8]. Thus, we have constructed an artifact that is capable of imagining in a nontrivial way. It does not merely reproduce stored images. It might be an artist. Is it creative, though?

NOTATIONAL SYSTEMS

In the previous section we have investigated the possibility of implementing imaginative behavior. To decide, however, whether we will succeed in constructing a device that is truly creative, we have to take a closer look at the relationship between the perceptual experience of an image and the symbolic representations that mediated its construction.

Depiction Versus Description

The depictive quality of an image does not depend merely on its congruence with visual reality but also on the organization of properties out of which the image emerges. This is even more obvious when nothing is represented in the referential sense. From this point of view, resemblance to visual reality can be best understood as the similarity between the experience of perceiving the image of the object and the experience of perceiving the object itself.

We might model the experience of an image mechanically by taking the exploratory activity as a description of the experience of an image. For instance, the visual exploration of an image can be expressed in terms of transition probabilities between the elements of the matrix of pixels.

Assuming the validity of this approach, does there exist a dual method of image synthesis? Can an artifact, having the experience of an image, infer its construction rules? As a historical note, Paul Klee made what he called 'Rezeptiv-Bildern' (reception images) using his visual scanning as a construction principle.

Production Methods

To avoid the referential problem, let us take music as an example. According to Sartre, in hearing a melody we practice an 'imaginative reduction' and make an 'ideal' object of the music by de-temporalizing it to its thematic configuration [9]. The other side of this process of imaginative reduction clearly is the process of composition. Related to the processes of experience and production, the role of notation in music is that of an intermediary: it allows one to identify a piece of music as a conceptual entity, apart from its history of production.

Music is the prime example of an art with a notation. From the point of view of music history, a score allows one to make a distinction between the constitutive properties or conceptual structure of the work and its accidental, contingent properties that differ from interpretation to interpretation. From the perspective of compositional practice, systems of notation provide a method of production.

Although I shall not attempt to give a precise formal account of notational systems, following Goodman [10] I will try to delineate what I understand by notational systems in a sufficiently precise way. A notational system consists of a symbol scheme and an interpretation that defines the extension of the symbols and their combinations. The notion of extension can be explained simply as follows: if a score contains an F-sharp, then the intended meaning is that an F-sharp will be played on the appropriate instrument. However, not all systems of symbols are notational. A notational system must adhere to certain restrictions. It must be *unambiguous*, in that one symbol does not denote several things at a time. It may, however, be redundant, in that one particular event is denoted by several distinct symbols. On a syntactic level and in a mathematical sense the system must be *discrete*. A nondiscrete or dense system allowing arbitrarily small differences between its symbols will lead to confusion. In summarizing, a notational system can be characterized as a system that is definite about its intended interpretation by being unambiguous and sufficiently differentiated. This does not exclude all freedom of interpretation, though, since for instance an instrumentalist may further differentiate between the indications given in a score. The early history of electronic music, as made in the analog studios, shows how the pursuit of exact control and density of sound led to an abolishment of notation as a vehicle for composition. In a sense, software sound synthesis reintroduced notation, although in a non-standard way, in the form of computer programs and input. Obviously, programs share with scores the property of being definite and discrete and hence repeatable. But one must note a shift in meaning here from a product-oriented to a more process-oriented interpretation of notation. In effect, if computer music is to be taken seriously, it is partly for overthrowing the monopoly of standard musical notation through the introduction of non-standard notation in the form of programs [11].

The Role of Notation in the Visual Arts

In the history of the visual arts there is no parallel to the development and use of notation in music. A sketch cannot be taken as the analogue of a score, since, in particular for non-representational paintings, none of the pictorial properties can be dismissed as irrelevant. Obviously, there is a problem of *density;* although we might digitize the image, we still have no conceptual abstraction of it. However, if we take a process-oriented view, we might be able to specify the method of production of the visual image in a sufficiently abstract way and thus create the opportunity for developing a notational system [12].

To find a notational system for the visual arts we must above all conceptualize the way an image is produced. In this respect, computational art forms a natural extension of the development of art in this century. Kandinsky, for instance, searched for a 'notation for painting', with which he could compose the score for an image—"correlating colors with musical sensations to depict the inner space of subjectivity". Cubism provides another example, as it achieved a certain independence between the 'representational' and the 'presentational' aspects of painting. Somewhat over-generalizing, one can say that reflecting on the method of production has given a constructivist turn to modern painting, thus preparing the way for computational art [13].

Any notational system for the visual arts unavoidably will have a strongly process- or action-oriented flavor. The use of the computer actually creates the opportunity for employing such systems in a definite and repeatable way. A notational system for the visual arts is a promise that only the computer has in store.

THE ALGORITHMIC GENIUS

An art-producing artifact must have aesthetic sensibility. If the device we envisage is going to count as a genius, it must have taste. The concept of notational systems allows us to describe the productive activity as the manipulation of the symbols of a formal system. To establish if what it produces satisfies its intentions, the device must have the capability of judgement.

The Notion of Artificial Taste

Gips and Stiny [14] have provided a computational solution to the problem of artificial taste. They propose taking as the measurement of the aesthetic value of an image the ratio of *visual complexity* to *specificational simplicity*. Aesthetic rating will be high with this method if a maximum of evocative effect is produced by as efficient means as possible. They obtain these measures by matching the image with the results of a generative system consisting of a number of primitive shapes and rules for composing more complex shapes out of those previously generated. Some refinements they built in include selection rules to determine what shapes are chosen and painting rules to govern the construction of compound shapes and the means to control the variability among the shapes that constitute the image. By selecting suitable shapes and applying the appropriate rules, one can generate an image that is sufficiently similar to the original image. As a measure of specificational simplicity we can then use, for instance, the number of rules used to derive the image.

The scheme proposed by Gips and Stiny relates the appearance of an image to the constructive intentionality from which it originated. Can this scheme be applied in practice? There is clearly a trade-off here between generality and feasibility. To put it differently, one can allow a very large range of possible images, but then the search space will likely be too large for all possibilities to be generated and tested. In addition, there may be a more fundamental defect to the solution proposed by Gips and Stiny. Their working hypothesis is, in effect, that one can identify basic elements, rules of construction and organizational principles governing the selection of rules and elements that uniquely determine the appearance of an image. However, I must note that the principal difficulty for developing a notation for the visual arts—density—may also preclude the mechanization of aesthetic sensibility: almost imperceptible changes in the basic elements might effect a completely different configuration.

Can the Machine Be Creative?

We can without doubt make our machine creative in the sense of its being able to produce novelty. In the theory of creativity, the creative process is often conceived of as consisting of a stage of incubation in which, so to speak, the ingredients of the work of art are being prepared, and a stage of illumination, in which the final concept is formed. The recognition of a new idea as valid can be explained psychologically by assuming that the idea has some excitatory value for the 'prepared mind' [15].

In order to implement creativity we must further restrict the generative system developed to give a computational description of taste such that at each step the choice that is made contributes to the novelty and 'interestingness' of the final product. Novelty as such is easily obtained by randomizing the choice. However, the use of stochastic processes, as for instance in serial music, is not very valuable unless the parameters over which they are varied are given a definite meaning and unless the range of variation is delimited in an appropriate way [16]. So we must insist that the novelty that is produced satisfies our criteria of interestingness and validity.

Since we have assumed that the imagination underlies any artistic activity, it seems necessary to reconsider this notion more carefully. In philosophical terms, imagination is a species of thought that is attuned to what is intrinsically meaningful [17]. Computational models that reduce this activity of thought to "mere representational activity in the absence of input" [18] clearly lack the valuational aspect of the process of imagining.

To incorporate this valuational aspect I propose installing some rules for assessing the interestingness of the image or idea. But this solution has some intrinsic limitations. A problem arises similar to that guiding the discovery of mathematical concepts: sooner or later the built-in heuristics for assessing the interestingness of an idea are not able to cope with the complexity of the newly generated ideas. The inability of the device to adapt its notions of interestingness and meaning is of an epistemological nature. When a range of concepts is delimited by built-in rules, a machine can only fill up the gaps. It can explore, if given sufficient time, all concepts within this range. It cannot, however, except to a minor extent, enlarge this range in a significant way. An artifact is not equipped to change its categorical framework because it cannot apperceive the meaning of such a framework in constituting possible reality.

Therefore, art cannot be automated. As Harold Cohen states [19], "art presumes [such] a flux of categories". A machine simply cannot be the agent of such a reflection. In other words, art is not an objective a computer can have, nor is progression in art an objective a computer can have. To complete this argument, consider it from a sociological point of view. Since art might have as a theme not only the form of an art product, but also the function of a work of art in society, art by an artifact can be fully appreciated only in a community of artifacts [20]. And what kind of community would that be?

Conclusion

We must admit that we have failed in our engineering task of constructing an artistic device. Our failure is due to the fact that we are unable to endow the machine with the taste and creativity necessary to an artist.

Nevertheless, we should not be disappointed, since we have encountered several valuable notions that clarify the possible use of the computer in the visual arts and music. It appears that the computer is an excellent notational device. Although, in effect, the computer can have no more than an instrumental status, it provides a hitherto unknown amplification of the constructive and combinatorial powers of the imagination. Moreover, the formalization necessary to make full use of the opportunities offered seems to be in line with the development of the arts toward a reflection on their methods of production. I have introduced the concept of notational systems to provide the means for describing an image in terms of its process of construction in an abstract but precise way. Taking *constructivity* (which includes the selection of the material and the procedures for manipulating that material) and conceptuality (which can be characterized as the awareness of such a choice as constituting artistic activity), I conclude that we must give the machine a chance. It lies in the hands of the artists to discover where this pursuit of a notation for the visual arts will lead us.

References

1. H. Cohen, "Some Notes on Machine Generated Art", in R. Cogarth, ed., *Aspekten: De Computer in de visuele Kunst* (Brussels: ICSAC, 1981).

2. Z.W. Pylyshyn, "What the Mind's Eye Tells the Mind's Body: A Critique of Mental Imagery", *Psychological Bulletin* (July 1973).

3. Cohen [1].

4. D. MacKay, *The Epistemological Problem for Automata*, Shannon and McCarthy, eds., *Automata Studies* (Princeton, NJ: Princeton University Press, 1956).

5. D. Lenat, "The Ubiquity of Discovery", *Artificial Intelligence* 9, No. 3 (1977).

6. P.H. Winston, *Artificial Intelligence* (Reading, MA: Addison Wesley, 1977).

7. Cf. W. Reitman, "Personality As a Problem Solving Coalition", in Tomkins and Messick, eds., *Computer Simulation of Personality: Frontier of Psychological Theory* (New York: John Wiley and Sons, 1963).

8. J.O. Wisdom, "Mentality in Machines", *Proc. Arist. Soc. Suppl.* **26** (1952).

9. J.P. Sartre, *L'imagination* (Paris: Presses Univ. de France, 1936).

10. Goodman (1976).

11. Cf. E. Karkoschka, *Notation in New Music* (Totowa, NJ: European American Music, 1972).

12. M. Bense, *Aesthetica* (Baden Baden: Agis Verlag, 1965).

13. Cf. A. Gehlen, *Zeitbilder zur Soziologie und Ästhetik der modernen Malerei* (Atheneum Verlag, 1960).

14. J. Gips and G. Stiny, "An Investigation of Algorithmic Aesthetics", *Leonardo* **8**, No. 3, 213–220 (1975).

15. D.O. Hebb, "What Psychology Is About", *The American Psychologist* (February 1974).

16. G.M. Koenig, *Observations on Compositional Theory* (Utrecht: Institute of Sonology, 1971).

17. R. Scruton, *Art and Imagination* (London: Methuen, 1974).

18. MacKay [4].

19. Cohen [1].

20. Cf. Burger (1974)

Additional Sources

M. Boden, *Artificial Intelligence and Natural Man* (New York: Basic Books, 1977).

B. Englert, "Automated Composition and Composed Automation", *Computer Music Journal* **5**, No. 4 (1981).

Establishing a Tonic Space with Digital Color

Brian Evans

ABSTRACT

Since Isaac Newton, colorists have, with little success, looked for ways to associate the vibrations of light and color with the vibrations of music and sound. Although the idea of proportion has been mentioned in these efforts it has never been studied thoroughly. This paper proposes, through use of computers and digital raster graphics, a means of measuring the color balance of an image through proportions of red, green and blue intensities. With this method of measurement it is possible to apply several theories of color harmony and balance to computer-based abstract imagery. Through the computer we get specific control of the process. If, through this technique, a quantifiable means of creating concordant color relationships is possible, then it makes color available to the composer as material for the coherent structuring of time. As in tonal music, movement in time can be established by movement in and out of balanced, consonant areas. An area of balanced color relationships could be thought of as a tonic space, functioning like the tonic pitch or key in tonal music.

In the search for harmonious color many conflicting ideas have been offered. With a borrowing of the concept of harmony from music, some theorists sought to map concepts of Western tonal music directly to the color domain. Others dismissed the possibility of direct correlation as frivolous at best, being based on emotional considerations and inconsistent from one person to the next.

While there appears to be no scientific relationship between the percepts of color and sound vibrations, evidence indicates that a large percentage of people experience color when listening to music [Karowski and Adbert; Simpson, Quinn and Ausubel]. This color-hearing or synesthesia by itself does not seem of practical use to the artist, but it encourages continued exploration of color/music relationships.

Goethe, who in his theories doubted any direct relationship, said, "Color and sound do not admit of being compared together in any way, but both are referable to a higher formula" [Goethe]. Writers on color theory from Aristotle to Newton to today have theorized about a possible candidate for this 'higher formula' but followed their speculation with little study. I again suggest this idea, simple proportion, as being a basis for associating color with music.

John Whitney, with his work in abstract animation, has long understood the value of proportion as a basis for correlating visual and sonic materials [Whitney]. With progression through simple ratios he establishes temporal motion similar to harmonic motion in Western tonality. Consonance and dissonance occur from movement through points of resonance expressed as abstract or physical manifestations of whole number (Pythagorean) ratios. Although his work deals more with aspects of motion than pure color, his 'digital harmony' based on proportion has proved itself through the austere beauty of his pieces.

This paper does not pretend to offer final answers to questions of color harmony but will discuss a means of measuring color on a computer image. This measurement, expressed as a proportion of red, green and blue color values, allows us to study relationships that might lead to qualification of color spaces as concordant or dissonant.

With dissonance wanting to resolve itself into a point of balance or consonance, a hierarchy is established. Like a pendulum at the bottom of its swing, consonance becomes a point of attraction. This attraction is expressed in Western tonal music by the tonic note or key center. In color this could be considered a tonic space, a point of color balance that creates what colorists call a harmonious effect. Simple proportions as found in nature provide a point of departure in the search for tonic color spaces.

TONIC SPACE

In general, tonality in music concerns itself with the successive and simultaneous relationships of tones or pitches. As the description of a tonal system becomes more specific, a hierarchy is established with a central pitch or tone given the top position. This pitch is called the tonic. All other pitches in the system are described in relation to this tonic. They are seen as moving away from or towards the tonic pitch.

The 'common practice' period in Western music (roughly the eighteenth and nineteenth centuries) further specified this hierarchy, giving pitches, and especially chords, functions that establish motion or relaxation of motion up and down the hierarchical ladder. The tonic center was expanded to mean scales such as C major or E-flat minor—a collection of pitches commonly called the key of a piece. Chords moved the music through different scales, departing and moving back to an established tonic center or key.

Colorists trying to relate color to music often tried to map hues with particular pitches, chords or key centers as understood in the 'common practice' tonal system [Jones]. This approach was doomed to failure for several reasons, the primary one being that there is a tenuous physical basis for Western musical harmony: it is a Western invention, not a discovery. We hear consonance and dissonance just as we characterize music as happy or sad—through acculturation. These associations, in a state of flux, have been established over centuries. That definitions of harmonic concord and discord seem to change from generation to generation is good indication of a weak basis in physical truth.

There are a thousand years of cultural conditioning that dictate our responses to music. Over that thousand years a sophisticated musical environment has been established, and for Western ears all music is experienced within that environment. Consider the difficulty many Western listeners have with the music of other cultures such as Chinese opera or Javanese gamelan. Both exist far outside the Western musical tradition. Color experience has its own established

Brian Evans, National Center for Supercomputing Applications, University of Illinois at Urbana–Champaign, Champaign, IL 61820, U.S.A.

Received 19 April 1988.

Pergamon Press plc. Printed in Great Britain.
0024-094X/88 $3.00+0.00

environment and traditions. Trying to map our musical traditions directly into color, without the same culturally built associations in effect, has proven a futile endeavor.

Nevertheless, putting aside cultural biases and emotional qualifications, it should be possible to consider the more general, abstracted case of a tonal system as a means by which dynamic time can be structured. This is done through creation and relaxation of tension, which is caused by movement away from and towards a tonic. This concept of tonality has been a part of Western music since its beginnings in plainchant with the *finales* of the church modes. It can also be found in the music of many non-Western cultures, as in the tonic drone of East Indian classical music.

Establishing this tonic area provides a basis for structuring time with sonic materials in music. If a similar tonic space can be defined in the domain of color, it should be possible to structure time with the materials of color. It should be possible to compose color-music. The work of color theorists over the past century or so indicates some possibilities for the creation of a balanced color space. With computer images and simple procedures for color measure, these possibilities can easily be explored.

METHOD OF MEASURE

Computer technology and raster graphics allow easy measurement of the color dimension. Raster images are made up of discrete pixels, with each pixel assigned red, green and blue (RGB) intensities and an address. If the graphic system uses a color look-up table, then each pixel holds a number associated with that table. The image becomes a digital paint-by-number canvas with the look-up table or color map containing the number-to-color palette. This paper concentrates on color map systems, as they are currently more prevalent and more affordable than the high color resolution RGB systems.

The measurement taken is that of proportions of the color primaries red, green and blue. In a color map this is done by summing all the values for each primary color. For a palette with 256 entries this can be expressed as

$$R = \sum_{i=0}^{255} \mathrm{r}_i$$

$$G = \sum_{i=0}^{255} \mathrm{g}_i$$

$$B = \sum_{i=0}^{255} \mathrm{b}_i$$

For the graphs used in this report each value is normalized so that the maximum possible value for each primary is 100, with R, G and B expressing the percentage of the maximum that is actually present in the color map. A map with 256 entries using one byte each for the R, G and B intensities will have:

$$\mathrm{MAX} = 256 * 28 = 65536$$

as the maximum possible intensity for each primary, giving

$$\mathrm{R} = 100\ (\mathrm{R}/\mathrm{MAX})$$

$$\mathrm{G} = 100\ (\mathrm{G}/\mathrm{MAX})$$

$$\mathrm{B} = 100\ (\mathrm{B}/\mathrm{MAX}).$$

The color measurement for the map is then expressed as the proportion triplet R:G:B.

As most images do not contain equal amounts of all colors from a palette, the map proportions should be balanced against the color map index distribution of an image. This is accomplished by creating a histogram showing how many pixels are assigned to each index of the color map. Each element in the histogram array H_i contains the number of instances of color map index i on the image. Each element is normalized to a number between 0 and 1, with 1 being equal to the total image space and H_i equal to the percentage of the total.

The R:G:B triplet for a raster image with a 256-element color map is then calculated as

$$R = 100[(\sum_{i=0}^{255} \mathrm{r}_i \mathrm{H}_i)/\mathrm{MAX}]$$

$$G = 100[(\sum_{i=0}^{255} \mathrm{g}_i \mathrm{H}_i)/\mathrm{MAX}]$$

$$B = 100[(\sum_{i=0}^{255} \mathrm{b}_i \mathrm{H}_i)/\mathrm{MAX}]$$

For a true RGB system the R:G:B triplet can be found directly by separately summing the values of each primary on all pixels. With n being the total number of pixels and allowing 8 bits each for R, G, and B values, the maximum possible intensity value for each primary is

$$\mathrm{MAX} = 28n$$

Keeping the maximum normalized triplet value as 100 and i equal to a pixel number, the R component will then be

$$R = 100[(\sum_{i=0}^{n-1} \mathrm{r}_i)/\mathrm{MAX}]$$

G and B values of the triplet are calculated accordingly.

The R:G:B triplet gives a measure of the proportions of the color primaries that exist on a computer image. Many theories of color harmony suggest that an equality or simple proportion of the primary colors can create a balanced color space. From this perspective the R:G:B triplet should prove useful as a means of quantifying the harmonic color balance of a digital image.

TOWARDS DIGITAL COLOR CONCORD

For over a century colorists have been working on the idea of color harmony: the establishment of balanced and concordant color relationships. From the ideas of balance and concord we get the concept of tonic space. For many colorists the fundamental tonic space is simple neutral grey. This is substantiated by the visual phenomena of successive and simultaneous contrasts.

If one stares at a color for an extended period of time one will successively see the color's complement, that is, the color's opposite on the color wheel. (When a color and its complement are combined in the right proportions the resulting color in light will be white; in pigment it will be black.) If, for example, the eye is fixed on the color blue and then on a light grey background, the color sensation of yellow, blue's complement, will occur.

With simultaneous contrast, also based on the principle of color complements, one will see a color's complement in neighboring areas after prolonged observation. For example, a light grey square surrounded by blue will appear yellowish. This phenomenon works not only for hue but for brightness as well. A light square surrounded by dark will appear lighter than it actually is and conversely the dark area will seem darker. It seems as if the eye seeks to create a balance if balance is not there.

These tricks of the eye give credence to the concept of neutral grey as a physiological point of balance in color perception. The eye appears at rest when seeing grey, or more importantly when seeing a collection of colors that equal grey if combined. This idea of color harmony can be traced back to Goethe, who said, "The whole ingredients of the chromatic scale, seen in juxtaposition, produce an harmonious impression on the eye." This gives a good point of departure for building a tonic color space when using the R:G:B triplet.

Using the color measure on a digital image we can easily tell when there is a balance of primary color values. When the R:G:B values are all the same the combined color should be within the grey scale. A neutral gray should be found at half of full intensity, midway between white and black.

Fig. 1 shows a plot of red, green and blue values over a specific color map along with the map's actual color content. It also shows the R:G:B triplet values for the map alone and applied to the image shown in Color Plate A No. 2. The triplets are shown numerically and graphically. The histogram of color index distributions is shown in the Color Plate. (The sample image in the Color Plate is an abstract fractal-based graphic derived from Newton's method for finding roots of the equation $z^7 - 1$.)

The map in Fig. 1 has been adjusted so the R:G:B distribution on the image will be equal to half of full intensity—a normalized triplet of 50:50:50. This is done using the simple color measure summations. With the proportion triplet 1:1:1 and a method for quantizing the color measure of a specific image we have a basis for defining and exploring tonic color space.

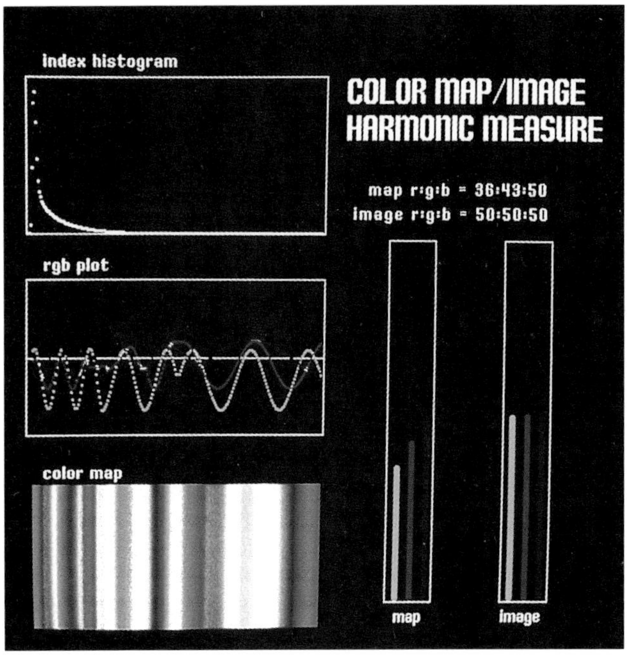

Fig. 1. Color measure of the fractal image in Color Plate A No. 2. All measurement components are shown including a plot of the color palette, a histogram of the distribution of color map indices over the Color Plate image, and the R:G:B triplet for the map and the image.

RESERVATIONS AND CONCLUSIONS

It would be naive to suggest that setting a balance of color primaries on an image will guarantee a consonant color space. Theorists have found other dimensions of color to be important in the search for color harmony, and none of these are considered in the R:G:B triplet measure.

Shade and tint gain prominence in some theories [Birren, 1934, 1937]. Munsell introduced color measure through dimensions of hue, value and chroma [Munsell]. His ideas have been adopted in many areas including methods of specifying digital color [Smith]. Renner dismisses the idea of balanced primary intensities, looking to balance and contrast of the other dimensions to create his color 'accords' [Renner].

The use of the R:G:B triplet does provide a tool where a color palette can be fine tuned with respect to a number of the other color theories, many coming from the ideas of Goethe. Of perhaps more significance is the ease with which imbalanced color spaces can be defined and then, using the R:G:B measure, altered and neutralized. Interpolation through these spaces in time suggests a wealth of material for structuring time and color. This is one area where work is continuing.

Accepting the other dimensions traditionally used in the study of color harmony, development of transformation functions from one method of a color space measurement to another is also an area where work is continuing.

The early work done with the R:G:B triplet measure has, at the very least, been fruitful enough to encourage continuing. Animation of these color progressions should indicate the most promising directions for further study.

For someone working in the ivory tower of art and aesthetics, all these ideas are of course subservient to whim, taste and artistic vision. Fine art has never felt compelled to follow any laws and, we can only hope, never will. Still, the idea of proportion has always been a useful tool for the skilled craftsperson, something every good artist must be.

Newton wrote, "May not the harmony and discord of colors arise from the proportions of the vibrations propagated through the fibers of the optic nerve into the brain, as the harmony and discord of sounds arise from the proportions of the vibrations of the air?" With proportion measurable and controllable through computer graphics and the R:G:B triplet measure, music composers and other artists working with time have new materials and new tools for working with these materials.

Acknowledgments

This research is being done with the help of a grant from the National Center for Supercomputing Applications at the University of Illinois at Urbana–Champaign. Images were made with the assistance of the Scientific Media Services at NCSA. Color maps were made using the ICARE color editor designed by graphic artist Donna Cox [Cox 1987].

Selected Reading

Albers, J., *Interaction of Color* (New Haven, CT: Yale University Press, 1963).

Arnheim, R., *Art and Visual Perception* (Los Angeles: University of California Press, 1974).

Birren, F., *Color Dimensions* (Chicago: The Crimson Press, 1934).

Birren, F., *Functional Color* (New York: The Crimson Press, 1937).

Cox, D.J., "Interactive Computer-Assisted RGB Editor (ICARE)", *Proceedings of the Seventh Annual Symposium on Small Computers and the Arts* (Philadelphia, PA: SCAN, 1987).

De Grandis, L., *Theory and Use of Color* (New York: Harry N. Abrams, Inc., 1984).

Goethe, J.W. v., *Zur Farbenlehre* (1810). In English: *Theory of Colors* (Cambridge, MA: MIT Press, 1963).

Itten, J., *The Elements of Color* (New York: Van Nostrand Reinhold, 1970).

Jones, T.D., *The Art of Light and Color* (New York: Van Nostrand Reinhold, 1972).

Karowski, T.F. and H.S. Adbert, "Color Music", *Psychological Monographs* **50**, No. 2 (Columbus, OH: Ohio State University, 1938).

Kueppers, H., *The Basic Law of Color Theory* (Woodbury, NY: Barrons, 1980).

Land, E.H., "The Retinex Theory of Color Vision", *Scientific American* **237**, No. 6., 108–128 (1977).

Munsell, A.H., *A Color Notation* (Baltimore, MD: Munsell Color Company, Inc., 1946).

Newton, I., *New Theory About Light and Colors* (Munich: W. Fritach, 1967).

Renner, P., *Color: Order and Harmony* (New York: Reinhold Publishing Corp., 1964).

Salter, L., "Tonality", in *The New Grove Dictionary of Music and Musicians*, Vol. 19, Stanley Sadie, ed. (London: Macmillan Publishers, 1980).

Simpson, R.H., M. Quinn and D.P. Ausubel, "Synesthesia in Children: Association of Colors with Pure Tone Frequencies", *The Journal of Genetic Psychology* **89** (1956) pp. 95–103.

Smith, A.R., "Color Gamut Transform Pairs", *Computer Graphics* **12**, No. 3 (1978).

Truckenbrod, J., "Effective Use of Color in Computer Graphics", *Computer Graphics* **15**, No. 3 (1981).

Whitney, John, *Digital Harmony: On the Complementarity of Music and Visual Art* (New York: McGraw, 1980).

The *Creation Station:* An Approach to a Multimedia Workstation

Henry S. Flurry

ABSTRACT

The Center for Performing Arts and Technology at the University of Michigan is developing the *Creation Station,* a workstation-based software package that will provide the artist advanced sound synthesis and graphics capabilities, as well as the tools necessary to create multimedia pieces of art. This paper discusses the design criteria, programming obstacles and implementation details of the *Creation Station.* Because the *Creation Station* is coded in Objective-C, a brief tutorial on Object-Oriented Programming Languages is included.

INTRODUCTION TO THE *CREATION STATION*

The Center for Performing Arts and Technology (CPAT) has been working for the past year on a multimedia electronic arts software product called the *Creation Station.* The team behind the *Creation Station* includes CPAT Director David Gregory, who first envisioned the *Creation Station,* and Associate Directors Hal Brokaw and Henry Flurry, principal architects and programmers of the *Creation Station.* This workstation-based package will provide the artist with advanced sound synthesis and graphics as well as the tools necessary to create multimedia pieces of art. We are attempting to present a unified environment that will reflect an intuitive understanding of multimedia integration while maintaining flexible and sophisticated storage, editing and performance capabilities. We also aim to provide a software foundation that will support different and perhaps yet-undeveloped aspects of computer-aided art, including computer-based art research.

The *Creation Station* will employ a graphics interface similar to that pioneered by Xerox and made famous by the Apple Macintosh. We utilize traditional musical metaphors to present a homogeneous interface that will allow control of many multimedia artforms. For instance, one window will contain the master recorder panel that will govern the performance and recording of all events. From this window, the button labeled 'PLAY' will perform any *Creation Station*–based piece consisting of musical elements, graphic elements or both. Other windows will display events contained in tracks of the hierarchical track structure, allowing the user direct control over the type of event stored within each track and the sequence in which tracks are performed.

Because of the simplicity of this interface, the average user will find the *Creation Station* straightforward. However, to the more experienced user or programmer, the *Creation Station* will reveal many layers of power and flexibility. This paper primarily discusses how this power and flexibility are achieved.

The first version of the *Creation Station,* to be announced during the summer of 1988, will include a composer's application, a choreographer's application and the Instrument Builder. The composer's application will provide a variety of musical output devices and a number of ways to input and edit musical events. The choreographer's application will allow a choreographer to design stage props, input and edit three-dimensional motion paths for objects (presumably, but not necessarily, dancers) and view in three-dimensional perspective the resulting choreography. The Instrument Builder (not discussed in this paper) will be an icon-driven, device-independent, sound design module. One version of the Instrument Builder will allow the user to program sounds on almost any MIDI synthesizer with system exclusive capabilities.

Later versions of the *Creation Station* will provide other artistic tools (such as theater set and lighting design simulation, interactive performance tools, and interactive video editing), educational tools (such as musicianship and other art form lessons), and research tools (such as large sound and video databases and applications supporting interactive testing of theories). Depending upon the complexity of the implementations, the *Creation Station* will run on either super-micro or high-power workstation class computers.

Fig. 1. In Object-Oriented Programming Languages, a single message may effect different actions when applied to different objects. This is called polymorphism.

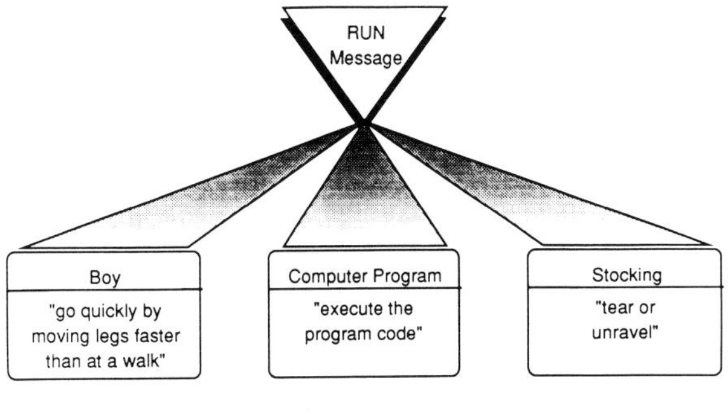

SOME SPECIFIC DESIGN CRITERIA

We aim to design an environment that will reflect the intuition of most artists but will also adapt to other creative styles. In view of this, we made the following design decisions:

- Tracks are hierarchical. Typically, an artist does not think of his/her creation as a single, indivisible chunk. A hierarchical track system allows the artist to organize

Henry S. Flurry, University of Michigan, School of Music, 1100 Baits Drive, Ann Arbor, MI 48109-2085, U.S.A.

Received 5 April 1988.

Pergamon Press plc. Printed in Great Britain.
0024-094X/88 $3.00+0.00

the creation into progressively smaller and more manageable groups.

- Performance order of tracks is not limited to the hierarchical structure of the tracks. This allows the artist to organize the creation within a structure not based upon time-span division.
- A single track may play in canon with itself, at any timing offset. This includes tracks containing either musical or non-musical events.
- The user may work in many different timing bases when editing events, editing conductor tracks and displaying real-time passage of performance time. This includes measures and beats, minutes and seconds, SMPTE, and user-defined timing bases.
- Tracks can follow whichever conductor track the user desires.
- The *Creation Station* will support third-party development of new types of artistic events, device drivers and editing environments.

POTENTIAL PROGRAMMING OBSTACLES

Even before coding of the *Creation Station* started, it was clear that these and other criteria would prove challenging. Some of the potential obstacles were:

- How to create a software package that would seamlessly integrate an undefined and potentially large set of event classes (such as music, animation, dance, etc.), their associated device drivers and the event editing environments.
- How to synchronize events of different timing schemes (such as measures and beats, minutes and seconds or SMPTE).
- How to synchronize events of different media—especially if some events take longer to realize than others.
- How to allow a single track to play in canon with itself. We need to prevent interference between two simultaneous performances of a single track.
- How to enable the integration of third-party extensions to the *Creation Station.*

Fig. 2. An object is presented as a single unified construct, where the methods of the object encapsulate the data of the object. Program code can only access an object's data through the object's methods.

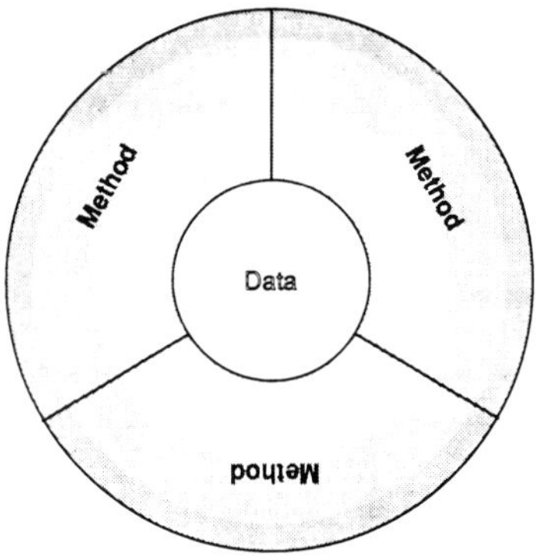

Although solutions to these and other problems could be implemented in many different programming languages, most programmers would agree that the complexity of the necessary code within languages such as C and Pascal would be almost too great to manage. However, in an Object-Oriented Programming Language (OOPL), many of the problems are diminished to the point of becoming trivial, and other programming tasks are conceptually simplified. For this and other reasons, we are developing the *Creation Station* in Objective-C [1].

INTRODUCTION TO OBJECT-ORIENTED PROGRAMMING LANGUAGES AND OBJECTIVE-C

In most programming languages, data is passed to a procedure to be acted upon. For example, the calculation of the square root of *x* might be executed by the procedure call:

sqrt(*x*)

There is, somewhere inside the program code, a unique function accessed by the **sqrt()** call. This function accepts its argument, evaluates the square root of the argument, and returns the resulting value. However, **sqrt()** is expecting a particular type of value—typically a double float number. It is the responsibility of the programmer to make sure that the **sqrt()** function is not passed a character, integer, or user-defined structure. Moreover, the user must make sure that the function's return value is assigned to a variable of the proper *type.*

Because so much of the burden of data typing and procedure management is placed upon the programmer, there is a 'complexity barrier' which prevents economical coding and maintenance of complex systems [Winograd, 1979]. We believe the complexity of the *Creation Station* would have approached this barrier.

OOPLs such as Objective-C encourage a different approach by blurring the distinction between data and code. To explain briefly the concepts behind OOPLs and the terms used in them, I will start by discussing the *object,* the basic construct of an OOPL. You may think of an object as analogous to any entry within the 'real' world. Like anything else around us, an object shows various properties and behaviors.

To command an object to do something, one sends it a *message.* As in the real world, the same message sent to different objects may mean different things. For example, commanding the objects 'boy', 'computer program' and 'stocking' to 'run' would generate three very different actions. In OOPLs this is called *polymorphism*—the use of a single message to evoke different actions from different objects (see Fig. 1).

Objects may be of the same *class* or of different classes. A class is simply a definition of an object's properties and behaviors. Objects of the same class exhibit similar properties and behaviors, whereas objects of different classes will likely display different properties and behaviors. 'Fred', 'Kevin', and 'Nancy' may be elements of the class 'people', and they will all exhibit certain similarities; however, these three people are unique, even if they are of the same class. In OOPLs an *instance* of a class is an object which belongs to that class but has a unique identifier.

At this point, it becomes necessary to discuss the structure of an object. Within a class definition, the programmer defines an object's *instance variables* and *methods.* Methods are the 'procedures' associated with an object. A message sent to an object invokes a method of the same name, executing the program code of that method and returning a value to the calling routine. Instance variables are variables that are accessible only by the methods associated with a class instance. One may liken the instance variables to the 'properties' of an object, and the messages and methods to the 'behavior' of an object. Thus, objects of the same class all respond to the same messages, execute the same methods and have the same data format for instance variables. However, different instances of the same class each contain their own copy of the instance variables, and the instance variable values associated with one instance may be changed without affecting the values of any other instances.

There are several other valuable characteristics of OOPLs, most notably encapsulation, inheritance and dynamic binding. The instance variables of an object can be accessed and changed only by the methods associated with that object. This process of information hiding, called *encapsulation,* has some obvious benefits to software design. Because the data of an object can be accessed only by that object's methods, there is less chance of accidental data corruption by outside routines. Once an object has been debugged, it can be used and reused as an entity with little concern for supporting code. In addition, the boundaries of class definitions help clarify the division of labor in group programming projects (see Fig. 2).

Inheritance is a natural by-product of the hierarchy of classes, in which all objects reside. In creating a class, the programmer defines only the differences between the desired class and the *superclass.* Instance variables and methods that are not redefined are inherited by the *subclass,* causing this new class to exhibit properties and behaviors similar to those of its superciass (see Fig. 3). Inheritance is a powerful capability of OOPLs. Valuable programming time is saved by writing only the code that is necessary to differentiate a new class from its superclass. Inheritance also extends the life cycle of an object definition by allowing a class to be tailored to the unique needs of other applications. A third aspect of OOPLs that is often overlooked is *dynamic binding*—the postponement of deciding what method to invoke for a particular message until run-time. Without dynamic binding, the ability to assign any object to a single variable would not exist, for the variable would have to be statically defined in order for the compiler to determine successfully which methods were bound to the coded messages. Dynamic binding also allows the creation of new classes that will work with existing precompiled code. Finally, dynamic binding will enable run-time linking with third-party extensions to the *Creation Station.*

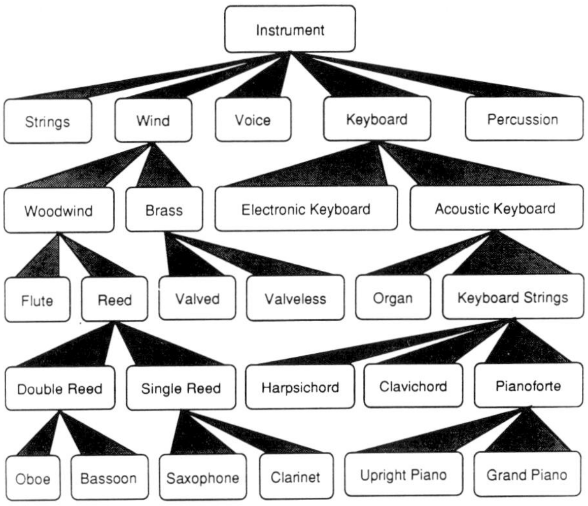

Fig. 3. In this inheritance hierarchy, Flute inherits from Woodwind instrument, which in turn inherits from Wind instrument. Flute would include only those methods and instance variables which differentiate it from Woodwind.

PROGRAMMING IN OOPLS

Many traditional programmers find it difficult at first to program with OOPLs. Two basic concepts useful in designing OOPL software are also useful for understanding many programming decisions presented in this paper:

- The methods of an object should closely relate to the data held within the instance variables of that object.
- Objects with conceptual similarities should be acted upon with a common protocol.

The first concept is fundamental to programming within an OOPL. For example, it might make sense to have an object representing a musical note be responsible for playing itself as staccato, but it would not make sense to have this same note object be responsible for deleting a file from a computer disk. This would be counter-intuitive and would make management of the programming project difficult.

The second concept is not as clear as the first. It does not dictate how to program in an OOPL as much as it displays the power of dynamic binding combined with polymorphism (dynamic polymorphism). Consider the generic class **Event,** which might encompass any type of performable event in which we would be interested. We can look at this group of event classes and begin to formulate a list of several conceptually common methods:

Event Classes:
- musical events
- dance events
- video events
- etc.

Possible Common Methods:
- perform next event
- return to real time of the next event to occur
- compare event attack-point timings of two individual events within the same class

Each event class would more than likely execute each method differently: the performance of a musical event might produce sound, and the realization of a dance event might generate visual images. However, the methods applied to the event classes share the same general concepts. Thus, if these methods carried a common protocol (i.e. respond to the same set of messages), it would be possible to write code that would control, for an object of any event class, many of the desired functions.

For example, to perform an event—be it musical or graphic—we could write the single line of code

```
[an Event performNextEvent]
```

which, in Objective-C, sends the message **performNextEvent** to the event object stored in the variable *an Event.* By changing the value of the variable *an Event,* we could perform any event defined within the *Creation Station.*

In fact, this is how we handle many objects of similar functions. Dynamic polymorphism allows us to define different 'genres' of objects, where each object of a single genre implements a set of messages in conceptually similar but physically different ways. We can then use the same code to control different objects of one genre to produce varying results.

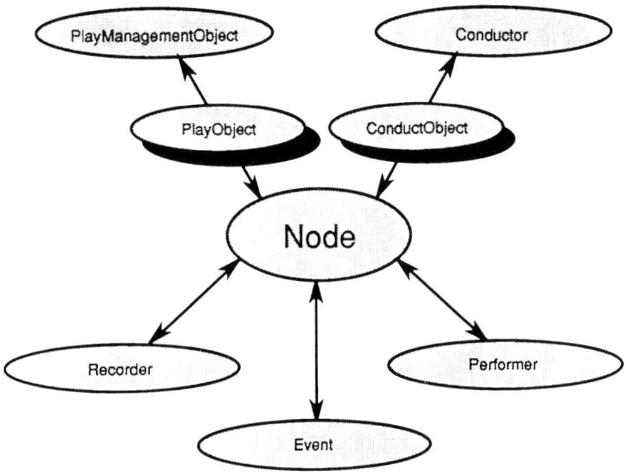

Fig. 4. The *Creation Station* communication channels. To maintain modularity of objects, the Node coordinates much of the inter-object communications. The PlayObject and ConductObject are little more than added levels of indirection of communication between the Node and the PlayManagementObject, and the Node and the Conductor.

THE *CREATION STATION* BASICS

There are six major objects that form the foundation of the *Creation Station.* These objects, to be further discussed later, are:

- Event: Objects of this genre store performable events and contain the code necessary for converting the stored events into a representation acceptable for a Performer.
- Node: A Node is the track of the 'hierarchical track tree'. A Node contains an Event list and provides links to the Nodes below and above it.
- PlayManagementObject: This object is responsible for sequencing during performance all of the events within the *Creation Station.*
- Conductor: An object of this genre is responsible for controlling the performance and recording tempos of any Node or set of Nodes.
- Performer: These objects are responsible for realizing at a specified time individual events received from the PlayManagementObject.
- Recorder: Recorder objects accept external input and translate this input into time-stamped events that may be stored within a Node.

The Event, Conductor, Performer, and Recorder objects all define genres of object classes, and different objects of the same genre may generally be interchanged. Two other objects, the PlayObject and the ConductObject, will be introduced later in this paper.

Time. There will be only one type of timing base used in communication between objects. If one object is to pass a time value to another object, then this time value must be converted to the 'standard timing base' and stored in a variable declared by the macro TIME or in an instance of the class *Time.* The rule is necessary for two reasons:

- All objects must be able to read and understand any timing values received from another object.
- The PlayManagementObject must be able to sort and sequence correctly multimedia events (such as music or video) that may be defined in different timing bases (such as measures and beats, or SMPTE).

The Node

As mentioned above, the Node contains an event list which may be played in synchronization with other event lists within the *Creation Station.* The Node stores the events in a modified AVL tree, a structure that I call the 'Linked Balanced Binary Tree'. This structure was designed to optimize the operations that would most commonly be applied to an event list: insertion, deletion, searching, changing, and sequencing (for performance). A strict AVL tree provides relatively fast insertion and deletion, optimal searching and changing, but slow sequencing [Wirth]. To accelerate sequencing, we modified the AVL structure so that each Node of the binary tree contains not only a link to the Nodes above and below it, but also to the Nodes sequentially before and after it. Sequencing through an event list is quickly accomplished by following the second set of links. Thus, the structure behaves both like an AVL tree and like a linked list.

To maintain maximum modularity, the Node coordinates much of the inter-object communications necessary for event performance and recording. The six objects described above—"*Creation Station* Basics"—must gather information from a number of other objects in order to perform their duties properly. If we allowed each of these objects direct access to the other objects containing pertinent information, we would begin to lose inherent modularity. Experience has shown that a system that loses its modularity becomes more difficult to maintain and more prone to failure. Thus, with the possible exceptions of the PlayObject and ConductObject (discussed later), the Node is the only object of the objects that communicates with more than one other object (see Fig. 4).

So, when the PlayManagementObject needs to know the performance timing of each event, the Node is responsible for communicating with the Conductor and the Event to get this timing. When the PlayManagementObject is ready to perform an event, the Node receives the timing back from the PlayManagementObject, retrieves the event data from an Event, and passes the two to a Performer object. During recording, a Recorder object passes received event data to the Node. The Node then requests its Event class to create an event instance, and the Node inserts this new event instance into its event list.

The Event

The Event is one of the objects that makes the *Creation Station* so versatile. An object of the Event genre is responsible for the following:

- Storing whatever information is necessary to define an event or set of events to be performed.
- Providing both the code necessary to convert the internal representation of an event into a construct acceptable by a Performer object and the code necessary to convert Recorder output into an Event object.
- Providing the code necessary to order two different instances of the particular class of Event (the **compare:** method).

- Sequencing events to be performed in the proper order (the **returnNextEvent:** method).

We can create a variety of events that, by conforming to the above rules and following the same messaging protocol as other event classes, may be used within the *Creation Station*. Beyond these guidelines, there are no restrictions to the event classes.

As an example, it is possible to create an event class where each musical event is timed in measures and beats. In order to have the Node store the events in the proper sequence, the event class implements a method named **compare:**, which examines the measure and beat timings of two event objects and returns a value indicating which object should be sequentially first.

In our choreography application, we implement an event class whose instances store four-dimensional splines (3-D space plus time) defining motion paths of dancers. When an instance of this class receives the message **returnNextEvent:** it calculates and returns a three-dimensional point in space based upon the performance time.

Finally, we could even define an event class which implements an interpreted programming language. Each event object might contain a line of code or a procedure within a user-written program. The **compare:** message of the Event class could sort the procedures or lines of code in the order they were input by the user. When an Event object is issued in the **returnNextEvent:** message, it would execute a segment of the stored program to construct the event to be returned.

The Performer

The Performer objects provide the link between the internal representation of events and the external realization of events. As in the Event genre, there may be many different types of Performer objects, where each of these objects connects the *Creation Station* to some artistic medium.

A Performer object accepts a request from the Node to perform an event at a particular time. The event to be performed is encoded within some construct the Performer object can parse, and the time is passed in the standard timing base. A Performer should make any lengthy calculations necessary for event performance, buffer the results or events for later realization and return control to the Node. There are a variety of ways to buffer events; two of the most common ways are for the Performer to arrange an 'interrupt' to occur at the time the event is to be performed, or, if the *Creation Station* is running on a multitasking machine, for the Performer to send the event to another process which would handle the event realization at the proper time.

Different Performers require various event constructs, and a Performer should not be sent an incompatible event construct. It is easy to imagine accidentally sending a choreographic event construct to a MIDI output performer. On the other hand, a Performer object should be able to accept event constructs from a multitude of similar event classes. For example, both an Event class which simply stores musical events and an Event class which computes musical events should be able to use the same MIDI Performer.

To solve these potential problems, the *Creation Station* implements a system which matches Event classes to compatible Performer objects. Each individual Event class has a 'Performance Format Name' (PFN), a string of ASCII characters which is unique to the type of event construct output by that Event class. Likewise, each Performer object has a PFN which specifies what type of event construct is accepted. When a user wants to choose a Performer for a Node, the Node matches the PFN of its associated Event class with the PFNs of the available performers. The resulting set of Performers is presented to the user, who presumably chooses out of this set a Performer object to realize the events stored within the Node (see Fig. 5).

With this system, it is easy to create new classes of Event objects which will work with pre-existing Performers. New Performers that work with existing Events can likewise be created to support new hardware.

The Recorder

The Recorder object is responsible for accepting input from an external source and converting it to an event construct acceptable to an Event class. It is similar to the Performer in that it needs to be matched with compatible Event classes. Both the Recorder objects and Event classes have 'Recording Format Names' (RFNs) associated with them. As above, the Node is responsible for matching its Event class with potential Recorder objects, and, also as above, it is easy to integrate a new Recorder class into the *Creation Station* if it matches an existing RFN.

The Recorder is additionally responsible for buffering its external input until the end of a performance is reached. At this time, the Recorder sends each event to its associated Node to be translated into an Event object and stored within that Node.

The Conductor

The Conductor is a very important object to the *Creation Station*. Not only does a Conductor provide a tempo map for performance within the *Creation Station*, it also can be employed by the user to define an arbitrary timing base. The main duties of the Conductor object are:

- To translate virtual time to real time, and vice versa, basing the conversion upon the tempo map stored within the Conductor instance.

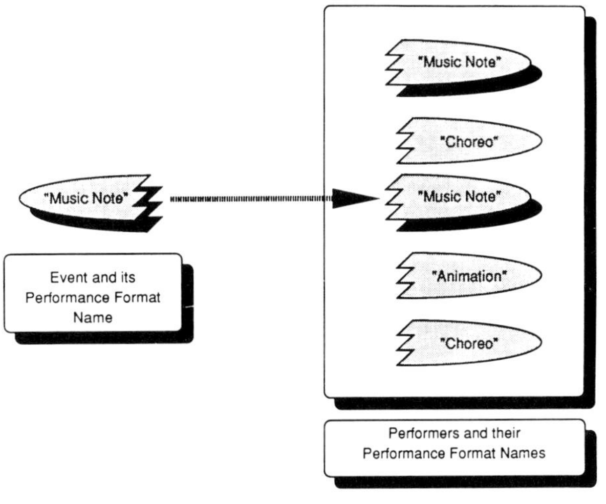

Fig. 5. The Performance Format Name is used to match up Events with compatible Performers.

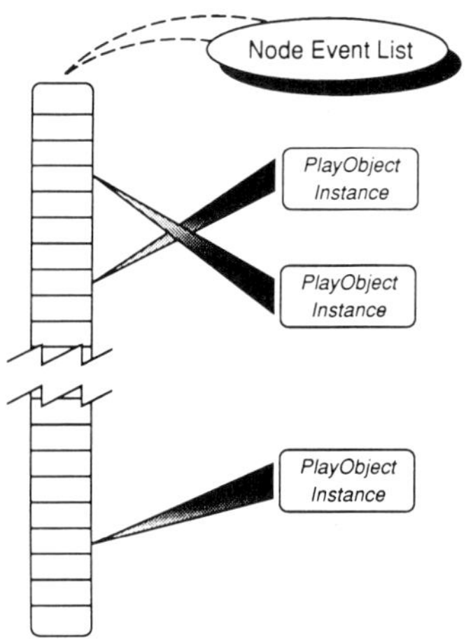

Fig. 6. The PlayObject can be thought of as 'saving a Node's place in an Event list'. Thus, a single Node may have several performances that overlap as long as there are PlayObjects to maintain each performance's place.

- To translate the user-defined timing base to the standard timing base, and vice versa.

There can be any number of Conductor objects active during a performance, with each Conductor controlling a single Node or a set of Nodes. In fact, it is entirely possible to have every Node within a performance following a different Conductor. In any case, the Node is responsible for coordinating the Conductor's translation of an event's virtual time to real time (for performance) and vice versa (for recording).

Before a user can input a tempo map into a conductor, he/she must define the timing base to be used. For example, the user might wish to create a tempo map for a piece of traditional Western music. In this case, the user would probably define the timing base as measures and beats and give the Conductor the number of beats in each measure before constructing the tempo map.

ConductObjects

One aspect of the Conductor and the Node not yet discussed is that of 'offset times'. The timings of events within a Node are all relative to the performance time of the Node. Thus, if a Node starts performing its events 3 seconds into a performance, the event within the Node set to occur at time 2 seconds will actually occur at $3 + 2 = 5$ seconds from the start of the performance.

In addition, in order for a Conductor to translate correctly between virtual time and real time, it must keep track of its offset time, the delay between performance start and Conductor start. To help with this, we have created the **ConductObject.** A ConductObject maintains the Conductor's time of start and any memory required by the Conductor to keep track of time translation—everything necessary to re-establish a Conductor's state of conducting. ConductObjects are always used by the Node to communicate with the Conductor, so the ConductObject can forward extra information to the Conductor along with the Node's message.

A Node may request a particular Conductor, or a Node may inherit a Conductor from a previous Node. In the latter case, the actual Conductor is not inherited, but rather the ConductObject, so that time translation remains consistent.

PlayObjects

During performance with the *Creation Station,* it is possible that the user may request that a Node be performed several times. It is further possible that these Node performances may overlap. This presents some potential problems: during a performance, a Node needs to store certain information, such as its performance offset and active ConductObject. Likewise, the Event objects may need to keep track of information. If two or more performances of a Node overlap, conflicts could occur among the data pertinent to each performance.

Similar to the ConductObject, the **PlayObject** resolves any potential conflicts by keeping track of performance states for the Node and its associated Event objects (see Fig. 6). The information stored in the PlayObject needs to be passed to the Node every time the PlayManagementObject wishes to communicate with the Node. This means that the PlayObject must receive and relay the appropriate messages from the PlayManagementObject to the Node.

The PlayManagementObject

The PlayManagementObject is a simple object with two purposes:

- Manage and sequence a list of PlayObjects during performance.
- Update the real-time display during a performance.

There is only one instance of the PlayManagementObject within the *Creation Station.* When a performance begins, the PlayManagementObject creates a PlayObject for the top Node in the hierarchical track system, which in turn creates PlayObjects for other Nodes within the tree. The PlayManagementObject keeps track of the events managed by each PlayObject and correctly sequences the events of the whole hierarchy until either no more events are available or the user interrupts the performance.

If, during the performance, the PlayManagementObject is well ahead of the Performer buffers, the PlayManagementObject will command an object called ScrollWindow to display the performance time. Each active ScrollWindow is associated with a ConductObject and displays the performance time in the user-defined timing base. This allows the user to have performance time displayed in any timing base desired, including measures and beats. If events are not being processed fast enough, the PlayManagementObject may never request the ScrollWindow to update the displayed time.

THE EDITOR AND EDITORUI

These two objects will provide the user with event list editing capabilities. Although these objects have not yet been created, they will follow many of the same ideas as other objects within the *Creation Station.* Objects of the Editor genre will contain the code that edits events of a certain class. Objects of the EditorUI genre (named for 'Editor User Interface') will be responsible for providing the graphics user interface to its associated Editor object. It is possible to have many EditorUIs that will work with a single Editor object, so we will implement a match system that works with the Editor Format Name (EFN). An Editor will have an EFN associated with it, and it will be matched with available EditorUIs of the same EFN. In this way, it will be easy to change the user interface while keeping the same editing functions.

CONCLUSION

As the *Creation Station* nears completion, it becomes increasingly clear how much our project has benefited from our using Objective-C:

- The *Creation Station* is easily expandable, with little or no recompilation of existing code. This includes easy addition of new Event classes and user interfaces, and easy integration of new hardware.

- The user interface is highly flexible, providing seamless integration and synchronization of a multitude of Event classes, device drivers and editing environments.
- Our program code more closely models how we conceptualize the *Creation Station.* In fact, most of the objects we generate have direct correlations within the user interface. This includes the Node, the Conductor, and the PlayManagementObject, which is directly linked with the master recorder panel.
- We have generated surprisingly little code in very little time to perform the desired tasks.
- Our code is highly reusable. In fact, we have been able to share objects that were originally created to support very specific tasks.
- General program management was much easier than expected.
- We soon expect to support third-party development for the *Creation Station.* This would not be possible without OOPL dynamic binding.

Many people have contributed to the *Creation Station,* and we have been able to implement innumerable ideas into one software package. Because the *Creation Station* is such a flexible system, we expect it to fill countless niches within the artistic world.

Note

1. Objective-C is a registered trademark of the Stepstone Corporation.

Bibliography

Brokaw, Hal, Henry Flurry, Phil Mackenzie and Jeff Stillson, "Center for Performing Arts and Technology Preliminary Documentation of Objects" (University of Michigan, 1988).

Cox, Brad J., *Object-Oriented Programming: An Evolutionary Approach* (Reading, MA: Addison-Wesley, 1986).

Gregory, David, "A Proposal for a Center for Performing Arts and Technology" (University of Michigan, 1987).

Krasner, Glenn, "Machine Tongues VIII: The Design of a Smalltalk Music System", *Computer Music Journal* **4**, No. 4, 4–14 (1980).

Ledbetter, Lamar, and Brad Cox, "Software-ICs", *BYTE* (June 1985) pp. 307–316.

Lieberman, Henry, "Machine Tongues IX: Object-Oriented Programming", *Computer Music Journal* **6**, No. 3, 8–21 (1982).

Pascoe, Geoffrey A., "Elements of Object-Oriented Programming", *BYTE* (August 1986) pp. 139–144.

Rodet, Xavier, and Pierre Cointe, "FORMES: Composition and Scheduling Processes", *Computer Music Journal* **8**, No. 3, 32–50 (1985).

Stepstone Corporation, "Technical Specifications: Objective-C Language Version 3.3" (Connecticut: Stepstone Corporation, n.d.).

Wirth, Niklaus. *Algorithms and Data Structures* (Englewood Cliffs, NJ: Prentice-Hall, 1986).

Computer Music Languages . . . and the Real World

Mathias Fuchs

The limits of my language are the limits of my world.

—Ludwig Wittgenstein

The language of the Canadian Eskimos has more than 10 different words for 'frozen water'. There is one for ice that melted and froze again, one for ice that is extremely cold and at least eight others. If one wants to have a conversation about frozen water in a Central African dialect, the conversation will be much more difficult. There are no appropriate words.

Yet the matter is even worse when one tries to communicate musical ideas on a digital computer. Such attempts have existed since 1957 and are known as computer music languages. A short survey should point out some of the problems in that field. Special notice will be taken of the state of the art of general-purpose programming languages at that time.

COMPUTER MUSIC LANGUAGES

MUSIC I (Mathews, 1957) made it possible to generate sounds of a triangle waveform on a computer. The tones could be controlled in pitch, amplitude and duration. As there were no means of defining structures on a higher level, the way of 'programming' a musical piece resembled the way programming in general was done at that time. FORTRAN was only a year old; therefore, most of the programs were still written on the assembler level. For that reason, the early programs for computer music contain all the ugly ingredients of 1950s programming technique, like GOTOs, mnemonics, numeric labels, and so on.

MUSIC III (Mathews, 1960) presented the totally new concept of unit generators. The program was a simulation of electronic modules, like the ones of the Moog synthesizer, which appeared at almost the same time. There are also parallels to programming techniques that became known at that time. Modular programming tries to build up a program structure from smaller, generalized units that fit into various applications.

MUSIC IV (Mathews, 1963) was programmed because the company changed the computer. It would be hard to find musical reason behind the redesign of the language. Mathews himself admits: "MUSIC IV was simply a response to a change in the language and the computer. . . . So in essence MUSIC IV was musically no more powerful than MUSIC III" [1]. There are many cases like that, where technical necessity rather than musical need controlled the development of music languages. Gottfried Michael Koenig, another pioneer of formal music languages, was forced to rewrite Project 1 from FORTRAN to ALGOL when he moved from Cologne to the Netherlands.

Mathias Fuchs, Elsa Beskowsgata 21, S-12666, Hägersten, Sweden.

Received 25 April 1988.

Growing discontent with the working conditions at a big university computer center prompted a number of composers to design portable systems in the beginning of the 1970s. Ed Kobrin's HYBRID system for voltage-controlled oscillators, amplifiers and filters was such a system running on a PDP 11/10. Others were the EMS1 system or HYBRID 0 for Moog modules and a CA minicomputer. In order to perform in real time, these systems ran very fast command interpreters to service the musician's instructions and the hardware interfaces. The only input source was, in many cases, the alphanumeric keyboard. Therefore, one of the main design criteria was an extremely abbreviated command language. For example, a line to set the oscillator 01 to the top tenth of the available frequency range was

01;8–9;I2;K;R <return>

One does not need to point out that such a cryptic code is only transparent to the experienced user.

The intransparency and the lack of self-explanatory strength led Xenakis to the design of the machine UPIC. Xenakis can claim to have one of the few computer systems whereby an absolute beginner immediately can start to make music in an intuitive way. This goal is accomplished through graphic programming. Instead of defining functions by numbers or mathematical relations, UPIC reads in lines that are drawn onto a graphic table and controls a software synthesizer according to the line's course. As soon as the line goes up, the pitch (or amplitude, etc.) goes up.

The problem with a complex system like UPIC is that it can be run only on a specific machine—in this case, the one at CEMAMu in Paris. Many composers would never be able to go there and experiment with the system for a reasonable time. These considerations were a starting point for the CDP (Composer's Desktop Project) in Great Britain, where an inexpensive system using the generally available Atari 1040 was built. The software is an integrated package of sound processing utilities, called GROUCHO. The link between the programs is a standardized file format. As all the programs use this format, it is easy to let the system grow. Any one of the project's members can add new software at any time. The design idea of an open system and some features of the user interface have their parallels in modern operating systems and in data exchange and communication programs. One could see this design as opposed to the totally defined languages, like PL/1. The open systems have their main domain in the home computer and PC field. Systems that resemble GROUCHO in some respects are the Californian

Pergamon Press plc. Printed in Great Britain.
0024-094X/88 $3.00+0.00

Table 1. Music Languages

Music Language	Author	Year of Implementation	Implementation Language	User Interface/Hardware	Representation of Objects
MUSIC I	Max Mathews	1957	Assembler	punched cards/big mainframe	numbers
MUSIC II	Max Mathews	1958			
MUSIC III	Max Mathews	1960			unit generators, simulation of electronic circuits
MUSIC IV	Max Mathews	1963	FORTRAN		
MUSIC V	Max Mathews	1968			
Project 1	Gottfried M. Koenig	1964	FORTRAN rewritten in ALGOL	command lines	numbers, strictly formatted (e.g. 4.783), lists
Project 2	Gottfried M. Koenig	1965	ALGOL 60	subprogram calls/multiuser system	numbers, lists
SCORE	Leland Smith	1972			
GROOVE	Max Mathews, Moore	1970		graphic input	
HYBRID IV	Edward Kobrin	1976	PDP Assembler	command lines/ mini comp. and piano keyboard	symbols for synth. units
UPIC	Iannis Xenakis, CEMAMu	1970s		dialogue via graphics tablet, CRT, tableau des fonctions	graphs
CHANT	Xavier Rodet, Gerald Bennett, Conrad Cummings, Yves Potard	1980	FORTRAN	parameters in dialogue	functions
BADA	Michael Hinton, EMS Stockholm	1970s	FORTRAN		
CARL	Stanford				
GROUCHO	Composer's Desktop Project, A. Bentley and others	1986	C	program calls/personal computer	

CARL (which actually served as a model for GROUCHO) and the Stockholm BADA package (see Table 1).

Proposal for Classification

Much of the systematic work on computer music [2] divides the object of investigation into two classes:
(i) sound generating programs and
(ii) programs for score generation.

The first ones are often called instrument definitions. Mathews argues that this hierarchy (in his case the categories are instrument, score, and performance or interpretation) emerges naturally from our concept of conventional music. For two reasons I do not want to keep this idea.

First, electronic music has ever attempted to cross the borders between the realm of 'sound' and 'compositorial structure' and has understood them as inseparable from each other. How can a systematic theory then hold up this difference? Second, since music languages contain certain features of the general purpose languages that are available at the time of their conception, I suggest a classification that takes into account the features of the 'unmusical' computer languages.

Classification for Programming Languages

There are at least four major families of programming languages, which differ in how they approach a programming problem (see Table 2).

(i) The first one could be called the systematic approach. ALGOL, Pascal, C and ADA belong to this family. These languages are characterized by total regulation by means of syntactic and semantic rules for any statement inside the language. Easy things are often complicated to express. Classes of objects are not permeable.

(ii) The second family was born out of the frustration caused by the first. BASIC was such a language, whereby simple tasks could be achieved in an easy way. APL is another example that shows how efficiently and briefly one can code as long as the language is flexible enough. One main aim in the design of these languages is efficiency.

(iii) The third family is fine for people who cannot read or write but still

Table 2. General-Purpose Programming Languages

General-Purpose Programming Language	First Published	Author(s)	Class
FORTRAN	1956		(i) systematic, algorithmic
ALGOL 60	1960	Backus et al.	
PASCAL	1971	Nickolaus Wirth, TH Zurich	
C			
ADA	1979	Jean Ichbiah, Honeywell Bull, Department of Defense	
BASIC			(ii) efficient
APL	1960s	Kenneth E. Iverson, IBM	
LOGO			(iii) graphic
SMALLTALK	early 1970s	Alan Kay, Xerox Palo Alto	
Framework	1984	Ashton Tate	(iv) integrated, open
Framework II with FRED programming language	1986		
OpenAccess			
1-2-3		Lotus Development Corporation	
Symphony	1985		

Table 3. Music Languages

Music Language	First Published	Author	Class
MUSIC I, II, III, IV, V	1957–1968	M. Mathews	(i) systematic, algorithmic
Project 1, 2	1964, 1965	G. M. Koenig	
HYBRID IV	1976	E. Kobrin	(ii) efficient
UPIC	1970s	I. Xenakis	(iii) graphic
GROUCHO	1986	CDP	(iv) integrated

want to be programmers. It is the family of graphic languages. LOGO is such a language, but the ideology reaches out into many modern operating systems, especially in the personal computer sector.

(iv) It was not long ago that the PC market was conquered by a type of software that became known as integrated packages. These programs, though not general-purpose programming languages in the original meaning of the word, come close to them when one regards standard applications for everyday usage. Programs like Framework, OpenAccess, Lotus Symphony and others offer many convenient functions to make programming easier. Usually, they contain some graphic utilities, a database, spreadsheet functions, a word processor and communication programs. A characteristic feature is their open design, which allows linkage to all kinds of programs. They are less hermetic, less concise, easier to use and easier to learn than the systematic high-level programming languages.

The classification proposed here reflects the way of handling the objects of the language. There are, of course, languages that fit into more than one group. SMALLTALK is one; though the graphic facilities are an important part of the language, one could place it as well in class (i).

Classification for Music Languages

If one applies the same classification scheme to computer music languages, one notices the degree to which design criteria for musical languages rely on design trends in the commercial field (see Table 3). It is certainly not by chance that the birth of the most interesting music packages, CARL and GROUCHO (Stanford and York, respectively), coincides with the birth of the Symphony/Framework class.

Conclusions

Language is a virus.

—William S. Burroughs

One of the myths computer musicians are living with is the idea that they can use the computer as a neutral tool that serves them in realizing their compositional ideas without influencing them. The opposite is true.

Musical output often seems closer to the computer system used than to the composer's ideas (if such were present). As a consequence, record covers and concert reviews are more often based on the technological background of the pieces than on aesthetics. The tool is not a neutral means of achieving an abstract aim; rather it should be regarded as an important factor in the process of musical creativity. This is no shame, neither is it new to the musical universe. It makes a difference whether one writes for trombone or for guitar. The impact of a computer music language on the process of composing therefore should be seen in the context of a given state of the art in programming techniques. Computer music languages have to do with sounds and with musical structures. But they also have to do with which software products are commercially available.

The German composer Herbert Eimert was angry once when somebody associated electronic music with electricity. He said, "Electronic music has more in common with serialism, than with the electric vacuum cleaner".

Apart from the fact that the concept of the vacuum cleaner seems to have a more lasting life than that of serialism, we should not hesitate to observe the importance of the hardware behind artistic creation.

References and Notes

1. *Computer Music Journal* **4**, No. 4 (1978).

2. For further information the reader is directed to the following works: William Buxton, *Design Issues in the Foundation of a Computer Based Tool for Music Composition* (Ontario, 1978); Lejaren Hiller, *Computermusik und Informationstheorie* (Mainz, 1963); Michael Longton, *Priorities in the Design of a Microprocessor-Based Music Program* (Victoria, 1981); Max Mathews, *The Technology of Computer Music* (Cambridge, 1969).

Further Reading

Ed Kobrin, *Computer in Performance* (Berlin, 1973).

Gottfried Michael Koenig, Computer Composition (Sonological Reports, Utrecht).

Barry Truax, POD 4,5 and 6 (Sonological Reports, Utrecht).

In addition, the reader should consult the diverse manuals and printouts of SCORE, BADA, UPIC, CHANT, Hybrid 0.

Computer Graphics and Animation as Agents of Personal Evolution in the Arts

Robin G. King

ABSTRACT

The author addresses a number of issues related to the potential of computer graphics and animation systems to enhance or reenforce the process of artistic creativity and evolution. Various constraints imposed by computer graphics systems are explored and the major psychological characteristics of creative thinking are described. Issues are raised regarding the impact on these characteristics by the properties and process inherent in computer graphics and animation systems and their potential as agents for personal evolution in the arts.

Many claims have been made, particularly in the visual arts, regarding the effects of computer graphics and animation technologies on the creative process. Unfortunately, there has been very little empirical research either to substantiate or to refute these claims. Many artists and writers have articulated the apparent, positive effects of using computer systems to explore their ideas [1]. A few have taken a somewhat neutral position (i.e. there is little or no effect on creative productivity) [2], but there is very little documentation to be found regarding the negative aspects of making images with these new technologies [3].

The picture is further distorted by the relative infancy of these media. Relatively few writers or researchers have articulated the aesthetic issues that characterize images produced with computer systems. Those who have attempted to deal with these issues have concentrated primarily on comparisons with traditional media, with the articulation of novel properties and characteristics, with classification or with aesthetic experience. Even less material has been published from a psychological perspective. Almost no empirical research has been forthcoming.

The purpose of this paper is to attempt to clarify some of these issues and, in particular, to raise questions regarding the potential of graphics technologies for accelerating or improving the creative process and hence the evolution of the artist and the visual arts. 'Computer art' is characterized as either mimetic, derivative, innovative or emergent, and these terms are explained.

THE CHARACTERISTICS OF 'COMPUTER ART'

Until the last few years, these technologies have been available to only a few artists because of their high cost. With the increased democratization of the technology, artists are currently able to access software with 'high-end' functionality at relatively low cost on microcomputer systems. A survey of the aesthetic characteristics of work produced with computer systems will, for the most part, reveal that most of it can be classified into one of four categories [4].

The *mimetic* category consists of replications of works of art originally produced in other media, e.g. paint, silkscreen, film photography, etc. This is probably the most common result of initial experimentation with the technology. By attempting to replicate, emulate or imitate established and traditional artwork, the artist is able to determine the characteristics, limitations and appropriate methodologies for the new tools. The artwork should be seen as a function of this experimentation, not as new or novel. The attempt to emulate traditional methods will always fall short of its goal.

Derivative computer artwork has the properties and characteristics of traditional art forms (typically work produced in an existing style or school) and meets established or traditional stylistic and aesthetic criteria. As the artist begins to master the techniques, there is often a period during which he or she makes variations by applying the technology to variations of known conceptual and artistic situations. It is perhaps to be expected that an artist will try to extend his or her working methods and stylistic preferences to new technology or to work in an established stylistic framework.

The *innovative* class of computer artwork demonstrates novel techniques, content or imagery through alterations or changes to the existing computer graphics paradigm. Most often these are the result of the development of new algorithms, but they also may be manifest as novel forms of imagery, for example, in the work of the better-known artists in this field.

The result of this approach is that the work, however monumental in its technical achievement, usually falls short of that which it tries to emulate. If it does come close, and it may be excellent in its own right, it is generally no better than the original. On the other hand, evolution is often achieved by incremental progress, and innovation serves to push development towards major change.

Emergent artwork is characterized by the use of the 'unique' properties of the media. It is this last category that has proved so difficult to deal with, for we have few analytical perspectives (particularly aesthetic ones) by which to categorize and critique the work that results from the application of techniques unparalleled in traditional art forms.

What are the unique properties of computer graphics and animation? To summarize other writers on this topic: there appears to be a general consensus that the uniqueness of

Robin G. King, Sheridan Computer Graphics Studios, Sheridan College, 1430 Trafalgar Road, Oakville, Ontario, Canada, L6H 2L1.

Received 5 May 1988.

Pergamon Press plc. Printed in Great Britain.
0024-094X/88 $3.00+0.00

the media may be characterized by interactivity (direct, immediate feedback), simulation (virtual three-dimensional space) and intelligence (the capacity of the technology to incorporate rules and constraints in order to incorporate decision-making strategies).

These four categories may be used to classify artwork, but care should be taken not to apply them in a way that may invalidate the integrity of, for example, mimetic or derivative work, providing the purpose for their production is appropriate to the situation, e.g. during education and training, as an extension of traditional work or as exploration. The problem is that much work has been produced without any emotion, without any purpose (other than exploration of technique), without novelty, without meaning and without an appeal to a broad cultural context or indeed to human issues [5].

THE CONSTRAINTS OF COMPUTER GRAPHICS TECHNOLOGY

With the introduction of any new medium, artists first must master the techniques of the medium and apply them to the solution of existing problems. This is often done by duplicating and imitating, stylistically and technically, traditional works of art. Indeed the very design of the technology is mimetic. The designers attempt to duplicate traditional working methods rather than to invent entirely new tools. This has even been extended to the development of a system designed to duplicate drawing with charcoal!

It is clear that the technology itself also imposes constraints on the aesthetic and stylistic characteristics of artwork produced in this manner. First among this list are the *hardware constraints,* and the most important of these are the characteristics of the hard-copy devices that are available, such as displays, film camera systems, printers, plotters, video technology and the like. These devices provide a very limited range of physical media with which to work, unless a process is developed to extend them or to interface them with other technologies, e.g. photography, ceramics or silk-screen.

In addition, to perhaps an even greater degree, there are *software constraints,* not only the particular characteristics of the system's primitive shapes, text, colors and attributes, but also the working methodologies. Every system is designed by a group of people who, through the combination of hardware selection and software development, leave their characteristic signature, and this signature often leaves its mark on the work of art.

In addition to the above, there are also *physical constraints.* At least for a significant part of the image-making process, the artist's body remains in a relatively static position, which limits the range of expressive gestures and movements available. The artist must maintain a high level of concentration on a bright, luminous monitor and must keep his or her eyes focussed in a narrow range.

In making the transition from traditional to digital media, it is important not to ignore the *emotional and intellectual effects* of working with computer systems. For the most part, artists report significant frustration while learning to use new and complex technologies, especially because the image-making methodologies required contrast sharply with those that they have used in the past and that form the basis of their working methods. The frustrations of not being able to express line, form and shape with the articulation that is available with paint and pencil probably have caused many an artist to reject the computer as a working tool. Breaking away from habitual techniques and replacing them with new ones often requires a painful transition. Many artists are disturbed by a medium that is so apparently logical in nature.

THE CREATIVE ACT AS PERSONAL EVOLUTION

Creativity may be defined as the transformational act of a human in the process of evolution [6]. Creative behavior occurs when there is a transformation or emergence of new ideas or artifacts resulting from a series of interconnected events. It is also the process by which the artist transforms him- or herself. In fact, it may be claimed that artwork is 'merely' a by-product of the process of personal evolution or restructuring. Rather than an end in itself, it is an indicator of the changes that have taken place during the reinvention of the self.

In a previous paper [7], I have suggested that there is a natural evolutionary process involved in the evolution of artistic constructs and skills, and that the hierarchical stages of personal development parallel the mimetic, derivative, innovative and emergent characteristics of artwork described above. These claims are made on the basis of empirical research using the Repertory Grid Technique.

First the artist must develop *skill,* becoming familiar with the materials and their characteristics. The artist builds a repertory of expressive techniques. These techniques are then *applied* to the solution of (usually familiar) visual problems. This step is followed by *novelty and innovation* as these techniques are combined with others or articulated by modification. Finally we may see the emergence of original elements, ideas or concepts. This emergence appears most often to be associated with moral concerns and constructs such as honesty and integrity.

For evolution to take place, for the emergence of the new, boundaries must be broken. For boundaries to be broken, there must be a degree of chaos or fluctuation in an open system. Artists often create chaos purposely in order to break out of their localized, conventional paradigm. Seldom do computer graphics systems have controlled randomness or chaos as a part of their design methodology (although it may often seem that way!).

THE CHARACTERISTICS OF CREATIVE PROCESS

In 1926, Wallas [8] formalized the stages of creative process as preparation, incubation and illumination; these terms still are used today. In general, traditional approaches to the development of descriptions and explanations of creative behavior have been limited to reductionist analysis rather than holistic synthesis.

The traditional approaches to research in the field of creativity have generally been limited to

1) descriptions of the various phases or stages of creative process,

Table 1. Comparison of the stages of creative behavior.

Taylor	King
Expressive	
Technical	Mimetic
Inventive	Derivative
Innovative	Innovative
Emergent	Emergent

2) psychological and behavioral characteristics of creative individuals,

3) observations regarding the nature of creative artifacts, i.e. style and aesthetic issues, and

4) the effects of the physical and psychological environment on the outcome of creative behaviors.

There have been many attempts to model the creative process from each of these perspectives. I have proposed a single structural model of creative process [9] that subsumes these traditional approaches by using general systems theory (specifically Catastrophe Theory) as a modelling device. This model has been applied to a variety of problems in computer graphics and computer graphics education.

Creativity is a fundamental part of artistic activity, yet it remains a paradox at the forefront of contemporary inquiry into the nature of human thought. Creative behavior is a synthesis of intuitive as well as intellectual thought, and intuition is not readily open to reductionist analysis. It is characterized by a process in which associations are made among 'remote' facts, concepts or insights in ways that, at least on the surface, appear unpredictable and not always of the individual's volition. While creativity is teleological or goal-oriented, there is often an infinite variety of ways in which the final objective may be reached.

From a variety of different perspectives, psychologists have identified a number of characteristics of creative behavior, both in terms of individual personality characteristics and in terms of process. The most important of these are summarized below, and their relationship to working methodologies in computer graphics and animation is discussed.

The process of divergent thinking (the ability to process ideas from different perspectives and contrasting frameworks) is a key characteristic of the creative process as well as an important part of the creative endeavor. During the formative stages of creative exploration the artist explores both the external world and the inner self in a psychological framework of *openness.* This exploration requires a number of critical capabilities, in particular the *ability to tolerate ambiguity and chaos, sensitivity to problems* and *a high degree of spontaneity.* The creative individual must develop a mental and physical environment that facilitates this activity. For maximum creative productivity, ideas must be produced with *fluency, flexibility* and *originality.*

In *Perspectives in Creativity* [10], Taylor describes a slightly more elaborate set of 'creative dis-positions' that characterize psychological processes similar to those I have described. These he describes as expressive, technical, inventive, innovative and emergent creativity. Table 1 illustrates these ideas.

The Computer as an Evolutionary Agent

The degree to which a computer graphics or animation system helps or hinders creative activity is of critical importance. At all stages of the creative process and during the evolution of ideas, we need the computer system to improve, supplement and enhance our articulation and manipulation of ideas rather than to cause mental, emotional or physical blocks to creative productivity.

From the start, we are working with a physical system that restricts access to physical and environmental stimuli. Because of this screen-centered activity, our mental faculties 'lock out', to a remarkable degree, our immediate surroundings. We are less likely to see or experience the environment that surrounds us. We are removed from the impact of other visual artifacts, tactile and auditory sensations and interaction with other people. The technology restricts our divergent thinking during the initial stages of idea development although it should be doing the opposite.

This process is intensified by the *interactivity* of the technology. We are seduced by its responsiveness. We lose a sense of time and place. Interactivity with an 'external' context coupled with the system's interactivity would appear to restrict the creative individual's opportunity to explore or to interrelate divergent concepts and images. In addition, computer graphics systems have significant expressive constraints. The tools available do not facilitate expressive gestures or tactile contact with the image. Hardware and software constraints may also have a negative influence.

On the other hand, the immediacy and interactivity of these systems provide a psychological framework much closer in some ways to that experienced by an artist during intense concentration during a production process. Computer graphics (and to some degree, computer animation) systems provide the artist with extended capabilities for improvement of both the fluency and the flexibility of image generation. They facilitate the rapid exploration of changes in image characteristics in both paint- and object-oriented systems, which are unparalleled in speed, flexibility and fluency by any other media. It is also possible to create, change and manipulate objects and process in ways that cannot be achieved by any other means. The artist can combine, rearrange and manipulate images from a wide variety of sources with great dexterity.

During the convergent stages of creative process (i.e. implementation) a similar situation exists. All of the individual's mental capabilities must be focussed on the process of synthesizing or 'distilling' ideas and concepts that have emerged (usually from the process of incubation and illumination). Again, current computer technologies appear in many ways to restrict the creative process at this point. The ease of production of many variations on a visual theme or pattern can serve to confuse the artist and make selection difficult. The artist also may become seduced into taking many of these variations seriously and may even be incapable of deciding what is important from such overproduction. On the other hand, variety, flexibility and ease of manipulation assist the associative processes, making it easier to combine remote visual ideas and concepts.

From these perspectives, the positive aspects of using digital systems are clear. Added to the above is the continued development of new modes of interactivity, representation and manipulation. Many of these new techniques come from advances in computer animation and allied technologies such as CD-ROM as well as developments in hard-copy technology. We also can expect to see the development of a wider range of both input and output technologies. As hardware increases in speed and storage capability, accessibility to large databases of imagery, viewable as multiple images on screen, should improve significantly the initial stages of creative exploration. Fast, high-capacity fibre-optic communications links will greatly assist the cultural and crosscultural exchange of both imagery and data.

At the educational level, major advances in artistic and design training could be made. Unfortunately, there is virtually no *systematic, empirical experimentation* available that could form the basis of applying these technologies to the evolution of either technical or conceptual skills. There is an urgent need for such work, if only to arrest the haphazard, poorly conceived tendency in many art schools to submit to the first high-pressure salesperson who sets foot in the door. We need an international task force to design and develop appropriate approaches to these problems and to share concrete experiences and perspectives; otherwise the negative effects of technological change may overcome the positive. This should be done not to standardize but to provide opportunities for divergent approaches and innovative exchange.

As far as the individual artist is concerned, while personal statements about the effects of computer graphics and animation systems of personal creative change are useful, there has been no systematic effort to document and to articulate the issues surrounding the transition process, the effects of these systems on creative behavior or the evolution of technique and ideas. Computer graphics and animation can affect creative activity positively at every stage, by improving the initial, divergent stages of exploration, by providing the means for accelerating the manipulation and articulation of ideas and by providing innovative frameworks for the synthesis of original imagery and concepts.

References

1. Cynthia Goodman, *Digital Visions: Computers and Art* (New York: Abrams, 1987); A. Michael Noll, "Computers and the Arts: A Retrospective View", in *ACM SIGGRAPH 1982 Art Show Catalogue* (Boston, MA: 1982); Frank Dietrich, "Five Aspects of a Theory of Computer Art", in *Panel Notes: Aesthetics of Computer Graphics. ACM SIGGRAPH* (San Francisco: 1985).

2. John Pearson, "The Computer: Liberator or Jailer of Creative Spirit", in *Proceedings NCGA 1988* (Anaheim, CA: 1988).

3. Jack Burnham, "The Panacea that Failed", in *The Myths of Information*, Kathleen Woodward, ed. (Madison, WI: Coda Press, 1980) pp. 200–215; Kenneth Knowlton, "Why It Isn't Art Yet", in *ACM SIGGRAPH 1986 Art Show Catalogue* (Dallas, TX: 1986); Gene Youngblood, "A Medium Matures: The Myth of Computer Art", in *ACM SIGGRAPH 1983 Art Show Catalogue* (Detroit, MI: 1983).

4. Robin G. King, "Aesthetic Experience, Creativity and Computer Art", in *Proceedings NCGA 1988* (Anaheim, CA: 1988).

5. King [4].

6. Robin G. King, "A General Systems Model of the Creative Process", in *Proceedings of the 25th Annual Meeting of the Society for General Systems Research with the American Association for the Advancement of Science, Toronto, Canada, January 2–5, 1980* (Toronto: Society for General Systems Research, 1980).

7. King [4].

8. G. Wallas, *The Art of Thought* (New York: Harcourt, 1926).

9. King [6].

10. Irving A. Taylor, "An Emerging View of Creative Actions", in *Perspectives in Creativity*, Irving A. Taylor and J.W. Getzels, eds. (Chicago: Aldine, 1975) pp. 295–325.

Storing Art Images in Intelligent Computers

Joan L. Kirsch and
Russell A. Kirsch

ABSTRACT

Images of artworks can be stored in media that preserve different characteristics of the original. Differences exist in the extent to which we can preserve color, three-dimensionality, surface texture, fine structure, tonal gradations, temporal variations and other characteristics that lend uniqueness to individual artworks. Usually, we are willing to sacrifice some of these characteristics in exchange for the permanence and recoverability offered by storage media. Thus, a color slide (diapositive), which is a common medium for storing images of artworks, compromises all of the above properties to different extents but is nevertheless considered useful for the archival properties it offers for images of artworks. Digital storage media used in conjunction with computers offer new opportunities and demand new compromises in storing art images. An unusual challenge is offered by the possibility of providing intelligence to a computer. The authors make clear the sense in which we may ascribe intelligence to the computer and how this may be used to 'perceive' the image of an artwork. The computer then uses its knowledge of the artwork with respect to a large class of such works not only for archival storage but also to achieve economy in the use of the storage medium. The authors illustrate the achievement of storage economy as much as tens of thousands of times greater than storage without intelligence. The intelligence is provided to the computer as syntactic descriptions of classes of artworks. The syntactic descriptions incorporate insight from the art historian, critic or artist who uses innovative tools like shape grammars to provide the computer with a small part of the intelligence that the educated human viewer brings to the perception of the artwork.

Any reproduction of a visual artwork creates a representation that fails to capture some properties of the original. Since most art is not sufficiently portable to make it available to all possible viewers, we accept the necessity of making reproductions with the consequent loss in properties, some of which may be vital to the proper appreciation of the artwork. Photography is the most well established of these reproduction methods. Critical viewers know that photographic reproductions fail to capture color, texture, three-dimensionality, surface texture, tonal gradations, fine detailed structure, and movement. Still, we make photographs and use them for teaching, scholarship, archiving, criticism and conservation of visual art materials.

Other reproduction methods are newer and less familiar, presenting new opportunities and demanding new compromises. Two notable such methods are the analog representations used on video discs and the digital representations used on optical discs for storage of art images. These methods differ in important ways from photography, notably in their ability to capture movement and to be rapidly searched among large collections of such images; however, their spatial resolution is poor compared to photography.

We could continue to list other methods of representing artworks, but almost all common methods we might list share one important property—they ignore the art by being passive with respect to the content of the image. To suggest that a photograph or a video disc recording ignores the artworks recorded is to imply that there is an alternative. Can a storage medium look at a work of art in such a way as to be said to perceive it? We would hesitate to answer 'yes', unless some intelligent process had intervened in the recording so as to show some evidence of understanding. Ordinarily, we think of understanding associated only with human capabilities. However, great advances in the field of artificial intelligence over the past three decades of research have en-

Joan L. Kirsch, The Sturvil Corporation, Clarksburg, MD 20871-0157, U.S.A.
Russell A. Kirsch, The Sturvil Corporation, Clarksburg, MD 29871-0157, U.S.A.
Received 7 April 1988.

Fig. 1. Albrecht Dürer, *Melencholia I*, engraving, 240 × 187 mm, 1514.

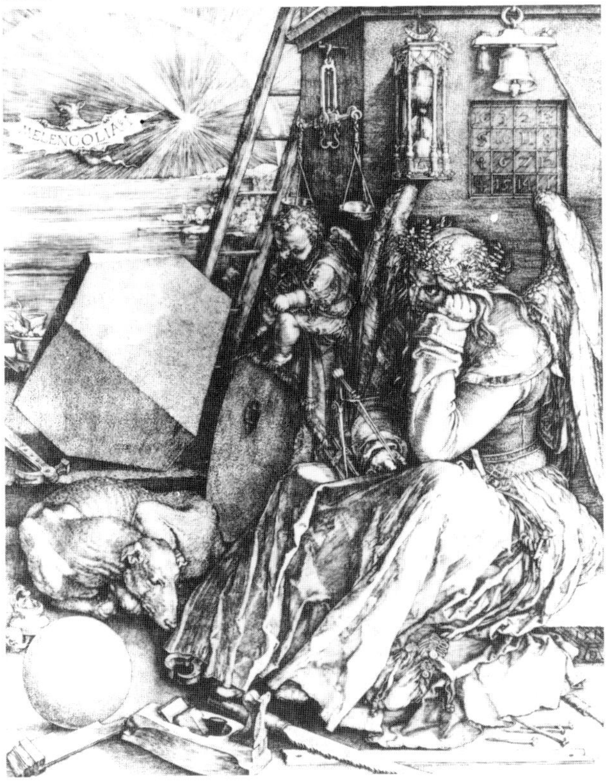

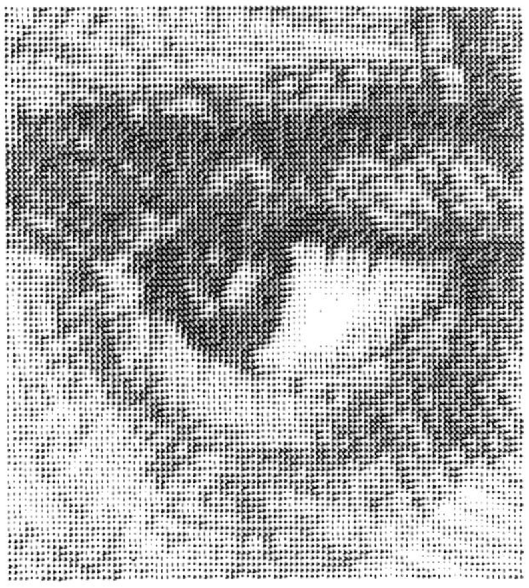

Fig. 2. Computer scanned and reproduced detail with a scanning resolution of 50 micrometers. Eight levels of grey tone are shown in individual pixels.

Pergamon Press plc. Printed in Great Britain.
0024-094X/88 $3.00+0.00

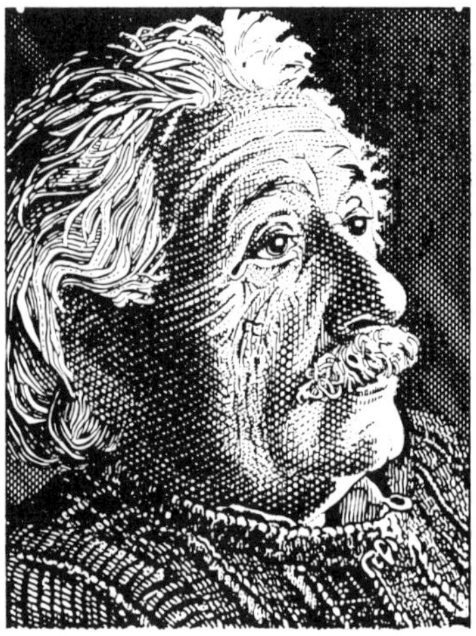

Fig. 3. Einstein postage stamp, issued 4 March 1979, U.S. Treasury, Bureau of Printing and Engraving.

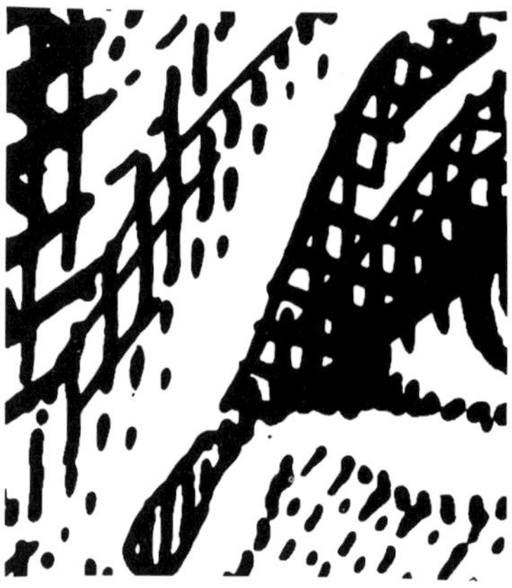

Fig. 4. Computer scanned and enlarged detail from below the eye in the Einstein engraving.

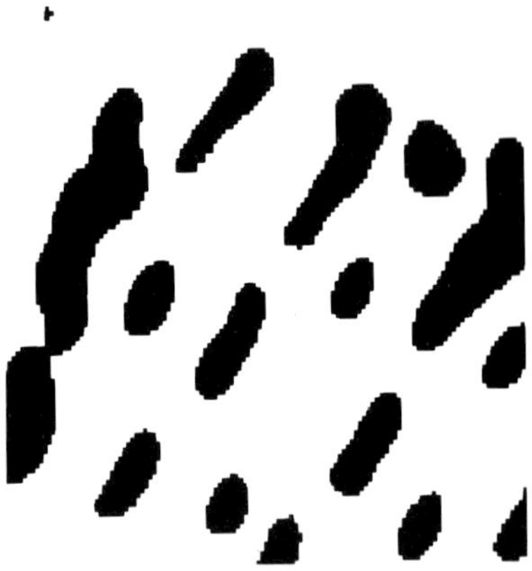

Fig. 5. Extreme enlargement of detail below the eye in the Einstein engraving.

couraged us to think of computers as having some degree of understanding in many disciplines. We see no reason why these insights from artificial intelligence should be denied to the visual arts. And we might expect that there would be different degrees of understanding to which computers might aspire, ranging from the superficial to that of an art historian, critic, educator or artist.

The question we raise about computer perception is not moot because it has been demonstrated recently that storage media using computers in novel ways can exhibit some limited understanding of works such as the architectural drawings of Frank Lloyd Wright [1] and the fine art images of artists like Joan Miró [2] and Wassily Kandinsky [3]. Computer understanding has also been demonstrated for paintings by Richard Diebenkorn [4], for a comparison of paintings by Georges Vantongerloo and by Fritz Glarner [5], for woodcuts by the German artist Jacob Fauser [6] and for contemporary computer art by Harold Cohen [7]. For each of these artists, it has been shown that a computer can be said to 'understand' the artist's work in one of several senses. In the simplest case, the computer can classify an image upon viewing it. In a deeper sense, the computer can be said to understand the image by being able to place it in chronological sequence with images of other works by the same artist. In a still deeper sense, the computer understands the artwork because it has produced the work by itself. And finally, in the deepest sense, the computer can be said to understand an art image by being able to recognize its formal properties and by being able to synthesize other works that are stylistically similar.

All these capabilities have been demonstrated and are the subject of ongoing research. We therefore feel justified in saying that a computer need not ignore an artwork that it sees. If the matter ended there, we might precipitate discussions in aesthetics, or even in epistemology, without any necessary practical consequences. But there are many practical consequences that follow from computer understanding of art images. In this paper we discuss one of these: the ability of computers to reduce greatly the storage requirements needed for archiving such images.

The Storage Problem

Digital storage of images is more expensive than photographic storage. This expensiveness is apparent if we consider only the cost of producing a stored record. The reason for storing images is usually to perform subsequent operations on the stored images, ranging from the common case of retrieval of the image to the more esoteric cases of modification of the image and answering questions about the image. All of these operations can be done on photographic images by varying degrees of manual manipulation, but when speed is important, digital storage is more economical for retrieval of images. When automated operations of the more esoteric kind are desired, only digital storage allows us to perform such operations as image enhancement, pattern recognition, image comparison and searching of images directly without the intervention of a text-based description. We are therefore led to consider the storage of images of artworks in the form of digital records accessible to conventional computers.

The digital medium of choice has become the optical digital disc. Capacities for such storage range from 600 megabytes on 'compact disc read only memories' (CD-ROM), which can be read only by the user, to 2000 megabytes on the much more expensive 'write once read many' (WORM) optical discs, which can be recorded once by the user and read thereafter as often as desired, as can the CD-ROMs. Complementing the storage media is the technology for scanning images and for producing the digital signal to be recorded on the optical discs. This technology is much more mature, having been used with computers for over three decades.

It is useful to understand the relations among artworks, their scanned images and the storage requirements needed for recording those images. To make this relation clear, consider the engraving by Dürer (1514) shown in Fig. 1. A print of this engraving was scanned with a scanner having a resolution of 50 micrometers per picture resolution element (pixel). We can see the extent to which this black-and-white print is adequately resolved with such a comparatively fine scan by studying the eye detail shown in Fig. 2. Here we can see the individual pixels. We notice that the line work in Dürer's engraving, which resolves quite well on the original print, is poorly resolved at this scanner resolution. Nevertheless, the whole scanned image requires a storage capacity of 18 megabytes at this (inadequate) resolution. Furthermore, this image has been scanned to produce an image with about 65 times as much information as a conventional black-and-white TV image contains. It follows, therefore, that a scanned image of the Dürer print, using only the resolution common with TV cameras and videodiscs, will be quite inadequate if the fine structure of the engraved lines is to be resolved. However, if no detailed structure is needed in the stored image, the coarse resolution may be adequate.

Occasionally it is suggested that, for so-called 'line work', the use of computer graphics technology is more appropriate than scanned images. Certainly, there are images, of at least peripheral interest in the fine arts, for which line drawings can create adequate representations of the original works. The most obvious examples occur in architectural drawing. Here, the use of computer graphics line drawings can provide greater storage economy than can scanned images. There are commercial machines in the computer-aided design (CAD) field that scan architectural drawings and immediately convert them to line drawings for many purposes, one of which is storage economy.

We must be careful not to infer that other kinds of drawings can be susceptible to the same treatment. Again, an illustration will make the issue clear if we consider line engravings. Figure 3 shows a print from a contemporary fine engraving made for a postage stamp by a master engraver at the United States Treasury. Upon superficial inspection, it appears to be a line drawing and therefore capable of being represented by a sequence of line segments commonly used in computer graphics. But if we look at an enlarged detail of the image (Fig. 4), we begin to see, and can see more clearly in a further enlargement (Fig. 5), that the image is composed of complex shapes and not of lines at all. The engraver has control over line quality that goes beyond the control that can be exercised, for example, by an etcher.

To test whether the detailed structure of Fig. 5 is an artifact of high magnification or an essential part of the composition, we performed a simple test. We showed the detailed structure of Fig. 5 to the engraver who had made the original engraving a few years previously. We asked him to locate the detailed image of Fig. 5 in the whole composition of Fig. 3 without the helpful intermediate illustration of Fig. 4. He took about 2 minutes to describe the structure of Fig. 5, immediately concluding that it must occur at the edge of Einstein's eye, and then, in another minute, located the exact spot where the detail could be found. The conclusion from this simple experiment is something known to most artists: everything counts! And so the gratuitous proposal that this engraving be treated as 'nothing more' than a line drawing fails a simple test.

We expect that most true drawings in which line structure is important would similarly fail to be adequately represented by computer graphics line drawings. And therefore, for drawings, only the crudest representations, such as TV scans for images, can be achieved with the obvious use of the most readily available technology.

Recovering Images from Storage

When an image is scanned with a TV camera, there is a direct correspondence between the original image, the scanned version, the version stored in computer memory and, finally, the image that is recovered for display. For every pixel extracted by the scanner from the original image, a corre-

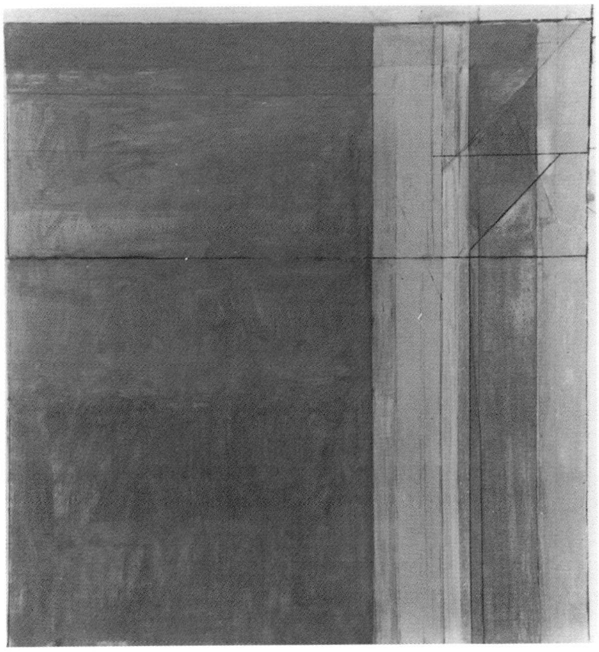

Fig. 6. Richard Diebenkorn, *Ocean Park #111*, oil and charcoal on canvas, 336.2 × 336.7 cm, 1978. (Hirshhorn Museum and Sculpture Garden, Smithsonian Institution, Museum Purchase, 1979)

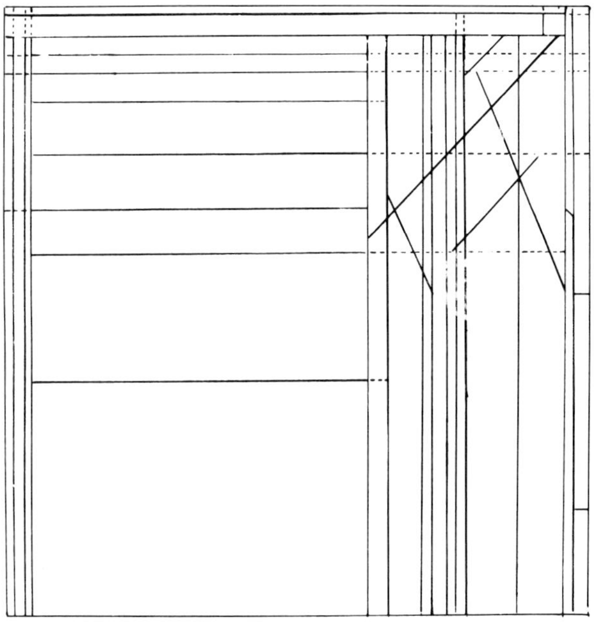

Fig. 7. A linear representation of the structure of Fig. 6.

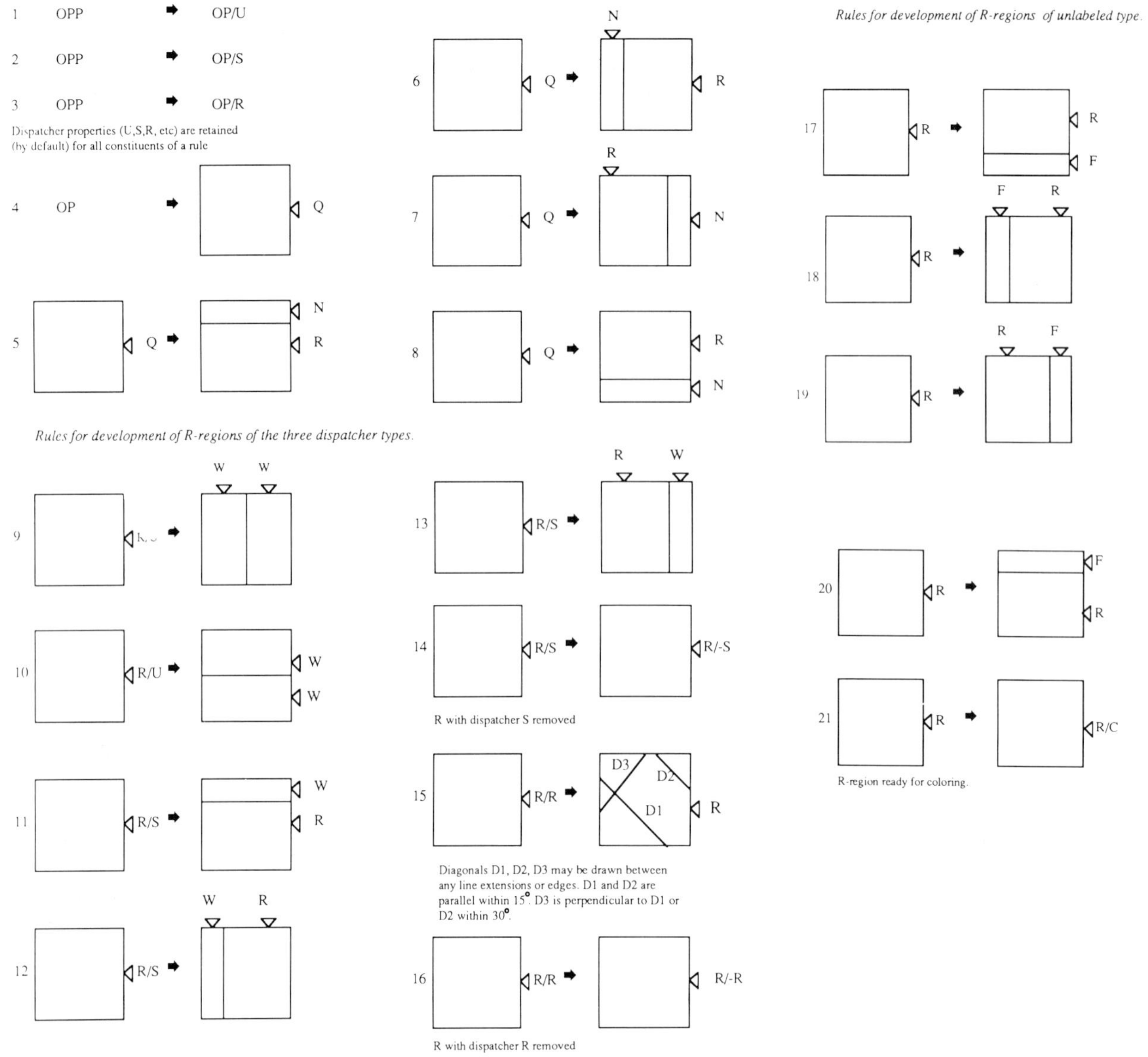

Fig. 8a. A grammar for the linear structure of Diebenkorn's *Ocean Park* paintings.

sponding one is stored in memory and a corresponding one is displayed. But this correspondence need not be so direct. It is acceptable for the stored image not to correspond to the scanned image, so long as the recovered image still has the direct correspondence with the scanned image. This is the approach taken with common code compression techniques. In code compression, the redundancy of the scanned image is exploited to save on storage requirements. What is stored is an encoded version of the scanned image in which certain commonly occurring arrays of adjacent pixels (such as all white or all black ones) are represented with a more economical code than would be used with more direct storage. Then, when the image is recovered for display, it is decoded to produce the correspondence between the displayed image and the original scanned image. The resulting storage economy can range up to a factor of about tenfold.

With encoded images, it is proper to speak of the displayed image as having been reconstructed from the encoded representation in storage. There are two kinds of such reconstructions, unique and approximate. The first kind reconstructs the scanned image identically; the second does not. The reason for using these two types of encodings is that unique reconstruction achieves absolute fidelity to the scanned image, but approximate reconstruction can achieve greater storage economy.

The cost of storage is determined by the kind of approximation one uses. A simple kind of approximation that is widely used depends on the degree of the fine structure in the image. This approximation starts by transforming the image into an entirely new image not apparently like the original. A useful property of this new image is that all the fine, detailed structure is located in one part of the image and the gross structure is located in another part. It is possible to recover the original image by a certain reverse transformation. But, first, the part of the transformed image containing the fine structure is removed. This yields a smaller image that can be stored more economically. To recover the original image, a reverse transformation is made, which yields an approximation to the original image. But the fine structure is gone. This so-called

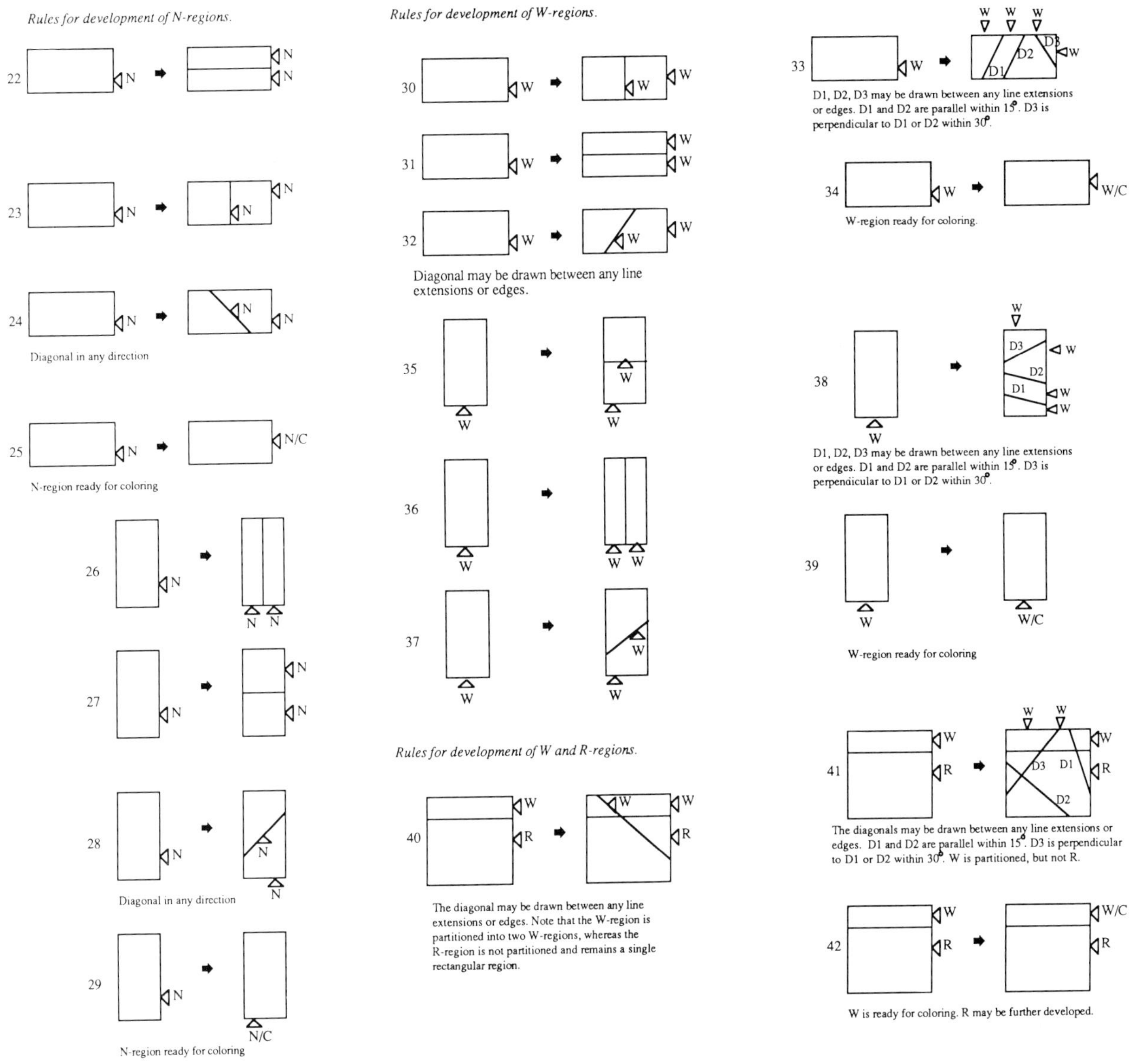

Fig. 8b. A grammar for the linear structure of Diebenkorn's *Ocean Park* paintings (continued).

'spatial frequency filtering' does not depend on any interpretation of the image. All fine structure is treated equally, whether it be a pimple on a nose or a pebble on the ground. And it can yield storage economy by as much as a factor of 10 to 100.

The appearance of a reconstructed image that has been spatial frequency filtered is easy to compare with the unfiltered image. The filtered one appears to be a blurred version of the original. Other kinds of approximate reconstruction are less easy to compare with their original images. One such reconstruction method, which claims to achieve large storage economy, uses fractals [8]. A fractal curve has a complex structure that is suggestive of, but different from, the structure of natural objects. To the superficial observer, images constructed from fractal curves often appear realistic. This property has been exploited in computer graphics research to create artificial images that lack the obvious geometric shapes often associated with computer-generated images. For example, pictures of flowers or mountains have been constructed with fractal curves to create a pleasing illusion that, nevertheless, is unconvincing to a botanist or geologist. Furthermore, even scanned photos that have been encoded for storage and reconstructed with fractal curves can create the illusion of being 'realistic' reconstructions. We would expect the pimples and pebbles would look realistic, but not like their originals. So, if we are willing to accept that once one has seen one pebble one has seen all pebbles, this method of achieving storage economy has some attractiveness—but only if we are tolerant of deviant pebbles! For those who would 'see the world in a grain of sand', such economy is less acceptable.

PROVIDING IMAGE INTELLIGENCE TO THE COMPUTER

The storage and recovery schemes thus far discussed exhibit a benign indifference to the content of the images dealt with. Even for images that have been approximately reconstructed, the approximation is not based on any understanding of the image content. Rather, the image's statistics constitute the basis for accepting and rejecting image properties during approximate reconstruction. Surely we can do better than this!

Indeed we can in several ways. We consider first a method whereby the computer clearly has some knowledge of the image content, although the knowledge is insufficient to reconstruct an image. Rorvig has shown how primitive-feature extraction procedures can be used by the computer to classify a set of woodcuts [9]. The primitive features consist of lines, angles and density distributions in the image. These were correlated with aesthetic judgments made by human viewers of the same set of images. Close correspondence between the human judgment and the machine ranking was seen to be possible. Clearly, the simple primitives provided to the computer were insufficient to characterize the images completely or to reconstruct them. This procedure, nevertheless, could provide the computer with an elementary component of understanding of an image similar to the understanding by a human viewer.

A much larger step in the direction of computer understanding of art images occurs in the work of Harold Cohen [10]. The images he provides to the computer do not come from any external source but, in fact, are generated by the computer itself. A program written by Cohen uses algorithms that represent principles of his composition. These are used to generate drawings both abstract and figurative. The drawings all have a readily identifiable style and can be produced in unlimited quantity. It is clear that the computer has sufficient intelligence to produce images that are both aesthetically interesting and consistent in style.

Since Cohen's images are generated *ab initio,* the storage problem for these images has a transparently simple solution. To reconstruct any image it is only necessary to know the algorithms for image generation and the specific options exercised by the computer in the production of the particular image. The storage requirement for this information, which is peculiar to any single image, is modest. So, in a sense, we have a case of a computer that knows almost everything about such an image and can convert that knowledge into economical storage of the image. Of course, Cohen's computer knows all about its own images and nothing about ones generated by any other artist. But it is interesting to speculate whether such a machine might be able better to understand drawings of other artists by using its demonstrated ability to generate drawings of its own! At present that question is quite open.

If the computer's knowing a class of images (in the sense that the whole class of Cohen's drawings can be generated) leads to great storage economy, it is important to know whether that approach can be achieved when we are dealing with pre-existing images. The question was answered affirmatively in 1964 [11]. The technique introduced was drawn from computational linguistics but modified to deal with images: the use of picture grammars. It was shown that a large class of images could be described succinctly by a grammar that successively transforms two-dimensional shapes into final forms that correspond to recognizable images. The resulting field of syntactic analysis of images developed many tools, the most productive of which was the shape grammar [12].

Although shape grammars are important conceptual devices for describing images, they have made more tangible contributions. Beginning in 1977, architects created shape grammars for a wide range of disciplines, including buildings [13,14], landscapes [15], furniture designs [16] and window patterns [17].

The schematization required by shape grammars poses little limitation in design areas such as architecture, where schematic drawing is already widely accepted. Consequently, grammars have been readily accepted in these cases. As we might predict, great economy of representation can be achieved because each grammar implies a large, or infinite, set of designs. To store the description of a single design, it is necessary only to specify, within the grammar, the options exercised that distinguish that design. As

Fig. 9. Six stages in the generation of Fig. 7 according to the grammar of Fig. 8. The notation 11^2 denotes rule 11 applied 2 times.

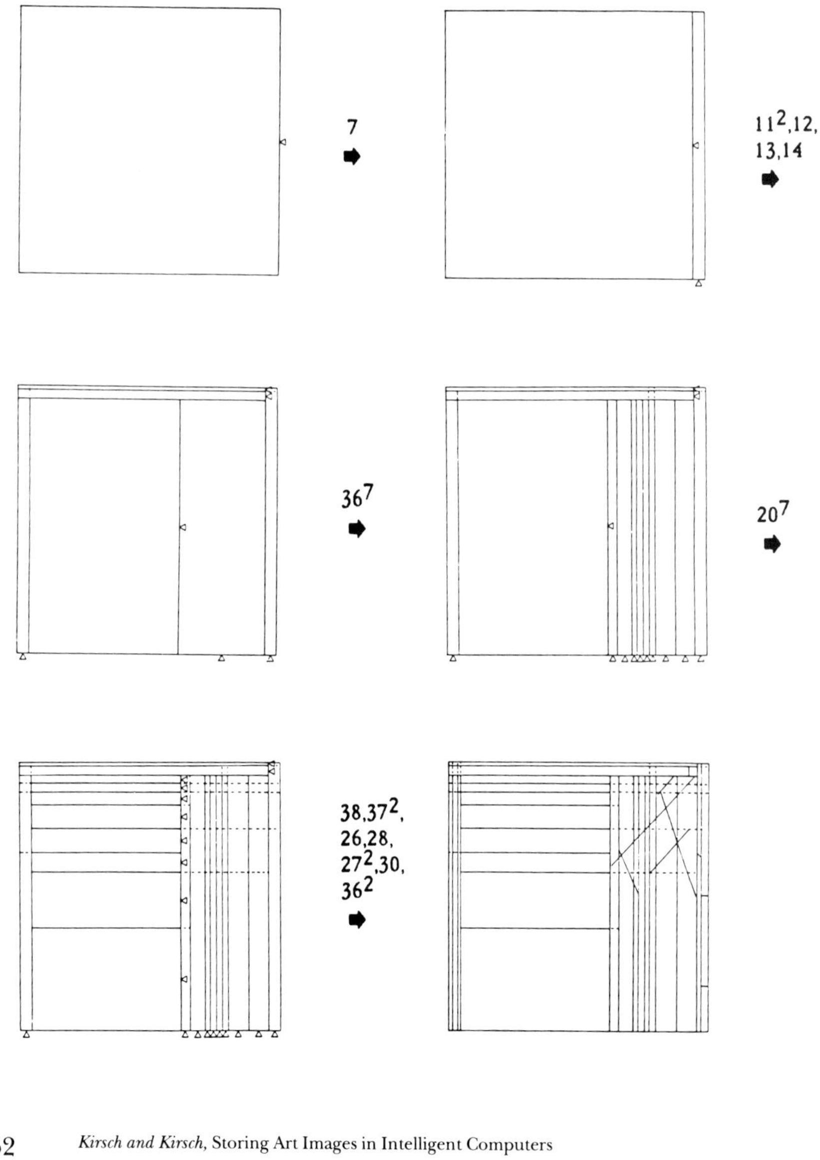

before, such a specification is orders of magnitude less costly in storage than would be a scan of the drawing for a design.

These architectural examples were the first practical use of grammars to describe a very large class of images in such a way that the images could be regenerated from the class description. But the question still remained whether images such as paintings could be treated this same way. Again, we have answered this question affirmatively by constructing a grammar for Diebenkorn's *Ocean Park* series of paintings [18]; the question has subsequently been answered also by Knight, who constructed a sequence of grammars for the successive stylistic periods of Vantongerloo and Glarner [19]; and by Lauzzana and Pocock-Williams, who constructed a rule system for the skeletal organization of Kandinsky's paintings [20]. All these examples provided the computer with sufficient understanding of the target class of images for us to credit the computer with substantial understanding of the style of the artists. And it is this understanding that can be exploited for many purposes, among them the economical storage of the approximate representations of the images described by the grammars.

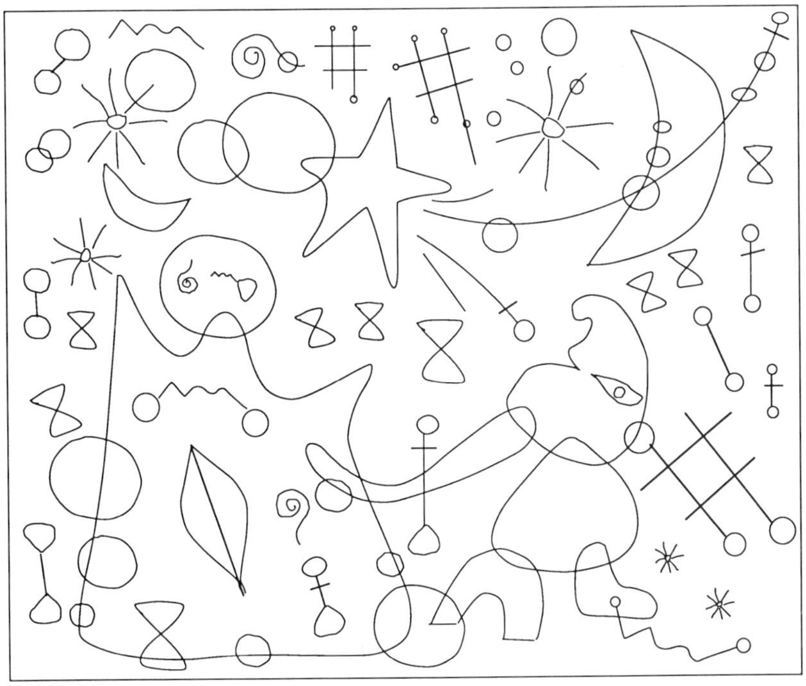

Fig. 10. An artificial Miró composition based on a catalog of prototype shapes.

Economy Resulting from Intelligent Image Storage

We wish, now, more specifically to calculate the economy that results from storage of images in an intelligent computer. We will start with Richard Diebenkorn's paintings and determine how much storage is needed for an image described by the grammar [21]. Because the grammar contains recursion, there are an infinite number of paintings described (all of them purportedly in the style of Diebenkorn). For any such painting, there is a sequence of rule applications that, when applied in the proper order, will result in a representation of the target painting. At certain points in the process, the grammar provides a set of alternatives among which a choice may be made in producing a picture. We must use information to specify which choice is to be made. If there are N alternatives offered by the grammar at that point, making such a choice always can be done by specifying no more than the logarithm (to the base 2) of N bits of information. Thus, if there were eight choices, any one of these could be specified with no more than 3 bits of information, four choices with 2 bits, two choices with 1 bit, etc. Then, by summing the information associated with each of the choices made in the production of the picture, we determine how much information is needed to specify the whole picture, with respect to the grammar.

For an example, we will choose the picture of Diebenkorn's *Ocean Park No. 111* shown in Fig. 6. The representation to be used is shown in Fig. 7. Such representations of the paintings are provided by the grammar taken from Kirsch [22] as shown in Fig. 8. The process of generating Fig. 7 from the grammar is shown in Fig. 9. Here we see six of the 32 stages in the generation process.

We start with a blank canvas as shown in the first image of Fig. 9. Corresponding to this image is the starting symbol of the grammar, OPP. We notice that there are three rules (nos. 1, 2, 3) that provide options for developing this blank canvas. On the average, with $\log(3) = 1.58$ bits of information, we can specify our choice, which is, for this picture, the second rule. Now, the grammar confronts us with a single rule for further developing the resulting OP/S that resulted from rule 2. This single rule (no. 4) creates a blank canvas labeled with a Q. Since there are no choices provided, no information need be specified, and the cumulative total information remains at 1.58 bits. At this point we are confronted with a set of four rules (nos. 5, 6, 7, 8), any one of which may be invoked. For the intended picture, we choose rule 7 by specifying $\log(4) = 2.0$ bits of information. This raises our cumulative total to $1.58 + 2.0 = 3.58$ bits of information. We thus far have produced the second image in Fig. 9.

To produce the third image in Fig. 9, we first invoke rule 11 twice to produce the two top horizontal bands ($2 \times \log(4)$), rule 12 once to produce the vertical band on the left ($1 \times \log(4)$), rule 13 to produce the medial vertical band ($1 \times \log(4)$), and finally rule 14, which removes the /S subscript that allows the previous rules to be applied ($1 \times \log(4)$). This adds 10.0 bits to yield a cumulative total of 13.58 bits.

The fourth image in Fig. 9 is produced by seven applications of rule 36. Each such application represents a choice among five alternatives, yielding a contribution to the total of $7 \times \log(5) = 16.25$ bits.

Then the fifth image is produced by seven applications of rule 20, which is chosen among five alternatives, yielding $7 \times \log(5) = 16.25$ bits.

Finally, the target image is produced from rule 38 (2.32 bits), rule 37 twice (4.64 bits), rule 26 (2.0 bits), rule 28 (2.0 bits), rule 27 twice (4.0 bits), rule 30 (2.32 bits) and rule 36 twice (4.64 bits). The cumulative total is thus 68.0 bits.

What the above calculation shows is that, if we provide the computer with the intelligence to understand the whole class of Diebenkorn compositions represented by the grammar of Fig. 8, any picture thereafter can be specified very economically. The example requires only 68 bits, or less than 9 bytes, of data to store it. This number should be compared with the storage requirements for an ordinary TV scan of the same painting, which would require about 0.25 million bytes. The dramatic difference in storage requirements is accounted for not only by machine intelligence but also by the fact that two different kinds of representation are being compared.

It is important to point out that these two kinds of representation also elicit different levels of understanding from people and machines. For the computer, a TV scan carries no meaning whatsoever. However, a grammatical representation does furnish it with a degree of understanding. Of course, for people, the TV scan is immediately comprehensible. The grammar is a human artifice created with great effort and insight, but it can produce a schematic representation that can be understood by both people and machines. If we wish to use the computer for operations upon images such as automatic searching of a large collection of images rather than textual descriptions of these images, then the grammatical approach is the only one of the two storage methods that makes such a search possible.

The extreme storage economy available for the Diebenkorn paintings, in an intelligent computer possessed of a grammar, results from our generosity in accepting the linear schematization of his works that we see in examples like Fig. 7. Like any representation, such linear schematization results in a loss of essential information from the original painting. But the loss achieves the dual gains of storage economy and intelligent understanding by the computer.

How might we preserve more information in a representation? An obvious approach is to help the computer to understand shape. Since shape does not appear essential in the Diebenkorn paintings, we can consider an artist like Joan Miró, for whom shape is essential. In a recent article, we discussed how artificial Miró compositions can be constructed based on a catalog of Miró shapes [23]. A typical such example is shown in Fig. 10, which may be compared with another example shown in Fig. 8 of the aforementioned article and with a photograph of a Miró in Fig. 9 of the same article. These compositions in the style of Miró can be represented very economically since each shape is drawn from a small catalog of prototypes, each of which can be specified with about 5 bits for identification, another 20 bits for size and another 20 bits for location. With those 45 bits representing each shape, a composition containing N shapes can be represented with $45 \times N$ bits.

While this method results in much greater economy of representation than TV scanning, we have arrived only at an ad hoc solution. Leyton [24] and Jakubowski [25] have suggested better ways to represent shape. Leyton's scheme uses a grammar for the shapes themselves just as we have used one for the compositional arrangements in Diebenkorn. He has devised grammar rules that correspond to the successive deformations that transform a simple circle into elaborate shapes with invaginations and evaginations that occur at maxima and minima of curvature. We currently are investigating a first such grammar for Miró shapes. This grammar allows us a wide choice of shapes as well as a natural characterization of how the artist draws and how the viewer sees.

CONCLUSION

We have seen several examples of how a computer may be given the intelligence to perceive representations of artworks. We have also seen how expensive it is to provide raw scanned images to a computer storage system. These scanned images are effectively invisible to the computer, a fact deceptively easy to forget since those same images are readily visible to the human viewer.

Once the large investment in providing appropriate intelligence to the computer has been incurred, many rewards accrue to the art historian, critic, educator, archivist and artist. We have directed our attention only to the question of economy of storage. But it is reasonable to expect that a computer that can view images intelligently in one way can do so in other ways, too.

Acknowledgement

We wish to thank Harry Rand and Sanford Ressler for pushing us toward the asymptotes of English and truth.

References and Notes

1. H. Koning and J. Eizenburg, "The Language of the Prairie: Frank Lloyd Wright's Prairie Houses", *Environ. and Planning B: Planning and Design* **8**, 295–323 (1981).

2. R.A. Kirsch and J.L. Kirsch, "Describing Painting Styles to a Computer", *Leonardo* **21**, No. 4 (1988) (forthcoming).

3. R.G. Lauzzana and L. Pocock-Williams, "A Rule System for Aesthetic Research in the Visual Arts", *Leonardo* **21**, No. 4 (1988) (forthcoming).

4. J.L. Kirsch and R.A. Kirsch, "The Structure of Paintings: Formal Grammar and Design", *Environ. and Planning B: Planning and Design* **13**, 163–176 (1986).

5. T.W. Knight, "Transformations of De Stijl Art: The Paintings of Georges Vantongerloo and Fritz Glarner", *Environ. and Planning B: Planning and Design* (forthcoming).

6. M.E. Rorvig, R. Helfer and S. Fitzpatrick, "Automatic Image Classification by Psychrometric Mapping", (Working Paper 87-2, Graduate School of Library and Information Science, University of Texas at Austin, 13 November 1987).

7. Harold Cohen, Becky Cohen and Penny Ni, *The First Artificial Intelligence Coloring Book* (Los Altos, CA: William Kaufman, Inc., 1984).

8. M.F. Barnsley and A.D. Sloan, "A Better Way to Compress Images", *Byte* (January 1988) pp. 215–223.

9. Rorvig, Helfer and Fitzpatrick [6].

10. Cohen, Cohen and Ni [7].

11. R.A. Kirsch, "Computer Interpretation of English Text and Picture Patterns", *IEEE Trans. Electronic Computers* **13**, 363–376 (1964).

12. George Stiny and James Gips, *Algorithmic Aesthetics* (Berkeley, CA: Univ. of California Press, 1978).

13. Koning and Eizenburg [1].

14. F. Downing and U. Flemming, "The Bungalows of Buffalo", *Environ. and Planning B: Planning and Design* **8**, 269–293 (1981).

15. G. Stiny and W.J. Mitchell, "The Grammar of Paradise: On the Generation of Mughul Gardens", *Environ. and Planning B* **7**, 209–226 (1980).

16. T.W. Knight, "The Generation of Hepplewhite-Style Chair Back Designs", *Environ. and Design B* **7**, 227–238 (1980).

17. G.Stiny, "Ice-Ray: A Note on the Generation of Chinese Lattice Designs", *Environ. and Planning B* **4**, 89–98 (1977).

18. Kirsch and Kirsch [4].

19. Knight [5].

20. Lauzzana and Pocock-Williams [3].

21. Kirsch and Kirsch [2].

22. Kirsch and Kirsch [2], [4].

23. Kirsch and Kirsch [2].

24. M. Leyton, "A Process Grammar for Shape", *Artificial Intelligence Journal* (1988) (forthcoming).

25. R. Jakubowski, "A Structural Representation of Shape and Its Features", *Information Sciences* **39**, 129–151 (1986).

The Making of a Film with Synthetic Actors

N. Magnenat-Thalmann

ABSTRACT

The author explains how to create a film involving synthetic actors and describes in particular the making of the film *Rendez-vous à Montréal.* The scenario of the film and the construction of actors are presented. The animation of actors is separated into three parts: body animation, hand animation and facial animation. The choreography of the complete film is then explained: decors, cameras, lights and actors.

Rendez-vous à Montréal [1] is an animated film that uses advanced computer techniques to achieve such effects as reincarnating the film stars Humphrey Bogart and Marilyn Monroe. It was directed by N. Magnenat-Thalmann and D. Thalmann and produced with a team of 10 people. The main purpose of *Rendez-vous à Montréal* is to show that true synthetic actors can be created. The film represents a technological breakthrough that opens new vistas in motion pictures, television and advertising. With this technique it will be possible to produce short films or motion pictures featuring any celebrity in any situation.

The film premiered in May 1987 at the Canadian Engineering Centennial Convention, which was attended by about 3000 delegates; excerpts were shown on six television channels the same week. Outside Canada, the first show was at CG International '87 at Karuizawa, Japan, and large excerpts were shown on the NHK channel 9 news program. Since that time the film has been shown at several festivals, including the Banff Festival, the Hiroshima Festival, the Montreal World Film Festival, the Women Film Festival in Hollywood, the Rio de Janeiro Festival, the Abitibi-Temiscamingue Festival, the Monte-Carlo Festival and the Stuttgart Festival. It was shown throughout the summer of 1987 at Montreal's EXPOTECH, the largest scientific exhibition ever held in Canada. An exhibition about the making of the film was shown in Canada and Europe.

SCENARIO

The movie begins in the hereafter, where Humphrey is bored and longs to live again. He thinks of Marilyn; he calls her many times and begs her to return to earth with him. The head of Marilyn grown old appears; she accepts. Humphrey then sets up a rendezvous with her for the next day at 10:00 PM at the Bon-Secours market in Montreal. Both actors disappear in the night while making faces at each other.

They come down from a starry sky into the Bon-Secours market; we hear footsteps and the sounds of the city in the background. We do not see Humphrey but we hear him think out loud. He hesitates, he looks about for the entrance, he finds it and enters the building. We come to a room where we see a clock that strikes 10 times, reminding us that time is a factor again.

Marilyn appears motionless and made of marble. She has not returned to life yet. In reply to Humphrey's questions, she turns into gold. Humphrey fancies her and sends her a kiss that awakens her. She appears in all her splendor. They take each other's hand and the romance begins.

CREATION OF THE ACTORS

Planning

Since modifications of an existing synthetic object are very expensive in terms of design time, it is important to plan the construction of a synthetic actor carefully. Consideration should be given to how the object will be divided into parts. Should the hand, for example, be constructed in one piece, or should the fingers be separated? If a part has a symmetrical axis, it is more economical to construct only

Fig. 1. N. Magnenat-Thalmann and D. Thalmann, *Rendez-vous à Montréal.* Plaster model of Marilyn's head.

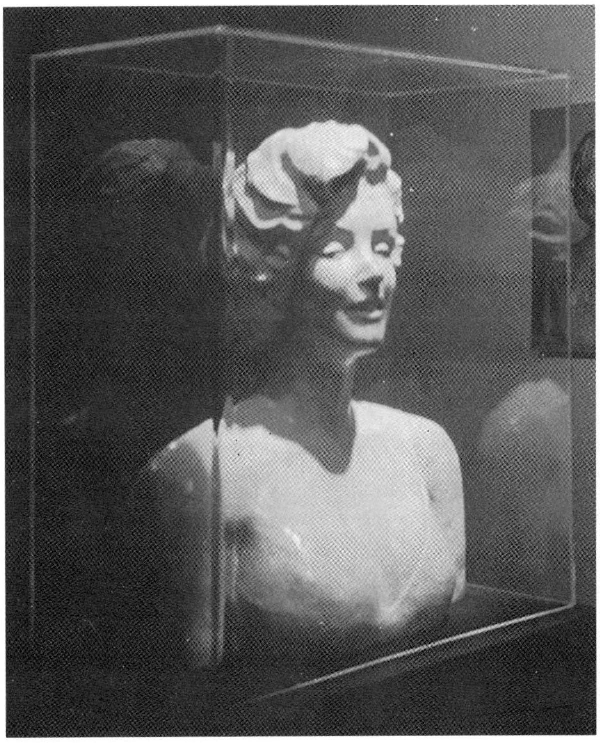

N. Magnenat-Thalmann, MIRALab, HEC, Université de Montréal, Montréal, Québec, Canada.

Received 7 June 1988.

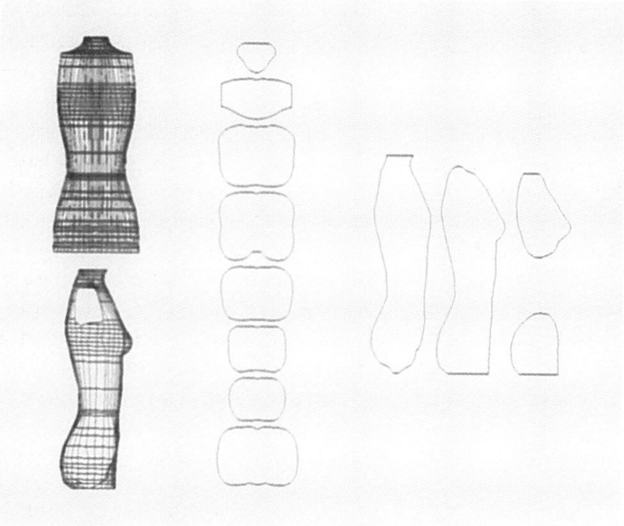

Fig. 2. N. Magnenat-Thalmann and D. Thalmann, *Eglantine*. Slices and reconstructed torso in wire-frame.

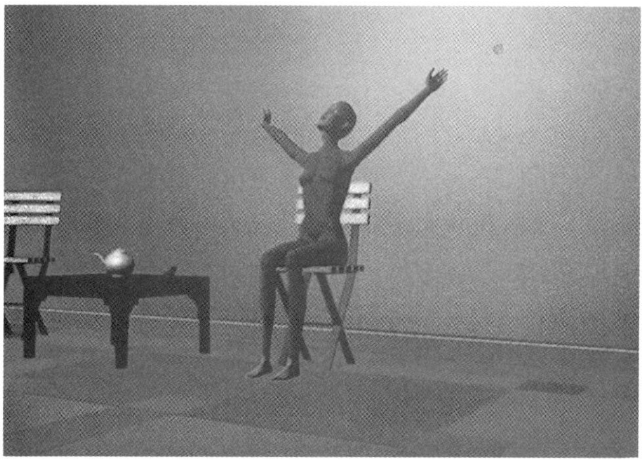

Fig. 3. N. Magnenat-Thalmann and D. Thalmann, *Eglantine*. Completely reconstructed actor in shading.

half of the part and then use a symmetry operation to get the whole. Although faces are not perfectly symmetric, they are generally considered as symmetric. Such are the choices of the designer and the animator. Their decisions will depend on the details required for each object, which in turn are strongly related to camera motion. When all the parts of a synthetic object have been created, they should be composed to generate the complete object. Although the separation into parts should be planned at the beginning, the composition process is only performed at the end, when all the parts are completely constructed. Once a satisfactory model is complete, we apply the digitizing technique. The model or object to be digitized should be large enough to allow the drawing of facets and vertices on it but small enough to be easily photographed. Any material may be chosen for the object; however, the surface should be of a light color and non-reflective to allow the drawing of lines and photographs.

To indicate to the computer the character's figure, we need to have either the actual person or a plaster model (life-size or reduced). In the case of actors who are dead, we rely on both photographs of the actor at a certain age and a live model who has about the same dimensions. The methodology differs according to the part of the person to be reproduced. For the head, teeth, hands, arms and fingers, a sculptor creates plaster models from the photographs of the real person (Fig. 1). As an aid, the computer has in its memory the three-dimensional shape of the character. The sculptor then can ask the computer to display the character according to several viewpoints. The cast of the body is made from the live model.

Digitizing

The most direct 3D digitizing technique is simply to enter the 3D coordinates using a 3D digitizer. Three types of such devices are now available: devices based on three orthogonal magnetic fields, devices based on three sound captors, and devices based on laser light [2].

A classical way of creating 3D objects is by 3D reconstruction from 2D information:

1. Significant points or grids are drawn onto the object.
2. Four orthogonal pictures are taken of the object.
3. An appropriate coordinate system is drawn for each picture.
4. Each point is identified by a number. Points have to be identified in at least two pictures to compute the X-, Y- and Z-coordinates of each point.
5. After placing the pictures on the digitizer, the user marks points that determine the boundaries of the pictures and those that identify the coordinate systems.
6. For each point, two different positions are successively marked.
7. Connections between the points are identified by numbers: this defines the strokes of points in wire-frame models and grids in facet-based models.

Another popular method consists of reconstructing an object from a set of serial cross sections, like tracing the contours from a topographic map. Several reconstruction methods are possible. This technique was used in the film *Eglantine*, directed by N. Magnenat-Thalmann and D. Thalmann. Figure 2 shows the slices and the reconstructed torso in wire-frame. Figure 3 displays the complete actress in a scene.

Facet modeling

The best-known technique of object representation describes an object by a collection of polygons [3]. Although often expensive in terms of CPU time, polygonal models of 3D objects are the most common. In these models, all objects are decomposed into polygonal faces. For objects such as cubes or regular polyhedra, this decomposition is very effective. But objects such as spheres or revolution surfaces require approximations. Unfortunately, large numbers of polygons often are needed to represent satisfactorily even comparatively simple shapes. In addition, the essential character of surfaces such as spheres is lost when they are approximated by collections of polygons.

To define an object using a polygon-based model, lists of vertices and polygons are specified where each polygon is defined by its vertices, identified by their rank in the list of vertices. A surface like the human face is irregular and composed of reliefs and depressions. It is important to choose vertices at the high points of reliefs and the bottoms of depressions. Dramatic angle variations between adjacent facets should be avoided, because they cause undesirable variations in shading, a physical phenomenon known as the Mach effect. The only solution consists of increasing the number of facets in regions where the curvature is significant. Because of the rendering process, the choice of facets to be drawn on the plaster model is very important. Facets should be planar, especially for shadow processing; for this reason, triangles are often chosen. However, it should be noted that quadrilateral facets require fewer vertices for the same number of facets. This may reduce the computer time considerably.

At this point, we turn our attention to the animation. First, the camera location must be considered: any curve (sequence of edges) that is shown from the side must have numerous vertices. As the camera eye nears the vertices, the number of vertices must be increased to make the surface smoother. The motion of the actor also enters into consideration. A curve (sequence of edges) may vary in animation. In this case the number of vertices should be increased for the maximum of curvature, to avoid any discontinuity of the surface during the motion.

ANIMATING THE HUMAN BODY

Skeleton

When the animator specifies the animation sequence, he/she defines the motion using a skeleton. A skeleton is a connected set of segments, corresponding to limbs, and joints, as shown in Fig. 4 [4]. A joint is the intersection of two segments, which means it is a skeleton point where the limb that is linked to the point may move. The angle between the two segments is called the joint angle. A joint may have at most three kinds of position angles: flexion, pivot and twist. *Flexion* is a rotation of the limb that is influenced by the joint and causes the motion of all limbs linked to this joint. Flexion is made relative to the joint point and a flexion axis that must be defined. *Pivot* makes the flexion axis rotate around the limb that is influenced by the joint. *Twist* causes a torsion of the limb that is influenced by the joint. The direction of the twisting axis is found similarly to the direction of the pivot.

In order to animate fully three-dimensional characters, the animator has also to position the skeleton according to the body of the synthetic actor to be animated. Apart from digitizing the shapes this procedure is probably the most time consuming. However, it is very important because all the mapping of the surface shapes is based on the skeleton position relative to the surface shapes. If a skeleton point is poorly positioned, the joint probably will cause abnormal surface deformations in the animation. This process is described in depth in another paper [5].

When the skeleton has been correctly positioned, the HUMAN FACTORY software will transform the character according to the angles required by the animation without any animator intervention. Figure 5 shows an example.

The mapping of surfaces onto the skeleton is based on the concept of Joint-dependent Local Deformation (JLD) operators [6], operators that control specific local deformation depending on the nature of the joints. They control the evolution of surfaces and may be considered as operators on these surfaces. Each JLD operator is confined to some uniquely defined part of the surface, which may be called the domain of the operator. The value of the operator itself is determined as a function of the angular values of the specific set of joints defining the operator.

Animation techniques

There are three main types of 3D computer animation [7]:

1. Image-based keyframe animation [8, 9]. Actors are characterized by their vertices; motion is specified by keyframes. Each keyframe consists of a series of values corresponding to the vertices for that keyframe. In-between values are calculated by applying an interpolation law for each corresponding vertex in the two keyframes.
2. Parametric keyframe animation [10, 11]. Actors are characterized by parameters such as joint angles; motion is specified by key values for each parameter. In-between values are calculated using an interpolation law.
3. Algorithmic animation [12, 13, 14]. Actors are objects with a motion defined by a list of transformations. Each transformation is defined by parameters. These parameters may change during the animation according to any physical law.

The body, hand and facial animation described in this paper is based on parametric keyframe animation. In this method, the animator creates keyframes by specifying the appropriate set of parameter values; parameters are interpolated and images are finally individually constructed from the interpolated parameters. For each parameter, interpolation has to be computed using appropriate software programs. To animate (to move) a human body, it is necessary to use a specific program for human motion (in our case, HUMAN FACTORY). This program runs using a certain number of key values provided by the user. These key values are angles between the various body parts at certain times. For example, to animate an arm bending, it is necessary to give to the computer the angle of the elbow at different selected times. The software is then able to find any angle at any time. In-between values are calculated using bicubic splines. The animator may look at parameter values for any keyframe or interpolated frame. He/she may also obtain a wire-frame view for any frame.

Methodology of animation

The first step consists of determining the various key positions in terms of location in space and time; that is, for each key position, the position of a fixed point and the values of the vertebra joint angles are found. It is essential to be sure that the vertebra joint angles are perfect for the entire sequence before determining the other angles, because any modification of

Fig. 4. A basic skeleton. The legs are represented twice, in order to show feet with a correct orientation.

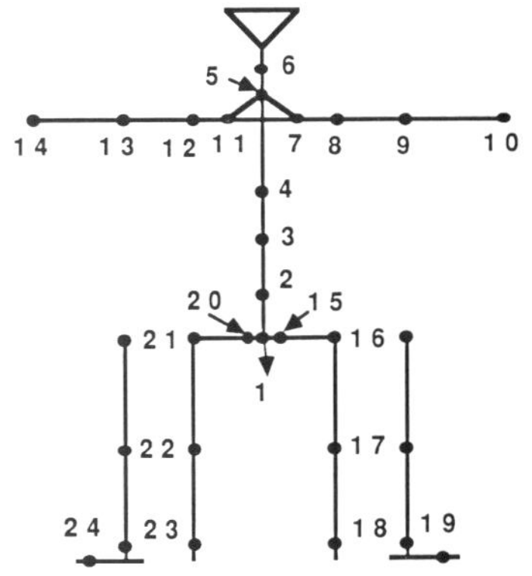

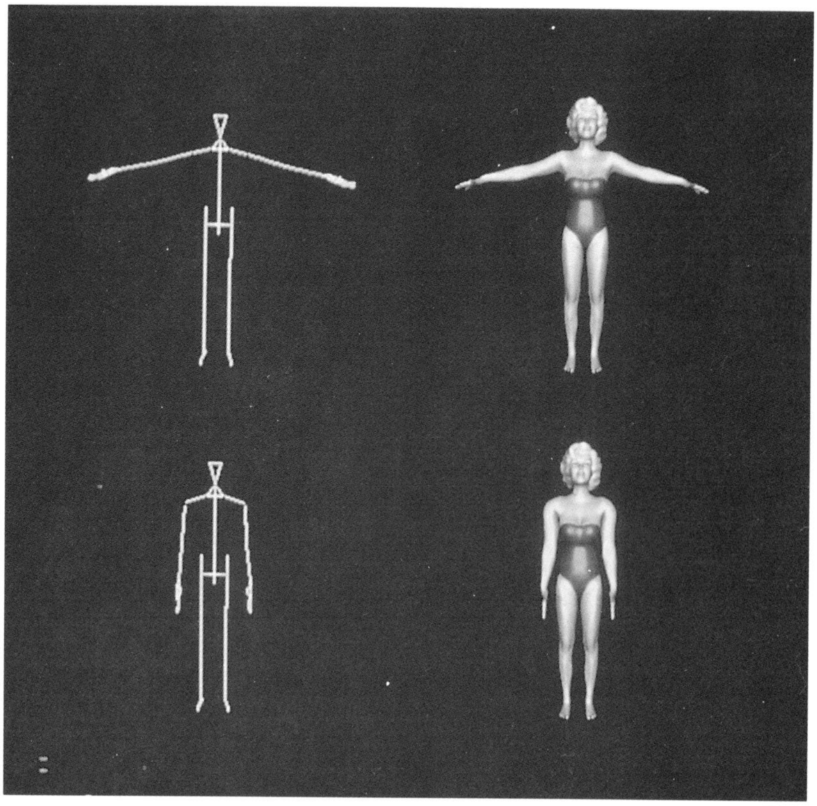

Fig. 5. Body mapping: basic skeleton (top left), basic actor (top right), skeleton with bent arms (bottom left), actor with bent arms (bottom right).

the vertebra joint angles generally implies a modification of the angles of other joints. Once the vertebra motion is defined, other angles are defined in a logical way moving from the center to the extremities (for example, vertebrae, shoulder, clavicle, elbow, wrist, fingers).

The problem of interpolation may be summarized as follows: given a certain number of points, find a curve passing through these points. The simplest method consists of joining the points by straight lines. However, if this method is used for animation, it causes a lack of smoothness that considerably alters the motion. A better interpolation is based on piecewise continuous interpolation of the curve by cubic functions. The interpolating curve must be continuous at the given points only up to a certain order. The Kochanek-Bartels method of spline interpolation allows control of the curve at each given point by three parameters: tension, continuity and bias [15]. A time value should be added to each control point to control the motion. The method is valid for interpolation between scalar values such as angles and vector values such as positions. We shall use this technique for calculating the interpolation of angles in the animation of human bodies, the interpolation of facial parameters and the interpolation of control points for the design of camera and light paths.

Fig. 6. Skeleton of a left hand.

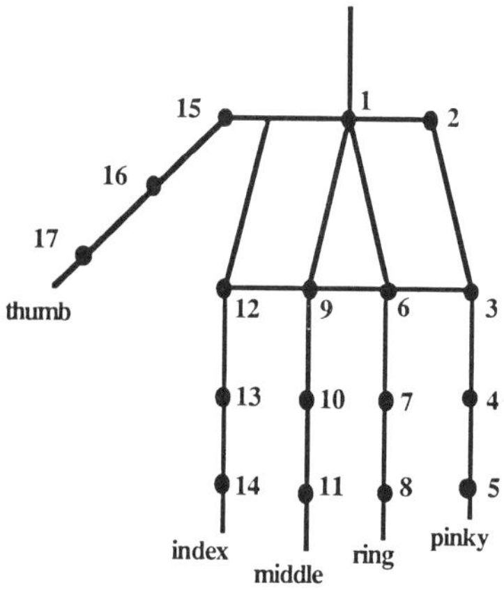

ANIMATING THE HANDS

Technique of hand animation

Hand animation is also produced using angle key-values. The transformations are more complex, however, because fingers inflate when they bend and the palm deforms (tenses, contracts). For the animator, the hand is simply composed of five fingers made of three jointed line segments, linked to the palm; 15 different angles control the finger movements. The animator selects key-values and the HUMAN FACTORY software automatically computes the in-betweens required to complete the motion. HUMAN FACTORY also determines finger inflation and palm shape based on angle values.

As shown in Fig. 6, the hand skeleton is a connected set of segments and joints. A joint is the intersection of two segments. The angle between the two segments is called the joint angle. There are three kinds of hand joints: the metacarpal joints (#1 and #2 joints), the joints between metacarpus and fingers (#3, #6, #9, #12 and #15 joints) and the finger joints (all other joints). Metacarpal bones are the small bones linking joints 2 to 3 and 1 to 6. The flexion of metacarpal bones may vary from 0 to 20 degrees. Metacarpal joints are important for the palm animation and other joints for the finger animation. All hand joints have a flexion angle, but joints between metacarpus and fingers also have a pivot angle. Figure 6 shows the left hand skeleton and Fig. 7 an example of hand animation.

Hand covering

Once the motion of the 3D character is designed, the hand needs to be covered with surfaces. As for the rest of the body, we try to separate completely the topology of the surfaces from the skeleton. This means that the hand may be constructed using any method: surfaces by sweeping, free-form surfaces or 3D reconstructed surfaces obtained from digitized projections. Our system transforms the surfaces into the wire-frame model, ensuring an automatic continuity between the different surfaces. This correspondence is based on a changing of coordinate bases that are independent of the segment length. This means that for the same set of surfaces, several bodies of different sizes may be obtained according to the segment length in the wire-frame models. In our approach, the animator has only to position his/her hand relative to the skeleton hand.

The mapping of surfaces onto the skeleton is also based on the concept of Joint-dependent Local Deformation operators. The case of the hand is especially complex, for deformations are very important when the fingers are bent, and the shape of the palm is very flexible. Figure 8 shows the hand mapping for the sequence of Fig. 7. Segments of fingers are independent and the JLD operators are calculated using a unique segment-dependent reference system. For the palm, JLD operators use reference systems of several segments to calculate surface mapping. In order to make the fingers realistic, two effects are simulated: rounding calculations at the joints and muscle inflation.

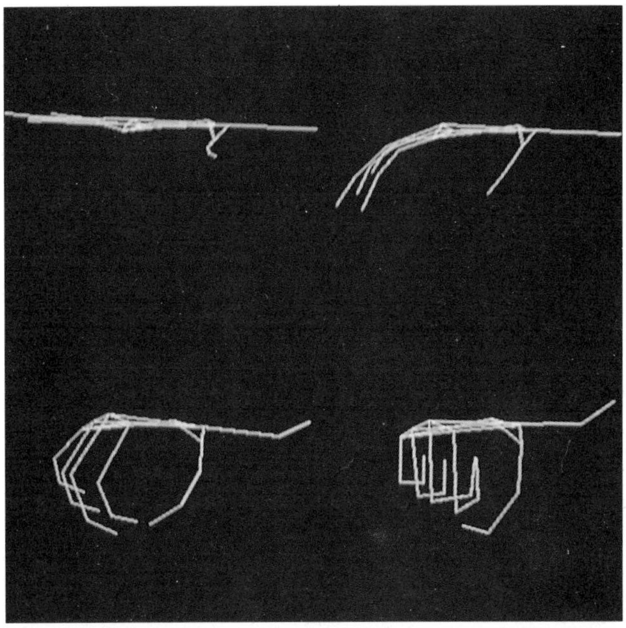

Fig. 7. Hand animation: skeleton.

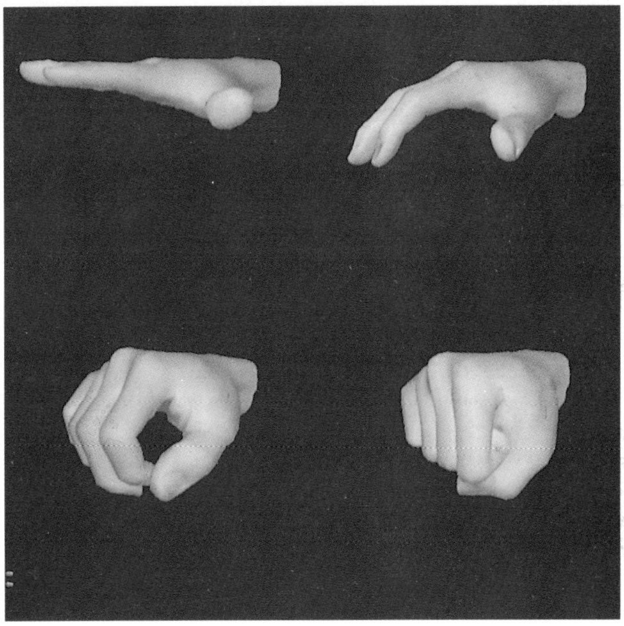

Fig. 8. Hand animation: mapped surface in Gouraud shading.

Object grasping

The animator may indicate to the HUMAN FACTORY software that an object has to be grasped. He/she provides the contact points between the hand and the object; then the software automatically determines the sequence of angles required to grasp the object.

To grasp an object, the hand has to be used, and the joints of the hand must move correctly. Two actions should be distinguished:

1. The various joint angles necessary to grasp the object must be determined. These angles should be defined to avoid any space between the hand and the object, and also to avoid any intersection between the hand and the object.

2. Once the object has been grasped, it has to be associated with the hand. For example, if the synthetic actor Marilyn grasps a book, it is obvious that the book has to move with her hand. When she turns her hand, the book must turn along with her hand. Yet it is the arm that essentially guides the hand to grasp the book and move it to a new position. So once the book is in Marilyn's hand, all her movements will make the book move too.

Positioning of the object may be controlled in two ways:

1. The animator manually selects the angles in order to grasp the object; the system indicates to the user when the fingers and the object have a common intersection.

2. The animator determines the vertex on the hand and the three vertices belonging to the facet of the object to be grasped. The flexion angles are automatically computed in order to make contact between a specific hand vertex and the object to be grasped. This calculation is performed using a binary search in order to make the distance between the contact point and the object less than some threshold value.

Generally, the animator starts his/her animation specification by positioning the hand at the best location relative to the object, without bending the fingers. This means that the chain 'shoulder-elbow-wrist' is defined with the maximum accuracy. Then one of the above methods is used.

ANIMATING A HUMAN FACE

Principles of facial animation

Facial animation of synthetic actors corresponds to the task of an impersonator. Not only should the actors be realistic in static images, but their motion should be as natural as possible when a series of images is displayed in the form of a moving film. The face is a small part of a synthetic actor, but it plays an essential role in communication. Humans read faces for emotional and intentional meanings; some literally read lips. Imitating these often subtle signs is a particular challenge.

A synthetic actor must speak and display facial expressions at specified moments. This leads to the concept of a script for facial animation, that is, a sequence of facial expressions in time. For example, at time 0, the face is neutral, at time 3 the face is smiling and at time 5, it is angry. This means that to animate an actor's face, the animator must first build a certain number of facial expressions specific to the actor's character. The expressions are built by specifying those facial deformations caused by actual muscle movement: jaw opening, eye opening, face folds, etc. These deformations vary from one person to another. For instance, if we ask several people to open their mouths as wide as possible, we find the maximum aperture is not the same for everyone.

Phonemes

A facial expression for a synthetic actor is made up of a percentage of actions for each active facial parameter. There are two types of facial expressions: phonemes (speech) and emotions (joy, grief, etc.). A phoneme uses only the muscles of the mouth, to create those specific sounds we call speech. Each phoneme corresponds to a lip motion and a tongue position. For our film *Rendez-vous à Montréal*, we chose 28 basic phonemes from the symbols categorized by the International Phonetic Association. In our particular case, however, we ignored the tongue position to simplify the technical problems. For example, for the phoneme 'I' (as in 'KID'), the teeth are slightly open and the commissures are horizontally pulled toward the sides of the mouth (risorius muscle). To produce the sound 'I', we select 10% of the vertical jaw, 50% of the left risorius and 50% of the right risorius.

Once the animator has built the expressions, he/she animates the face by indicating to the computer specific expressions at selected times. For example, 'KID' will be pronounced by a character beginning with the phoneme 'K' followed by the phoneme 'I' a short time later and then the phoneme 'D'. The software then progressively will transform the facial expression corresponding to the phoneme 'K' to obtain the facial expression corresponding to the phoneme 'I' and then the one for the phoneme 'D'.

In addition to creating phoneme expressions, however, we also must imitate the natural human rhythm of speech. For this it is essential to study a real human voice, ideally the voice of the true actor (if there is one) corresponding to the synthetic actor. For example, we establish the vocal rhythm of the synthetic actor Marilyn by studying the actual voice of Marilyn Monroe. We use a magnetic tape player of the actor pronouncing a few words or syllables and measure the length of the tape corresponding to these sounds. From this length, we easily can compute the required time for each phoneme.

Fig. 9. Facial expressions.

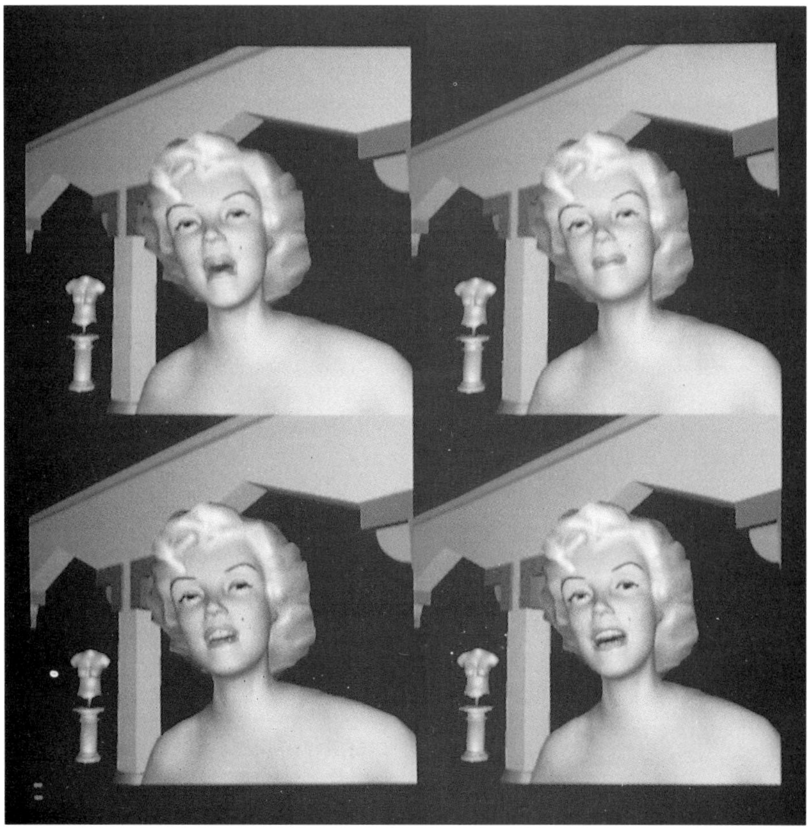

Levels in facial animation

From the considerations above, we distinguish three levels of interaction for the animator: The first and lowest level is the level of control of facial parameters; the animator may decide how a basic deformation will appear on a specific synthetic actor. At the second level, the animator creates specific expressions based on the facial parameters. For example, he/she creates phonemes, a smile, a loving look. At the third level, the animator decides the timing of the animation by fixing certain expressions at various points.

As an example, at the first level, the animator may decide how the synthetic actor Marilyn will open her mouth, that is, its maximum horizontal and vertical openings, which are facial parameters. At the second level, the animator may decide to contribute these facial parameters to an expression like a smile. At the third level, the animator makes Marilyn smile at a certain moment. In other words, an animator may work only at the script level; however, in this case, he/she controls only the timing and the duration of expressions or series of expressions. He/she cannot create completely new expressions, except when they are combinations of existing expressions. The parameter level is not necessary when basic facial parameters for a synthetic actor already exist, as, for example, those for Marilyn Monroe and Humphrey Bogart created for *Rendez-vous à Montréal*. In this case, the animator can create any new scene involving the same actors. At the expression level, new expressions can be created using the facial parameters. Figure 9 shows examples of facial expressions.

Realistic Aspects

Colors

Once digitizing is finished and all facets are known from the computer, it is possible to color the actor or even to color each facet. The number of available colors is hardware-dependent; it may vary from two colors (black-and-white terminal) up to about 16.7 million colors. For realistic images, light plays an active role. When we consider, for example, a complex red object, we realize that many red tints are required to represent the object. In general, the production of realistic images using transparency, texture and shadows requires a very large number of colors.

But how do we select colors? If we limit ourselves to eight colors, we may use the standard color names; but for the thousands (or even millions) of colors need to produce a realistic image, numerical systems are essential. The most well known are the RGB and HLS systems.

Drawing style

Three types of drawings are possible on the screen:

1. The computer draws the edges of all facets—this is a wire-frame drawing.
2. The computer colors each facet according to the light source selected by the user.
3. The computer colors each object using a gradation based on light calculations. This is the most realistic representation. Unfortunately it is also the most complex and the most expensive in terms of computer time.

Reflectance and highlight for synthetic actors

Human skin is difficult to render because of its complex texture. However, its aspect may be considerably improved by using a suitable reflectance factor. Theoretically, there are two extremes of surface type: *ideal specular reflectors,* which are like perfect mirrors (e.g. polished brass, still water) and *ideal diffuse reflectors,* which correspond to dull matte surfaces (e.g. cork, chalk). In fact, most real surfaces are neither ideal specular reflectors nor ideal diffuse reflectors. For this reason, illumination models have been developed. These models break reflection into three components—ambient, diffuse and specular.

The *ambient* component of light does not come from any single source but is an overall illumination that comes from the surroundings (walls, other objects); it represents in fact a completely distributed light source. The *diffuse* component consists of light that emanates from a point light source but is scattered equally in all directions. Objects possessing only diffuse lighting attributes appear to be made of a dull, smooth plastic. The *specular* component simulates the reflection of light from a surface in some distribution about the angle of incidence. This represents the highlight, i.e. light concentrated around the impact point of the incident ray. The highlight has the color of the source light. There are typically two parameters to control the specular component: (1) the reflectance factor and (2) the highlight width w. The highlight width depends on the surface and determines how glossy this surface is; typically w varies from 1 to 200 and would be infinite for a perfect reflector. Large values of w correspond to metallic and shiny surfaces, while small values correspond to nonmetallic surfaces like paper.

A reflectance factor of 0.5 seems too plastic, because it is too reflective. For the synthetic actor Marilyn, the following values were used: skin, eyelash and eyebrow: 0.1; beauty spot and pupil: 0.01; nails: 0.9. The value of the highlight of the pupil has been set at 1; the default value of 5 is applied to the rest of the character.

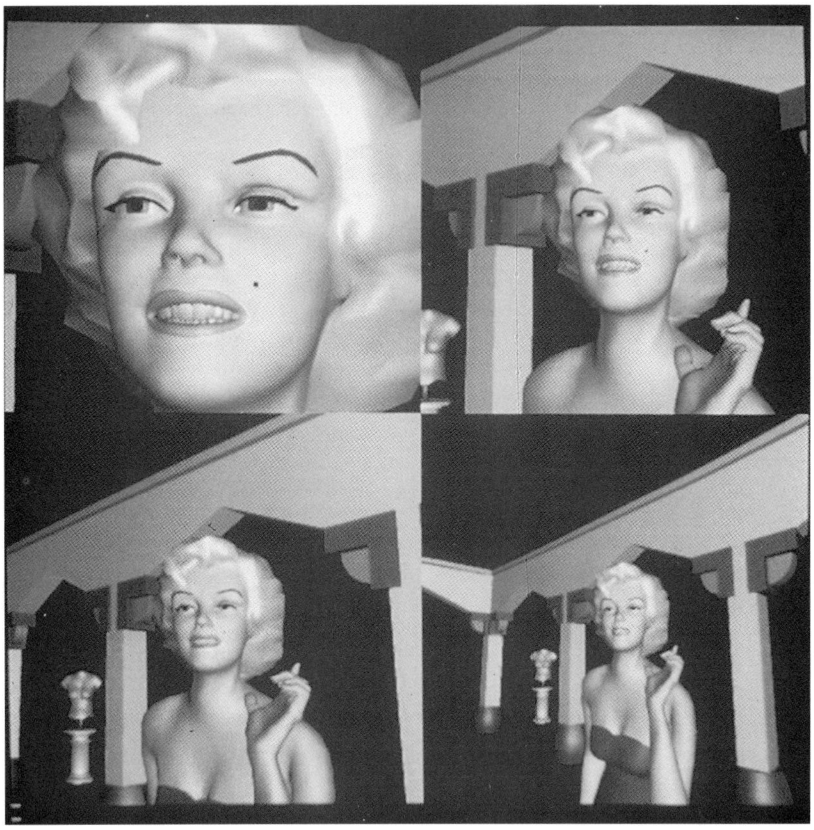

Fig. 10. Facial expressions with zoom, illustrating variations of the camera view angle. Top left: view angle = 15°; top right: view angle = 30°; bottom left: view angle = 45°; bottom right: view angle = 60°.

SYNTHETIC CAMERAS AND LIGHTS

The role of synthetic cameras

One of the most impressive effects in computer-generated films is rotation around a three-dimensional object or entrance into a complex solid. Although these effects appear spectacular, they are in fact quite easy to produce. Typically, these effects are based on the motion of a synthetic camera. A synthetic camera is a software entity that uses a few input parameters to display, like a real camera, a 2D view of a 3D scene. This means that a synthetic camera performs all the geometric transformations needed to convert three-dimensional points into points in the two-dimensional image plane. A basic synthetic camera is characterized by at least two parameters: the eye point and the point of interest. The eye is a point that represents the location of the camera. The point of interest is the point toward which the camera is directed. A view angle also may be defined to control the width of the observer's view, as shown in Fig. 10.

A synthetic camera can simulate such typical effects used by camera operators as panning, tilting, tracking, zooming and spinning. Special effects such as the wipe effects produced by optical printers in conventional animation also can be produced using synthetic cameras.

Design of a camera path

One important task of the animator is to design the movement of the camera; the typical camera motion consists of guiding the eye and/or the interest point along a path. A path is in fact a curve containing time and space information. One of the best ways to create a path is with the use of splines. They are created as follows:

Step #1: Positioning of the first camera. The animator first decides the initial characteristics of his/her camera: eye, interest point and view angle.

Step #2: Creation of the first control point of the spline. Once the camera is well positioned, the animator defines the camera eye as the first control point of the spline.

Step #3: Creation of the other control points. A second point is then selected by moving the camera eye. The new camera eye is then inserted as the second control point for the spline. Other control points are created using the same procedure.

Step #4: Editing of control points. Each control point may be modified and new control points may be inserted between existing control points.

Step #5: Time control. A time can be defined either at each control point or at only the first and last control points.

Step #6: Spline visualization. All in-between points should be displayed for control purposes.

Step #7: Definition of spline parameters. Default values for bias, tension and continuity should have been defined at each control point. Now the animator probably should change the spline by modifying these values.

Step #8: Creation of the spline.

A spline for the point of interest of the camera also may be created using a similar procedure. In this case, the point of interest of the camera is used to generate the control points instead of the eye.

The role of synthetic lights

Generally, four kinds of synthetic light sources can be defined to illuminate a three-dimensional scene:

1. ambient light, defined by its intensity, corresponds to light that is uniformly incident and is reflected equally in all directions by the surface.
2. directional light, defined by intensity and direction.
3. positional light, defined by intensity and location.
4. spotlight, defined by intensity, location, direction and concentration. Spots are light sources with a direction that may be controlled independently of the source location. A factor may determine the spatial concentration of the directed light source, allowing spotlights and floodlights to be simulated.

For any realistic computer-generated image, light sources have to be considered key elements in the scene. However, unless the light source is unique and located at an eye-point or the illumination is very diffuse (as from an overcast sky), images are not complete without shadows. Unfortunately, algorithms for shadows require considerable computation time.

References and Notes

1. N. Magnenat-Thalmann and D. Thalmann, "The Direction of Synthetic Actors in the Film *Rendez-vous à Montréal*", *IEEE Computer Graphics and Applications* **7**, No. 12 (1987).

2. N. Magnenat-Thalmann and D. Thalmann, *Image Synthesis: Theory and Practice* (Tokyo: Springer, 1987).

3. Magnenat-Thalmann and Thalmann [2].

4. N. I. Badler and S. W. Smoliar, "Digital Representation of Human Movement", *ACM Computing Surveys* (March 1979) pp. 19–38.

5. N. Magnenat-Thalmann and D. Thalmann, "Creation and Animation of a Synthetic Actress", *Proc. EUROGRAPHICS '88* (Nice, 1988).

6. Magnenat-Thalmann and Thalmann [1].

7. D. Zeltzer, "Towards an Integrated View of 3D Computer Animation", *The Visual Computer* **1**, No. 4, 249–259 (1985).

8. N. Burtnyk and M. Wein, "Computer-generated Key-frame Animation", *Journal of SMPTE* **80**, 149–153 (1971).

9. W. Reeves, "Inbetweening for Computer Animation Utilizing Moving Point Constraints", *Proc. SIGGRAPH '81* **15**, No. 3, 263–269 (1981).

10. F. I. Parke, "Parameterized Models for Facial Animation", *IEEE Computer Graphics and Applications* **2**, No. 9, 61–68 (1982).

11. S. N. Steketee and N. I. Badler, "Parametric Keyframe Interpolation Incorporating Kinetic Adjustment and Phrasing Control", *Proc. SIGGRAPH '85* (1985) pp. 255–262.

12. C. W. Reynolds, "Computer Animation with Scripts and Actors", *Proc. SIGGRAPH '82* (1982) pp. 289–296.

13. N. Magnenat-Thalmann and D. Thalmann, "The Use of High Level Graphical Types in the MIRA Animation System", *IEEE Computer Graphics and Applications* **3**, No. 9, 9–16 (1983).

14. N. Magnenat-Thalmann, D. Thalmann and M. Fortin, "MIRANIM: An Extensible Director-Oriented System for the Animation of Realistic Images", *IEEE Computer Graphics and Applications* **5**, No. 3, 61–73 (1985).

15. D. Kochanek and R. Bartels, "Interpolating Splines with Local Tension, Continuity and Bias Tension", *Proc. SIGGRAPH '84* (1984) pp. 33–41.

Towards a Universal and Intelligent MIDI-Based Stage System: A Composer/Performer's Testimony

Philippe Ménard

There is a straight line linking the 'cybernetic' paradigm of the mid-1950s to the various 'robotic' applications of the 1980s. During the last 3 decades, in the most vital research in sound synthesis, sound processing and sound recording, there have been continual attempts to bring 'control' and 'auto-control' into the field of music. I remember, in the early 1970s, when I was still a student, being thoroughly impressed by Peter Beyls's and Joel Chadabe's experiments; they were real 'control-voltage sorcerers' to me. During that glorious period in analog electronics, the role of electronics was huge compared to that of digital technology. This ratio has been completely reversed since then.

In the past decade there has been an explosion of control experiments, as never before—an eagerness to apply to the arts, and especially to music, what had been or was being developed in other, usually less peaceful fields, such as the military/industrial field. I am thinking in particular of pattern and speech recognition, artificial vision and audition, and the like. I suspect that one of the main reasons for this explosion is the shift from heavy electronics to digital computing and microcomputing. A great deal of electronic operations have shifted to programming, making this world accessible to many more people. I would say, ironically, that the control field has become affordable to 'ordinary' researchers, in the sense of 'computer-literate individuals not necessarily supported by large research and teaching institutions'.

The MIDI standard probably opened the last door for access to this robotic world, one more step in the direction of easier and better material and human communication. I am not saying that things have become so easy that research on control has been trivialized. On the contrary, I would say that complexity and heterogeneity remain the 'trademarks' of this research, but that, without the pretext of all kinds of technical difficulties, researchers no longer have an excuse not to be really inventive. I make the hypothesis that it is probably easier today for an artist to realize his or her robotic ideas than it was just a decade ago. As far as my own work is concerned, the microcomputer, assembler language, MIDI standard and some electronic expertise have proved affordable enough to make my dream of SYNCHOROS come true: a way to give the human body control of the music, and ultimately of the whole stage environment.

Philippe Ménard, 5982 rue Durocher, Outremont, Québec, Canada H2V 3Y4.
Received 5 May 1988.

ROBOTICS IN SYNCHOROS

Control is certainly the key word of cybernetics and its robotic applications. Actually, a system designed and built on detection or external data retrieval, on decision-making or 'artificial intelligence' and, finally, on task execution, corresponds to what I consider a 'robot system'.

SYNCHOROS is basically a system belonging to the family of the new MIDI systems. In the hands (literally) of a performer, it 'shrinks' to a 'simple instrument', but I shall leave that matter for later and focus instead on SYNCHOROS as a collection of units in a communication network, which has had from the beginning the complexity inherent in any cybernetic system. SYNCHOROS is not just one more MIDI product on the market, but rather a new, organic way to have MIDI instruments interrelate to each other. It is a new organization of separate, common MIDI instruments.

SYNCHOROS is a robotic system and, at the performing stage, a robotic musical instrument, in the following sense: its inputs are a combination of artificial perceivers and sensors, sending real-time information. These sensors, artificial equivalents of the human eye, ear, members and whole body, are actually sensors of light, color, weight and movement. The outputs may be combinations of various sound synthesis and processing units or, more generally, a combination of any sound-and-image synthesis or processing unit. In the middle, to interrelate one to the other, to bring the output into straight dependence on or full interdependence with the input, is located a 'decision-maker', the seat of artificial intelligence, processing input information and controlling output units according to a set of conditions listed in an aesthetic protocol designed by the composer.

This is not the place to describe the fabulous history of art and electronic technology. But 'educated' musicians know that even as pioneers like Shannon, Weaver (1949), Von Neumann (1951), Wiener (1954), Ashby (1956) and Foerster (1960) were establishing the new science of automata, artists like Xenakis, Barbaud, Hiller, Mathews, Nicolas Schöffer and many others were borrowing the concepts for artistic applications, first in the fields of analysis and composition, and a bit later in synthesis, processing and real-time performance. Actually, with SYNCHOROS, I feel close to Mathews's experiments with GROOVE and to his ideas on "conducting the computerized orchestra", and of course still closer to Buxton's ideas embodied in the SSSP system. Chadabe and Beyls, discovered in the 1970s, always have been important beacons. But since that time, I found a new hero named Michael Waiswitz, who questions this control domain at the level that interests me. In his performances

0024-094X/88 $3.00+0.00

he demonstrates clearly that serious research can result in an exciting performance and thorough communication with the audience (or what research can be like when undertaken by a researcher with a performer's approach or frame of mind). These people, among others, are probably the top figures in the line of continuity cited above from cybernetics to contemporary robotics.

SYNCHOROS IN THE CONTINUITY

As a system designed for real-time audiovisual shows, taking as its stimuli the usual stage devices (light, color, sound, space, movement, etc.) and driving sound or/and image generators or processors, SYNCHOROS, I believe, has a place on this historical line, as a system designed from a performer's perspective. Where I see the continuity is in giving the human gesture the power of control, in increasing the musical efficiency of the gesture in conducting the electronic orchestra and, consequently, in improving the chance for real communication in a performance situation. I think that this question of the means of control is certainly at the heart of current research in general and musical research in particular. There certainly are new means of making music, of performing it, of controlling total environments, beyond the traditional keyboards or the more recent 'mouse'. There are ways of freeing the hands of the pianist, for example, from material contact, to allow a more immediate response in space —to stay as instrumental as before, but with more power, more choice in the various levels of operations. From this performer's point of view, I discovered that working with lamps and photocells, and, lately, with sonars and cameras, was a way to give gesture more freedom in space, without any material contact.

Freeing the hands from the traditional keyboard is significant for different reasons: hands on the keyboard are visible; being a sort of hand-dance, the gesture is necessarily more dramatic; it adds a layer of interpretation or description, in the sense that, according to the music being triggered, the gesture patterns change dramatically, like dynamic envelopes: soft or hard attacks, short or long resonances, points or waves, straight or humorous, etc. For communication with the audience, this synchronicity between gesture and sound is vital, for otherwise the magic is lost. We have a long experience of instrumentalists causing sounds with their hands or mouths. The same fascination is at work for real-time computerized instruments. Not only can we deceive an audience but we have to work even harder to produce an effect on it because of the nonacoustic nature of our instruments.

The power gained from such programmed systems lies in the shift from unicity to multiplicity. Contrary to the pianist's or trumpeter's world, this is a new world of musical control where one gesture can generate many types of sound objects. Thanks to compositional software, the same gesture can trigger an individual note or a whole sequence of notes, not to mention the fact that it can be used to define one sound parameter (microscopic level) or to increment a counter for a delayed sound event. This is real power in the hands of a performer and it has an immediate effect on the audience. Not only can the performer's gesture be dancelike, dramatic or theatrical, but it also can produce, for each sensor, a variety of musical responses in a way that is very perceivable to the audience. This concept of moving in the hierarchy is central to both composition and performance in SYNCHOROS.

To me, the major difference between real-time and non-real-time performances (e.g. taped performances) is this concept of risk, of danger, of possible errors. I think that this almost sadistic pleasure of the auditor in feeling somebody else suffer on his or her instrument, taking risks in performing with it, with equal possibilities of being impressively good or bad, is the basic support of performance communication. Musical or instrumental gesture has always existed in 'mediated' music, by which I mean studio music. I have been involved in electro-acoustic music for years, and instrumentality in the studio always has been the basis of my musical methodology. This is probably the strength of this musical school going from Schaeffer to Dennis Smalley, to mention one of the virtuosos of the genre: most of the time the music is less architectural than instrumental, or at least equally one and the other. But this instrumental gesture is not live and stays outside the circuit of performance communication. Unfortunately, I must admit that in such a situation the communication is only partial, which could explain (partially) the failure of 'mediated' electro-acoustic music to seduce even small audiences. I think that qualities in performance such as concentration, intensity and presence are not empty words and have a real, almost physical impact on an audience. I tested this with SYNCHOROS and found that because of the concentration required at any moment of performing, the rhythmic precision, the variety of gestural patterns and the musical invention in improvising, it is obvious to the audience that a human being is controlling the machine and not the opposite. It is not a 'technology-left-to-itself' situation, but a humanly satisfying situation where technology is subdued for artistic production and communication goals. It seems that we will accept musical machines in our living room but not in the concert hall. It is one of the musicological mysteries of this electric century, which too few musicologists are questioning, in my opinion.

Musical automata on stage do not have more appeal than taped performances. At least, conscious of the lack, many electro-acoustic composers compensate by refining distribution systems, and with great success in some cases, even to the point of being spectacular. With the exception of really big environments (public places, museums, monumental sculptures, public-controlled installations, etc.), musical automata on stage never conquered audiences. They were rapidly felt to be too 'square', too cold, too repetitive, too little moving—tedious, in a word. Even astonishing mechanics cannot fulfill this appetite of humans to 'consume' another human in total control of mechanics. These last three decades have been the history of more than less deceiving attempts in this matter.

Automata combined with human or instrumental gestures seem to be a more winning combination. The human being, already present in the music stored in digital memories and in the compositional rules listed in the software, is above all present in the performer's real-time, instantaneous gesture, controlling the time and space coordinates of the whole machine.

I stressed in the preceding pages the 'soloist shape' of SYNCHOROS. Actually, it was the shape that I preferred, given the money available; and, from a performer's point of view, it was the shape that could offer the most interesting challenges for renewed instrumental gestures. But there are many other possible shapes, all based on the same SYNCHOROS concept, that is, the same software and some of the hardware, the rest having to be adapted to each new production. Among the other possible configurations are the group or 'chorist' shapes intended for dancers, mimes and actors and the crowd or 'agorist' shapes, to be used in public-controlled installations, for example. It is easy to understand that what is triggered by a performer's hand also can be triggered by a dancer's whole body or by a single visitor at a monumental sculpture. If the organizational or compositional core of the system is neutral enough, not too biased aesthetically, it can fit any composer's intentions for any show format.

It is an additional strength of a software-based system that it can be expanded in different ways. One way is to keep working with the same physical devices but improve the compositional software, from 'dumb' to 'intelligent'. This is being achieved in the current development of SYNCHOROS. Another way is to modify the physical devices themselves. To shift from a soloist configuration to a chorist one means to change the sensors, their spatial location, etc., without necessarily changing the existing compositional software, which may be sufficiently complex already.

The Current SYNCHOROS System

In May 1988, for my participation in the Second Festival of Art and Technology in Rennes (France), SYNCHOROS will consist of eight lamps, eight photocells and two sonars as input devices and, as output devices, a set of synthesizers and samplers as music generators (mainly one DX-7, one 8-unit TX-816, one or two Mirages) and a set of slide projectors as picture generators, as well as three different programs: the MIDI Sequencer, the Composer and the Performer, all three running on my oldie-but-goodie Apple IIe. Each of the thousand instruction lines has been written in assembler language, a sine qua non for running on the microprocessor 6502. Apple IIe has proven to be a good choice, allowing us to develop a real expertise in MIDI protocols and especially to refine our musical ideas. Every day, as the software develops, we bump into memory and time limits; every day, while composing with the system, I must sacrifice some interesting musical ideas because of the size of the memory. But I am used to coping with constraints in my work as a composer; they have always been positive stimuli. On the other hand, I am more than ready to switch to a higher-performance machine, and I certainly would not complain about the facilities and musical capabilities of a Mac II, for example.

In this paper, I will skim over the input and output devices, assuming that most readers know enough about photocells, sonars, synthesizers and slide projectors to figure out how they can be used in SYNCHOROS. There is a little more to say about their interfaces with the computer. Until now, the input interface was a non-MIDI, TTL custom-made card: the output interface was a MIDI Passport Design card—24 clicks/quarter-note. But we are now designing our own MIDI boxes as input/output universal interfaces, so that it will be possible to build a cascade of input and output MIDI boxes. These boxes will be operational in May 1988. This represents a major step in universalizing the system.

Of the Sequencer, I would say frankly that it certainly performs less well than most of the commercial sequencers, but it is our own, it suits our needs, it never bugs, and it includes many valuable services: memory allocations for 64 sequences, a standby option for recording or playback, any combination of sequences in recording and playback together, erase and copy commands, variation of tempo, etc. A custom-made sequencer allows one, above all, to master the smallest detail of the MIDI code. Editing capabilities are still totally absent, which makes the correction process quite awkward, the user being obliged to make time or pitch corrections, for example, directly in the Apple monitor. This will be changed, of course, in the next phase of development. In the present phase, the emphasis was put instead on time efficiency in the Sequencer and the Performer, and above all in the Composer. The playback codes (looped or not) can have two parallel control sources: the computer keyboard, also used to simulate performance situations in the absence of lamps or sonars, or the Performer Software, in operation during a live performance. The keyboard always stays active during a performance, giving an operator the opportunity to share control with the performer.

The real nature of the SYNCHOROS Sequencer is less to be a 'tape recorder' than to store a collection of musical, visual or other structures to be combined during live performance. A sequence in SYNCHOROS may have multiple meanings: it can be a musical sequence directed to a synthesizer, but it also can be a visual sequence directed to a slide projector, and a macro-command called at the beginning of each movement.

The Composer Program

In the present system, the organizational software, or Composer Program, is basically 'patchware', that is, a program to bridge or interrelate the individual input sensors to the individual output sequences. The 'personality' of the system probably lies in the various functions available in the menu. This program includes eight acts or parts or movements, that is, a pool of eight instant patches between 32 sensors, and 64 sequences or MIDI files. We plan to attach lists of conditions in this patching process, but we will not do so before the next phase on the Mac II. This is part of our dream of making this patchware intelligent. For now, it is a one-stimulus/one-response situation. But, once again, within these limits, the variety of assignations is great. These assignations include five different start/stop modes with two statuses related to these modes: Loop and Sustain. There is an additional 'Effect' mode that allows the sensors to be used as MIDI parameter modifiers: Tempo, Channel, Timbre, Velocity, Volume, Transposition, etc. The numerous combinatory processes fall between these two extremes: at one end, only one sequence with a maximum of sound modification or processing (that is, one sensor for start/stop of a sequence, and the rest for processing it), and at the other end, each sensor starts/stops one sequence, with no room left for processing. There is very little room for randomness. This software demands that the composer carefully evaluate the kind of association he or she could make between the musical structures and the different start/stop modes or parameter modifications. Before making any decision, the composer must answer these question: How would I like to play live with these given musical structures? For what kind of musical result? The composer has to figure out how he or she is going to 'improvise' with this material. Gradually ways to edit or to mix this material will come to mind, and the decision the composer makes will constitute the organization of an act.

Of the Performer Program, I will say little, even though it is the one and only support for real-time performance. The program runs as soon as an Act Number from 1 to 8 is called. It is a scanning program of the input sensors. As soon as a sensor has shifted, informed about its number and the Act Number, the program reads the patch table of the Composer Program and triggers the selected sequence according to the content of the patch table.

METHODOLOGY: A NEW MUSIC–MACHINE RELATIONSHIP

Needless to say, a new physical environment induces new creative strategies. I remember when I experienced, with my whole body, the 'Schaefferian' experimental method in electro-acoustic composition; I was convinced that it was, in comparison with the paper-and-pencil method, a real compositional revolution. With SYNCHOROS, I had to start anew, but with an accumulated musical culture.

It is probably clear from the preceding paragraphs that SYNCHOROS has two time periods, a 'before-stage' time period and an 'on-stage' one. In the before-stage period, SYNCHOROS stores preorganized or precomposed music, which is not completely music yet, but which will become real, definitely structured music under the on-stage, real-time performer's control.

The reality of musical creation with SYNCHOROS implies three levels of musical involvement. The first level is a collection ('bank') of sound materials, synthesized, sampled, processed and stored on individual machines. The second level is a collection of 'structured sound materials'. At this level, assisted by SYNCHOROS Sequencer, the composer records the basic musical structures, made of 1 to *n* sound events. Working with this sequencer, the user probably will encounter many constraints: only 64 sequences can be defined and the memory left for their allocation is rather small (about 20K bytes). For the moment, we simply cope with these constraints as positively as possible. For example, the memory constraints strongly bias the composer towards short structures, either as individual complex sound objects or as repeatable structures. This is certainly an aesthetic bias, but there is a great deal of music that can be done with that. Then at the third level, the level for the collection of musical rules, the composer applies compositional rules to the lower levels, establishing a set of possible relationships between structured sound materials and the various performance modes. At this level, where music is at the final stage before existing, it is important to understand that the composer installs the boundaries within which music is going to exist. In other words, integrating these three levels, the composer says: I know well enough what this piece is not going to be, but within the specified boundaries there is a set of possible pieces, among which only one will come out through the performer's instrumental gestures.

As a musical creator, I have two different feelings according to which I act as system designer or composer with the system. I think that designing a composer/performer's system is truly a creative act, but at a meta-level, in the sense that one offers a sort of 'meta-music' or a nest of 'possible actual works'. As a composer, I go from meta-music to actual works, but still the organizational works imply a set of possible musics. It is only as an improviser/performer that I can say I really am the composer of this and only this piece.

INTERDEPENDENCE OF THE MUSICAL LEVELS

These working steps seem to be totally independent of one another, and they can be. But I think music happens when they are not. Actually, we are in a network with the possibility of complete interdependence of the levels. It is a question of choice: from complete independence to complete interdependence, through degrees of interdependence. For example, I might decide to work out sound material without any kind of relationship to the following levels, as I might decide to select sound material with a certain degree of foreknowledge of the following steps. In this case, I would select a type of sound as a function of a specific sequence, itself thought of as a function of a specific sensor/sound interconnection, itself selected as a function of a specific real-time performance mode. This could be represented in simple mathematics as follows:

$$M = f(S)$$
$$S = f(I)$$
$$I = f(P)$$

where M = material, S = sequence, I = interconnection, P = performance. In reality, this process is truly bi-directional. The reverse process is as true. Types of sound materials often suggest types of sequences, which inspire types of interconnections, which in turn suggest performance modes. Before working with SYNCHOROS, I had already experienced this power of sounds in orientating us to specific musical patterns. It often happened that a musical improvisation would be triggered by only one timbre. It is still true with SYNCHOROS, but in a more complex network.

I make the hypothesis that there could be categories of sequences more 'tuned' (concordant) to given sound materials, categories of interconnections more tuned to both of the preceding levels, and, similarly, categories of performance modes more tuned to the three preceding levels. The more tuning there is among them, the more efficient will be the connection with the audience; we can imagine the artistic communications as going through a line from sound material to sequence to interconnection to performance with the composer/performer having the choice to stay close to or deviate from this line (see Fig. 1).

Musical reality is certainly more complex than that. There is nevertheless a grain of truth in this hypothesis,

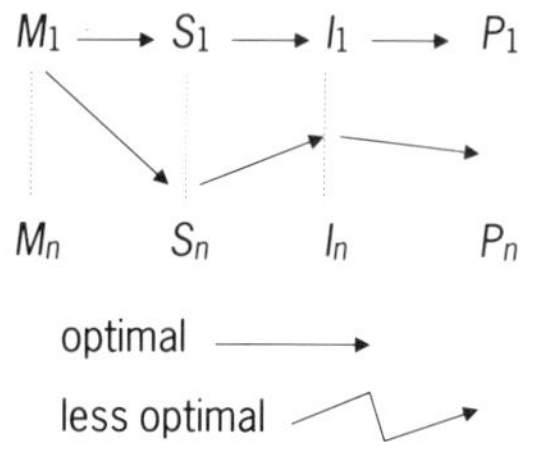

Fig. 1. Flow of artistic communications from sound materials to performance.

according to my musical experience. As part of this reality, I have noticed as musical facts that I am inclined to distribute the musical events on the sensors in a way that is easy for my limited human memory, and that I really perform within a feedback loop, in the sense that my gestures are not totally 'programmed' or rehearsed, but dependent on the real-time preceding sound objects.

Development of the System

On the basis of the present set-up of SYNCHOROS, we are progressing towards a universal and intelligent stage system. How universal and how intelligent (in the universality) is what we are going to examine.

Our ideal system would be universal in the sense that any stage 'stimulator' could become a MIDI informational source for the system, with some places planned for feedback loops. Every input or output device would be interfaced through MIDI boxes to the micro-computer. The prototype of the MIDI box is under construction. There will be four possible informational outputs—the microphone for sound environment, the camera for visual environment, our existing lamps (or any photocell device) and sonars (or any other distance sensor)—with at least two possible feedback circuits through the microphone and the camera.

In the near future (December 1988), the decision-maker of this system is going to be a Mac II supporting MIDI LISP. It is certainly the best development tool available, given the facts that (1) every input or output is going to be MIDI coded and (2) we are taking an artificial intelligence (AI) orientation.

Finally, at the output, to the actual music set will be added, step by step, slide projectors, video monitors and a stage lighting system, all driven through MIDI code.

The system will be universal mainly through the universality of the software. SYNCHOROS software from the beginning has been designed so that it could embrace any figurable stage device. When we go to the Mac II, I think that it will be easy to adapt the software, both to a new machine and to new stage devices.

How Intelligent?

The current system is only a part of what is planned to become an 'artist-system', in the sense of an 'expert system', that is, a system capable of the 'best possible' artistic decisions. My model for that is the live composer/improviser, who has composed and memorized all the sound materials and structures for a specific show and who, under live stage stimuli, gives them an instantaneous definite shape. By completing and refining the present sensor input system, by formalizing the implied musical expertise, I think that, given the existing skills, SYNCHOROS is on the way to becoming at least a good assistant/consultant. Ultimately, what interests me is how to formalize, in order to imitate, this composer/improviser involved in a live, interactive musical organizational process.

Liberty Scale

If we try to come closer to what the decisions could be like, we are introduced to a central concept in this whole process, which is the 'liberty scale' or, according to the expression borrowed from Emile Leipp, a French acoustician, the "degrees of liberty". This concept applies to the musical organizational mode during stage activities. Concerned with a true cybernetic complexity, with being as close as possible to a true artistic model, I thought of relating the input causes to output effects on various levels. At one extreme, the most simple level could be associated with positive or negative incrementation, a numbered value available for any algorithm at any moment. In this mode, incrementation could produce a delayed event, without any immediate and perceptible relationship to the initial sound or image. At the other end, each sensor could define one and only one parameter. All of them together would 'synthesize' the sound, in all of its constituent spectral and temporal parameters. It would be instant creation without any assistance from the organizational memories. And in between lie all the intermediate degrees, more or less polarized by triggering or synthesizing.

The triggering mode can give way to situations as different as an individual note and myriads of events. A first refinement is to introduce various start/stop modes; a second, to produce parameter modifications in the triggered sequence, such as Timbre, Tempo, Velocity and Transposition. This intermediate world is made of many possible musics. In pitch processing, for example, one can go from pure randomness to pure bi-univocality (one sensor/one pitch). This compositional method is comparable to Umberto Eco's 'open work', conceptualized and widely practiced in the 1970s (by Pousseur, Stockhausen, and others).

Very little of this plan has been implemented. For now, I am triggering sequences according to five start/stop modes, allowing a great complexity in real-time editing and mixing, with such real-time sound processing as Timbre, Sustain and Channel Assignation. To evolve within the liberty scale, the patchware will have to be injected with a set of knowledge and rules.

It is on the basis of this knowledge base and list of rules that the 'intelligent' patchware will be capable of patching decisions. The conditional lists could be based on such input variables as

(1) two-state or scaled voltage. In this case, one could specify conditions according to voltage segments, as in the example shown in Fig. 2.

(2) speed of moving bodies or objects.

(3) combination of input events. If event A,B,C triggers Effect 1,2,3, one could say that the combination of A and B would produce Effect 4, and so on.

(4) time related to counted number of sensor's detections. For example, within the first 10 minutes, if the number of detections is less than or equal to 50, then Effect 10, else Effect 11.

Combining all these variables we could solve the following problem: "If light rays nos. 1 and 3 are interrupted

Fig. 2. On the basis of its knowledge base and list of rules the 'intelligent' patchware will be capable of patching decisions. The conditional lists could be based on input variables such as two-state or scaled voltage. In this case, one could specify conditions according to voltage segments.

Cause: ADC Volume — Segment

a b c d e

MIDI: 0 127

Effect: Transposition — Octave

1 2 3 4 5

in speed segment C and the number of actions on no. 3 is 5, then read MIDI file no. 9 in loop and file no. 15 in start/stop mode no. 1; each detection of no. 7 would mean a timbre change by incrementation of a pile."

This is a 'dumb' execution of a stage situation that we would like to be processed with more 'artistic intelligence'. To achieve this, we should provide the system with the following:

(1) for the MIDI sound file, two complementary information 'banks': one of detected quantitative variables (measure = 4/4; tempo = 120, etc.), and one of qualitative variables written by the composer (qualities such as swing rhythm, calm ambience, urban or rural environment);

(2) at input, two parallel data retrieval systems: a system of discriminating sensors for quantizable values, and a base of knowledge related to stage activities (this part is pianissimo, exotic environment, etc.);

3) for decision-making, an Inference Motor capable of processing synonyms, metaphors and logic operations like implications and exclusions.

Thus equipped, the system could solve this problem: "If a dancer is moving very slowly from behind to the front of the stage, in a blue-lighted ambience, play a very meditative repetitive music to follow him."

With the addition of knowledge and conditional rules, we lift the system a step higher from bi-univocality mode to multivocality mode, according to which, under information reception, it must test a whole list of conditions before making any decision. It is this decision-making center, seat of 'intelligence' or 'talent', that promises spectacular developments, inasmuch as we will succeed in formalizing a maximum of knowledge and rules and in quantizing a maximum of input sensor information, that is, in reflecting as well as possible a real musical situation.

With the developments we envisage, SYNCHOROS, seen as a 'stage robot', may be the beginning of a new type of stage manager. Actually, a system asked to generate in real-time sound material, sound distribution, light, color, pictures, etc., is without any doubt a dramatically improved production system; not a passive dispatch production, which lets sounds or lights come in and out at previously determined moments, but an interactive production capable of inventing environmental objects for stage action, on the basis of a fine analysis of this action and of a set of memorized sight-and-sound sequences. It is what we could describe as a real, qualitative leap towards universal and intelligent control.

Geometric Image Modelling of the Musical Object

Michel Naranjo and
Assuh Koffi

ABSTRACT

Contemporary music is often thought of in terms of musical objects where tonic notes, appropriately clustered, give a mass corresponding to height and tessitura criteria. A mathematical characterization of a musical phrase permits various visualization techniques of the figure. In accord with philosophical concepts, the pattern is perfectly represented by an envelope which is a tangent surface at a set of notes in a polyphonic score. Two image models are discussed in this paper. The first is based on the B-spline surfaces smoothing a discrete musical event set in the space: height-duration-timbre. The second performs the Discrete Fourier Transform signature of the digital musical signal.

Since Pierre Schaeffer's works, contemporary music is often thought of in terms of musical objects. Schematically tonic notes appropriately clustered do not give a chord, but a mass corresponding to height criteria and to a tessiture more or less fair [1]. Ligeti's second quartet, for example, can be seen as "a large moving shape of jagged texture and opaque tonal mist". Stephane Goldet translates this as "a pure music of tessitura, smoothed surface moving like a lava flow which little by little curdles . . . ", where "Ligeti breaks with the traditional discontinued register which exists between one instrument and the other and establishes the timbral tessitura notion where every timbral individual expression is exhausted" [2].

On account of the sound richness found by new musical material frequently associated with traditional orchestral instruments, the composer often needs tools that are necessary in structural description and monitoring. Philippe Manoury thinks the aid of Artificial Intelligence and cognitive science is indispensable [3]. Scientists easily sympathize with Marvin Minsky's suggestion that music is an ideal subject for the study of human knowledge representation [4]. It is not by chance that the first examples used to illustrate the perceptual rules of pattern came from music.

THE PATTERN, THE RHYTHM AND THE IMAGE

The connection between pattern concepts and rhythm is ancient. Benveniste finds its etymological roots in Greek antiquity: Plato divided the primitive significance of pattern into a spatial, stable pattern (which later became the 'Gestalt notion' or figure) and a fluid pattern, or 'order in motion', which became the word 'rhythm' [5]. In terms of images, the figure is perfectly represented by an envelope determining a tangent surface on a set of discontinuous events. They define within this surface the singular points and that one fixes their continuity [6]. Rhythm provides motion in image. This metaphor introduces a relation between music and drawing. Using mathematical rules like philosophical concepts, the composer Iannis Xenakis abstracted patterns and then used them in musical and architectural creations. In "Metastasis" (1954), he introduced a simple relationship between drawing and music. In Brussels in 1958 this graphic musical imagery was transmuted into architecture in three-dimensional space where the lines of glissandi generated hyperbolic-parabolic surfaces on the Philipps Pavillion [7]. The assistant composer machine UPIC (in French: Unité Polyagogique Informatique du Centre d'Etudes de Mathématiques et Informatique Musicale) resembles a drawing board connected to electronic equipment capable of translating into sounds any graphic design (point, line, curve) traced on the drawing board with a special electronic pencil. The sonic equivalent of the draw-

Michel Naranjo and Assuh Koffi, Electronics Laboratory, Blaise Pascal University of Clermont–Ferrand, B.P. 45, 63170 Aubière, France.

Received 19 April 1988.

Fig. 1. "Tetras" by Iannis Xenakis, measures 378–389 (Salabert Editor).

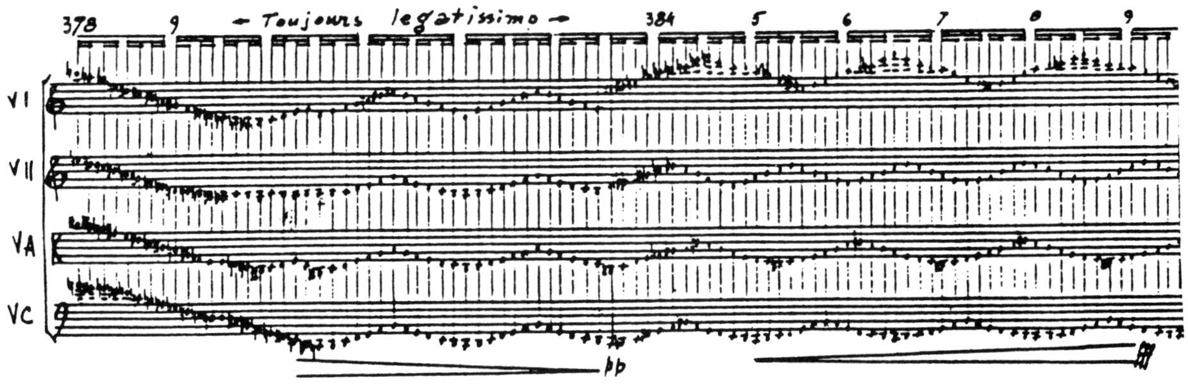

Pergamon Press plc. Printed in Great Britain.
0024-094X/88 $3.00+0.00

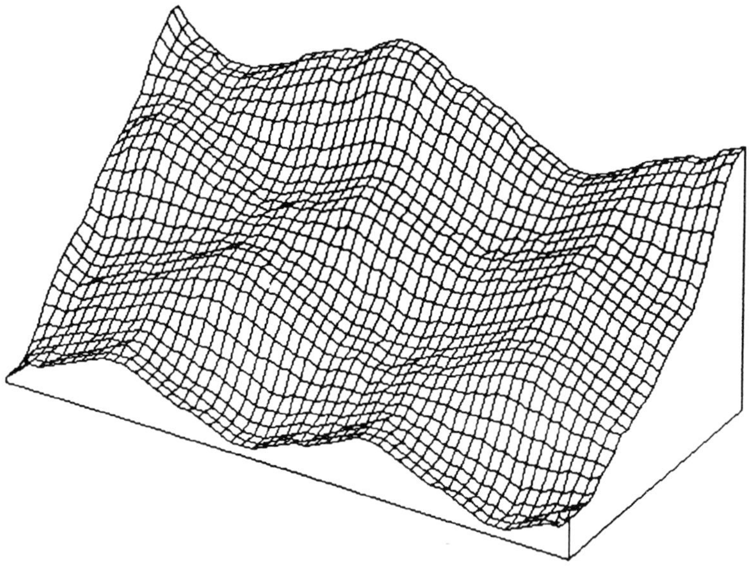

Fig. 2. Perception of mass of the string quartet.

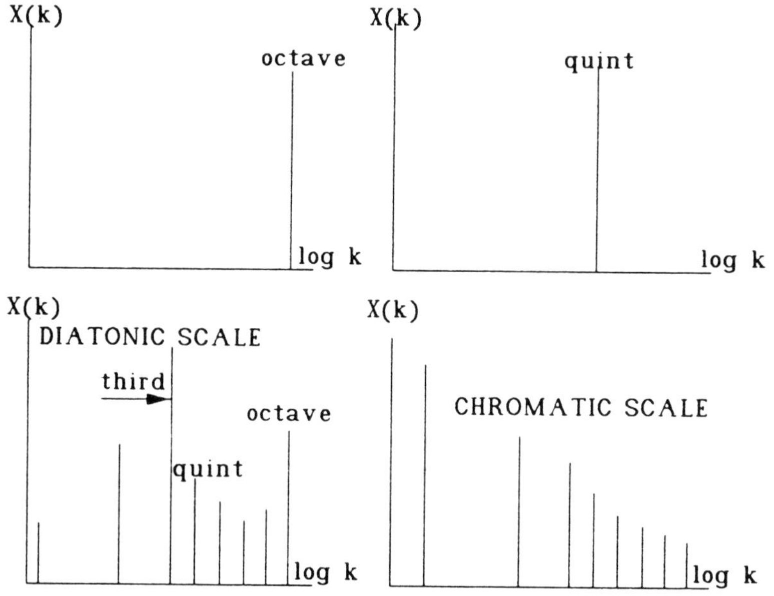

Fig. 3. Discrete Fourier Transform of an octaver, quint, diatonic and chromatic time-repetition.

ing is immediately calculated by the machine and made audible, permitting instantaneous control of the sound and sequence that have just been drawn. It is not, therefore, a matter of transforming the drawing into music, but actually conceiving the music graphically. The UPIC user quickly learns how to establish a relationship between the sounds and becomes capable of drawing these curves according to the sounds wished, even if the operator is a child.

Graphic Representation of Musical Knowledge

The recent evolution of graphic systems permits us to realize new composers' assistants where the plane representation is substituted for the 3-D space. A. Bogornovo and G. Hauss analyze the 3-D surface generated by two variable functions in order to control the resultant waveforms [8]. C. A. Pickover implemented a 3-D representation of melody patterns using topographic spectral distribution functions [9]. The dynamics of musical structures existing between several successive notes or sounds are being visualized by J.P. Boon and A. Noullez using 3-D schemata [10]. Musical aspects of fractal geometry are studied by B. Degazio in applications to automated musical composition [11].

In our representation system the images that we manipulate are synthesized using digital signal processing concepts; a melody is a signal in the plane: height-time, and a polyphonic phrase is a 2-D signal in the space: height-timbre-time. The composer introduces into the computer keyboard a set of discontinuous sound-components such as note sequences, their duration and their timbre. For instance, a phrase from Xenakis' "Tetras" (Fig. 1) is introduced line by line and each note is represented by three symbols: name-octave-value. The software transforms this string of characters into real points in the height-time plane and the timbre is given by the number of the line. David Ehresman and David Wessel show us that timbre can be classified by function of proximity criteria in a plane: spectral variations (brightness)–temporal evolution (attack) [12]. We believe it exists for an instrumental set, given a particular axis where all instrumental representative points are projected.

For reasons of simplicity and considering the timbral proximity of a string quartet, we have classified this timbre as a function of the register utilized in the partition. So the polyphonic phrase given in Fig. 1 is transformed into an array of points:

[V_{ij}] where:
V_{ij} is the MIDI code of the note played during the
ith elementary duration by the
jth instrument.

In the example in Fig. 1, the elementary duration is the triple quaver and

$j = 1$ for violin 1,
$j = 2$ for violin 2,
$j = 3$ for alto,
$j = 4$ for cello.

This array of points constitutes the singular elements set of the phrase, and a smooth surface gives the continuity of the figure. We have used a B-spline algorithm [13] in order to obtain the parametric surface

$$Q_{44}(u,v) = \sum_{i=0}^{m} \sum_{j=0}^{n} N_{i,4}\ (u)_{j,4}(v) V_{ij}$$

where:
m is the total number of timbres,

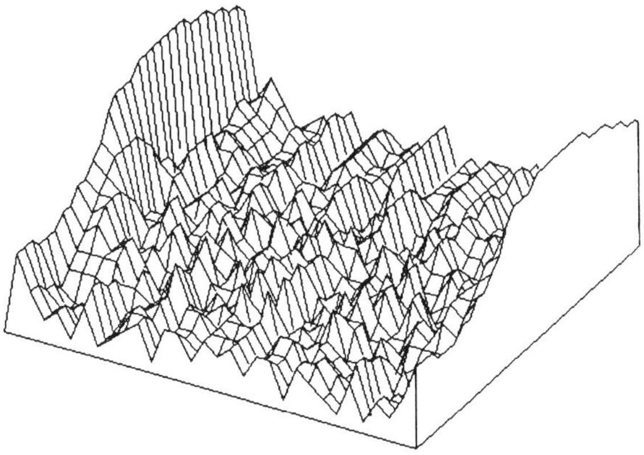

Fig. 4. Discrete Fourier Transform of "Tristan's Solo" by Wagner.

n is the total number of elementary durations,

$N_{i,4}$, $N_{j,4}$ are the order 4 basic functions for a cubic approximation of, respectively, the scale timbre and the scale duration given by the following recursive procedure [14]:

$N_{i,1}(u) = 1$ for $i \leq u \leq i+1$

$N_{i,1}(u) = 0$ otherwise.

$$N_{i,k}(u) = N_{i,\,k-1}(u) \cdot \frac{u-i}{k-1} + N_{i+1,\,k-1}(u) \cdot \frac{i+k-u}{k-1}$$

The synthesized image generated by the phrase given in Fig. 1 from measure 385 to measure 389 is given in Fig. 2. This image is a translation of the perception of mass where it exists as a shifting in the wave heights of the different instruments.

It is possible to utilize an inverse B-spline algorithm which gives us the singular geometric points of an image. In musical composition these points can be the height of the sounds. We shall use this representation for manipulating the musical phrase: first, detecting any particular line or curvature; second, manipulating the detected line or curvature as any rotation or translation; and, third, generating a new image derived from the initial image but made using the transformed line or curvature. This final work is now in progress [15].

Graphic Spectral Representation of the Musical Phrase

There are many instances where signal processing involves the measurement of spectra. For example, in speech recognition problems, spectrum analysis is usually a preliminary step to further acoustic processing [16]. Development of a comprehensive theory of spectrum analysis is made difficult by the fact that nearly all such measurements are taken over finite time intervals, and the length of this interval is usually determined through intuition and experience. In music, this difficulty is avoided because of the discrete nature of composition and because the elementary duration of a partition can be a basic sampling.

The Discrete Fourier Transform (DFT) is a mathematical function that performs the operation of breaking down a digital signal, such as a digitally recorded sound, into its spectrum. The DFT of a finite duration sequence of M heights is defined as

$$\{x(m)\},\ 0 \leq m \geq M-1$$

$$X(k) = \sum_{m=0}^{M-1} x(m) e^{-j\left(\frac{2n}{M}\right)mk}$$

$k = 0, 1, \ldots, M-1$ spectral scale sampling.

Figure 3 gives the DFT of an octaver, a quint, a tierce and a diatonic scale repetition. This experimentation shows the increased ray number and permits the spectral axis rating.

The image given in Fig. 4 is synthesized using the DFT of Wagner's melody "Tristan's Solo" (English horn). The third dimension is obtained by windowing the partition through a rectangular function.

This result is comparable with images synthesized by Pickover but with analogic definition of the Fourier Transform [17]. Our transforms are computed with a radix 2 FFT's algorithm which reduces the computation time [18]. Our investigation continues toward a 2-D DFT transforming polyphonic phrase:

$$X(k,l) = \sum_{m=0}^{M-1} \sum_{n=0}^{N-1} x(m,n) e^{-j\left(\frac{2n}{M}\right)mk} e^{-j\left(\frac{2n}{N}\right)nl}$$

with a height sequence (M basic durations and N timbres),

$k = 0, 1, 2, \ldots, M-1,$

Fig. 5. This synthesized image represents the Discrete Fourier Transform of the "Tetras" phrase given in Fig. 2.

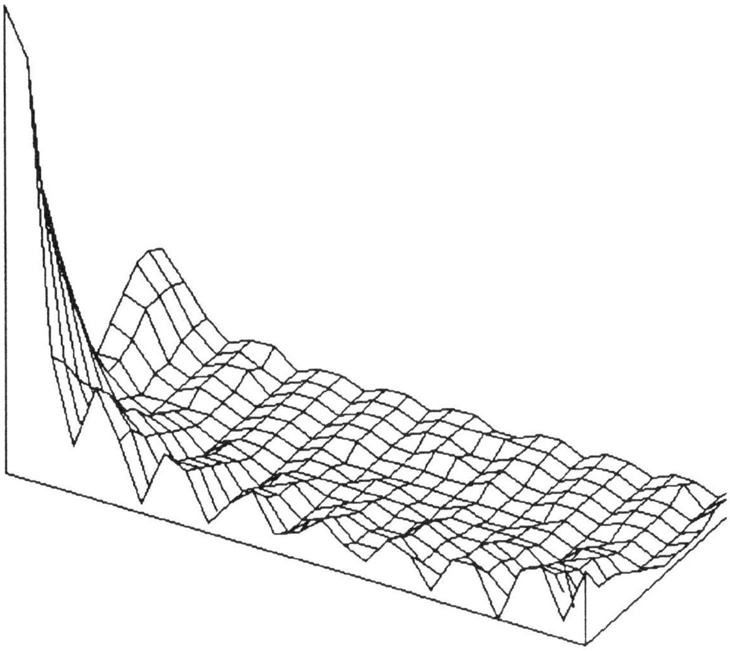

$l = 0, 1, 2, \ldots, N-1$.

We have illustrated this formula with the synthesized image of Fig. 5, which represents the DFT of the "Tetras" phrase given in Fig. 2. The chromatic aspect of the partition explains the important border rays.

Conclusion and Future Applications

Today Computer Science permits fundamental world transformation. Thus, musical research must be multidisciplinary in order to progress in this and other art forms concerned with scientific discipline.

Our research, materialized by a geometric representation of the musical object, could result in the realization of an assistant composer machine. Beyond the space representation height-timbre-time, it will be possible to introduce new dimensions: rhythm and dynamic exploration of the graphic possibilities of color and motion. This new composer's assistant is another step towards introducing the camera to the musical creation process [19].

References

1. Pierre Schaeffer, "Traité des objets musicaux—Essai interdisciplinaire" (Paris: Seuil Editor, 1966; revised 1977) pp. 519–521.

2. Stephane Goldet, "Quatuors du 20ème siècle" (Paris: IRCAM/Papier, 1986) pp. 107–108.

3. Philippe Manoury, "La part consciente", *Consequences,* No. 7/8 (Fall 1985/Spring 1986) pp. 67–74.

4. Tod Machover, "Quoi, Quand, Comment? la Recherche Musicale", Christian Bourgois, ed. (Paris: IRCAM, 1985) pp. 137–163.

5. Emile Benveniste, "Problèmes de linguistique générale" (Paris: Gallimard, 1966) pp. 327–328.

6. François Nicolas, "Visage du temps: rythme, timbre, forme", *Entre-Temps,* No. 1 (April 1986) pp. 35–57.

7. Iannis Xenakis, "Musique-Architecture" (Paris: Casterman, 1976) pp. 8, 133.

8. Aldo Bogornovo and Goffredo Hauss, "Sound Synthesis by Means of Two-Variable Functions: Experimental Criteria and Results", *Computer Music Journal* **10**, No. 3 (Fall 1986).

9. Clifford A. Pickover, "Representation of Melody Patterns Using Topographic Spectral Distribution Functions", *Computer Music Journal* **10**, No. 3 (Fall 1986).

10. Jean Pierre Boon and Alain Noullez, "Musical Structure and Complex Dynamics", *Symposium on Music and the Cognition Sciences* (Paris: IRCAM, 1988).

11. Bruno Degazio, "Musical Aspect of Fractal Geometry", *ICMC 86 Proceedings* (The Hague: Royal Conservatory, 1986).

12. David Ehresman and David Wessel, "Perception of Timbral Analogies", *IRCAM Report,* No. 13 (Paris: 1978).

13. Assuh Koffi, "3D-Graphic Representation of the Musical Object". Thesis in submission (September 1988).

14. Briand A. Barsky, "A Description and Evaluation of Various 3D-Models", *IEEE Computer Graphics and Applications,* **4**, No. 1 (1984).

15. Koffi [13].

16. Lawrence R. Rabiner and Bernard Gold, "Theory and Application of Digital Signal Processing" (Englewood Cliffs, NJ: Prentice Hall, 1975).

17. Pickover [9].

18. Rabiner and Gold [16].

19. Henning Lohner, "Interview with Iannis Xenakis", *Computer Music Journal,* **10**, No. 4, 50–55 (Winter 1986).

The Computer: Liberator or Jailer of the Creative Spirit

John Pearson

ABSTRACT

This presentation covers some of the historical and aesthetic questions raised by the fine arts community regarding the use of computers by artists. Before addressing issues related specifically to the computer, the author gives a preamble that provides a context and creates a texture for the comments relating to the computer and its role in the visual arts. Comments are offered on the role of technology, science, mathematics, the humanities and aesthetics in the visual arts.

PREAMBLE

It is fair to posit that technology is being looked to as the solution to all of our problems: medical, agricultural, political, educational. It is viewed as the new 'Savior', as our salvation. Unfortunately technology becomes self-perpetuating, building upon itself, becoming an indispensable factor in every facet of daily life, controlling the quality and mode of life to a frightening degree while offering increased liberty and the illusion of greater independence. Computers have become the new backbone of this technological syndrome and thus it is not surprising that certain artists are beginning to investigate them, assess their impact on the visual arts and either adapt—capitulate—to their magnetic powers or assimilate/appropriate their power and make it serve the purposes and needs of the visual arts.

THE HISTORICAL ROLE OF TECHNOLOGY IN THE VISUAL ARTS

Technology has always been the handmaiden of the visual arts because, as is obvious, a technical means is always necessary for the visual communication of ideas, of expression, or the development of works of art—tools and materials are required. Without tools and some understanding of the basic physical and chemical properties of certain materials, sculpture and painting could not have developed. Without this development not only would societies not have progressed but neither would the arts. Casting made for more effective weapons for hunting and protection but also provided tools for the making of objects that fulfilled practical, aesthetic, intellectual or spiritual needs. While bodily demands were being met, a need existed to satisfy spiritual and intellectual requirements. Thus, a fabric of understanding regarding the realities of the environment became woven, the strands of this fabric being spun from relationships based upon fantasy tempered by personal experience and the observation of natural events. By the nineteenth century, carving, casting, painting, printmaking, weaving and pottery had become quite sophisticated as the mechanical and chemical technologies involved in these processes had developed. Since the middle of the nineteenth century, welding, photography, film, resins and plastics, and electronics media have provided artists with alternative approaches that have profoundly affected the visual arts. Now the computer has entered the scene and has been appropriated by artists because it offers exciting new means for expressing their ideas. All of the above technologies, except perhaps photography, however, were not developed by the artistic community for artistic purposes but by science and industry to serve the pragmatic or utilitarian needs of society. With the introduction of the assembly line facilitating mass production, the development of mass communication and advertising, and the development of mass distribution via air, rail and road, there has grown up a new society of consumerism that apparently has an insatiable appetite of global proportions. The technologies necessary for satisfying this appetite, and the attitudes it has sired, all are fair game for artists to use as they see fit. Computers are simply another one of these appropriations/utilizations.

THE ROLE OF SCIENCE AND MATHEMATICS IN THE VISUAL ARTS

Science

A major function of the visual arts, as of other disciplines, is to try to formulate an understanding of the nature of truth and reality. At different periods in history, for a variety of reasons—practical/material, political, etc.—certain disciplines have appeared more attractive or have been more successful than others at articulating these formulations and understandings. Philosophy, psychology, physics, mathematics and engineering have all been placed in the driver's seat and their ideologies have permeated all aspects of society including the visual arts. In great cultures of the past there was little separation between the humanities and the sciences. Art, mathematics, philosophy and science seemed integrated, exchanged ideas, learned from each another much more than today; but perhaps this is changing again as Eastern thought and quantum mechanics each increasingly echo the thinking of the other. However, since the rise of industrialization, the arts and sciences have regarded each other with suspicion and misunderstanding, and a

John Pearson, Department of Art, Oberlin College, Oberlin, OH 44074, U.S.A.

Revised version of paper originally presented at the Ninth Annual Conference and Exposition of the National Computer Graphics Association, March 1988. Published in *NCGA '88*, Vol. III of the Conference Proceedings. Reprinted by permission.

Received 25 April 1988.

Pergamon Press plc. Printed in Great Britain.
0024-094X/88 $3.00+0.00

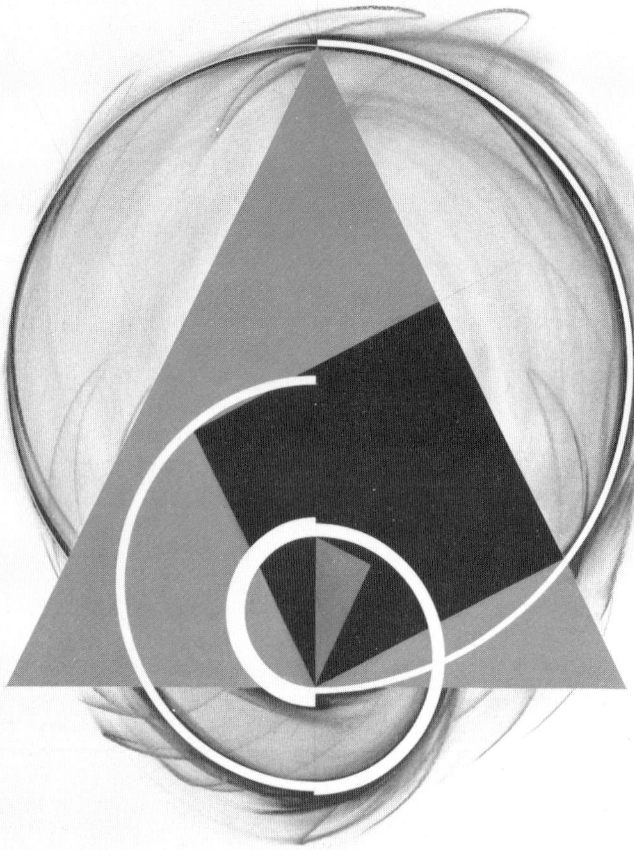

Fig. 1. ***Arc/Area/Section: Spiral-Flip 'A'*****, conte, charcoal and pencil on paper, 38 in × 50 in, 1983. (Photo © 1983 Brenda L. Lewison)**

chasm has come to exist between the two, which is not only unfortunate but also quite counterproductive.

Relativity theory also had its indirect influence on art, giving rise to Cubism. Heisenberg's notions not only heralded new attitudes in physics but influenced the visual arts, leading to the idea of the 'open system' in the artistic process and to the exploitation of randomness in certain forms of Surrealism and the Abstract Expressionism of Pollock. In this century, electronic engineering and chemical engineering (resins, polyesters, fiberglass, etc.) have had a profound influence on the images that artists create to express their ideas.

Today the most powerful modes of visual or audio communication are electronic, and the instantaneous transmission of images from one part of the globe to another has caused reality to wear a different mask. These communication modes are heavily invested in new electronic media and tools such as film, videocassette, television transmission and lasers; the computer is pivotal to the operation and performance of most of these electronic processes. Perhaps because this technology has entered the mainstream of life via its application through electronic entertainments, video recorders, video games, MTV and the home computer, the chasm is being reduced and the rift between art and science eliminated.

Mathematics

Throughout history artists have consistently attempted to discover mathematical truths underlying the visual harmony and beauty of the ideal, from the architects, ceramists and sculptors of classical Greece, to Renaissance painters such as Leonardo da Vinci, Piero della Francesca and Cimabue, to twentieth-century figures such as Seurat and Le Corbusier. Perspective is a mathematical method of conveying the illusion of the third dimension—a mathematical construct describing optical distortion in time and space. Perspective was developed by the Renaissance architect Alberti, facilitating the next few hundred years of artistic involvement with creating works of art that echoed the optically perceived world as reality, the *eye* taking over from the *mind.* Conversely, because of the religious ban on images in Islamic culture, highly complex patterns were developed using simple geometric concepts as a point of departure. The obsessive nature of these patterns, covering the walls, floors and domes of Islamic mosques, produces a visually rich and intense aesthetic experience. Repetition and modularity as means of artistic expression have been used in other contexts, such as in the works of American quilt makers, the paintings of Andy Warhol and the highly retinal perceptual abstractions of Bridget Riley. Geometry has consistently appeared in the visual arts, whether as a means of generating regular patterns on fabrics or tiled walls or as a way of echoing the order and harmony, observed or intuited, in nature. The Greeks and the Egyptians used the Golden Mean of 1.618 in their architecture; during the Renaissance it was reintroduced as a design element, and it continued to be used by such seventeenth-century classicists as Poussin. Such applications have not been confined to the visual arts but have appeared also in music, an example being Schönberg's work. Today, Mandelbrot's fractals offer possibilities for the visual arts through the linking of fractal geometry to computer science, particularly image generation, manipulation and animation.

In short, artists have always been aware of not only the spiritual and intellectual climate of their times but also the technological, scientific and mathematical climate. They have either embraced it, absorbed it by osmosis and thus reflected it in their work or process, or added to the intellectual and technological development of their times, their symbiotic relationship to their times being inevitable. Today's artists have to face the computer if they are to be a part of these times and make a meaningful contribution.

Is There a Relationship Between Art and Aesthetics?

The linguistic root of the word 'aesthetics' can be traced to ancient Greece, where its meaning dealt with perception: "things (material as opposed to thinkable) perceptible to the senses". In the 1750s the German philosopher Baumgartner extended and distorted this strict meaning so it served that branch (science) of philosophy that dealt with the criticism of taste. While this extension was protested by many, most notably Kant, by the 1850s it was in common use, and the term was generally accepted as pertaining to the philosophy of taste, the theory of the fine arts, or the science of beauty. Today it is often posited that aesthetics basically translates as taste. But what is taste? Is it acquired? And if so how is it acquired?

At a recent lecture a young Chinese scholar, Hang Wu, related an incident that clearly illustrated taste to be based on cultural conditioning. He explained that in 1979 he curated an exhibition of both Western and Eastern portrait paintings and supervised its tour of villages throughout China. When villagers were asked which of the portraits were most objective—that is, most realistically rendered—without exception they selected the Chinese portrait paintings. When pressed for reasons as to their selection they replied that "there are no smudges of brown, or other colors, on the faces of real people". Such 'smudges' they found only in the Western portraits. It appeared that although the portraits of the Chinese personages in the Chinese paintings were all quite similar and could bear little, if any, physical resemblance to the particular facial characteristics of the sitters, they were viewed as being more objectively realistic. The scholar who arranged the exhibition had been trained in painting and also was a Western-style painter who had lived in the U.S. for 16 years. He was used to (had been conditioned to understand) the rules of Western painting and thus was surprised at the above responses.

This story aptly demonstrates that the visual interpretation (translation) of images is based on cultural conditioning. It is also possible that we unwittingly learn, i.e. are taught, to think in particular ways that condition our communication of information via visual means. When children are asked to draw a landscape to include the sky, grass and flowers, they work in an abstract manner. They will draw green on the bottom of their paper and may even have flowers growing out of the bottom edge of the paper. The sky more often than not will be a blue band at the top of the page. If asked why they have left a large empty space in between the sky and ground they will make statements that in effect say that that is the way the real world is—there is only space between the ground and sky. In short they are depicting what they *know* to be true as a complete realistic physical experience and not depicting only an accurately observed *optical* experience. It would appear, then, that the mind understands experience holistically, engaging and synthesizing the subtle nuances of all of the senses, rather than perceiving only information transmitted through (seen or sensed by) our visual organ, the eye. Artists—visual as opposed to audio—try to discover methods for translating the experiences of all of the senses into a singular, purely visual language. This language is constructed from numerous experiences—personal, local, regional, national, international, physical, psychological, cultural, sociological, political, racial, religious, etc.—which have been filtered, consciously and unconsciously, through emotional and intellectual fabrics, again both personal and cultural. I believe that it is this same process that determines both personal and cultural taste. Thus patterns are established that determine aesthetic judgment.

It is generally accepted that Darwin's theory of evolution—the theory

Fig. 2. ***Arc/Area/Section: Double Flip*****, conte, charcoal and pencil on paper, 38 in × 50 in, 1983.**

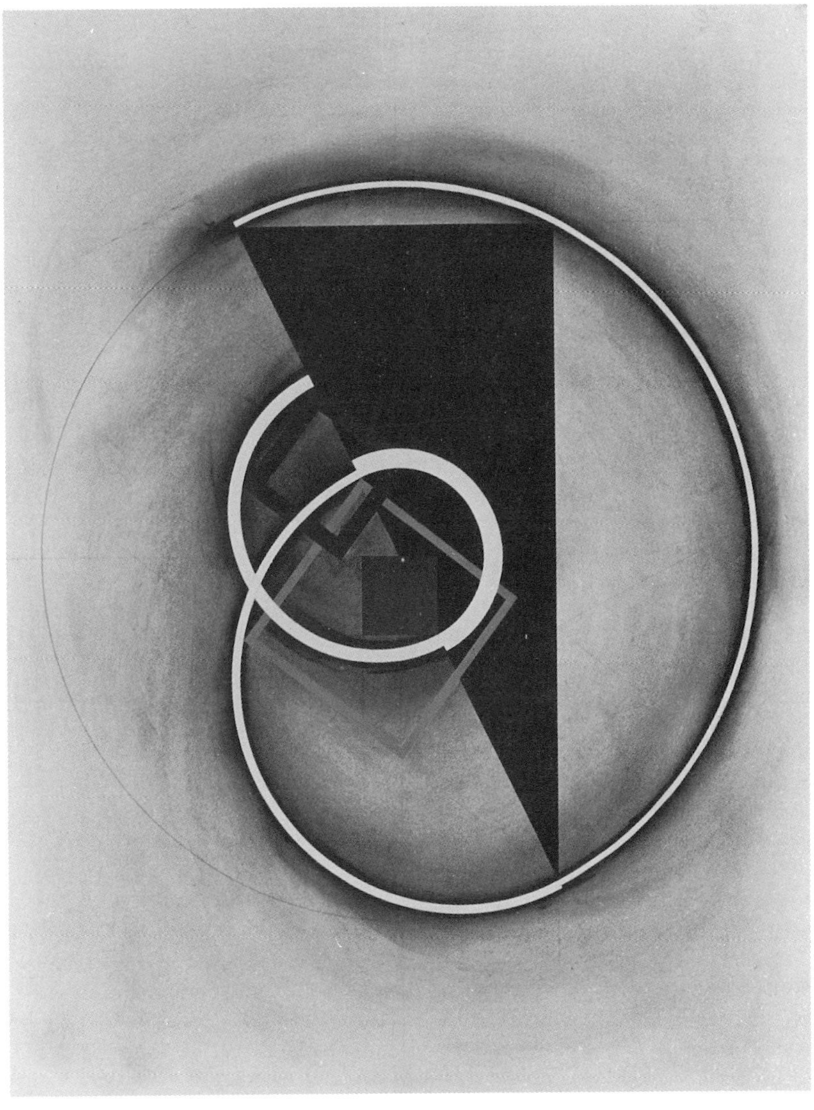

of natural selection, the notion of the survival of the fittest—is the best explanation to date of how the human species developed. Perhaps an analogy could be made whereby Darwin's 'model' could be applied to aesthetics. The story of the Chinese portrait exhibition reminds us strongly of the cultural differences between East and West. The history of the cultural evolution of both is not a topic we can cover here but it is fair to say that each has quite different and yet highly developed cultural traditions. These traditions color intellectual and emotional assessments of all circumstances. Breaks with these traditions—digression, whether growth or regression—are viewed with suspicion, often fear.

The word 'connoisseur' usually means a person well acquainted with one of the fine arts, a critical judge of art or matters of taste (wines, delicacies, etc.). A connoisseur of art acquires judgement or taste by continued dedicated interest in, and study of, art within a given set of parameters—the parameters of extant objects enveloped within understood traditional cultural values. These may be political, moral (Michelangelo was attacked for the nudity of his figures in the Sistine Chapel), philosophical, religious or aesthetic. Fashion is a perfect example of the latter: hemlines up/hemlines down, tight pants/baggy pants, long hair/short hair, etc. Because we are closest to contemporary art there is a tendency to think of it as the most controversial, but all advanced art of the past has suffered from contemporary criticism and quite often outright rejection, many if not all new ideas would appear to suffer this fate. However, it is via persistence and consistent qualification that new attitudes ultimately become accepted and synthesized into the culture's mainstream of life and thought.

New concepts that bring new images and new materials are usually in conflict with the accepted aesthetic of the status quo precisely because there are few if any criteria against which they can be measured. They do not fit the standard aesthetic yardstick. Thus they are perceived as a threat to established traditions, and here lies the crux of the matter. Art deals with ideas, concepts. Aesthetics deals with taste, and it is aesthetics that causes rejection. A New York art dealer once indicated to this writer that art must be a threat—it must be confrontational to either ideas or taste. And recently someone said, "If it looks like Art, it probably isn't." Thus we have a conflict between art and aesthetics, and the relationship between art and aesthetics is at best tenuous. To quote Barnett Newman, "Aesthetics is for artists like ornithology is for birds".

Computer imaging is only 25 years old. It has no tradition. Not enough time has elapsed for the cultural conditioning necessary either for this new process to be added to our aesthetic storeroom or for it to become modulated to fit current critical/evaluative criteria. So who is to say that the images we are now being bombarded with—the endless logos we are 'flown' through on TV commercials, the glitzy still lifes, the lifeless landscapes, the mechanical figures—are not art or do not already have their own aesthetic?

Is There a Computer Imaging Aesthetic?

Given that there are strong similarities in the appearance of images produced whenever the computer has been involved in the generative process, given that it seems most difficult to shun the label 'computer art', and given that the art establishment continues to reject these 'computer' images, it would appear that the answer to the above question must be 'yes'. What is it, then, that identifies and differentiates these images? The answer is simple yet complex.

The simple answer might be that there is still a serious but narrowly focused fascination on the part of the artist, artist-engineer and artist-computer scientist, as well as the public, with the technical process, with the 'magic' of this machine. Few seem to be able to go beyond or transcend this hypnotic fascination. The public still attaches too much significance to the *power* of the computer. This leads to the myth (or is it a myth?) that because the computer *assists* in solving problems, in reducing tedious labor, in executing a work, it has the power, the capacity, to *generate* or create self-generated works. How often have we heard "that was done by computer", as if this validates a work's existence? Technically it may be interesting, even most impressive, but from a conceptual, intellectual or artistic point of view the work does not withstand analysis. Only the creative imagination of the artist, cultivated from a solid conceptual base and tempered by a sophisticated visual sensitivity, can develop and resolve the problems of art.

With traditional art media there is a much more direct involvement of the artist with the medium—a tactile and scale involvement—where there is direct feedback from at least two sensory organs: the eye and the hand. The sense of touch is very important to artists, and it is finely tuned. The painter, for instance, must build from scratch and add everything. He/she therefore learns to develop a direct response to his/her eye-hand-intellect-emotions, a direct link between seeing, thinking and feeling. The photographer does not have this luxury, however. When he/she establishes an image (I use the term establish on purpose because the photographer learns how to organize and control via light and editing) he/she takes a chaotic world and organizes it with his/her trained eye. In one sense the photographer edits out information from the plethora of images presented, creating a focus so that the image serves his/her intentions.

The artist, no matter what medium he/she chooses, is a decision maker. If he/she uses a computer, it is as a tool or, as I like to think of it, an assistant, a conduit, a means of transmitting/expressing ideas visually. Questions must be raised, therefore, regarding the quality of the ideas and the quality of the decisions being made when images are produced by electronic means. If the ideas simply revolve around demonstrating the technical virtuosity or prowess of the machine or programmer, then the artist-technician has simply become an extension of the machine, in a sense its slave. In this case, only technology is served, for the work is a closed system involved only with technology. The machine should be an extension of humanity, of human senses, ideas and vision, not the other way around. Technology, in and of itself, is not art. Technology for technology's sake is as redundant and meaningless as the idea of art for art's sake. Art or technology should be for the people's sake, society's sake; it should serve some purpose—intellectual, spiritual or even functional. Even paintings by Morris Louis, Kenneth Noland, Jules Olitski and Helen Frankenthaler or the Lyrical Abstractionists of the late 1960s (Showel, Poons, Walker, Seery, Snyder and Christianson), works that appear to be only about paint or color, served not only as individual expressions but more importantly as metaphors of the heroic, the poetic, reflections of the inner self of the artist, representations of the unseen but deeply felt inner human reality.

At this juncture it is probably important to be reminded that the development of imaging systems was by and for industry and covered a wide range of industrial applications: graphic design, medicine, film, TV, etc. It was not developed with the fine arts in mind. Thus software development was specifically directed at these pragmatic-minded, 'client-oriented' industries. The software determined that the images produced, being 'client-oriented', would have clarity and little ambiguity and would be clean, crisp, efficient and practical. As in early photography, detailed accuracy was equated with factual truth.

The whole gamut of historical developments in art, from perspective to realism, has been re-invented by computer scientists (technicians) re-enacting the same painfully slow visual evolution and patterns of growth experienced by the artists who first dealt with these problems. Why do images created by ray tracing seem accurate but mechanical and unreal, far from natural or realistic? Why is it that computer-generated landscapes are recreated (represented) almost diagrammatically, as 'sky is blue, grass is green, trees are brown'? The Impressionists and color photography taught us that 'local color' has no absolute value because all color is activated, and modulated, by the ever-changing conditions and circumstances of light. Further, the aim of art is not to recreate visual (retinal) objective reality only. Realistically rendered images serve as only one part of the artist's expressive vocabulary, and quite often deviation from optical reality becomes a must in order that a painting echo the artist's intentions or create a more cohesive resolution that is both expressive and has visual plasticity. In computer-generated imagery, local color becomes an absolute. In painting it is the modulation of color that gives the painting its plastic unity. In computer-generated imagery, adherence to local color via ray tracing and stiff paint systems results in a lack of plastic unity—the separate objects remain as separate objects and are not convincingly unified in any plastic way.

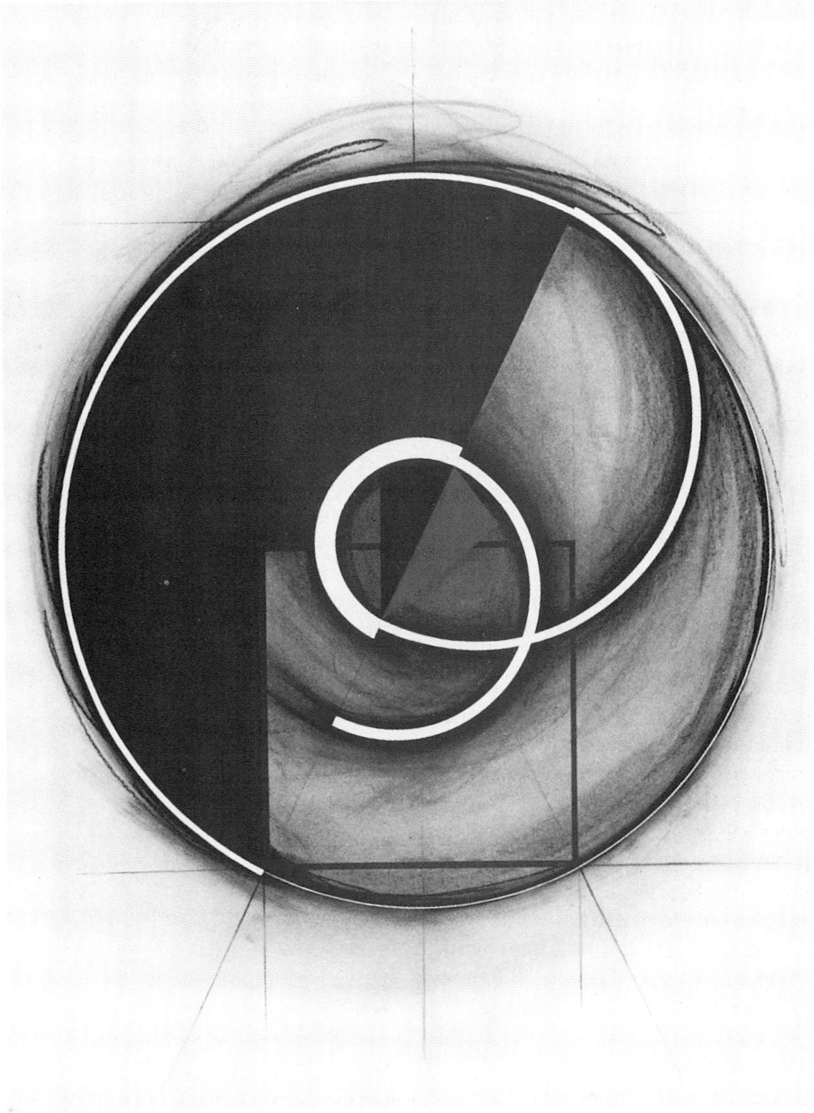

Fig. 3. ***Reassess #2*, conte, charcoal and pencil on paper, 38 in × 50 in, 1984.**

Donald P. Greenberg in an article in the February 1988 issue of *Communications of the ACM* makes all of this clear. In his superb article he indicates that strides are being made to rectify this problem by focusing upon color 'interactivity'. Referring to it as 'the hermicube radiosity approach', he cites the research being carried out at Cornell University that attempts to come to terms with this color plasticity problem. Another stylistic manifestation of many computer-generated images is that when they are formula-written they tend to have a rather simplistic, predictable, patterned structure—predictable in the sense that the final resultant images within their structure have no visual surprises.

Tom Linehan pointed out in a talk at SIGGRAPH '85 that with computer imagery the artist begins with a three-dimensional void. Within this void pure fantasy can be created and very effective special effects generated via animation. Animated TV logos are extremely effective, and while one might become a little tired of flying in and out of letters of the alphabet, they are eye-catching, visually engaging for the moment and therefore most effective for the 'client'. They are carriers of specific but limited information; there are no metaphors. They are in effect mindless. Each time we view them we gain no new information, no new insight: in short we are not educated or experientially revitalized. We contribute nothing, our involvement is passive. Computers are most adept at producing this type of image, and it is the type archetypically associated with the computer. It is hard for artists to shake the perception that computers can only, or must always, create such images.

Conceptual art of the 1960s explored and challenged the linguistic base of art; much recent painting has concerned itself with social issues, angst, politics, etc. Neither deals with technical issues, and in fact such issues are not considered relevant to the art idea. Thus in conceptual art we see a totally desensitized, nontactile, colorless set of objects—most often with no image attached, as in the work of Lawrence Weiner. At the other extreme, in recent painting we see surfaces exploding with tactile, gestural, densely colored images full of metaphoric or literal information. Yet the technical means are only the means to an end; the technical facilitates the bridge to the conceptual roots of the work, the poetic, spiritual essence of the work. As outlined above, in computer-generated images the technical often seems to be a closed loop, a pipeline back to the technical. There is a great temptation on the part of artists who use computers to try to retain the imprint of the computer's involvement and thus to inform us that their images are arrived at through sophisticated electronic means. In other words they are reluctant to let the image or idea stand by itself. The question we must now pose is, Is this any different from painting? If so, how?

Painters in the last half of the twentieth century, from Jackson Pollock to Chuck Close, from Brice Marden and even Robert Mangold to Sigmar Polke or David Salle, are concerned with the appearance of the paint—the revelation of the process of painting. If the quality of the paint plays an important role in how we assess the worth of a painting, should the qualities produced by images developed electronically be treated differently? The answer of course is that they should not. The surface qualities of any medium should support, indeed be integrated into, the holistic concept of the work. They should not be the only thing that our mind focuses upon. Unfortunately, with electronically developed images this is perhaps what happens all too often.

Electronic tools are still resistant and clumsy and do not facilitate working in a direct and expressive manner. The software has been written to eliminate unevenness of line or any other accidental marks. It could be posited that charcoal is also a clumsy tool. Drawing with charcoal, as we see so beautifully in Matisse, involves a great deal of trial and error, a great deal of learning, of programming. Charcoal is both clumsy and primitive as a tool but in the hands of the right person, with training and sensitivity as well as imagination, it becomes a conduit, a means, by which sensitively rendered images expressive of the artists intentions and emotional state can be produced with tremendous effectiveness. When an artist uses a material or tool long enough, when the artist is thoroughly familiar with a tool, it becomes, in a sense, an extension of the self, instinctive and thus invisible. Currently this directness is not available with computers.

Computer imaging today could be compared to the disciplines of printmaking and photography, which are also technical processes involving intermediaries. In fact, the best prints today seem to be produced for artists by print workshops. This collaborative approach might well be productive for artists in terms of computer imaging. Both photography and printmaking (especially silkscreen) offer extremely efficient methods of creating a multitude of variables of an image quite rapidly. The changes or choices and decisions regarding the images produced by these processes are arrived at by direct, hands-on, tactile involvement where 'accidents' occur, the unexpected happens and the eye and mind build on these accidents by acceptance or rejection. This leads to my final point. It would appear that, because there is little or no evidence of the hand in computer-generated imagery, such imagery is dismissed as not being art.

This argument has consistently been leveled against photography. Photography had to learn to transcend its fascination with its technical capabilities, which limited conceptual evolution. Photographers, as well as the general public, were enthralled by the capability of their medium to capture every minute detail of any subject, albeit in black and white, in their photographs. In fact it was thought to be irresponsible to manipulate images, the implication being that the artist thus would be manipulating the truth. Today we know differently, and photographs are manipulated by the artist in a multitude of ways at the service of his/her vision. However, the fact remains that initially artists and photographers were impressed by the technical attributes of their medium and only later were able to transcend this limiting fascination with technology. In a parallel way, computer imaging has to overcome its fascination with its own technology; it must stop looking solely inward at its own capabilities and begin asking serious questions about its purpose beyond its commercial applications. It must address issues and ideas concerning the nature of art and the purposes of art.

WHAT DO WE MEAN BY 'COMPUTER ART'?

A major problem with the label 'computer art' is that it is linguistically and semantically incorrect. We do not say 'sculpture art' or 'painting art'. What then should we call images created with a computer? Perhaps they should be called computer or digital images, and the process, computer or digital imaging, and if these electronic images are successful in communicating artistic intentions they should then be called art.

Computers are machines that are engineered to be extremely precise and incapable of making mistakes and to follow only the strict logic of their circuitry and of the instructions of their software written to utilize this circuitry. But as Sol LeWitt said, "Artists jump to conclusions that logic cannot reach"[1]. Thus, if one accepts LeWitt's statement, computers cannot be artists, they cannot alone make art. This may lead to the assumption that there can be no such thing as computer art.

LeWitt's point is well taken, and I have chosen it to stress that the *computer* does not make art. However, in the hands of the artist it can become a tool, perhaps also the material, to serve the creative ambitions of the artist. Tools and materials, whether welded or cast metal, photograph, charcoal on paper, or paint on canvas, radically affect the resultant appearance and therefore the projected meaning of a work of art. Each of these materials has a history, a tradition, which also colors or affects the appreciation and understanding of a work of art. When we look at a Rembrandt portrait, for instance, we understand it on many levels at once: we perceive the subject because of the particular history of the sitter; but we can also perceive the formal construction of the painting, the use of light and shade and texture and how the artist has manipulated the paint itself. We finally comprehend and appreciate it holistically as a painting, understanding that the paint has been modulated to communicate the complete, as opposed to simply the literal, meaning of the artist's intentions. We appreciate it in this manner in large part because painting has a tradition, and the history of that tradition cannot be obliterated or denied when we see paintings. Our aesthetic, our taste, is tempered by this tradition.

The historical tradition of computer imaging spans a mere 20 years, but as outlined above, computer imaging seems to have certain stylistic tendencies. These stylistic tendencies have been determined by factors outside of art, and they strongly affect the appearance and therefore the understanding of the images created. Yet at this point computer images mostly seem to mimic art executed with traditional art materials. Artists who use computers seem to retain their own personal history of materials. Thus they fight the computer's potential by trying to force this historical will upon it.

Computers can be employed, like any tool, to make art. Computers by themselves do not make art. Perhaps the software that makes possible the attributes that then become available to the artist is where the art of computers resides.

ADVANTAGES AND DISADVANTAGES OF THE COMPUTER FOR THE ARTIST

Advantages

1) That the PC and software development have made the computer accessible is a given.

2) The computer offers the artist the possibility of testing a range of ideas very rapidly within a given set of parameters.

3) Images can be generated by paint systems, digitizing or formulas or by any combination of these.

4) Images can be stored and retrieved almost instantaneously. This allows for the storing of an image when it is at a successful stage yet allows for further development of that same image. If a series of erroneous decisions is made during this further development, the initial, successful image can be recalled and nothing has been lost physically. In fact, taking risks need not be a disaster; this results in expanded, new learning experiences.

5) In formula-written images an artist can see a tremendous range of possible configurations developed within the strict parameters of his/her concept. Thus the artist can develop a much larger database than by traditional means.

6) Images can be easily transported using optical disc, floppy disc or tape.

7) The structure of an image, its color, shape, size, location, density, etc., can be manipulated in real time and much faster than by traditional physical means.

Disadvantages

1) The artist can become obsessed with the technology, be seduced or hypnotized by it, and simply become an extension of the technology.

2) Unless the artist is somewhat sure of the conceptual terrain to be explored, the information overload could be overwhelming. It is also possible that, if the artist is not sure of the purpose of using the computer, the technology will again seduce, and the artist will be taken over by the technology.

3) A major problem of the computer is scale. The artist is limited to the size of the monitor and the ideas quite often suggest much grander scale. Thus, scale is virtually lost on the computer.

4) The artist can have no experience of surface, no real tactile involvement with the work.

5) The uniformity of the system's attributes is overpowering: a line cannot be emphasized or inflected in a direct, emoted manner. While one feels the different tensions in one's hand and arm and in one's emotional makeup, the line on the monitor screen remains totally unmodulated. Software

Fig. 4. *Sectional Open Spiral—Flipback*, conte, charcoal and pencil on paper, 38 in × 50 in, 1984.

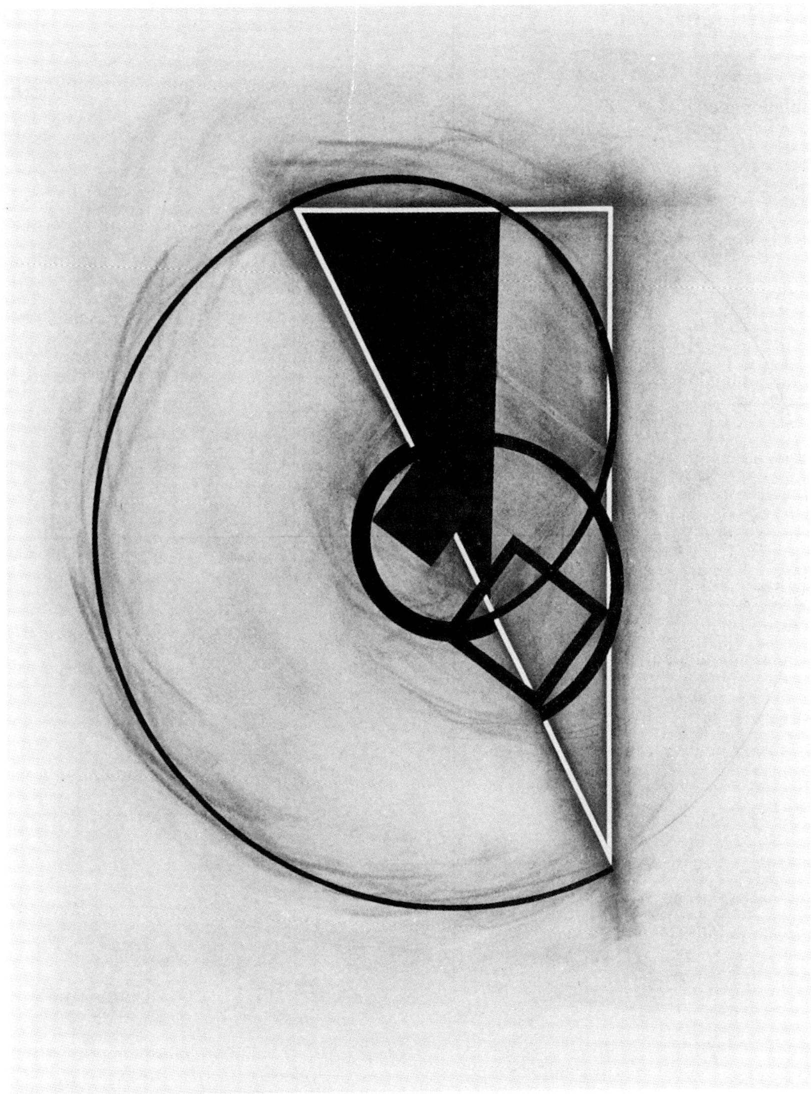

needs to be written or hardware developed to address this issue.

6) Finally and most importantly, the computer is capable of generating so much information within a narrow set of parameters that it would be quite easy to stay within that narrow set of parameters and thus stop any further intellectual/conceptual growth or development; ideas can ossify. In my own work, for example, I have generated over 14,000 individual linear drawings that I could use ad infinitum probably for the rest of my life without advancing one iota conceptually. I would simply be creating variation upon variation of a well-established and well-known structure. The poetry would surely exhaust itself.

In summation it is clear that the *computer* is neither liberator nor jailer of the creative spirit. The artist's attitudes are what will decide that issue. The manner in which the artist approaches this challenging and exciting technology will determine whether or not the creative spirit is limited or enhanced.

My Own Work

Since 1973 I have developed a fickle 'love/hate' relationship with the computer, because it always has seemed to command too much of my time in learning its 'language' or its technical attributes and/or limitations. Currently I view the computer as an efficient tool in much the same way that I viewed power tools in the early 1960s. Not wishing to become a 'slave to the machine', and given my priorities, I have resisted the desire to learn programming, although I have some knowledge of Pascal. At the same time, however, I recognize that it is perhaps in the creative development of imaging software that the essence of art resides for the computer. I also do not wish to be a slave, introspectively limited, to my ideas, and the computer is most useful in this regard. It is an efficient tool that can clear out ideas expeditiously. Beyond that it has 'taught' me, challenged me, to be much more open and adventurous by revealing that even a simple idea can be multifaceted. At a purely intuitive and subjective level many of these facets would have been overlooked.

The computer generates a tremendous amount of visual information. This creates a dilemma, or perhaps a paradox: while the computer seems to save time, it generates far more information than can be absorbed, and thus it seems impossible to keep the information under control. The computer is a tool that differs in a major way from previous tools. It can present the artist with accurate alternatives to variations of the original image while remaining solidly embedded within the parameters of the main concept. However, while it works to generate new visual variations, it is confined to the set parameters and *cannot generate new ideas.*

Technical Reference for My Own Works

It is ironic that, while technology offers to be an efficient servant, ultimately it seduces rather than serves the artist, who, like society, becomes a slave to the technology. It is important to escape this trap.

I have been using computers interactively by using the results achieved with the computer with other traditional artists' materials for many years. The following explains my process, although from a technical point of view only.

Simple Image Generation and Plotting. The software was written in Fortran by Ken Ghiron, rewritten in C by Mike Ashley. This software allows for the generation of all possible permutations of a set of simple geometric shapes which are related according to the Golden Mean. Each of these shapes is consistent in surface area (according to Fresnel). Images were first generated on a Tectronics 4013 terminal. Images were plotted on a CAL-COMP Graphics Drum Plotter #563, each plot containing 256 unique linear images for a total of 11,880 images. The host computer for the CAL-COMP Plotter was a Xerox Sigma 9. Pastel/pencil/charcoal drawings (38 in × 50 in) were then hand-executed from these plots whereby the original generative and underlying structure, plus minimal color and gesture, were added (see Figs 1–4).

Digitizing and Image Manipulation. The above pastel drawings were digitized (using filters to achieve pseudo-color) into a COMTAL VISION 1–20 (3M) system with a 512 × 512, 8 bits monitor. Software was developed by Ed Angel, David Gold and John Brayer of the VAX Research Center of the University of New Mexico. The host computer for the COMTAL VISION 1–20 was a VAX 11/780 by Digital Equipment Corp. Digitized images were manipulated; the structures and color were altered. Emphasis was placed on color manipulation. Slides of the manipulated images were automatically recorded using a Matrix Instruments Image Recorder (Color Plate B No. 1, bottom). Pastel/pencil/charcoal drawings (38 in × 50 in) were then hand-executed using the slides of the digitized images as models or points of departure (Color Plate B No. 1, top).

Colored Plots. These plots were executed on a Hewlett Packard plotter HP7475A using software developed in C by Mike Ashley for use on an AT&T PC6300 with a TARGA 16 board and 20-megabyte Hard Card coupled to a Sony CPD1201 color monitor. Large shaped and relief paintings were also created using these plots as points of departure.

Reference

1. This famous dictum is quoted from Sol LeWitt's 25 statements on art, 1968.

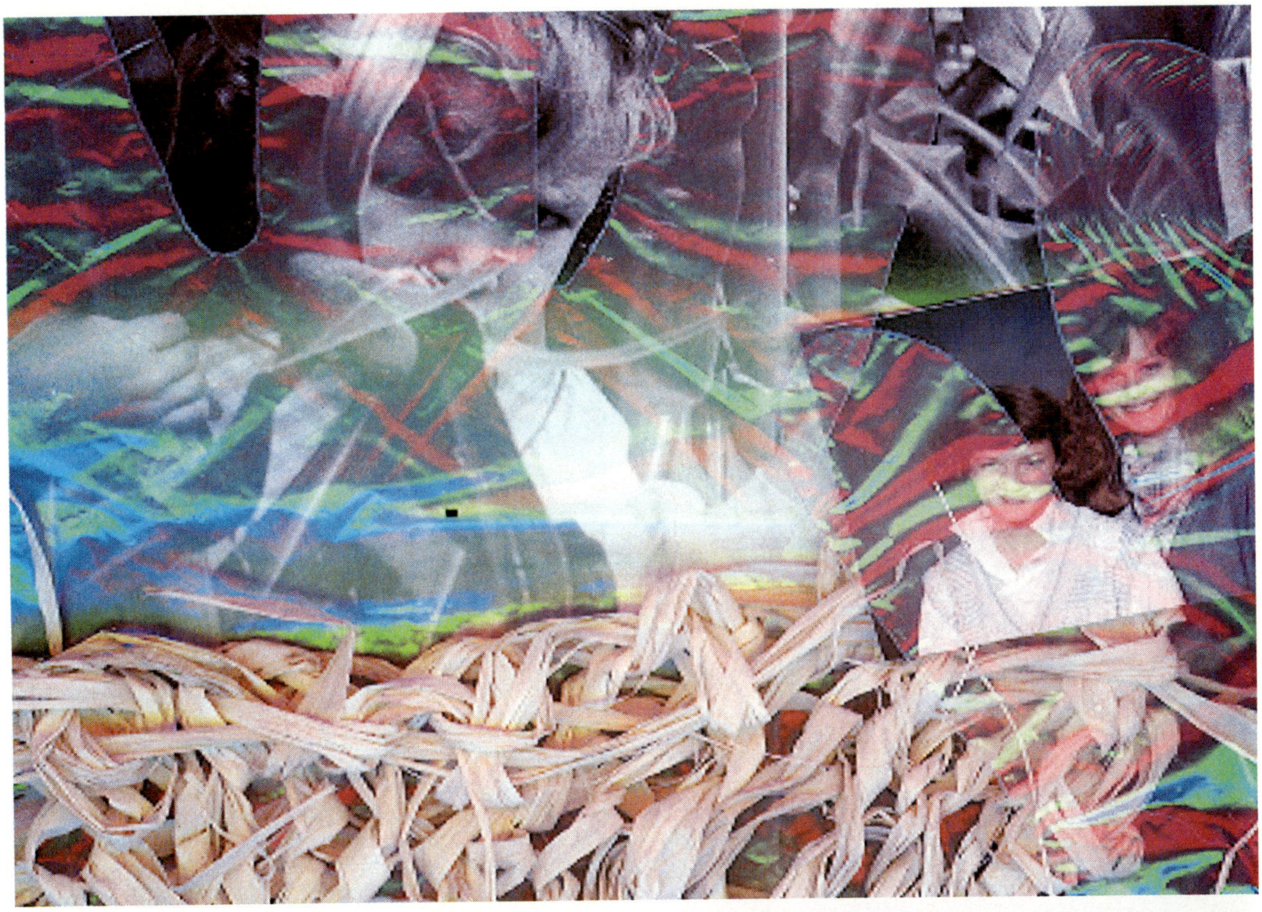

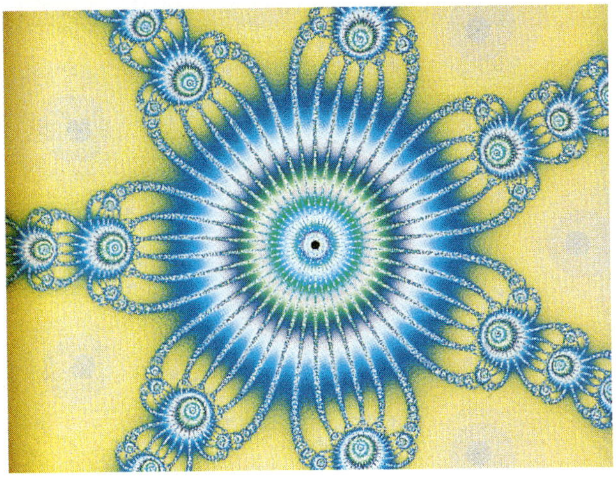

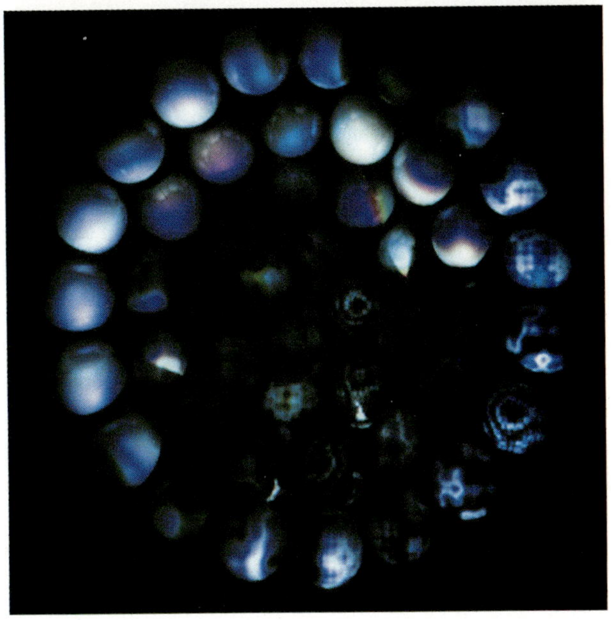

COLOR PLATE A

No. 1. Top. Joan Truckenbrod, *Time Knit*, digital photograph, 24 × 26 in, 1988.

No. 2. Bottom left. Brian Evans, fractal image created using Newton's method for finding roots of the equation $f(z) = z^7 - 1$. The RGB triplet measure for this image is 1:1:1 with total intensity at half of full.

No. 3. Bottom right. Richard Wright, *Parameter Space*, software: artist's software in 'C'; hardware: VAX 11/785, Gems Framestore, Dunn Film Recorder; format: 35-mm slide of computer-generated image. 1987. A fractal sine function was used to solid texture map a conical arrangement of spheres. Computer algorithms can take arbitrary sets of data and fuse them together to create an object that possesses the quality of tangible reality.

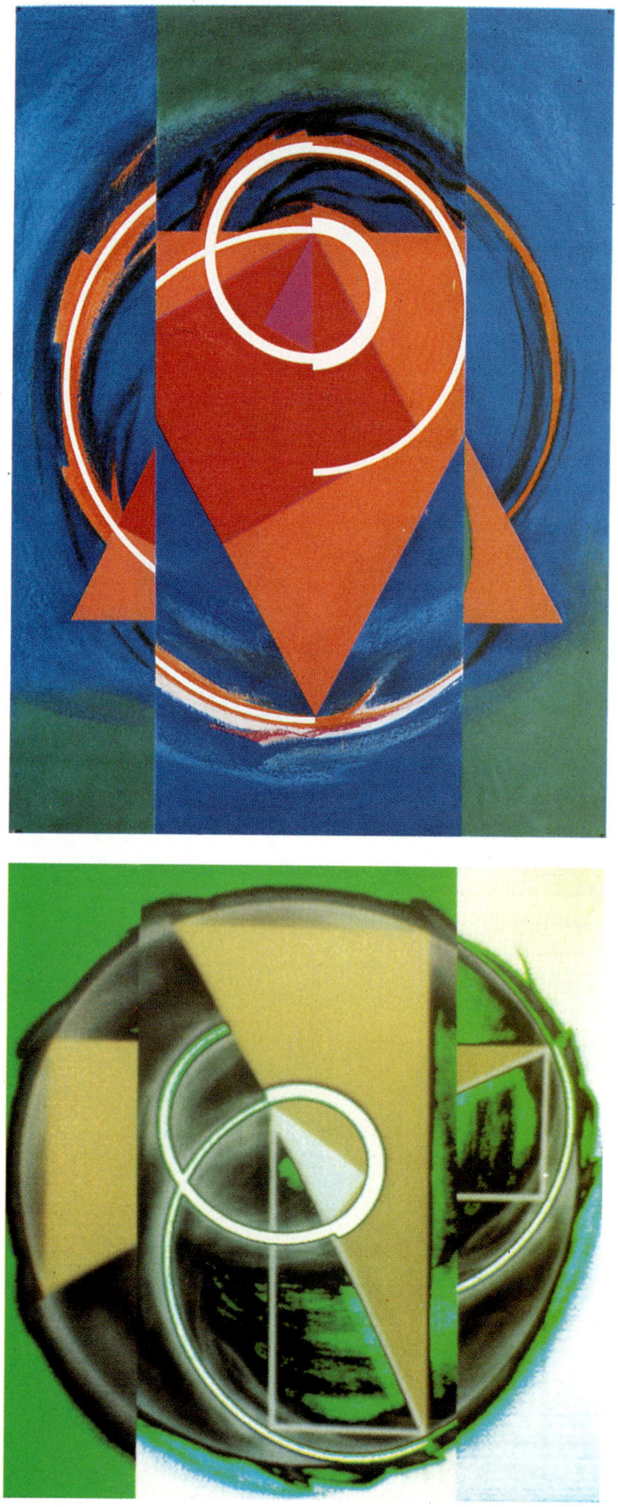

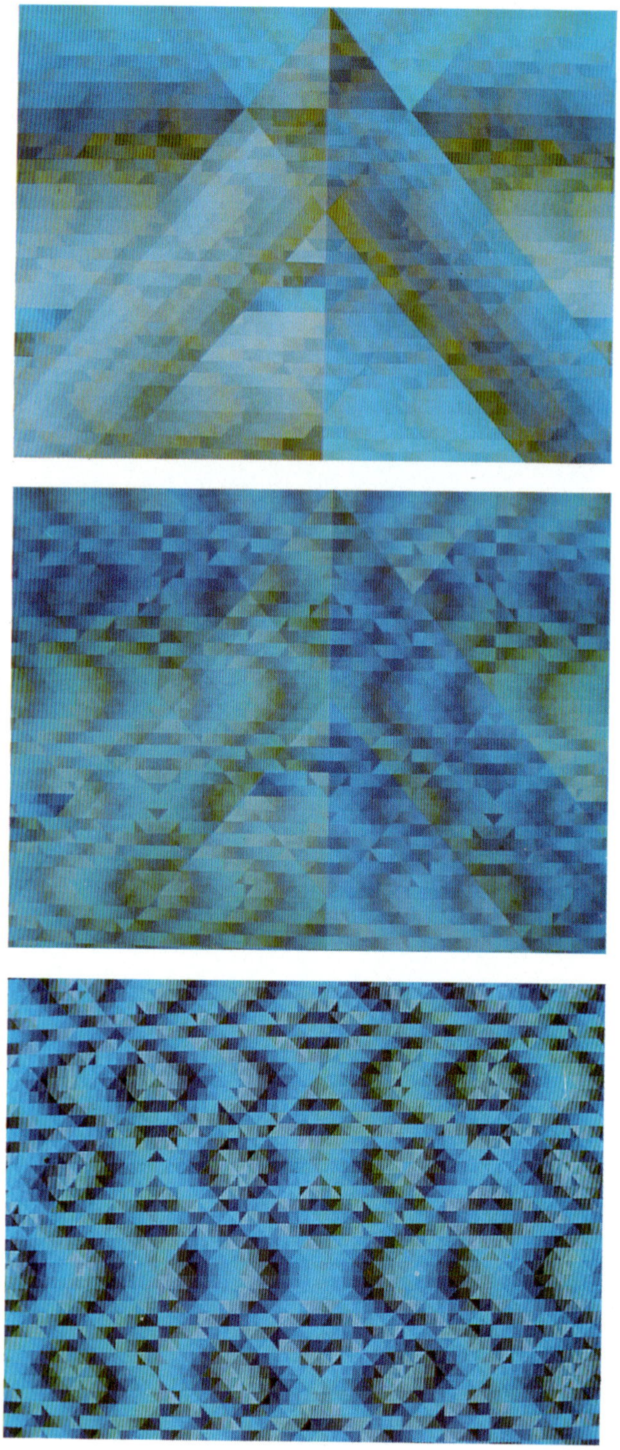

COLOR PLATE B

No. 1. Left. John Pearson, (top) *Finale #3*, pastel and pencil on paper, 38 × 50 in, 1988; (bottom) *Fresnel Proposition: UNM Series #8*, electronic (digital) image and 35-mm slide, 1985.

No. 2. Right. Edward Zajec, (top to bottom) a thematic dissolve is shown. Two transparencies can be displayed concurrently on the screen and layered and unlayered at will. The thematic character of the dissolve comes to light when the action of the underlying transparency (the ray in this case) weaves itself into the upper transparency's action. Important here is the temporal nature of the dissolve, which involves structural changes that closely interrelate motive development with color modulation.

The Aesthetics of Exhibition: A Discussion of Recent American Computer Art Shows

Patric D. Prince

ABSTRACT

Artists are using technological advances in their artmaking processes and are concerned about the difficulty of getting their work exhibited. The author discusses the aesthetics of exhibition and the nature of computer-aided art as seen in recent important exhibitions, as well as the problems associated with mounting these exhibitions. A brief history of computer-aided art exhibitions is presented, including the earliest exhibitions, the developments of the 1970s and recent major museum exhibitions. The author compares concepts and traditions in exhibition design to those that will be needed in the future, and finally discusses why certain art forms are exhibited.

The nature and purpose of art dictate how and where it is seen. The history of Western culture has witnessed a development that has taken art from the realm of the spiritual to the realm of the secular. The secularization of art has changed our understanding of art. This progression of art also has effected changes in the nature of art. The didactic replication of religious subjects was well understood by the medieval Christian faithful who contemplated the images for their personal salvation. The traditional Christian subjects that artists used, e.g. a Pietà, required only that the viewer followed the teachings of the Church. In the intervening centuries, as art has become more and more secular, it has become esoteric.

The viewing public has needed to become educated in art theory to understand the meaning and purpose of art. Modernists' concepts of art have led to a refining process in the understanding and appreciation of the arts. It takes an informed viewer to comprehend the abstract formal elements of twentieth-century art. Tom Wolfe in his book *The Painted Word* implies that Modern contemporary art has become so esoteric and literary that only a few cognoscenti understand it. Future art objects may be eliminated altogether, with only the conceptual elements of art existing [1]. The nature of Conceptual art and the current fashion for ephemeral art objects does affect the public's understanding of 'modern' art.

Although much contemporary art has an esoteric quality that some viewers may find obscure and meaningless, there are aspects of computer art that are extremely appealing to a large segment of the population [2]. Interactivity as an aspect of computer-aided artmaking, coupled with realistic imaging, mathematical visualization and the growing availability of implementation, make computer art interesting as an expressive vehicle.

Patric D. Prince, Fine Arts Administration, 901 Sixth Street, S.W., Number 914, Washington, DC 20024, U.S.A.

Received 3 May 1988.

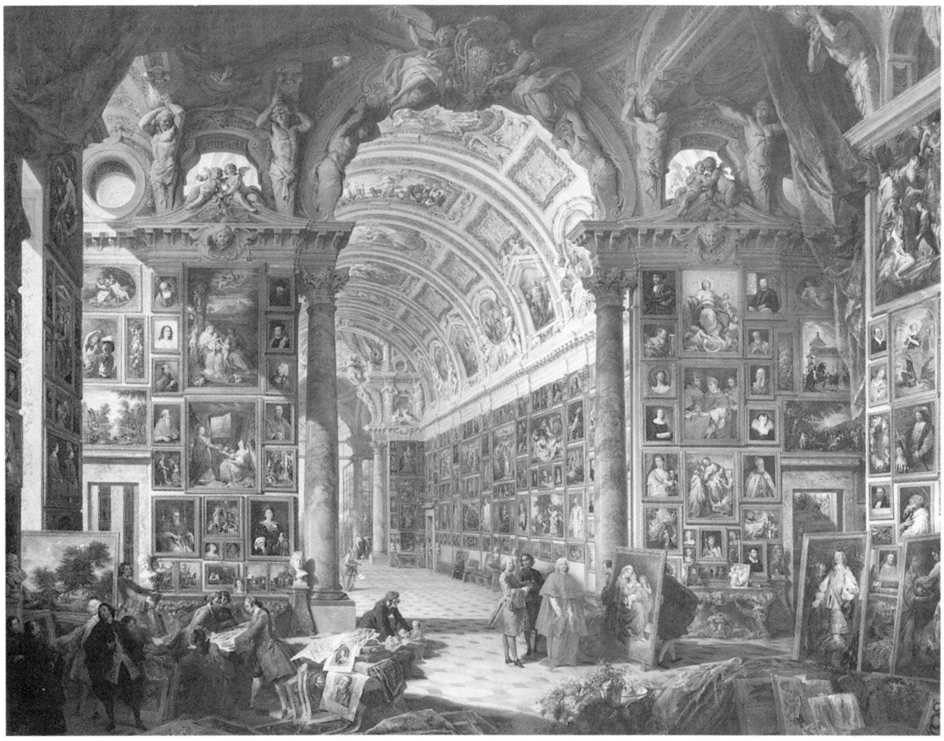

Fig. 1. Giovanni Paolo Panini, *The Gallery of Cardinal Valenti-Gonzaga*, oil on canvas, 78 × 105.5 in, 1749. (Wadsworth Atheneum, Hartford. The Ella Gallup Sumner and Mary Catlin Sumner Collection) Panini's painting demonstrates the early Salon exhibition style. This method of stacking paintings one above another on the wall was popular until early in the twentieth century. This painting is of an imaginary collection of artworks from the eighteenth century.

Pergamon Press plc. Printed in Great Britain.
0024-094X/88 $3.00+0.00

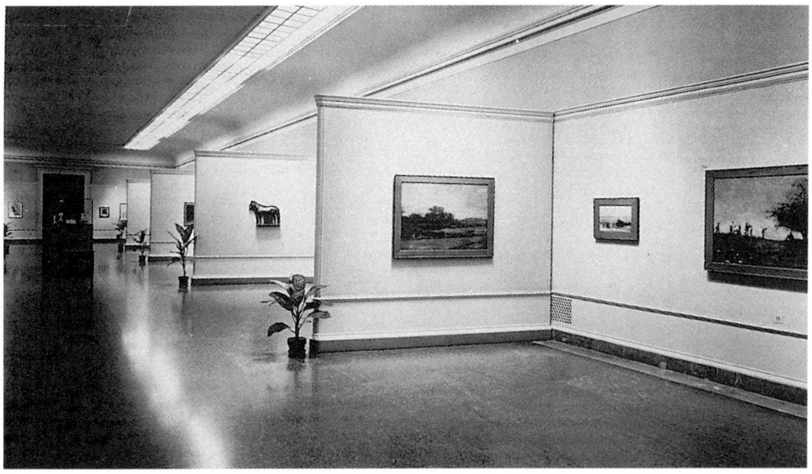

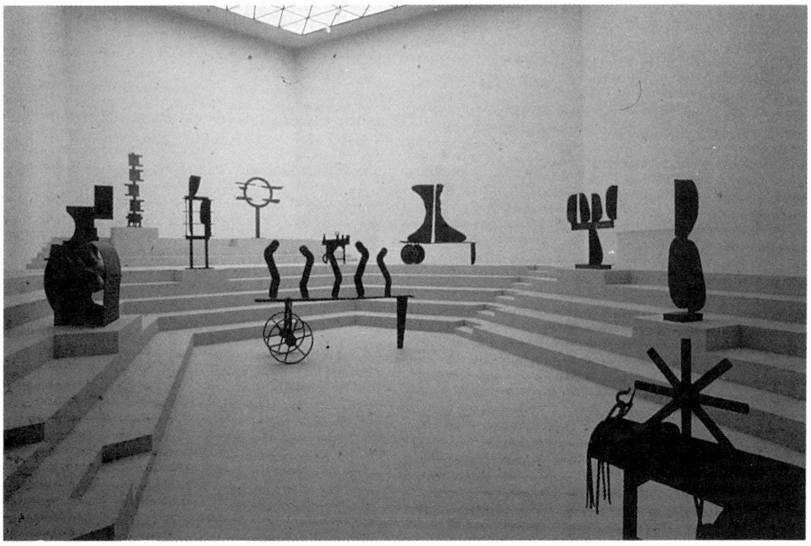

Fig. 2. Two installations from the National Gallery of Art in Washington, DC. Austere designs for displaying artworks evolved as contemporary museum architecture affected interior spaces and as Modernism became a prominent style. (Courtesy National Gallery of Art)

The evolution of art includes an interest in the processes involved with creativity as well as the aesthetic experience.

A Historical Approach to the Display of New Art

The method of display of technical art is connected to the history of the development of museums and, in particular, to the development of the 'modern' museum. The Museum of Modern Art in New York was the first museum created for the display of contemporary artworks. After its founding in 1929, the display techniques of individual artworks became increasingly modern as well. "Beginning with the Museum of Modern Art, the first art gallery of world importance to be designed in a wholly contemporary style, American museums have immeasurably encouraged the acceptance of architecture relying on new technology and exploiting the potential of new materials" [3]. The earlier technique of stacking artworks was eliminated and single works of art were displayed in a clear, neutral setting (Fig. 1). A.W. Melton wrote in 1935:

> Whereas the museum can increase the frequency with which visitors see a specific object by increasing its isolation, by placing it in a favorable position within the gallery, and by placing it in a gallery visited early in the museum visit, it cannot increase the concentration of intensity of the visitors' interest in it by such manipulation. In order to do the latter it must resort to the use of printed labels which explain or interpret the art object [4].

In the modern museum an artwork is no longer viewed in its context as in the medieval Christian church but is seen as an isolated work. The main thrust of twentieth-century art exhibition design has been towards creating isolated, well-lighted spaces (Fig. 2).

A Brief History of Computer Art Shows

In 1965 several computer art exhibitions were mounted. The first was held in the Gallery Wendelin Niedlich at the University of Stuttgart in January 1965 and featured the works of Georg Nees. In April 1965, A.M. Noll and Bela Julesz had a show of their work at the Howard Wise Gallery in New York. Georg Nees and Frieder Nake mounted another show in November at the Niedlich Gallery in Stuttgart. In addition, artworks were published in the June issue of *Computers and Automation,* which held an annual art contest from 1963 to 1979.

In 1968 Jasia Reichardt curated an important art show that was held at the Institute of Contemporary Arts from August through October. A catalog was published that illustrated many of the works shown.

> Cybernetic Serendipity was mounted in a gallery of 6500 square feet, involved 325 participants and was seen by 60,000 people. The exhibits showed how man can use the computer and new technology to extend his creativity and inventiveness. These consisted of computer graphics, computer-composed and -played music, computer-animated films, computer-texts, and among other computer-generated material, the first computer sculpture. There were also cybernetic machines such as Gordon Pask's 'colloquy of mobiles', television sets converting sound into visual patterns. Peter Zinovieff's electronic music studio with a computer which improvised on tunes whistled into a microphone by the visitors; there were robots, drawing machines and numerous constructions which responded to ambient sound and light. Six IBM machines demonstrated the use of computers, and a visual display provided information on the history of cybernetics [5].

Following *Cybernetic Serendipity* the influential exhibition *The Machine as Seen at the End of the Mechanical Age* was held at the Museum of Modern Art in New York from November 1968 to February 1969. This exhibition was significant because of its survey of art and technology artifacts and because it included computer-aided works by

Schwartz, Harmon, Noll, Fraenkel and Raskin. The catalog from the exhibition has become a collector's item.

Technical Art in the 1970s

After 1970, many exhibitions of computer art were organized all over the industrialized world, from Japan to Brazil. There were several notable museum shows of the work of individual artists, including Harold Cohen and Jeff and Colette Bangert. Vendors of computing equipment sponsored art exhibitions and travelling art shows. Exhibitions were held regularly by the Computer Arts Society in London and the Association for Computing Machinery (ACM) in the United States (Fig. 3.) [6].

SIGGRAPH Art Shows

The Special Interest Group for Graphics (SIGGRAPH) of the ACM has sponsored computer art shows as an adjunct activity to the annual conference since 1981. These art shows have involved hundreds of computer artists and have been an important venue for technical art. Since 1982, an art show catalog has been printed to document the exhibitions [7]. The early SIGGRAPH exhibitions of computer imagery combined works showing technical innovations with fine artworks. The 1984 exhibition was devoted exclusively to computer-aided design (CAD). The 1985 art show was complex, involving installations held in conjunction with several San Francisco museums. The 1986 art show was an international retrospective of computers in the arts surveying the development of its use by artists over the last 20 years or more. More than 450 artworks were presented in all media. The 1987 art show was concerned with the 'unusual' in computer art. The SIGGRAPH art shows have consistently involved innovative exhibition design because of their use of temporary facilities. The art selected has reflected SIGGRAPH's focus on new technologies. One aspect of this focus has been the mounting of new art forms. Many of the installations supported by the SIGGRAPH art shows would have had no other venue.

The earliest computer art shows were held in conventional exhibition spaces, with temporary panels dividing the works into compartments. The original organizers of the SIGGRAPH shows were computer artists who were determined to make an effort to create the best possible viewing space for art that not only depends upon electronic light but also is interactive (Fig. 4).

Major American Museum Shows

In 1987, there were three major museum art shows featuring computer-aided art. The Bronx Museum of the Arts held the *Second Emerging Expression Biennial: The Artist and The Computer* from 17 September 1987 to 24 January 1988. The show was curated by Louis R. Cancel, the director of the museum, and juried by Shalom Gorewitz and this author.

In his introduction to the catalog Louis Cancel states,

> This catalog documents The Bronx Museum of the Arts' second exhibition (the first was in 1985) that seeks to capture the extent to which computers are being utilized as creative tools by visual artists.... All of the artists selected for this exhibition are pushing the boundaries of media, going that extra mile, and helping to establish a path where technology and art can converge in the creation of new tools for human expression [8].

More than 75 artists, technicians and programmers exhibited work in the show, which included installations, musical works, video, animation, sculpture and two-dimensional artworks. The museum has several galleries, two of which were set up for the show. The spaces were tall and elegant. Special areas were created to hold the works that required a low-light environment (Fig. 5).

Computers and Art opened at the Everson Museum of Art in Syracuse, New York, in September 1987 and is to travel to several galleries, including the IBM Gallery in New York in April 1988. Cynthia Goodman curated this survey. The show is ambitious and includes works by 150 artists, which are documented in Goodman's book *Digital Visions, Computers and Art* [9]. The works were selected for their suitability for inclusion in a museum show. Goodman's research led her to many well-known artists from New York who dabbled with technology as well as artists admired by their peers in the computer world. The interactive selections in the Everson show were wonderful and innovative. Many works of historical interest were shown, including an updated version of *Proxima Centauri* (1969) by Lillian Schwartz, Per Bjorn and Arno Penzias and *Computer Sculpture* by Georg Nees.

The museum devoted most of its gallery space to the show. It was displayed in several adjoining galleries, in a multilevel plan. The architecture of the Everson had its impact on the viewer's appreciation of the show. It

Fig. 3. A photograph of an exhibition sponsored by IBM in 1974–1975. (Courtesy IBM) The Art and Skill of People Using Computers exhibition featured artworks by several computer artists including Jeff and Colette Bangert. This exhibition toured several sites in New York and New Jersey. Many early computer art shows were seen in environments similar to this space.

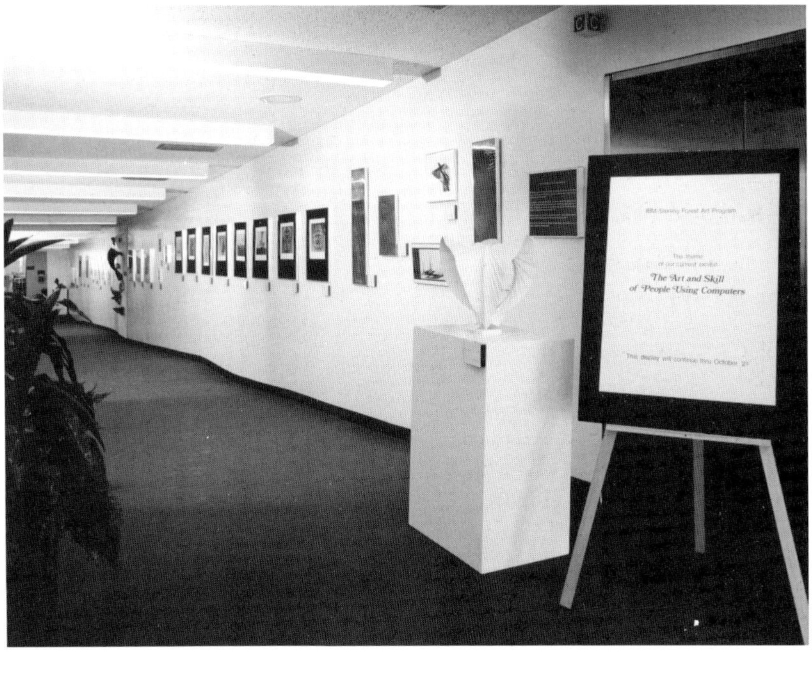

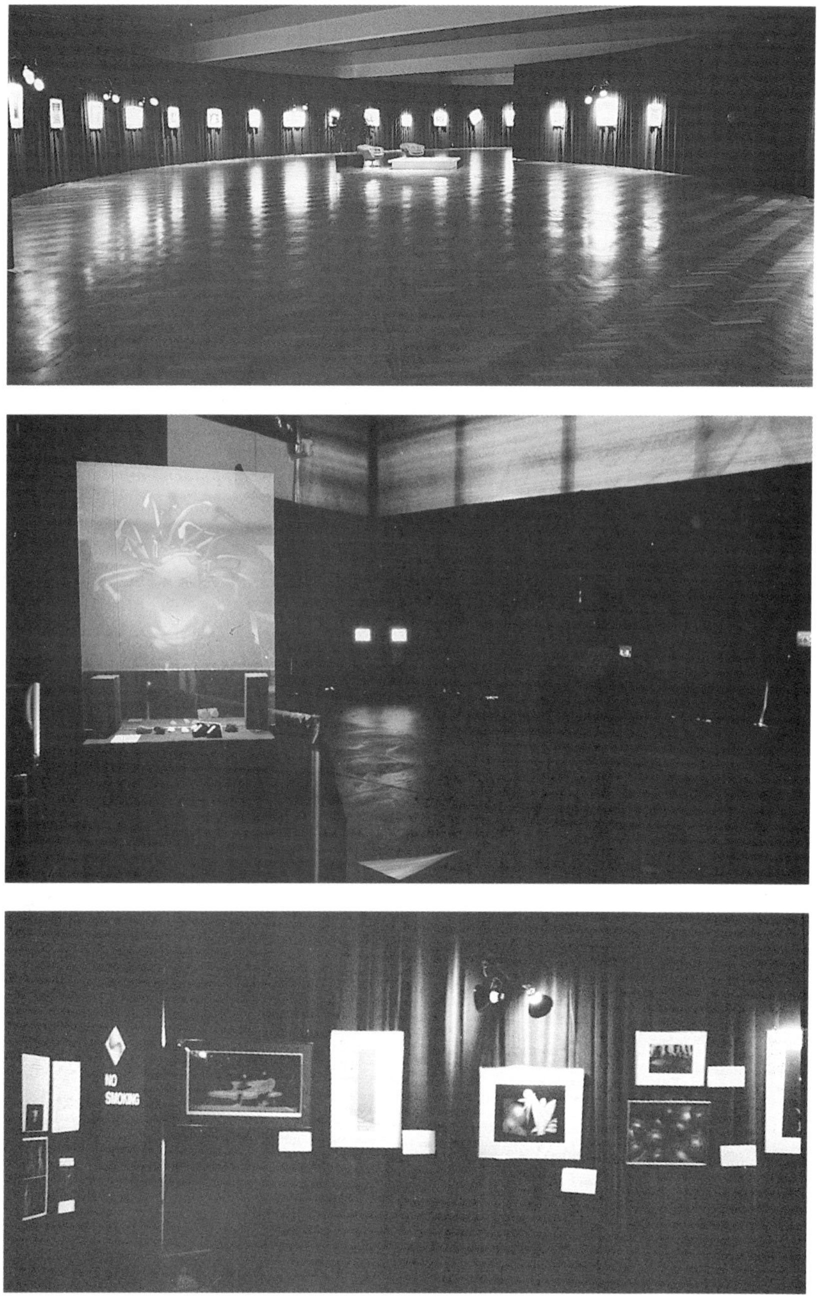

Fig. 4. SIGGRAPH art shows. (a) 1983, Detroit, Michigan, showing the low-light effect on the 2-D art (Photo: Copper Giloth); (b) 1986, Dallas, Texas, installation section with a large hologram (Photo: P. Prince); (c) 1987, Anaheim, California, showing the site and the nature of the art selected (Photo: P. Prince).

was far more interesting to snake around and down spaces than it would have been to see the work in a single large space (Fig. 6).

The Interactive Image, a computer graphics and imaging technology exhibition, was presented by the University of Illinois at Chicago College of Engineering and Electronic Visualization Laboratory. The exhibition opened at Chicago's Museum of Science and Industry and ran from 24 October 1987 until 10 February 1988. It will travel to SIGGRAPH 1988 in Atlanta, Georgia, in August 1988 and will become a permanent exhibit at the Computer Museum in Boston, Massachusetts. The show was curated by Thomas A. DeFanti, Dan Sandin and Maxine D. Brown of the Electronic Visualization Laboratory. The whole show is intended to be seen and used by 'participants'. It consists of 18 computer systems chosen to illustrate the "experiences and concepts of electronic visualization to a museum audience. Visualization is the art and science of creating images on electronic screens" [10].

The exhibition was designed by Vicki Putz. She worked on more than one level of design. All of the individual works have a similar control structure; they all have the same user interface, in terms of hardware (five buttons and a joy stick), and menu structures. The individual menus are varied for the sake of interest.

> The Interactive Image is a hands-on computer graphics and imaging technology exhibition that encourages museum visitors to learn about science and technology through interaction with computers. . . . The public is encouraged to create animations, manipulate four-dimensional spaces, discover the art of mathematics and explore astrophysical phenomena without fear of making mistakes, breaking the equipment, or getting lost in the software [11].

This show is art masquerading as science. It was obviously necessary to lean towards an 'educational orientation' to get support for the project. For example, DeFanti says, "The Interactive Image is Art and Science and . . . all the works were programmed by art students and faculty". The systems development was facilitated by computer science students. He also states that "the proper use of aesthetics gets more out of the science". The displays were of major concern to the curators and to the artists. Sandin says, "It didn't look like a computer art show, it looked like something else. It looked new, like Broadcast T.V." (Fig. 7) [12].

Gallery Shows

A recent example of a small gallery's computer art show was held at the Dundalk Gallery, Dundalk Community College, Baltimore, Maryland. It was curated by Harold McWhinnie, and it took place in March 1988. The show consisted of computer-aided works by 24 artists. The Dundalk Gallery is small, about 600 square feet, and located in an active community college. Janet Anderson, the director of the gallery, says that "the computer art reflects the interests of the college, which has three computer laboratories on campus". She did not consider this show to be an avant-garde exhibition, but said that "it was an ordinary show. College art galleries should include the introduction of new art forms" [13]. McWhinnie states,

> Exhibitions such as this will explore the world of technology and the arts, which as the last years of the 20th century are now upon us, will become an even more important arena for crea-

tive and artistic activities. . . . The show is not necessarily a show of computer art. Not all the works are made by the computer, in fact many of the works appear to use standard artistic mediums. The emphasis is upon the use of computer technology at some stage in the creative evolution of the individual artist's work [14].

The Dundalk Gallery has an irregular, pentagonal floor plan: a single long wall, three short walls and a long glass window. Panels were hung from the ceiling to provide additional wall space for two-dimensional works. The computers for the interactive display, which were loaned to the gallery from laboratories on campus, were set up on tables along one of the short walls. A VCR and monitor were placed on a trolley and there were pedestals for three-dimensional objects. It was a simple design intended to involve the viewer with first-hand interactive experience and close-up contact with artworks (Fig. 8).

THE CHALLENGES INVOLVED IN THE MOUNTING OF COMPUTER ART

It has been very difficult for artists to get their computer art accepted by curators and juries. Museum and gallery staffs do not have technical backgrounds and cannot determine what the works will look like from the slides submitted for consideration. Curators need to have an understanding of the nature of the art form. For example, Cibachrome prints are not just photographic reproductions; Cibachromes involve a combination of photographic processes and dyes and are regarded as originals.

Another problem is the question of what is the original in many works of computer art. An aspect of this type of work is the challenge associated with art that is not concrete. There is no artifact in digital art. The images exist only in the computer's memory and are called up to be viewed on a monitor; they are pure visual information. Curators and directors have a genuine concern about hanging the 'original' work of art. It is that which makes the art unique. It may be an outmoded concept, but it still exists.

Another concern of the contemporary curator is the scale of much conventionally produced computer-aided art. Most of the two-dimensional artistic production seen is diminutive in scale as compared to contemporary work seen in other media. Plotter drawings are usually limited by the size of the plotting surface.

Recent technological advances allow for larger-scale production of works, but these facilities are not yet widely available. Robert Mallary relates an experience he had during an interview with the director of a New York gallery. Mallary was showing him his vector plots, and they were being warmly received, until the director asked Mallary, "What do you have that is big?" Only works of a certain scale were ever hung in the gallery. Mallary refers to this incident as "the Castelli factor" [15]. Harold Cohen and Mark Wilson create large-scale two-dimensional computer art by taking advantage of custom software in the production of their works involving automatic drawing.

For those artists who create complex large-scale works, especially multidimensional artworks, there are always other concerns related to mounting an exhibition. Large-scale works are costly to fabricate, to move and to install, and they occupy vast amounts of space. The electronic equipment that controls many of these works frequently gets damaged in transit.

Fig. 5. Bronx Museum of the Arts 1987 show, site and works, illustrating the nature and quality of the light in a museum setting. The walled-in space to the right contains a multidimensional sound installation. (Photo: P. Prince)

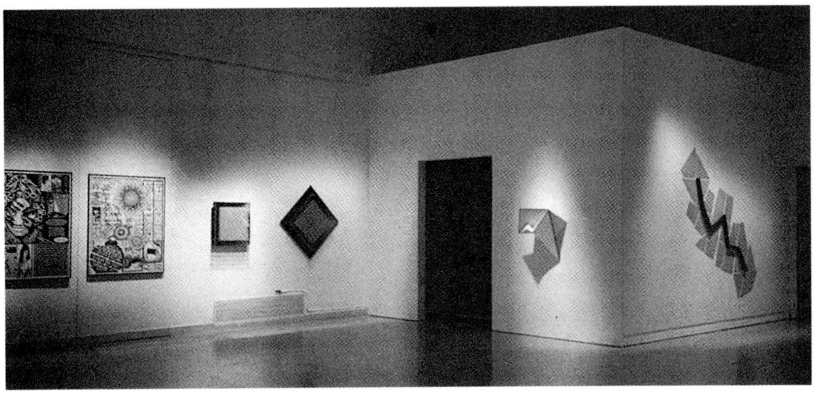

CONTEMPORARY ART SPACES: STATIC VS. DYNAMIC

The bright light that is required for an exhibition of conventional art forms contrasts with the low light that is required by much technical art. Modern art spaces have developed into white temples of light. "The art museum of the early 20th century is probably best symbolized by the placement of the Philadelphia Museum of Art as a Greek temple placed high on the hill above the city" [16]. How does the designer create totally darkened space in a 'white temple'? How does the gallery manage the large numbers of viewers in total darkness and still comply with fire regulations? In conventional gallery spaces, if a low-light environment is required, the standard solution is to create a static, theater-like design where the people are secured, usually by seats, and the art moves before them. Milton Komisar's large-scale computer-controlled sculptures involve electronic light and need total darkness in order to be viewed. He considers his works to be 'intimate' in nature; they need a space in which the viewer can become involved and explore the dimension of the work.

Display and Setup Requirements of Technical Art

Once complex technical works have been selected for exhibition, it is necessary to fabricate suitable environments. For multidimensional art pieces, there exist several layers of design and fabrication. There are external fabrications to be manufactured, software to be designed so that various displays relate to each other and equipment configurations to be arranged so that it all functions properly. There are problems involved in the acquisition of electronic equipment, although as industry standards are defined, no doubt, electronic equipment will become as commonplace as audiovisual equipment is now. Curators may have a reluctance to organize the specialized set-up required for this equipment. It is one of the fac-

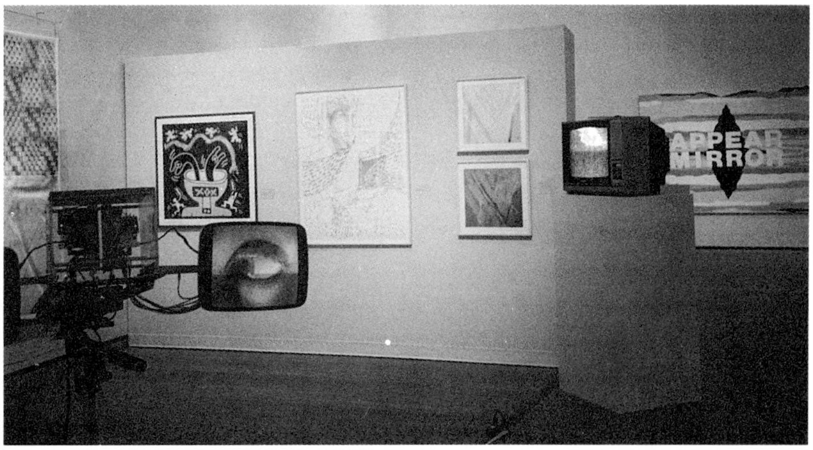

Fig. 6. One of the larger spaces at the Everson Museum displaying a variety of artworks. Several pieces were interactive. (Photo: P. Prince)

tors that increase the costs involved in the display of computer art. Museum and gallery staffs will include professionals who are capable of mounting any type of artistic production, but who may not be sufficiently trained to install software and to maintain continuity so that these works can be seen. This is one of the advantages that artists have when their work is exhibited in connection with technical conferences; systems experts are usually available to offer advice. Galleries, on the other hand, must either rely on the artists themselves or hire consultants to perform this essential function.

The trend in museum design is towards specialized environments for art exhibitions, especially for the 'block-buster' travelling shows like the *Treasures of Tutankhamun* show that toured Europe and the United States in the late 1970s. Each museum treated the event in the context of the expected crowds and revenues. In San Francisco, for example, there was a "record of over 1,300,000 visitors" [17]. The differences here are that with much multidimensional art the curator has no choice. In order for the work to be seen, specialized environments must be constructed. Some of the recent exhibitions of technical art have been seen by large numbers of viewers, but few have warranted the expense of fabricating environments based solely on the attendance [18].

Sound in Technical Art

Sound is another aesthetic element of technical art that creates problems. Even though many computer-controlled artworks include a sound component, few galleries are prepared to offer effective sound equipment. Artists complain that they have to use alternate and in many cases inferior setups for auditory experience. Nicole Stenger reports that her composer collaborator insisted that she use earphones in one particular project because the environment was not suitable for broadcast of the sound [19]. Gallery curators must be concerned about noise pollution when works include sound. At SIGGRAPH '86, the organizers were very careful about the spacing and audible levels of sound installations; they sought a dynamic atmosphere, not sound intrusion. It is a difficult physical problem for a gallery because if a sound-tight space is obtained, it may not suit the flow of the exhibition. Future galleries will have to address this problem and find suitable solutions, such as glass enclosures that do not block sight lines but enclose the sound. Many exhibits of multidimensional art suffer from sensory satiation because of noise pollution. This is probably from the use of inferior equipment that allows only a single sound dimension. There is a need for auditory dimension controls in galleries.

There are other complications to the exhibition of technical art that I will only list here; they include specialized power requirements, separate insurance policies for the equipment (aside from the artworks), licenses for laser use (which are required in some states), fire safety considerations for low-light spaces, and the specific expenses related to the technology. These additional expenses include the cost of shipping the equipment to and from the site, the cost of fabrication of specialized environments and the cost of equipment maintenance. Specialists are needed to set up the equipment, and constant maintenance is required in order to keep it working. There is also the time necessary for the education of museum staff, so that docents are able to discuss the works.

What Gets Viewed

The majority of art pieces seen in formal exhibitions of technically advanced art have been conventional aesthetically. They relate to and conform to Modernist theories. The mediums are also understandable: print forms (ink-jet prints, screen prints, lithographs, engravings), paintings based upon computer-generated sketches, plotter drawings and sculpture (computer-assisted, computer-made, computer-controlled). Many exhibitions of digital art include micro-computer stations with interactive pieces, where the viewer becomes a partner in the process. Video walls and animation screenings are installed regularly in exhibitions.

The unconventional forms of computer art seen in recent exhibitions include laser light shows, computer-controlled environments (sound and visual), holograms and on-line art. A few exhibitions included 'frame buffer' shows, bringing in the complete computer system to display the works as originally conceived. Many contemporary art shows now have walls of written material explaining the art and giving artists' statements. Esoteric Modernist art is not yet in the domain of public comprehension; because most museums are public institutions supported by public funds, they are obligated to appeal to the public in the broadest sense. Most museum visitors relate to conventional art forms, that is, art forms that are imitative. If technological art is to be available to the general public, museum staffs and gallery directors must understand it first. That knowledge then can filter down to a mass audience as part of the ongoing historical development.

Software was an ambitious exhibition of technical art mounted at the Jewish Museum in New York City. In 1970, Karl Katz, the director, and Jack Burnham, the curator, put together a show using mainframe computers. There was a catalog printed to document the exhibition. However, so many problems occurred with the logistics of the exhibition that the pieces were hardly ever viewed [20]. The first really successful mainframe show was not seen until 1982 at the SIGGRAPH art show in Boston.

The trend, however, is towards a more experiential art exhibition. The 1988 SIGGRAPH art show is directed towards interactivity and animation. It also will feature many of the works from the *Interactive Image* show from Chicago. The next Bronx Museum of the Arts computer art show will focus on environmental work and 'on-line' stations. The 1988 *artware* exhibition is devoted to "large-scale installations, many of which employ highly complex state-of-the-art equipment" [21].

Art Galleries of the Future

Art forms of the future will involve a unity of the senses and will involve the participant in interactivity. Art galleries of the future will have to continue to expand our knowledge of what *is*, as well as to put what *was* (art of the past) into context. The purpose of the museum or the gallery is to inform viewers, not to limit access to new art forms, and these repositories will move forward with the times to overcome the physical limitations that relate to computer art.

Experiential and multidimensional art forms have led us towards an active participation in the viewing of art. A static relationship between the artifact and the viewing participant is no longer satisfactory. Since the turn of the century, artists have discussed the rejection of museums and galleries as sites for their art. This attitude was once part of a revolutionary gesture promoting the avant-garde in art. Because of the difficulties in putting together exhibitions of technically advanced art, artists are re-evaluating alternative display sites out of necessity. Advanced art such as that envisioned by the late Stan VanDerBeek, who publicized the idea of the 'Culture Intercom' that places the production and distribution in different continents that would be linked via satellite [22], and works by Tom Klinkowstein linking artists via telecommunications would be almost impossible to 'mount' in a static gallery under any circumstances. These artists are examples of those who have sought alternative methods of communicating their art to the public. Their work relates more to performance art than to conventional art and is part of the movement toward multi-sensuous experience.

David Carrier, in a *Leonardo* article, suggests that "the proper location for the type of art published in *Leonardo* is not a physical space at all, but in this journal" [23]. Stephen s'Soreff describes art experiences and sites using new materials, concepts and technology because "it simply takes too much time to travel to see firsthand all of the art being made today. Art criticism has become for many the only way to experience some artworks, and thus the magazine has become a de facto medium of art exhibition" [24]. s'Soreff's reviews of future works that he calls 'post-conceptual' describe visionary new art including attempts to interest the Army Corps of Engineers in poetry, 'Teleprivateering', freezing sound in paint, and weather art.

Jürgen Claus, Fellow of the MIT Center for Advanced Visual Studies, suggests that the proper place for technical art may be 'media centers' such as the Cologne Mediapark. In his words, this "project is meant to be based on a connection of research and development, for example in the field of applied computer science, telematics, education and further training in art and culture in the interface divisions. . . ." He believes it is possible that this type of center might become the new 'Electronic Bauhaus'. Claus also believes that "advanced art has no choice but to confront itself with contemporary research. This would at all events be much easier if we established

Fig. 7. ***The Interactive Image*, Museum of Science and Industry, Chicago, illustrating the specialized fabrication of environments. The video wall installation repeated forms along a continuous plane. The space was designed to capture the viewer's curiosity through changing directions. (Copyright Electronic Visualization Laboratory, University of Illinois at Chicago)**

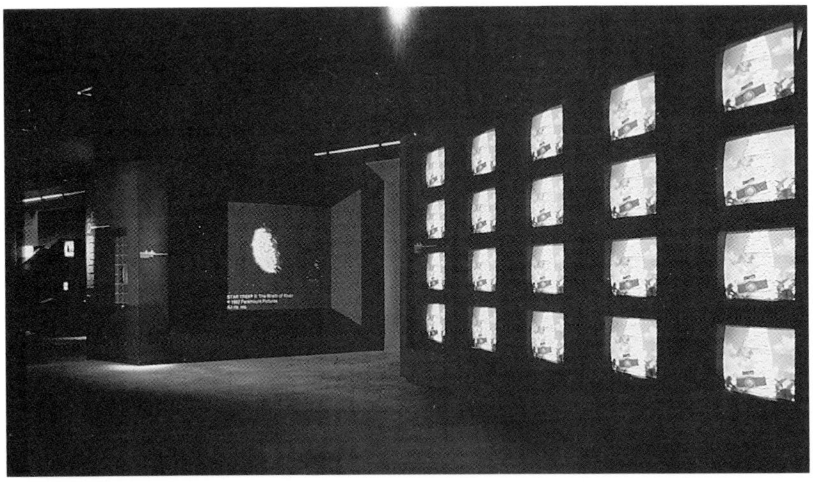
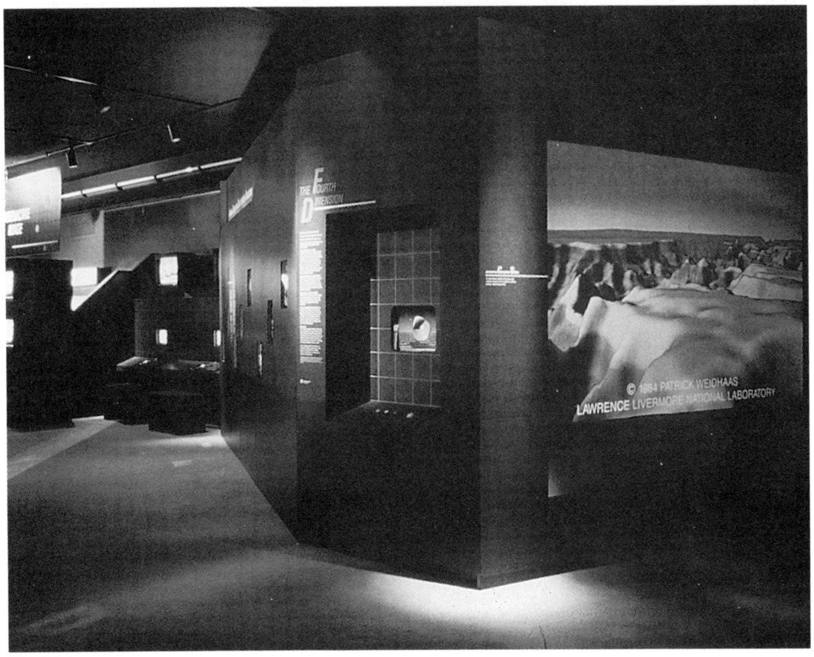

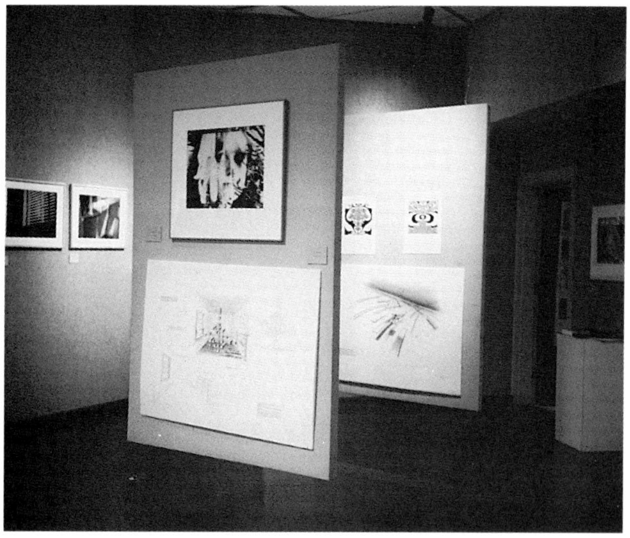

Fig. 8. Hanging panels from the Dundalk Gallery exhibition where Stephen s'Soreff's drawings of future art experiences are visible. (Photo: P. Prince)

appropriate conditions—in education, museum 'policy' and criticism—under which such discussions could be carried on in a well-informed, intelligent manner and with high demands as regards the visual field" [25].

Harold McWhinnie has expanded André Malraux's idea of the 'Instant Museum', that is, that all artifacts will be available photographically in a universal museum, to include the concept of the electronic museum. McWhinnie's concept involves an electronic bulletin board and an outer space site: "Works of art would be stored in an information retrieval system and could be beamed back and forth to the museum spectator both on earth, or under it in an art museum, and on other space stations as well" [26]. He has established three electronic 'museums' on floppy disks. Several large institutions have been working to develop systems that will offer the visual information suggested in McWhinnie's paper [27].

The exploration will continue and exhibition sites will evolve as the artist and the viewers/participants redefine what is needed. Whatever is invented in the future for an art exhibition will include art spaces. The evolution of experiential work demands more than that which currently can be given to the viewer in pure electronic experience. The tactile qualities of art are still very rich. Michael Fehr, Director of the Karl Ernst Osthaus Museum in Hagen, West Germany, in his essay "The Art Museum as Critical Locale for the 'New Media'" points out that in spite of the criticism aimed at museums as institutions, they are the appropriate sites for new art forms. Because museums are concerned with historical perspectives, the limited space is part of the timely process of delimiting art and therefore creating 'memorable images', and, because of the museum's individuality, it is not "accessible to arbitrary intervention" and can therefore be a fundamental site [28].

The important issue is the quality and the changing nature of communication between artist, artifact and the viewer/participant. Artists who create inaccessible art or predictable art because the process of creation is more important to them than the artifact or the experience must involve and communicate their ideas to the viewer. Conceptual artists wrote about their art. This literary adjunct to contemporary art is not totally satisfying. Perhaps in the future all viewers will be so well educated that art theories, technical concepts and digital processes will be fully understood; until that time the artist using technology must transform the viewer's reality as well as create or transform new art forms. This is part of a historical continuum dealing with process in art. Twentieth-century artists became intrigued by and involved in the process of creation. The viewer/participant will become more involved in process art in the future. In order to be seen and appreciated, artworks must be compelling, must address the viewer on some level—visually, emotionally, spiritually, intellectually, or in some unique way yet to be discovered.

"The past is prologue."

References

1. Tom Wolfe, *The Painted Word* (New York: Farrar, Straus and Giroux, 1975).

2. See Patric D. Prince, "COMPUTER AESTHETICS: New Art Experience, or the Seduction of the Masses", *ACM SIGGRAPH '86 Art Show Catalog* (New York: ACM/SIGGRAPH, 1986) p. 41.

3. Karl Ernest Meyer, *The Art Museum: Power, Money, Ethics: A Twentieth-Century Fund Report* (New York: Morrow, 1979) p. 128.

4. Arthur Weever Melton, *Problems of Installation in Museums of Art* (Washington, DC: Publications of the American Association of Museums, New Series, No. 14, 1935) p. 268.

5. Jasia Reichardt, *Cybernetics, Art and Ideas* (Greenwich, CT: New York Graphic Society Ltd., 1971) p. 11.

6. *Event One* (London: Computer Arts Society, 1969).

7. *SIGGRAPH '82 Art Show Catalog* (New York: ACM/SIGGRAPH, 1982); *SIGGRAPH '83 Exhibition of Computer Art* (New York: ACM/SIGGRAPH, 1982); *Computer Support Design Exhibition* (New York: ACM/SIGGRAPH, 1984); *ACM/SIGGRAPH '85 Art Show* (New York: ACM/SIGGRAPH, 1985); *ACM/SIGGRAPH '86 Art Show Catalog* (New York: ACM/SIGGRAPH, 1986); *SIGGRAPH* (New York: ACM/SIGGRAPH, 1987).

8. Louis R. Cancel, "Introduction", in *The Second Emerging Expression Biennial: The Artist and the Computer* (Bronx, NY: The Bronx Museum of the Arts, 1987) p. 7.

9. Cynthia Goodman, *Digital Visions* (New York: Abrams, 1987) pp. 22–34.

10. Dan Sandin, interview with author, 19 April 1988.

11. Maxine Brown, *Notes on The Interactive Image* (Chicago, IL: Electronic Visualization Laboratory, University of Illinois at Chicago, 1987) p. 1.

12. Brown [11] p. 10.

13. Janet Anderson, interview with author, 22 April 1988.

14. Harold McWhinnie, "Dundalk Catalog" (1988) p. 2.

15. Robert Mallary, interview with author, 14 April 1988.

16. Harold McWhinnie, "A Gallery for the Art of the Next Century" (1987) p. 4.

17. McWhinnie [16].

18. Lora Hopman, interview with author, 15 February 1988; Tom Piche, interview with author, 21 April 1988; Maxine Brown, interview with author, 21 April 1988.

19. Nicole Stenger, interview with author, 27 April 1988.

20. Jack Burnham, "Art and Technology: The Panacea that Failed", in *The Myths of Information* (Madison, WI: Coda, 1980) pp. 200–215.

21. David Galloway, *Artware Kunst und Elektronik* (Hannover, F.R.G.: Messe AG und Siemens AG, 1988) p. 48.

22. Jürgen Claus, "The Digital Alphabet", in *Artware Kunst und Elektronik* [21] p. 49.

23. David Carrier, "Theoretical Perspectives on the Arts, Sciences and Technology", *Leonardo* **20**, No. 1, 83–86 (1987).

24. Stephen s'Soreff, "The Malleable Memory of Avant Garde Art Review (AGAR): A Post-Conceptual Artwork", *Leonardo* **20**, No. 4, 387–390 (1987).

25. Claus [22] p. 54.

26. McWhinnie [16] p. 8.

27. *Grant Program* (Los Angeles: The J. Paul Getty Trust, 1986) p. 10.

28. Michael Fehr, "The Art Museum as Critical Locale for the 'New Media'", *Artware Kunst und Elektronik* [21] p. 57.

The Staging of Leonardo's *Last Supper*: A Computer-Based Exploration of Its Perspective

Lillian F. Schwartz

ABSTRACT

The question of perspective posed by Leonardo da Vinci's *Last Supper* has been addressed by an analysis supported by a computer-aided multi-processor. A three-dimensional space was built within the computer to explore the notion that Leonardo used the 'trickery' of the theater in constructing the non-traditional perspective of this Fresco. In this investigation, the compositional elements were manipulated in the computer-created space, and the resulting images were projected into the plane of the Fresco. The analysis compared these projected images, as seen from various points in the Refectory, to the painted ones in Leonardo's mural. The results clarify Leonardo's use of an accelerated perspective in his construction of the staging of the *Last Supper* and locate the vantage points at the door and in the viewing plane of the monks, who sat along the side walls of the Refectory.

This paper describes the creation and use of a three-dimensional computer model that encompasses both Leonardo da Vinci's *Last Supper* (Fig. 1) and the Refectory at Santa Maria delle Grazie, where it is painted (see Fig. 4).

In the painting (Fig. 1), there are four key lines. The strong lines of the tapestries must be an extension of the design in the Refectory in order to cause the illusion that the mural is a real room. The orthogonal lines of the ceiling intersect at the center of the vanishing point to the painting, at the level of Christ's face. From this vantage point, the borders on both of the Refectory walls line up to make the mural 'look right'. But this point is more than 15 feet above the floor.

The analysis addresses the major issue that has provoked scholars for over 500 years: How was the painting meant to be viewed? Why did Leonardo position the true vantage point above the viewer? Is there a place from the floor of the Refectory where the painting appears to be an integral, three-dimensional part of the actual viewing space?

Some 75 years before this work was painted, Filippo di Ser Brunelleschi demonstrated that linear or 'true' perspective is simply what a viewer sees when looking at a scene through a window[1]. To perform this demonstration, Brunelleschi stood with his back to the Baptistery, held up a small flat mirror to reflect the building and painted the reflected image of the Baptistery on a small wooden panel propped up on an easel in front of him [2].

Once Brunelleschi completed his painting, he made a hole in the panel in order to look through it and begin his experiment. With one hand, he held the back side of the panel close to his eye, and with the other he held up a mirror to reflect the painting. The reflected image of his painting produced the same effect as the one from the Baptistery itself. In exhibiting the illusion of depth, Brunelleschi's

Lillian F. Schwartz, 524 Ridge Road, Watchung, NJ 07060, U.S.A.

Received 7 April 1988.

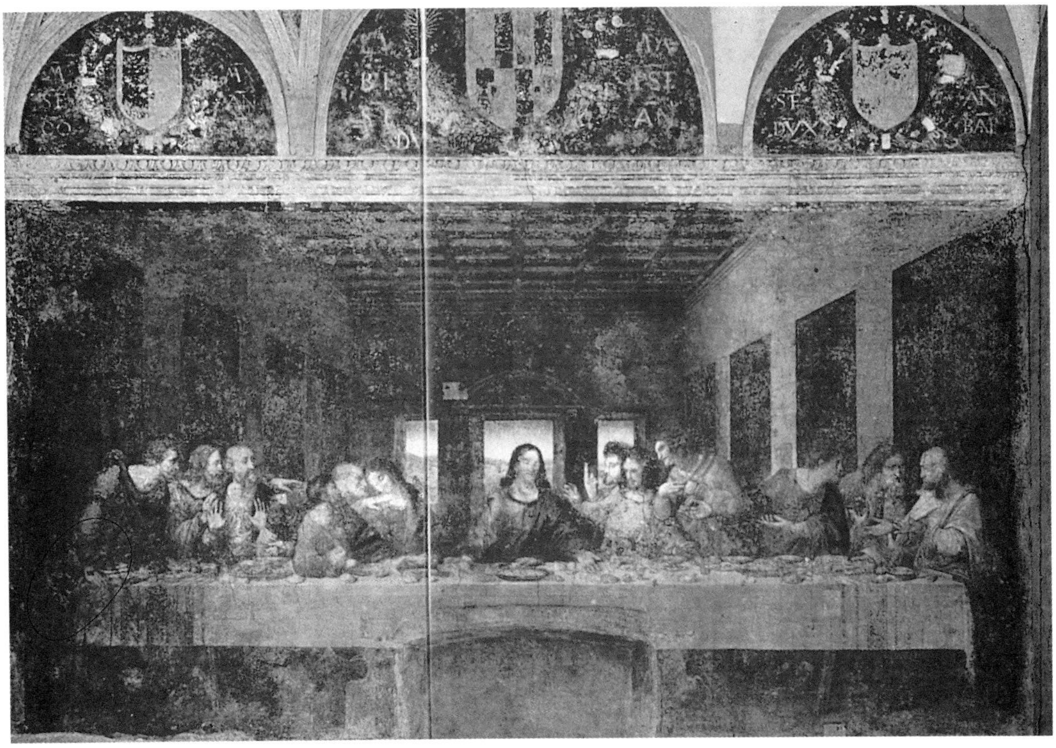

Fig. 1. Leonardo da Vinci, *The Last Supper*, 1498 (Refectory, Santa Maria delle Grazie, Milan, after World War II. Courtesy Soprintendenza per i Beni Artistici e Storici of Milan.)

Pergamon Press plc. Printed in Great Britain.
0024-094X/88 $3.00+0.00

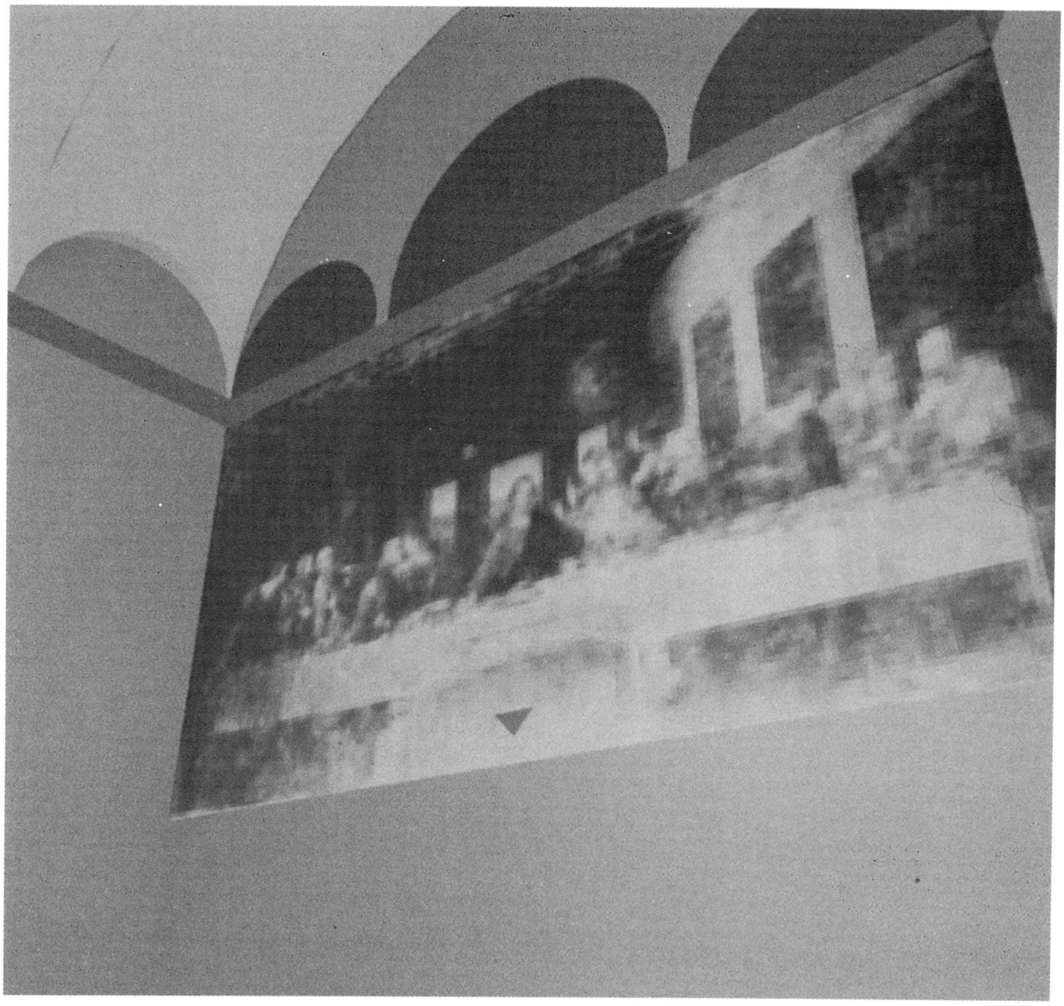

Fig. 2. XYZ = position of eye 9.8, 1.75, 29.0; XYZ = position of where to look 4.42, 5.86, 35.5. The viewing position is at the vantage point near the entrance and looking up at the Fresco. The eye is drawn to Christ's hand, to Christ, to the upper left corner of the picture and, finally, out into the Refectory. All vertical lines slant inwards, emphasizing the position of Christ. Since the viewer is closer to the brighter wall, the wall looks larger than from a frontal view. (Copyright Lilyan Prod. Inc., 1988)

'peep-show' yielded a procedure that painters could follow. These concepts were formalized and published 10 years later by Leon Battista Alberti [2] and ever since have been commonly referred to as 'Albertian perspective'.

Since Leonardo had applied Albertian or 'true' perspective to earlier works [3] and, according to Naumann [4], wrote notes that "resemble Alberti's treatise", some scholars have attempted to interpret the *Last Supper* in the context of these laws but have failed to achieve a conclusive thesis [5]. In addition, Leonardo's own *Treatise on Painting* misleads scholars by specifying that the vanishing point in a mural should be positioned "opposite the eye of the observer of the composition". But, as noted by Pedretti, "whoever looks at the *Last Supper* is far below the axis perpendicular to the vanishing point (in the Christ's head), no matter how far back one can step" [5].

Controversy over the scheme of the Fresco's construction continues to the present day. One historian asserts that there is no exact position to take in the Refectory "to make the picture come right" [6]. On the other hand, another historian states that "each of the monks sitting at any place of the long tables in the Refectory could view the *Last Supper* with the illusion of standing in front of it in the center of the room" [5]. A third disagrees with both opinions, concluding instead that the perspective for the *Last Supper* not only distorted Leonardo's own written rules of perspective [4] but was so uncommon "that it cannot be generalized or turned into rules" [7].

The apparent inadequacies of descriptions based upon 'true' perspective have led several recent authors to suggest applying an 'accelerated' perspective instead—one in which the scene converges towards the vanishing point more rapidly than it would in the real world [4,5,7].

In this study, I have used the accelerated perspective employed in stage design [8,9] as the basis for comparisons between a computer-generated rectilinear model and the projected plane of the painting in question. This same model contains provisions for the manipulation of viewing points to examine the relationship of the Fresco to the Refectory. This model is described in the sections that follow the discussion of the painting itself.

THE *LAST SUPPER*

The *Last Supper* (Fig. 1) was painted in the late 1400s, at the command of Ludovico il Moro, for the Refectory of the Convent of Dominican friars at Santa Maria delle Grazie, Milan. It was immediately hailed as a masterpiece, but one that quickly became the center of scholarly debate. In particular, its perspective construction evoked a host of contradictory interpretations, which remain unresolved to the present day. Even at the level of the vanishing point, where the mural can be viewed as an extension of the Refectory, Steinberg noted that "the projected perspective is disjunctive" [6]. Since the conventional tools of artistic investigation have not enabled researchers to reach a satisfactory conclusion, a resolution of the puzzle appears to require a premise outside the normal laws of perspective.

I began the present investigation by searching for clues in the few preparatory drawings of this work that survive. Leonardo used conventional rules for perspective in at least one preliminary sketch [10]. This sketch was drawn in 'true' perspective, displaying an interior with figures seated along a long wall beneath arches that matched the architecture of the Refectory. But a later sketch was drawn in a more distorted manner, showing figures standing behind a table sloped at an extreme angle [11]. However, in this sketch, an architectural design behind the figures was omitted. What led Leonardo to reformulate these elements in different ways?

In confronting the Refectory's interior, Leonardo faced problems like those found in the theater. The hall was long and narrow. The audience (the monks and prior) sat along the perimeters of the walls, far below the 'stage'. The entrance to the hall was through a small door, near the right side where the Fresco would be painted. The audience of dignitaries and their retinue, the monks and the prior, would gain their first view of the stage at the door [12].

Leonardo's genius permitted the audience to participate in the painted action. All who entered through the doorway at the right perceived the left hand of Christ gesturing towards them in welcome (Fig. 1) [11]. When Goethe visited the Refectory, he visualized the monks and their prior seated at the tables along three sides of the Refectory and, on the fourth wall—that of the Fresco—Christ and the Disciples at the "table . . . as though they belonged to the company. At suppertime it must have been an impressive sight, when the tables of Christ and the Prior confronted each other as counterparts, . . . the sacred company was to be brought into the present, Christ was to take his evening meal with the Dominicans in Milan" [7]. In order to achieve this effect, the perspective projection had to produce the illusion that audience and stage were united. However, as many scholars have pointed out, this illusion was unattainable with 'true' perspective. A rectilinear room, located in front of an audience, high above their heads, clearly marks the separation of stage and audience.

The required projection shared many features with the Renaissance theater. The theatrical stage in the late 1400s was a dynamic art. Instead of a 'real' room on stage, the audience was pulled into the performance through the stage designer's use of non-rectilinear rooms to achieve 'accelerated' perspective [8]. The Renaissance stage usually was enclosed by an ornamented architectural facade that obscured the transition between the setting and the audience. A horizontal strip at the top completed a rectangular proscenium. Stage design followed the form of the Roman acting-platform with a narrow acting-area directly in front of the audience. The sets usually were built on a sharply raked platform [8]. A typical platform held the setting of a city street or square, built up with houses placed near the front. To achieve the perspective effect, the size of the houses diminished rapidly towards the rear of the stage, where they stopped at a wall or canvas that was parallel to the front of the stage. To avoid shattering the perspective,

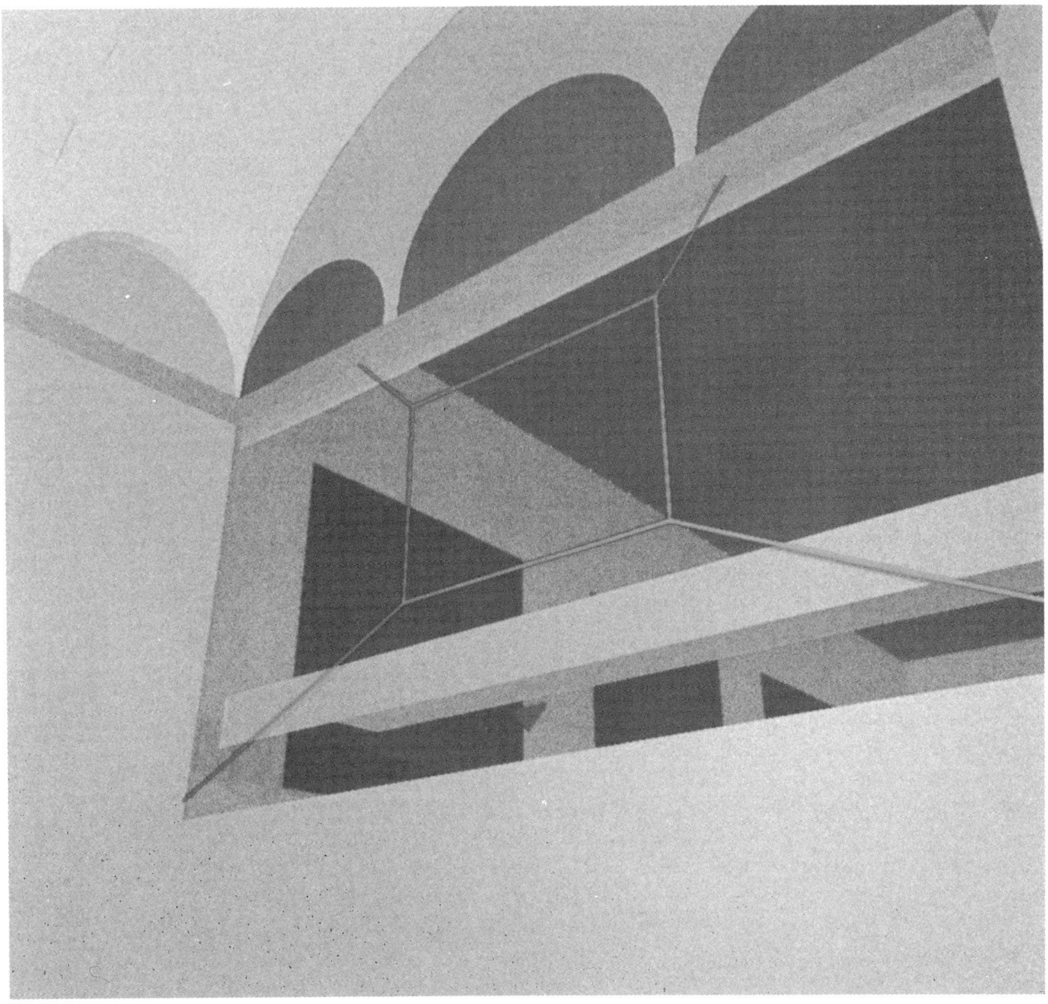

Fig. 3. XYZ = position of eye 9.8, 1.75, 29.0; XYZ = position of where to look 4.42, 5.86, 35.5. The vantage point is located at the entrance to the Refectory. Lines representing the Fresco are superimposed over a rectilinear room. The floor, right wall, and top of the table are not visible in the rectilinear room, whereas the lines representing the painting show that the floor, ceiling and walls are visible. (Copyright Lilyan Prod. Inc., 1988)

the actors performed *against* the scenery at the front of the stage, rather than in the scene, where they would appear too large for the setting.

Since Leonardo had constructed numerous stage settings in Milan for Duke Ludovico and had drawn a study for the stage set of Baldassare Taccone's *Danae* of 1496 [13], we may assume that he was familiar with the novel concepts of perspective used in effective stage design. Furthermore, he probably knew of the writings of Vitruvius or of Alberti's study *De re aedificatoria,* popular at the time, which emphasized theatrical experiments [13].

The distorted perspective of the theater thus could have provided Leonardo with the opportunity to create a new way of handling a painting in the Refectory [5]. His genius allowed him first to construct a linear perspective of the main structure of the room and to position the vanishing point for Christ's head. Then, to accommodate the eye-level vantage point from the doorway—for the most instantaneous perception of the work—he bastardized this perspective. He hid the lower part of the back wall and most of the floor lines and he changed the left orthogonal ceiling line to a transversal that no longer intersected the vanishing point. The mural still appears legitimate, even though it is geometrically incorrect.

Leonardo painted the back wall the minimum size that could contain windows large enough to reveal an impressionistic landscape, one that appears far away, yet with a clearly defined horizon. He built a work in the style of a classical stage where he had the freedom to change sizes of objects. The actors on a stage cannot be changed in size except by costumes and props, but since he was constructing a painting at the end of a long, narrow hall, he needed to adjust the relative sizes of his actors for the most metaphorically significant impact on his audience. Even the gestures of the figures are designed as if directed for the theater (Fig. 1) [11].

To dress this stage, Leonardo had to use the same elements of theater in order to place Christ and the Apostles in the positions that would not destroy the perspective. He raked the stage so that Christ's feet are displayed in an upright position and tilted the table to expose everything on it. The freedom provided by theaterlike distortions also gave him the opportunity to introduce a strong depth effect [15].

In medieval and Early Renaissance representations of the same subject, the table is usually round or square, compelling the artist to depict some of the Apostles from behind [10]. If Leonardo had used either the round or square table for this setting (or moved the table around and seated Christ at the end of the table), the perspective would have changed, diminishing Christ. Instead, by using theatrical ideas to stage this event, locating the 'actors' up front, almost upon the audience, thrusting Christ into the Refectory by making Him larger than the Apostles and, at the same time, maintaining a spiritual distance by placing the table in front of Him, Leonardo avoided turned backs and blasphemy.

Theatrical lighting in the late 1400s meant bathing the audience in the same light as the stage, while the props were painted to simulate other bright-

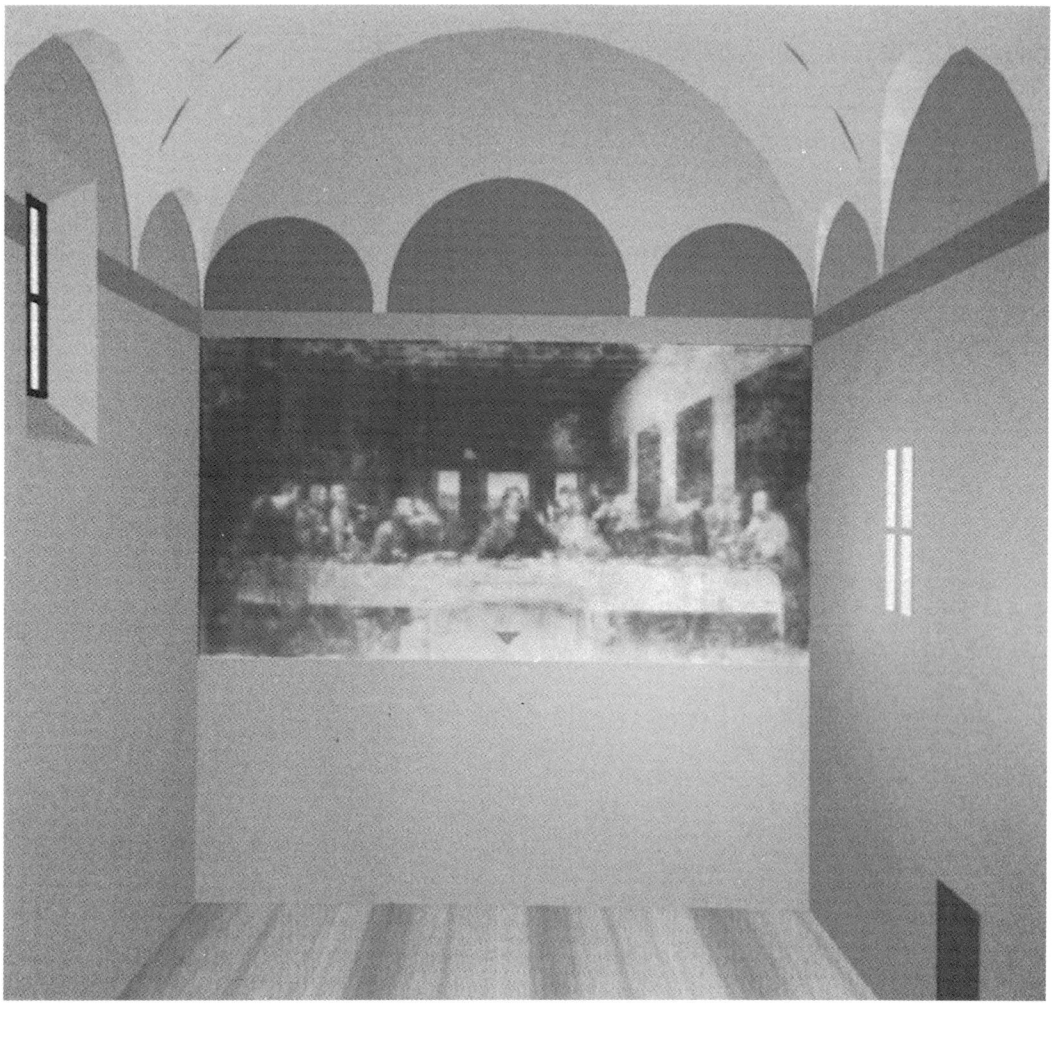

Fig. 4. XYZ = position of eye 4.4, 4.5, 20.0; XYZ = position of where to look 4.4, 4.5, 35.5. The vantage point is placed at the vanishing point behind Christ's head. The tapestries line up. The entrance on the right wall is indicated in black. The lighting is calculated at dusk, 21 April 1500. (Copyright Lilyan Prod. Inc., 1988)

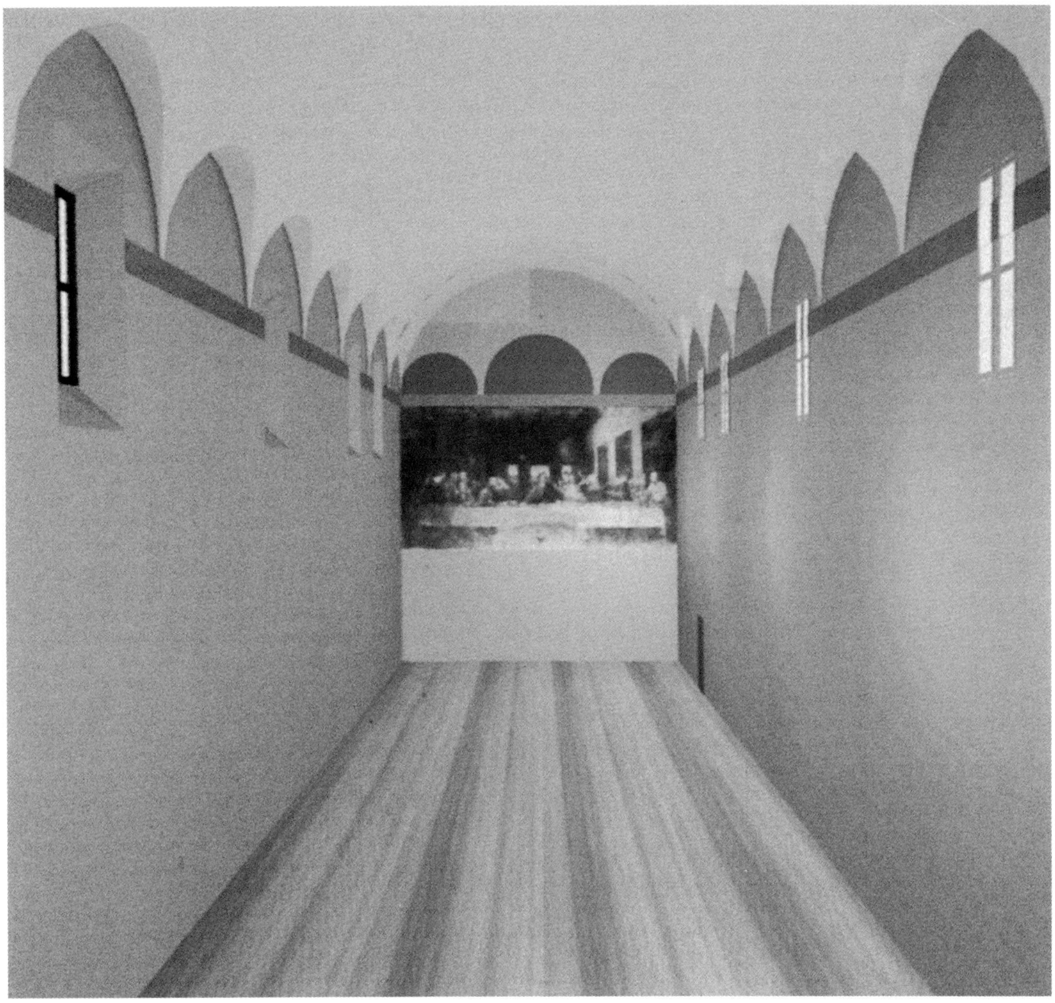

Fig. 5. XYZ = position of eye 4.4, 5.5, 1.0; XYZ = position of where to look 4.42, 5.5, 35.5. The distance is so great that it is difficult to view the painting in any detail, but the brighter wall, the table and a silhouette of Christ's head can be discerned. (Copyright Lilyan Prod., Inc. 1988)

ness or shadow [8]. Leonardo used the trickery of theatrical light in his scenery as well as available ambient light to enhance the perceptual illusions. Steinberg described the light as being "the most magical feature of Leonardo's illusionism. . . . Even today the effect sometimes returns at the hour of dusk" (see Fig. 4) [7].

The painting captivated visitors even while Leonardo worked on it. The first view of the work was at the entrance to the Refectory through a doorway about 18 feet from the painting. When Francis I visited Santa Maria delle Grazie in 1515, he noted that the "viewer's attention would soon be focused on the particular loaf of bread in line with the left hand of Christ, open in a gesture of offering directed to the entrance door" [11]. Leonardo directed Christ to reach out in welcome to all newcomers as they entered the Refectory. As will be shown, Francis I, standing at the door of the Refectory, unknowingly unraveled the secret of how to perceive the *Last Supper* less than 20 years after its completion.

PERSPECTIVE MODEL

A three-dimensional computer model was built using a high-performance, multi-processor computing system [16] to track the perspective of the Fresco's relationship to its painted wall and to the other walls of the Refectory to determine whether Leonardo used a theaterlike 'accelerated' perspective in the construction of his *Last Supper*. The computer model provoked the analysis of the work in question and permitted an 'observer' to view the painting and its setting from any point in the hall. To locate the different positions, we defined 0,0,0 at the lower left corner of the model. The first set of coordinates XYZ is the 'position of the eye'. To take photographs of what the viewer would see, we positioned the second set of coordinates XYZ at 'where to look'. For example, if we are looking at Christ's hand, we input the XYZ coordinates of that location. To avoid distortions, we kept the view the same as if we were looking through a pinhole camera without a lens, and with a normal field of view and an angle of 50°.

A model of the Refectory, called 'Viewing Room', was constructed using standard computer programs. The dimensions for 'Viewing Room', such as length = 35.5 meters, height = 11.74 meters, width = 8.82 meters, position of door = 5.5 meters; size of windows and their frames and depth of walls [3] were defined as before World War II, when the floor was lower [17] than it is today. Since it is important to show how the strong line of the tapestries matches up with the designs on the long walls of the Refectory, we calculated the position of these designs and marked them with solid colored bands. This same color was selected for the border and the designs above the Fresco.

In 'Viewing Room', a wall, called 'Main Wall', corresponds to the wall with the Fresco in the real situation and allows for two different views: the painted replica called 'Fresco' and a three-dimensional rectilinear room called 'True Room'. 'Main Wall' is 3.57 meters from the floor to the bottom of the Fresco. The space for the

Fresco and the 'True Room' is 4.59 meters.

For 'Fresco' we digitized [18] a photograph of the Fresco (resolution 1280 × 1024), which was then texture-mapped [19] onto the North Wall of 'Viewing Room'. A triangle, representing Christ's feet, was positioned on the digitized painting as based on an early copy of the work [11]. (Christ's legs and feet were eliminated in the 1700s by a door that was cut into the painting.)

We then constructed 'True Room' with the dimensions length = 28.0 meters; width = 9.7 meters; and height sitting up from the floor = 8.16 meters, based on a system of measurement that Leonardo had used, where a unit is equal to about one-third the height of a person [14]. But when I tried to align the back wall of 'True Room' with the back wall of the Fresco, the length was insufficient. It was necessary to extend the length to almost 80 meters to match up the walls. (When 'True Room' is 80 meters long, the ceiling lines match the Fresco. However, it was necessary to 'shorten' the room to accommodate the props essential to the accelerated perspective of the 'depicted' room.) 'True Room' extends beyond 'Main Wall' as in a real three-dimensional room and always is seen in 'true' perspective from any position in the Refectory. In addition, we superimposed lines—positioned as in the ceiling, floor and walls of the Fresco—over 'True Room'. As we moved our point of view, we then could compare the position of the Fresco lines with those in the rectilinear room. Since in the 'depicted' painting the upper ceiling, the top half of the wall lines and only the ends of the floor lines at the bottom of the Fresco are visible, we extended the lines on the lower half and connected them to reveal the differences between the 'true' and 'accelerated' projections.

We began our study by using the model to view the Fresco from different locations to find a position from the floor where the Fresco would appear to be an extension of the actual room. We located the position of the eye at X = 9.8, Y = 1.75, Z = 29.0; and the position of where to look at 4.4, 5.86, 35.5. As soon as we located a vantage point at the door of the Refectory in Fig. 2, it became clear that Leonardo chose this position to lead the viewer to Christ and then to the tapestries on the left wall where they would line up with the design on the Refectory wall, earmarking the illusion that the Fresco is an extension of the real world. All vertical lines appear to slant inwards, emphasizing the position and size of Christ and His hand ushering us in. Once the vantage point was positioned at the door we continued along the same Y-axis of 1.75 to find that the monks' perception of the painting also allowed for the illusion that the Fresco appeared to be an extension of the Refectory.

For Fig. 3, the vantage point was positioned at the door as in Fig. 2: XYZ = position of eye 9.8, 1.75, 29.0; XYZ = position of where to look 4.42, 5.86, 35.5. A comparison of the elements in 'True Room' with the superimposed lines of the Fresco in 'True Room' reveals that the floor, right wall and top of the table are not visible, whereas the Fresco lines show the floor, ceiling and walls.

For Fig. 4, when the position of the eye is 4.4, 4.5, 20.0 and the position of where to look is 4.4, 4.5, 35.5, the tapestries line up. If the Z coordinate is changed while the X and Y coordinates remain the same, the tapestries continue to line up. However, in order to see this view, the spectator would have to stand on a stepladder 4.5 meters above the floor. The entrance on the right wall is indicated in black. The same model positioned the lights to determine whether the ambient light would fall on the right, brighter wall of the Fresco. It has been noted that Leonardo took advantage of the light streaming in from the windows to illuminate his painting as if the real light were cast on it, thereby enhancing the illusion that the 'depicted' room extended beyond the Refectory [7]. This study was not completed at the time of this paper, but when we calculated the light at noon, at 3 o'clock and at dusk, in April and in September, we found that the light from the windows was cast on the east wall of the Refectory, away from the mural as in this figure. The lighting is calculated at dusk on 21 April 1500 [20].

In Fig. 5, the vantage point for the back of the room is raised above the vanishing point from 4.5 meters to 5.92 meters. The lines of the tapestries and the design in the real room appear to line up, but as Steinberg noted, "A spectator tight-roped on the hall's longitudinal axis 15 feet above ground would see nothing wrong; the real and the depicted perspective would appear to him in undisturbed continuity" [7]. It is unlikely, given Leonardo's concern with the perspective and the viewing position, that such a viewing height was his intention. This viewing distance was so great, however, that any angular change did not make a big difference (see Figs. 4 and 5).

The illustrations show that the best views from the floor have been located. Leonardo makes clear his intent in engaging the viewers' perception at the doorway of the hall where they see the painting for the first time. By slanting the ceiling lines at such a sharp angle (the angles are 10% higher in absolute size on the right than on the left), Leonardo could provide a viewing plane at eye level where the spectator is drawn first to Christ's hand, then to His figure and, finally, along the orthogonals from the vanishing point to the tops of the tapestries, which then appear to line up with the designs in the actual room, providing a view of the Fresco as a three-dimensional room. The monks along either wall view the Fresco as a continuation of the Refectory. Leonardo sacrificed the view from the back of the room to attain the proper height for the vanishing point to satisfy the requirements needed to insure the view at the door and along the side walls.

Leonardo may have composed the Fresco by following his own written rules for perspective. But once he determined the locations for the viewing positions at the door and along the perimeters of the hall, the ceiling lines had to be moved. He could afford to relocate the strong lines of the ceiling to modify the linear perspective—disregarding the requirement for converging all parallel lines at the vanishing point—since he did not intend for the mural to be viewed on the horizon of the vanishing point. He would have destroyed the mirage at eye level if he had used 'true' perspective. Fig. 3 shows how little of the panorama would have been visible. Even for the viewer moving back into the room, much of the Fresco would have been out of sight from the sidelines. The essential elements in the mural could be projected only by an 'accelerated' perspective. Leonardo needed to display the floor in order to see Christ's feet, but he also needed to obscure the lines of the floor where they would abut the walls. If he had not hidden these lines—behind the table and figures—the distortion caused by these lines

(Fig. 3) also would have destroyed the total illusion. In addition, if the floor lines could be seen, the viewer's attention would have been diverted away from Christ and the strong vertical orientation of the painting, which is essential to the eye-tracking paths dictated by Leonardo as described in the following section.

DISCUSSION

Since the procedure for finding the true vantage point is usually to position oneself at the level of the vanishing point, the search for the correct position for viewing the *Last Supper*—from a position on the floor—as an extension of the Refectory was directed away from the side entrance. The strong vertical line of Christ also misled scholars into looking for the vantage point from the frontal view, at the level of Christ's head. But the results of this study demonstrate that the painting 'comes right' only when viewed obliquely [15] or at the level of the vanishing point, more than 15 feet above the floor.

Once Leonardo positioned a vantage point for the viewer's first impression, at the entrance to the hall, he had to modify the linear perspective construction, which could not show the entire display of his interpretation of the symbolic and sacramental story. He turned to an accelerated perspective projection to provide a view of all the elements in the *Last Supper,* as well as to provoke the effect that the Fresco appeared to be an extension of the Refectory.

After Leonardo drew the ceiling and tapestry lines, from the point of view of the door and the eye level along the walls, and determined the size and position of the rear wall behind Christ, then everything else was fixed. All Leonardo could do was to connect the rest of the lines and link them to the back wall, effectively building a raked stage with raked walls, ceiling and floor (Fig. 4). However, while the upper lines of the ceiling are visible, the lower lines of the floor, and therefore most of the floor, had to be obscured to insure the desired effect. Steinberg noted that "he leaves just enough floor in front of the table to satisfy the literal requirement of an autonomous space" [7].

Once Leonardo 'fixed' the perspective construction to cause the entering viewer to see the entire panorama as if it were staged in a three-dimensional room, the monks along the side walls could be included in this same plane. He then turned to the prior's seat, at the back of the room. Leonardo was aware that this viewing position is not a serious problem since the further away the viewer is from the mural the smaller the angular change, with the result that the view is still quite acceptable (Fig. 5). Once Leonardo took care of the viewing positions, he then combined his skill as a painter with the artifices of the theater.

In the theater set, the figures usually are positioned for a transient moment. The action directs us in how we follow the performance. In painting, however, the artist creates the action by influencing the viewer's eye movements [21]. Leonardo choreographs our eye-movements, not only from the moment we first see the mural at the entrance to the hall but from whatever position we take.

As we enter the 'theater' by walking through the doorway, our eye is directed towards Christ and then to the left corner on the wall behind Him. Then a group of lines and objects carries our eye around the *Last Supper:* the tapestries; positions and hands of the figures; the converging lines directed out from Christ's feet [7]; the lines leading to the vanishing point behind His head; and then immediately forward to Christ Himself. The strong vertical line of Christ that draws us from Christ's upper torso and down to His feet guides our eye up and down before the direction is changed either by zooming off to the left on one of the converging lines from His feet that catches our eye or by the orthogonals that pull us to the left side of the painting. Even though we have a number of visual directions away from Christ, we finally have no choice but to start the tracking on the left wall (Fig. 1).

As Steinberg noted, "while the tapestried wall on the left slopes predictably downward, the corresponding slope on the right seems to climb [7]. The wall on the left not only is darker than the wall on the right but also is longer. Furthermore, the tapestries on the right change in size in a more radical way than do those on the left.

The eye reaches the upper right corner of the largest-appearing tapestry on the right wall and is then directed to the center vertical again by following the converging lines to the feet and straight up to Christ, or by latching onto the hands of the Apostles which point to (and carry the eye back to) Christ.

Because the image is blurred during the movement [21], our eye may start the trip down the tapestries or, at times, be fooled into following a line of a design painted on the Refectory wall that appears to be an extension of the line at the top of the tapestries in the painting. The eye may move back and forth on this line before continuing down the left side of the room to travel the path back to Christ.

It is widely noted that Leonardo painted the margins on the sides of the Fresco in an unclear manner to cause conflicting readings of the position of the table [7]. Therefore, as we track the painting we may be influenced by how we interpret the margins as to whether we view Christ and His table in our space, or whether He is seen positioned in a space of His own. If we see the margins as part of the side walls of the Fresco, then the walls come forward enough to include Christ and the table. But, if the margins appear to be frames outside the Fresco, Christ and His table are halfway between the painted room and the actual space. Besides blurring the contours of the margins, Leonardo again hid his intentions by applying his *sfumato* [22] technique to Christ, the Apostles and the table to hide the discrepancies in their relative sizes.

To add to the ambiguity of the depicted room's relationship to the Refectory, Leonardo painted a top frontispiece to make it more difficult to connect the real and painted ceiling lines. The depth of the ceiling and the disappearance of the coffers beneath the fake painted molding pull us into the Fresco's room, while at the same time keeping us outside. The molding is analogous to the frame in a theater. Just as stage designers disguise their sets, Leonardo resorted to the above devices, as well as to the unevenly sized tapestries on their contrasting 'walls', to add a final dimension to the depth-illusion presented by this unique work of art.

SUMMARY

In creating a painting as if setting a stage, Leonardo tilted the floor, painted an over-sized table and tilted it, designed side walls of uneven lengths with tapestries of different sizes and spacing, disguised the margins and the disparate sizes of Christ and the Apostles, and positioned his lighting to create the strongest illusion for the desired effect—the visitor's first view of the painting. From that key first impression, the spectator is drawn into the Fresco by Christ's hand. When the monks took their seats along the walls, these principal locations continued the illusion and, in addition, provoked the feeling that Christ was in the room with them.

The view depicts Christ along a vertical line as if crucified. The viewer's eyes are drawn downward to His feet, splayed on the raked stage, as if nailed to the cross. But this is no ordinary crucifix. This is a stage—raised before the viewer—that foretells the events to come. Leonardo gave all who entered the Refectory a window onto that stage. In Leonardo's theater, as in a successfully designed and directed theater, the audience feels part of the production rather than outside it, by the artist's ingenious handling of the accelerated perspective of a stage set, as described above.

The capabilities of a high-performance, multi-processor computing system have allowed us to re-create Leonardo's stage to examine and view the Fresco from any position in the Refectory. We could compare linear and accelerated perspective projections. The results suggest Leonardo's use of 'false' perspective in the staging of his *Last Supper.* He plucked from the theater the elements of this type of projection to draw his audience into the work. His ploys were disguised by the application of unique artistry.

The analysis, along with the computer model, shows how Leonardo was led to design his own perspective scheme to construct the *Last Supper,* altering the laws of linear perspective so that they could be integrated with the 'accelerated' perspective used in theater. This construction provided optimal vantage points for all who entered at the door as well as for the monks who sat along both sides of the Refectory [23, 24].

Acknowledgments

I thank Mauro Broggi and Eugenio Battisti for architectural drawings of the Refectory; Gerard Holzmann, Michael Potmesil and Dave Gibbon for help with the image processing; Douglas McElroy for assistance with "Sky" program; Douglas Blewett for programs; David Burr, Joe Condon, Tom Duff, Thrasyvoulos Pappas, Thomas Papathomas, Dave Slepian and Frank Sinden for discussions; the Pixel Machine™ developers; Leonard McMillan for rendering the raytracing of the model; Thorsten von Eicken for the interactive tools; and Jack and Laurens Schwartz for editorial assistance. I also thank Donna McMillan, for help in constructing the data base for the three-dimensional model, and Arno Penzias, who gave excellent advice in the writing of this manuscript.

References and Notes

1. Michael Kubovy, *The Psychology of Perspective and Renaissance Art* (Cambridge University Press, 1986) pp. 32, 140, 149.

2. Samuel Y. Edgerton, Jr., *The Renaissance Rediscovery of Linear Perspective* (Harper & Row, 1975) pp. 5, 42–49.

3. Leonardo's Perspective Study for the *Adoration of the Magi* (Original: Uffizi, Florence) and pen-and-ink sketch for the *Adoration of the Magi* (Original: Louvre, Paris) are reproduced in Bruno Santi, *Leonardo da Vinci* (Scala Books, dist. by Harper & Row, 1981) pp. 19 and 20.

4. Francis M. Naumann, *The 'costruzione legittima' in the reconstruction of Leonardo da Vinci's "Last Supper"* (Arte lombarda, 1979) pp. 63–89.

5. Carlo Pedretti, *Leonardo A Study in Chronology and Style* (Harcourt Brace Jovanovich, 1982) pp. 68–76.

6. Frederick Hartt, *Italian Renaissance Art* (Harry N. Abrams, 1979) p. 401.

7. Leo Steinberg, "Leonardo's *Last Supper,*" *Art Quarterly* **36**, No. 4, 297, 355–401 (1973).

8. Allardyce Nicoll, *The Development of the Theatre* (Harcourt, Brace & World, Inc., 1966) pp. 69–92.

9. In the modern world, photographers achieve accelerated perspective through the use of a fish-eye lens. The exaggerated size of Christ in the middle of the progressively decreasing sizes of the Apostles, and the sharply tapered walls, ceiling and floor suggest that Leonardo, who understood the principles of lenses, employed some form of a fish-eye lens concept. However, the fact that the table line appears straight against this procedure because the use of a fish-eye lens leads to curvature. Instead, the absence of curvature in the Fresco leaves the possibility of an accelerated, rectilinearly based perspective.

10. The original drawing (at Windsor, 12542r) is reproduced in Ludwig H. Heydenreich, *Leonardo The Last Supper* (Viking Press, 1974). See pp. 32–41.

11. Compositional study for the *Last Supper* (c. 1493–94, Venice Academy, 254r) is reproduced in Carlo Pedretti, *Leonardo Studies for the Last Supper* (Cambridge University Press, 1983) pp. 28, 43.

12. Most likely there was a cat-walk or a raised step at the entrance, at the same level as the platform underneath the monk's tables and chairs, designed to protect from the cold beneath. (Such Renaissance catwalks survive to the present day.)

13. *Il Paradiso,* Leonardo's stage design, Codex Arundel 263, folios 224r and 231V, reconstructed for the Elmer Belt Library of Vinciana by Howard Kahl, Dept. of Theater Arts, UCLA; Metropolitan Museum of Art, *Sketch for scene from Baldassare Taccone's play "Danae",* 1490 by Leonardo.

14. Warman Welliver, "Symbolic Meaning in Leonardo's and Raphael's Painted Architecture", *Art Quarterly* **2**, No. 1, 37–66 (1979); 'True Room' is approximately 80.0 meters long by 9.7 meters wide by 7.25 meters high.

15. Rudolf Arnheim, *Art and Visual Perception* (Univ. of California Press, 1969) pp. 268, 269–270, 275, 276, 364, 365.

16. The Pixel Machine™ is a high-performance image computer, which offers super-computer power dedicated to three-dimensional graphics and image processing.

17. Carlo Pedretti, *Leonardo Architetto* (Milan, 1978; London, 1979); Eugenio Battisti, letter to L. Schwartz, 2-3-88: "Consider that the original floor was almost a meter below the modern one." Barcilon and Brambilla, "Il Cenacolo di Leonardo in Santa Maria Delle Grazie" (Olivetti, 1984) p. 4.

18. W.B. Green, *Digital Image Processing* (Van Nostrand Reinhold, 1983) p. 113.

19. Texture-mapping graphics: the addition of texture to an otherwise smooth surface. The digitized image (the photograph of the *Last Supper* was translated into binary form) was positioned on the 'wall' of the 3-D model of the Refectory.

20. Robert Morris, *Sky:* a program that calculates the azimuth and elevation from the latitude, longitude, date and time of day. *UNIX Programmer's Manual* (AT&T Bell Laboratories, 1981).

21. Mark Fineman, *The Inquisitive Eye* (Oxford Univ. Press, 1981) pp. 130, 131.

22. Lillian Schwartz, "Leonardo's *Mona Lisa*", *Art & Antiques* (January 1988) p. 53.

23. The data from which the floor texture and the window dimensions were taken were derived inadvertently from a different epoch. These inaccuracies do not affect the analysis reported above.

24. Note added in proof: Recent findings reported by Pietro Marani, Soprintendenza per i Beni Artistici e Storici of Milan, now indicate that the Refectory floor was actually some 20 cm below the level adopted for the perspective models described above. This new result strengthens the conclusions of the present discussion by bringing the Renaissance viewer's eye closer to the point at which the painted tapestry comes into exact congruence with the lines of the real room.

State-of-the-Art Art

Seth Shostak

ABSTRACT

The author muses on the emergence of electronic art, especially computer animation, as seen from a technical perspective. The ability to make realistic imagery with computers is only a recent development, and, because of its newness, both access to and capabilities of electronic imaging are still limited. But comparison with earlier technical innovations gives some insight into how creative designers will likely react to this promising technology.

Hardware, Software and Art

Computer imaging began not with the artists but with the engineers. It is not so much that designers felt a need for computer graphics but rather that technical people saw a possibility for it. The first to use the computer to generate pictures were engineers and scientists. The former were interested in data display and the latter were keen to do image processing, a specialized discipline whose pursuit was the stimulus for much of today's graphics capability.

The earliest computer graphics systems were based on modified oscilloscopes, instruments that could rapidly draw freestyle lines on the face of a phosphor screen. These systems were designed to display data, for example the location of planes in the vicinity of an airport, and the degree of detail in the image depended on how fast the oscilloscope could be fed information.

Vector graphics, which refers to high-speed oscilloscope systems, was soon adopted by the early practitioners of computer animation. Although most suitable for wire-frame renditions, vector graphics could be adapted to simple filled-in images by drawing a multitude of lines to cover an area. Achieving color was a messy business: three separate exposures on 35-mm film were made through a red-green-blue filter wheel.

Although much fundamental work was done on vector machines, the big breakthrough in computer graphics occurred when computer and television technology were coupled. Unlike their high-speed, free-wheeling oscilloscope brethren, television displays are disciplined creatures of habit. Beginning in the upper left corner of the screen, they methodically trace out an image line-by-line until reaching the bottom. This they do a fixed number of times per second, irrespective of how fast or how slowly the input changes.

What television systems lack in speed (they are maddeningly slow for drawing simple lines) they make up in tonal and chromatic resolution. Grey scale and color are simply added. Furthermore, such systems are easily coupled to video recorders for later playback. The semi-discrete nature of television (a fixed number of horizontal lines) soon led to identifying each picture element on the screen with a memory location in a frame buffer. Raster graphics, the name given to television-based systems, forms the core of most modern graphics computers, whether they be two-dimensional paint devices or three-dimensional animation packages.

While only 5 years ago raster images of simple objects would elicit gasps of amazement, the rapid improvement in technology, in both hardware and software, has made such imagery commonplace. Amazement has given way to nonchalance and occasional cynicism: "Computer graphics, sure. But all those flipping logos? Where's the art?"

In the following I consider whether 'the art' is coming . . . and if so, when?

What Is Art, Anyway?

As one with a technical background, I am ill qualified to define 'art', although in this respect I appear not to be alone. Fortunately, recognizing art seems to be somewhat easier than defining it. As a functional definition, we might say that art consists of ideas that stimulate an emotional response, packaged in such a way that others can experience them.

Thus, good packaging is a necessity for art. But by itself, good packaging, or 'technique', is not sufficient. From paintings and photographs to computer animation, there is much imagery to be seen that is technically excellent, but that few would characterize as art.

It is the confusion of technique and message that leads to disputes over the value of electronic imagery. At first, the sheer novelty of electronically produced pictures was sufficient cause for excitement. The promise of a new technique generated widespread hope amongst those who saw in computer graphics a fresh medium to be exploited. Today, the technique has reached adolescence, and the novelty is gone. If there is disappointment or criticism, it is from those who now wish to see emotional content in the packaging. The medium is not sufficient as message.

It Has Happened Before

Beginning with the Industrial Revolution, major new techniques of imaging have appeared at intervals of about 40 years. In the early part of the last century, the camera obscura made it possible for dilettantes to trace out drawings of landscapes and other static scenes without the benefit of an artist's training or talent. Much like today's camera-toting tourists, the travellers of those days took along these primitive assemblages of mirrors and lenses to record as best they could the local views. Traditional landscape artists at first re-

Seth Shostak, DIGIMA Computer Animation, Kapteyn Institute, Postbus 800, 9700 AV Groningen, The Netherlands.

Received 5 May 1988.

Pergamon Press plc. Printed in Great Britain.
0024-094X/88 $3.00+0.00

jected but then adopted the camera obscura, ultimately finding it an aid to achieving realism, particularly in rendering perspective.

The problem with the camera obscura was that it still involved laborious hand copying of the image. This was solved with the development of photography, and for the first time traditional artists were confronted with serious competition. Their initial response was to reject the new medium as inadequate. But as photography improved technically (and, in the process, displaced much of conventional portraiture) artists accepted the inevitable and sought expression in alternatives to realism.

Later developments improved the accessibility of photography. Once it was no longer the exclusive province of those with technical flair, photography began to be explored by creative artists. Today, no one denies that this medium can be used for artistic purposes. It has been adopted as one more 'conventional medium'.

This push-pull cycle of technology and artistic application—rejection, acceptance, exploration and finally adoption—seems to be the natural form of interplay between creative artists and new engineering developments. A similar process is now underway for two-dimensional graphics. Two decades ago, pioneering research by Ivan Sutherland resulted in the first electronic 'sketch pad', a scheme for drawing with the computer. This silicon sketch pad had less resolution—spatial, tonal and chromatic—than a real sketch pad, and it was far less handy. Nonetheless, it had a potentially important capability: it allowed the artist to *edit*. He or she could endlessly reproduce objects drawn once, cut and paste seamlessly, erase and displace. Later technological developments reduced some of the resolution limitations while improving the interface and capabilities. An additional possibility of recent vintage is the ability to 'input' (via camera or scanner) external images for further manipulation. Suddenly, electronic montage was easy. What only a decade ago still was seen as a mere technological toy is now the workaday tool for many commercial designers. Rejection has given way to acceptance, and the appearance of 2-D paint systems in art academies signals the beginning of the phase of exploration by a wider group of artists.

Computer animation, involving as it does both motion and three-dimensional objects, is a far more intimidating medium than paint systems. Even today the best computer animation (in an artistic sense) requires considerable technical support. The construction of 3-D objects benefits from geometric insight and an analytic approach. Animation systems are still largely based on a key frame, a scheme that often suits the technologists better than skilled animators. Computer animation lags behind paint systems in terms of accessibility. Nonetheless, computer graphics, even animation, is apparently conforming to a well-established pattern. Born of the marriage of two technologies, it has seen its first efforts now improved to the point of being worthy of criticism. Rejection on esthetic grounds is giving way to its acceptance as a new medium, and some ambitious artists are already in the wings, anxious to begin exploration of its possibilities.

In this regard, it is probably fair to compare computer animation with the state of the motion picture at the beginning of the twentieth century. For a relatively long time after its invention, the motion picture was the exclusive province of the inventors. Screenplays were not filmed until 1903, and it was at this point, 15 years after Edison's first movie camera, that the new medium began really to develop its creative potential. Television experienced a similar history following its primitive beginnings between the world wars. Thus to ask "where is the art?" is premature. Where was photographic art in 1850, or cinematic art in 1890? The technology of computer graphics is still too young.

FUTURE TRENDS

Photography, cinematography and television were ultimately exploited by artists because they offered new creative possibilities. Computer animation can mechanize the tedious tasks of applying the laws of perspective and producing consistent lighting. The result is an opening of the screen with a convincing illusion of depth.

The problems of today's computer animation from the artist's point of view boil down to cost, complexity and lack of immediate feedback. Virtually all of the difficulties are engineering problems that will be largely overcome in the next decade. Creative designers will then have 'electronic clay', clay that, moreover, can move. Once the problems of accessibility have been overcome, we can expect that artists will once more begin to explore, and ultimately to adopt, this flashy new medium.

As an aside, it is worth noting that, despite the clear-cut analogy with earlier imaging technologies, not all is rosy for computer animation. The obvious future in which everyone can make animation at home (much as is the case with video today) is compromised by the difficulty of generating believable *human* characters, in terms of both shape and motion. Until this serious shortcoming is overcome, artists will have to content themselves with a medium devoid of living characters.

Computer graphics has generated a great deal of enthusiasm in its youth. But as it matures, some of the excitement inevitably palls. Attendance at last year's SIGGRAPH was down from a year before, and many of the technical sessions have become far too specialized and mathematical for the hordes of TV producers and graphics designers who used to attend. Firms specializing in computer animation have found a fickle market, and many have gone out of business. The technology is entering a new phase: one of greater accessibility, greater acceptance and less novelty. It is in the quiet backwaters of the first tidal wave of development that the art will be born.

A New Language for Artistic Expression: The Electronic Arts Landscape

Joan Truckenbrod

ABSTRACT

Are artists and electronic technology in harmony with one another? What is the character of the interface between artists and electronic technology? It is clear that electronic technology has made available to artists new modes of expressing ideas, feelings, emotions, insights, events and information and thus has expanded traditional means of artistic expression. However, the author observes, the integration of this technology into the creative process also has led to the development of a new language that provides a context for artistic expression with new modes of communication. The elements, the vocabulary, of this new language translate the nature of electronic technology into the realm of the artist, allowing the emergence of new experiential art forms. The language consists of elements that describe the creative process and influence the character of the final artwork. By means of electronic technology, this language can be used by artists to express and communicate multidimensional experiences involving sound, image and movement, permitting the expression of previously impossible syntheses and transformations of ideas. The resulting art is alive, responsive and interactive. Artists become choreographers synthesizing the numerous dimensions of human experience. The issue of how to get the spirit and soul of the artist into the computer—and back out into the world—is manifest in new visions of artistic expression in the electronic arts.

The intersection of artists and electronic technology is producing new art forms that differ from traditional art and are unique to the context of electronic technology. If we examine the process of creative expression in this context, it is clear that new modes of expressing ideas, feelings, emotions and insights have become available to artists. Thus electronic technology expands traditional means of artistic expression. However, the integration of this technology into the creative process also has necessitated the development of a *new language* that provides a context for artistic expression with new modes of communication. The elements of this new language translate the nature of electronic technology into the realm of the artist, allowing the emergence of new, experiential art forms.

A New Language

Because of the uniqueness of this technology in artistic expression, new modes of artistic communication and vehicles for artistic expression are emerging. These modes of communication form a new language for artists working in this area, and a new working vocabulary stimulates new artistic visions. There have been significant examples in other fields in which a new vocabulary of elements led to dramatic changes in the art and design work produced. In architecture, a significant transformation in design and building techniques resulted from the availability of new materials like steel. Ludwig Mies van der Rohe created a new approach to structural design with his steel-and-glass buildings. These buildings represented a major departure from traditional masonry structures. The structure became the design. These ideas are extended in the work of Helmut Jahn. His State of Illinois building in Chicago has a large and dramatic interior courtyard that extends the height of the building and provides a feeling of spaciousness. The outside becomes the inside with the architect's use of the glass skin of the structure. Offices are arranged around the perimeter of about half of the building. In this design there is a definition of the function and role of a building. This definition developed out of the new language in architectural design that emerged with the availability and use of steel building materials.

Another example of a new language resulting in new design forms is in the field of jewelry design and its extension into body adornment. Jewelry traditionally has been created from precious stones and metals. As jewelry designers have explored and experimented with new materials, such as plastics, wood, paper and polyester, a new design vocabulary has emerged. Carved polyester, for instance, gives rise to unique shapes and forms. The use of new materials also has extended the concept of jewelry to ornamentation in which body adornments also function as garments. New materials provide a new vocabulary for these designers in which innovative approaches to jewelry design are nourished.

One of the most striking examples of a new vehicle for communication or a new language of expression that expands the scope of a field is in music and its extension into electronic music. Electronic composers use a dramatically different musical vocabulary from that of traditional composers. Consequently, the nature of the process of electronic composition and the character of its sound images are a significant departure from traditional music. This set of new elements required the development of a new language, which facilitated the creation of innovative musical compositions. The evolution of electronic music is analogous to the evolution of two-dimensional, three-dimensional and four-dimensional electronic arts. Electronic devices provide a new mode of creating sound and new methods for creating and synthesizing sound images. Using these devices musicians can create sounds that could not be created with traditional instruments, opening up new dimensions of sound imaging and music composition.

Musicians can create sounds or sound images in a number of ways using electronic technology. Sound images can be created by digitizing sounds in the real world. Voices, notes played on instruments or noises, such as crumpling paper or popping open a soft-drink can, can be captured and manipulated for sound composition. In addition, sounds can be created by constructing the shape of a waveform that represents a sound. Thus, there are new acoustic elements available to artists and composers.

Joan Truckenbrod, Art and Technology Studies Program, The School of the Art Institute of Chicago, Columbus Drive and Jackson Blvd., Chicago, IL 60603, U.S.A.

Received 4 May 1988.

Pergamon Press plc. Printed in Great Britain.
0024-094X/88 $3.00+0.00

Sound sequences and music are created by combining and manipulating these electronic sound images. Sound is malleable and can be transformed easily. Sound images can be stretched or compressed in time by changing the frequency and the amplitude of the waveforms. Sound pieces or musical compositions can be edited in a manner similar to text editing or image processing. Segments can be cut out, moved around, repeated and reversed. Various aspects such as the octave, volume and speed can be changed easily. Sounds also can be mixed and repeated in various combinations to create new sound landscapes. For example, digital sound can be mixed with speech or sounds from the natural world. Mixing can be accomplished either by layering sound images on audio tape or through digital mixing, in which the sound waves of each individual sound are actually mixed together to create an entirely new sound. With electronic devices, musicians are working with a new vocabulary of sound images, using new tools and methods for transforming sounds and composing musical scores. This language of sound composition is analogous to, and part of, the new language emerging in electronic arts.

Fig. 1. (a) *Syllogism*, digital photograph, 24 × 26 in, 1986. (b) *Encoded Myth*, digital photograph, 24 × 26 in, 1987.

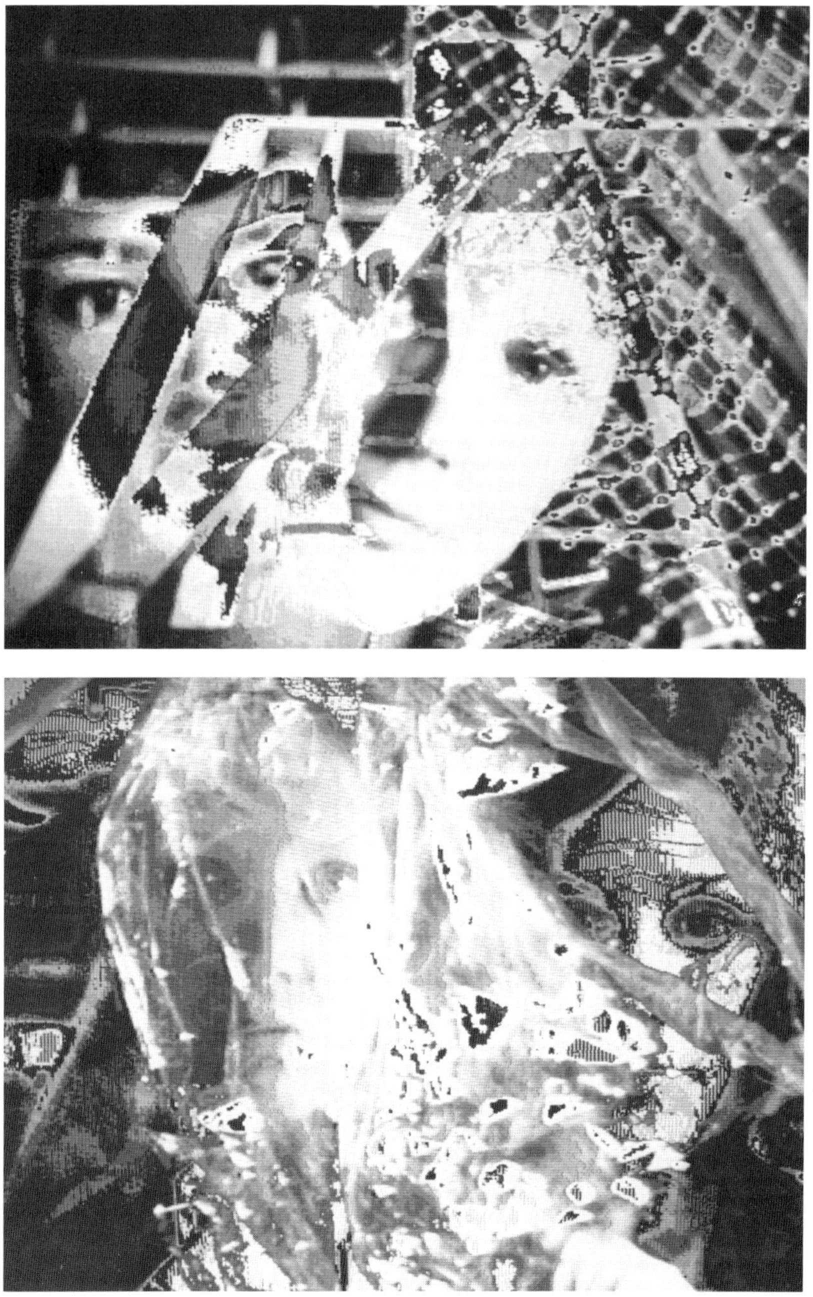

A New Vocabulary

Electronic technology provides a new communication landscape for creative expression in the arts. The electronic media are alive—titillating, experiential. The elements of this new landscape are malleability and transformability, responsiveness and transmittability. Artists create, synthesize and communicate experiences using this technology in a variety of ways. Artists communicate ideas and emotions by creating images, movement and sound with a variety of devices. Video digitizers and optical scanners facilitate visual communication with computers. Sound digitizers allow the artist to capture any type of sound image or event and transmit it to a computer. Electronic gloves and three-dimensional digitizers allow the artist to capture gestures: movement of the hand, arm or body sculpts in space, communicating form as well as movement to the computer. Emotions can be transmitted to a computer through the use of alpha and beta wave sensors. Thus electronic arts are experiential, for artists express ideas through visual images, sound sequences, body movement and emotions. Using electronic technology artists create experiences for the audience or participants that include visuals, sound and movement—individually or in conjunction with one another. Thus the electronic arts studio is a multidimensional studio environment that facilitates the creation of *experiential* art forms.

Malleability and Transformability

An important aspect of this new language is image and sound processing. Digital images and sound are infinitely malleable; consequently we have unlimited power to sculpt, shape and mold experiences into new forms. For example, any figure, object or environment recorded with a video camera or scanner can be transmitted to the computer, displayed on the screen and manipulated. In addition, the use of this video digitizer allows artists to create their own 'lenses' by specifying the way in which they want to see the world. Images can be captured as normal pictures, high-contrast images, contour maps or outlined figures. Scanning digitizers capture images during a time segment that allows the artist to create stretched, compressed or smeared images as well as multiple images in one frame. Changing the lighting during the scanning time creates unusual figure distortions. Images created in this manner are unique to computing systems.

In my own artwork I am processing and synthesizing images that express the complexities and dynamics of the relationship between parent and child. My current work confronts the fragmenting effects of differing behavioral roles. We assume various roles, as mothers, daughters, artists and friends, that push and pull us in different directions. Roles, as expected patterns of behavior, support certain behaviors and inhibit others. Consequently, they act as templates predetermining behavior that may or may not correspond to personal goals, dreams and fantasies. My work involves the process of resolving the multiplicity of roles, synthesizing personal experiences into a multidimensional model. The layers of patterns and screens in my images represent different roles and their undulating positions (see Fig. 1 and Color Plate A No. 1). At various times one of these 'role-planes' becomes predominant. Other time these planes recede into space, taking a secondary position. These role-planes also can act as an interference in some images as they block out or hide figures. The computer provides a vehicle for synthesizing these behavioral roles into digital portraits, making visible the complexities of psychological spaces that emerge between the multiple modes of behavior. My images are sensitive to the conflicts between roles and express the hidden dimension of the ongoing struggle to resolve these conflicts. The image in Fig. 2 expresses the anguish of the AIDS (acquired immune deficiency syndrome) epidemic and the trauma of the barriers between people that are necessitated by this disease. Plastic is used to separate people in times when people need closeness and support, representing the distancing between people that is occurring in this crisis.

Sound images as well as visual images are malleable. Students in my Experimental Computer Imaging class are currently exploring the nature of sound images and are creating sound landscapes by manipulating and layering sound images. I have students expressing ideas through sound in three ways and then synthesizing these sounds into a sequence or composition. Initially students work with

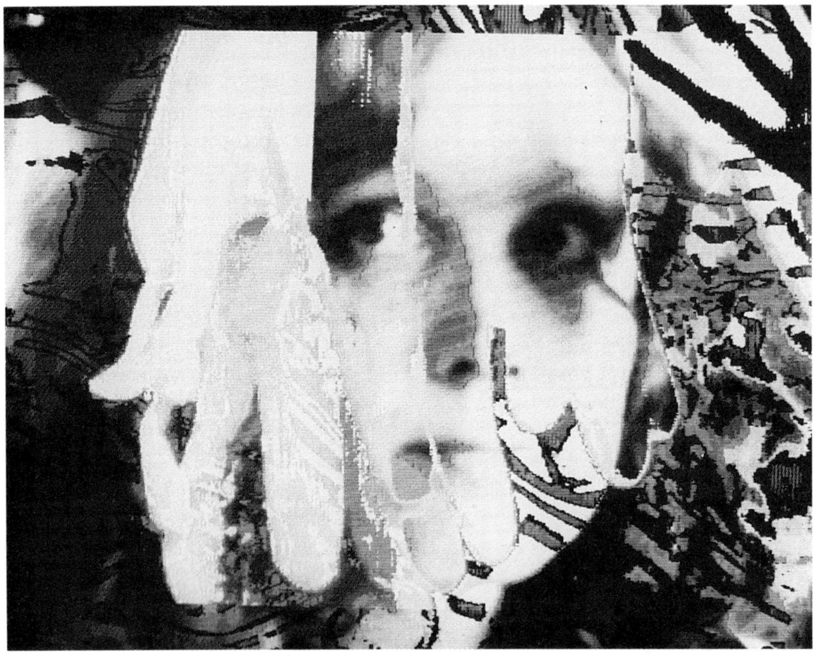

Fig. 2. ***Free Radical*****, digital photograph, 24 × 26 in, 1987.**

speech synthesis software, creating sound images or patterns using words, phrases or poems. By changing the tone, pitch, volume and accent they create interesting electronic sound images. In addition, they experiment with the sound of the repetition of letters and sets of letters. This process creates innovative sound images. Next students use an audio digitizer to capture the human voice and sounds from the natural world. These sounds are translated into a digital format and can be manipulated and processed. There is an interesting acoustical contrast between synthesized speech and the digitized voice that students explore and develop in their sound compositions. Finally, students work with music composition software to compose musical scores. Students approach this portion of the project visually as they create patterns on a grid or draw curves that represent the placement of sequences of notes. Using this software students can edit sound sequences through repetition, changing octaves and changing positions of notes.

After these three types of sound images are complete they are layered together on an audio tape into a sound landscape that undulates in time. Depending on the score created by each student, various types of sound fade in and out at different times in the composition. These sounds also can be digitally mixed to create totally new sound images. In addition to the sound landscape, students create visual images that correspond to the sound landscape. These visual compositions integrate the text from the audio tape with visual images. The students working on this project are beginning students in the electronic arts; they use Macintosh computers.

In addition to individual images and sounds, artists use computers to transform one type of experience into another type of experience. For example, sound can be transformed into images or images into sound sequences. Sound also can be transformed into movement in kinetic sculpture as sound can be used to create movement in a kinetic sculpture. Electronic technology provides a unique opportunity for artists to create art forms by transforming one type of experience into another.

Responsiveness

The interactive nature of electronic technology allows artists to create responsive environments or installations that engage participants in unique means of expression and communication. I have created an installation that uses the interactive nature of computers to create a responsive environment. This piece will be installed at the exhibition *Images du Futur '88, Art et Nouvelles Technologies* in Montreal during the summer of 1988. This project, titled "Expressive Reflections: Reflective Expressions", forms an 'experiential mirror' in which the voice and image of a participant undergo simultaneous related transformations. Participants experience their own speech transformed and played back through speakers and their own image transformed and concurrently displayed on a video screen. In this project I have fashioned an environment that transforms the world, giving the participants new ways of experiencing themselves through sound and image simultaneously. This installation provides an interactive experiential environment involving the essence of human experience expressed through sound/voice and facial images. The participant expresses an idea or feeling verbally and the installation captures the person's speech with an audio digitizer. At the same time the person's facial expression is captured using a video digitizer. The sound image—a word, phrase, song or noise—is then processed or changed and transmitted back to the participant via a computer program, to create a sound landscape that undulates in time. The visual image is simultaneously transformed and repeated on the display screen.

Initially the participant's voice is digitized and played back in its original form so the participant recognizes that a personal sound landscape is being formed with his or her voice. The voice pattern is manipulated, transformed and repeated to create a sequence of short sound landscapes. For example, the sound image is played more slowly, faster, backwards, upside-down, up an octave, down an octave and in combinations of these variations. The order of these sound transformations varies with each participant to create a sense of mystery about the nature of the phenomenon. Simultaneously the participant's face is digitized to capture the facial expression that corresponds to the expression in the voice. The digitized face is displayed on a series of video monitors and then is transformed in synchronization with the sound undulations. The image processing techniques used on the facial images include the formation of outlines, contour maps, negative and positive images, high-contrast images and various color transformations. The combination of sound and image provides an experiential mirror that captures the essence of an expression and creates multidimensional views of each participant.

Transmittability

Another element in this new language is the potential for transmitting an image or experience globally via telephone or satellite. That electronic arts are alive implies that images, sound and movement can be communicated anywhere in the world or into space. Ideas and experiences can be communicated instantaneously anywhere. These transmissions can be interactive since the receiver can work with an image and return it to the sender. In Vancouver in 1985 the Digicon Conference sponsored an international concert performed interactively via satellite by musicians in Canada, Germany and Japan. Theatre and dance events as well as contemporary performances can be choreographed involving performers who are in different geographical locations. Video teleconferencing has significant potential for innovative real-time performances that link distant locations. Another potential for electronic arts is the use and programming of public-access television stations. Art events can be created for distribution to a broad public audience. This is a very different context from traditional gallery exhibitions.

New Art Forms

Artists have new visions of artistic expression in the electronic arts studio. The new language of electronic arts is used by artists to express and communicate insights and sensitivities, to synthesize multidimensional experiences and to create a metamorphosis of ideas, images and experiences. Not only can the artist make statements individually in each of the areas of imaging, animation in form or video, kinetics, performance and sound composition, but the synergism of the computer studio allows artists to create experiences that involve a number of these components simultaneously. Computers offer artists the potential to convey the complexities of everyday life and culture. Images can be layered and synthesized in a manner that parallels the fabric of contemporary life. We live in an experiential world in which sound, speech, music, image and movement affect us at all times. Two-dimensional artwork attempts to represent our environment but does so in only one medium—a visual image; similarly, a concert represents only one facet of our environment. Since the computer allows the artist to choreograph sound, images and movement simultaneously, artistic expression via computer moves closer to the multidimensional experiences of our lives. The electronic artist will be akin to the Renaissance person exploring the fiber of human experience. Computers allow artists to create intimate, interactive relationships with their environment by synthesizing a multitude of sensory stimuli and sculpting this artistic sensitivity and perception into new art forms.

Bibliography

Anna Campbell Bliss, "'New Technologies of Art—Where Art and Science Meet': University of Utah Conference, 1985", *Leonardo* **19**, No. 4, 311–316 (1986).

S. Emmerson, ed., *The Language of Electroacoustic Music* (New York: Harwood Academic Publishers).

Myron W. Krueger, "*VIDEOPLACE:* A Report from the ARTIFICIAL REALITY Laboratory", *Leonardo* **18**, No. 3, 145–151 (1985).

Loren Means, "Digitization As Transformation: Some Implications for the Arts", *Leonardo* **17**, No. 3, 195–199 (1984).

J. Truckenbrod, *Creative Computer Imaging* (Englewood Cliffs, NJ: Prentice-Hall, 1988).

J. Truckenbrod, "Speakeasy", *New Art Examiner* (November 1987) pp. 13–14.

Stephen Wilson, "Environment-Sensing Artworks and Interactive Events: Exploring Implications of Microcomputer Developments", *Leonardo* **16**, No. 4, 288–292 (1983).

Some Issues in the Development of Computer Art as a Mathematical Art Form

Richard Wright

ABSTRACT

In this paper the author considers some of the issues that arise when mathematics is used to make art (predominantly visual art), in particular the possible conflicts between the role of the mathematician as artist and of the artist as mathematician. Mathematics in art can be approached in a number of ways, as analyses and 'simulations' of artworks and processes perhaps by artificially intelligent systems, as 'ready-made' mathematical objects appropriated by an artist, or as products of the creative imagination in their own right. These approaches are examined and criticised, and connections are made and used to highlight the difference between the mathematics *of* art and mathematics *as* art. The relevance of ideas in the theoretical history of computing and philosophy of mathematics is revealed and used to open up a critical context for this kind of computer art.

Mathematics has been an activity of crucial importance in human thought for many centuries, and no more so than now in this computer age. Yet its ways of thinking often seem an anathema to artistic values, its products remaining aloof, alien and detached from experience. Mathematics has also tended to stand apart from the empirical sciences. It does not seem to involve the same kind of inductive reasoning and the testing of theories against observation, but appears to be self-sufficient. In the great debate between the Rationalist and Empiricist philosophers of the eighteenth century, mathematics was the prime example of the human mind's ability to construct abstract theories of great power from pure deductive reasoning. Even when Kant tried to unite these tendencies of Western philosophy, he preserved the role of mathematics as the keeper of *a priori* logical truths.

"Mathematics is the science that draws necessary conclusions" was the definition attributed to mathematician Benjamin Peirce in 1881; it was a view echoed by many thinkers at the turn of the century [1]. Indeed mathematics does have this quality of certainty about it: its theorems follow inevitably from self-evident assumptions of axioms using the logical laws of non-contradiction. This feeling of completeness due to the conception of mathematics as a closed system causes many people to be surprised that there is such a thing as the creation of new mathematics at all.

The aim of this article is to reach an understanding of the nature of mathematical activity, a definition that might be useful to computer artists. We begin by asking what mathematics and art, as descriptions of the world, have in common. Firstly, how rational is art, is it a logical sort of process that just produces pictures instead of theorems, and can it therefore be appreciated in those terms? The answer to these questions will be neither yes nor no, but the discussion will be used to probe further the realms of mathematics and art.

Richard Wright, Centre for Advanced Study in Computer Aided Art and Design, Middlesex Polytechnic, Cat Hill, East Barnet, Herts, EN4 8HT, United Kingdom.

Received 27 April 1988.

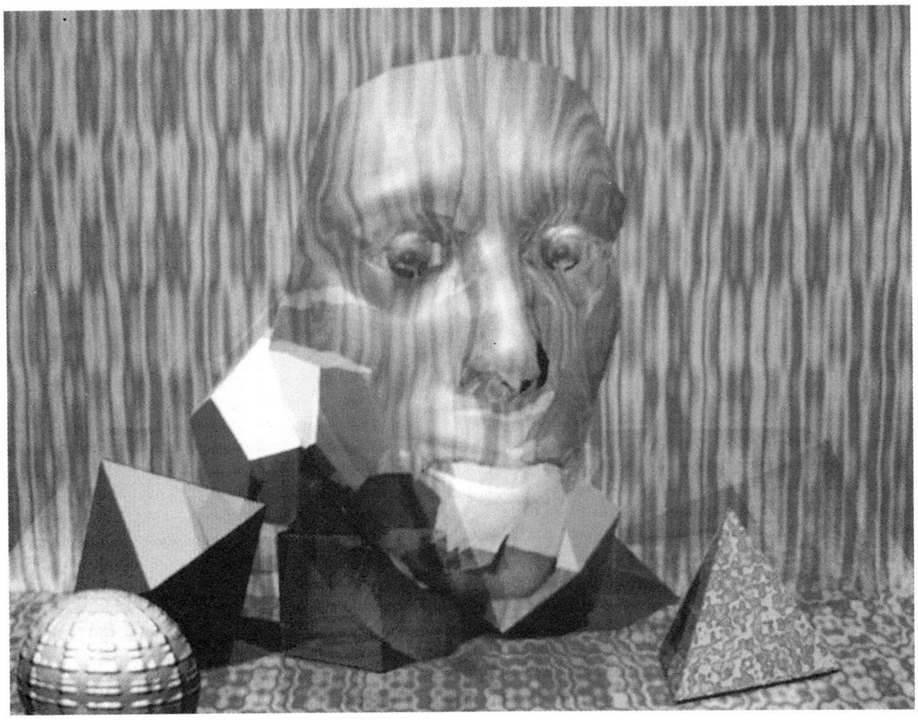

Fig. 1. Richard Wright, *The Disembodied Intelligence.* Face Model by Keith Waters. Software: artist's own software in 'C'. Hardware: VAX 11/785, Gems Framestore, Dunn Film Recorder. Format: 35mm slide of computer-generated image, 1988. The computer as a model of human intelligence is one essentially detached from its environment, existing somewhat out of context. In this image the familiar human visage is surrounded by objects symbolising the results of intelligence abstracting from the world it interacts with. These include the five regular Platonic solids as well as an irregular bump-mapped sphere and textured background. The face is rendered as transparent, to give a sense of both reality and unreality: an ethereal consciousness floating in a private world of mental constructs.

Pergamon Press plc. Printed in Great Britain.
0024-094X/88 $3.00+0.00

Mathematical models view the world as a sequence of precisely related events, and one might question whether art falls into this category or even if it is a relevant approach at all. Because art is regarded as reflecting the deepest experiences of the human mind, the mathematics of art might on the one hand imply a far-reaching explanation of the nature of psychological processes; on the other hand it might contribute just another theoretical tool to art-making, like colour theory did at the end of the nineteenth century.

The Computer as Artist

As part of the effort in recent years to explain aspects of human activity in terms of mathematical and computational processes, art and algorithmic aesthetics have received a certain amount of attention [2]. This has often taken the form of analysing existing artworks in order to reveal some mathematical structure in them, a structure perhaps not consciously intended by the artist but forming some subliminal deterministic basis to his or her artistic decisions. Before the advent of artificial intelligence research, the idea that aesthetic appreciation might have an underlying mathematical explanation was believed by many writers who sometimes conducted dissections of classical paintings to find some compositional format [3]. Just as the language of musical harmony was derived from geometrical ratios—legend has it by the philosopher/mathematician Pythagoras—geometry has often seemed an obvious starting point for a mathematical analysis of fine art, and developments this century have been no exception. Many of these attempts have since been criticised as being gratuitous, although it is well known that particular artists, especially of the early Renaissance, and some composers have used geometrical proportions as compositional aids [4].

The implication of much artificial intelligence work, however, is by extension to show that the mental processes going on inside the artist's head are also of an algorithmic nature and may also express themselves in artworks in the form of various mathematically defined characteristics. In order to be able to recognise a 'successful' creation of a work of art by a machine without having to wrestle with the philosophical problems of defining art explicitly, these scientists normally use a behavioural definition. It amounts to saying that if an art object produced by some 'artificial' method is generally accepted by its spectators as a genuine work of art, then it is so defined. Some early computer art was produced in a similar fashion by formulating a set of generative rules derived from a particular artist's style and then making them act upon a group of simple pictorial elements (e.g. A. Michael Noll's computer-generated 'Mondrians' [5]). The resultant images are then compared to actual examples of the origi-

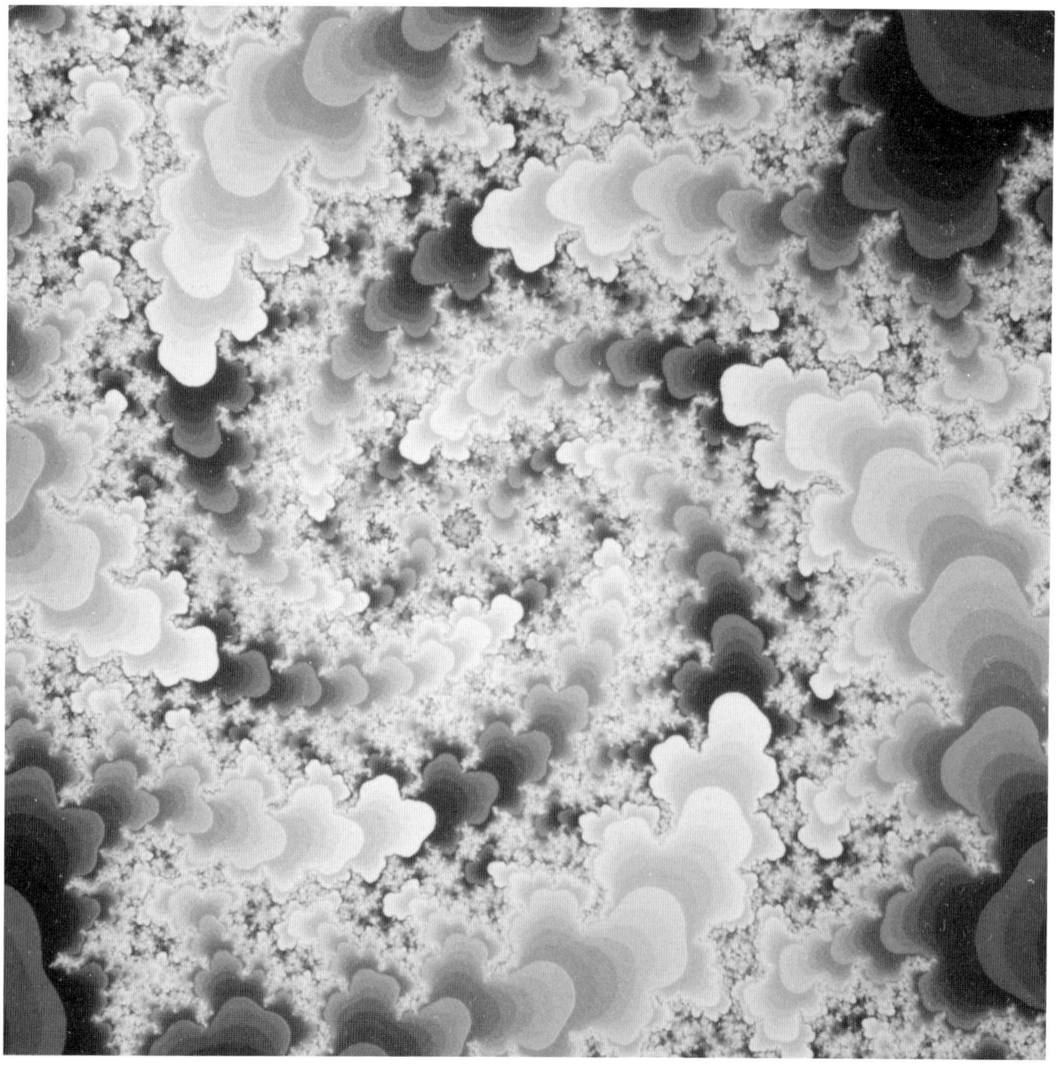

Fig. 2. Richard Wright, *Image from the Mandelbrot Set.* Software: artist's own software in Pascal. Hardware: IBM 4041, IBM 5080 Display. Format: photographic print of computer-generated image, 1985. An example of 'Map Art', mathematical objects produced and studied by mathematicians and also exhibited as art.

nal artist's work. More recently, and with substantial success, Harold Cohen has sought through his artificially intelligent program AARON to simulate the pictorial forms of his earlier painting style [6]. Though the program begins with basically random elements, it is guided by a highly sophisticated system of aesthetic rules that Cohen has built up by carefully observing his own artistic methods and preferences.

Instead of being the results of autonomous art-making, though, these works might be seen as an extended form of reproduction, of a pictorial style. What is the point of these mathematical 'forgeries', of computer-automated art, filling the world with plotter drawings like the model T Ford? The possibility of the computer as an 'original' artist does not in itself tell us much about what to expect from such art, what issues it would address. Although these criticisms might appear premature, the most obvious difference between this behavioural approach to making art and what artists actually do is something in philosophy called intentionality—it concentrates on *how* art is produced rather than *why* [7]. Attempts to explain why an artist might have chosen a particular style or what the artist hopes to achieve by engaging in this occupation are not considered relevant to the computer model. But is not this sort of criticism also vulnerable to the same argument that is used to construct it? Namely, that it in turn ignores the reasons why this attempt to re-create a work of art was undertaken by computer scientist/artists in the first place. Perhaps their implied belief that nature is mathematically determined is as good an artistic reason as any, though this would mean their having to include themselves and their motives in their model of art. So in what sense could a computer model an artist's behaviour? This leads us to a consideration of mathematics as a system of representation and of its limitations, especially as regards the problems of artificial intelligence.

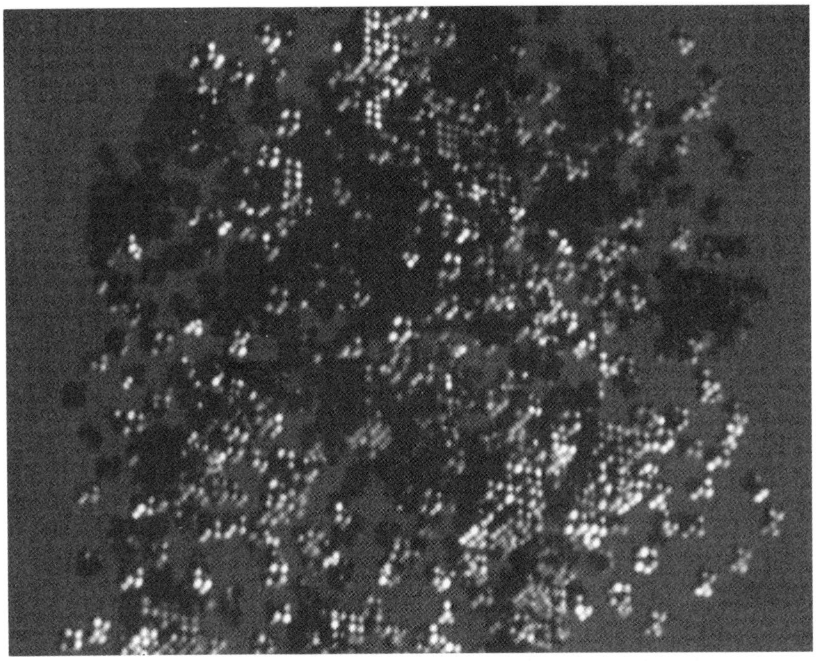

Fig. 3. Richard Wright, *Cellular Object No. 3*. Software: artist's own software in 'C'. Hardware: VAX 11/785, Gems Framestore, Dunn Film Recorder. Format: 35mm slide of computer-generated image, 1987. A set of data has been generated by a cellular growth algorithm, modeled using spheres and rendered using ray-tracing. The object is composed of several thousand individual particles, points picked out of a 3-D lattice, forming clumps of varying shapes and sizes. They were coloured by a solid texturing function to suggest an alternative form of coherence for this imaginary structure.

AI and Problems of Semantics

In his paper that has come to provide so much of the theoretical justification for artificial intelligence research, Alan Turing introduced a definition of intelligence by which machine intelligence could be assessed [8]. Turing proposed an operational definition of thinking called the Imitation Principle. He described a game in which an interrogator would have to decide which of two people, a man and a woman, was the woman on the basis of written replies to questions. Both were allowed any method of persuasion except practical demonstrations to try to convince the interrogator that they were the woman. The point was that the successful imitation of the woman by the man would not prove anything, because gender was based on physical facts not reducible to symbols. In contrast to this, Turing argued that the method *would* apply to intelligence, so that a computer would be displaying intelligent behaviour if the interrogator could not tell a computer apart from a man. There was no way of judging whether people were thinking intelligently other than by comparison with oneself, and he saw no reason to treat computers any differently.

As to whether the human senses, muscular activity and bodily chemistry were relevant to thinking, Turing wrote:

> It will not be possible to apply exactly the same teaching process to the machine as to a normal child. . . . one could not send the creature to school without the other children making excessive fun of it. . . . We should not be too concerned about the lack of eyes, legs, etc. The example of Miss Helen Keller shows that education can take place provided that communication in both directions between teacher and pupil can take place by some means or other.

For his proposed subjects for automation Turing chose only those that involved no contact with the outside world—chess, mathematics, cryptoanalysis, anything that was primarily a matter of technique. This approach assumed that the physical characteristics of the brain and body had no direct bearing on intelligent activity, that it was possible to abstract the essential properties of thinking and limit them to symbol manipulation. But the purpose of intelligent behaviour is to guide the human organism through its dealings with the outside world. Can there be such a thing as a disembodied intelligence, detached from its environment and existing somewhat out of context? Should a discussion of intelligence be limited to what goes on inside our heads or must it include an organism's entire way of life? Intelligence operates in order to effect changes in the world in which it lives; otherwise it is a meaningless game, devoid of a *raison d'être.*

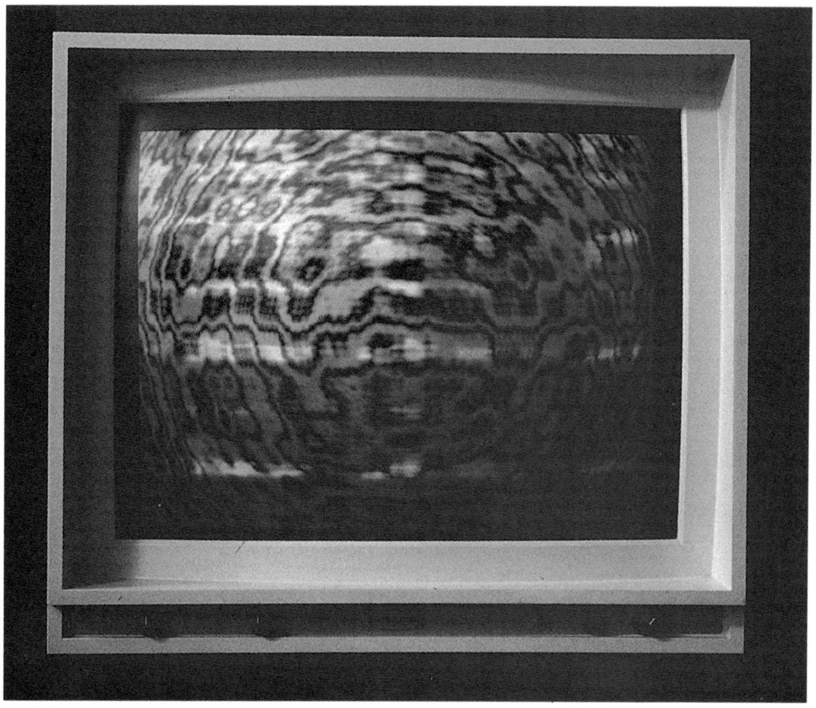

Fig. 4. Richard Wright, *Window*. Software: artist's own software in 'C'. Hardware: VAX 11/785, Ikon Framestore. Format: 35mm slide of computer-generated image, 1988. Two surfaces have been rendered in close-up in order to create an ambiguity between the image as a representation of a solid object and the physical reality of the picture plane. A transparent cover is shielding us from another surface beyond, like a view through the glass of the screen.

Turing anticipated some objections to his thesis:

> May not machines carry out something which might be described as thinking but which is very different from what a man does? This objection is a very strong one, but if we can construct a machine to play the imitation game we should not be troubled by this objection.

In any case the disembodied Turing machine would naturally display an intelligence very different from human intelligence. Building a thinking machine might be as appropriate as trying to breed a flower that barked like a dog.

At first it might seem justified to build a behavioural representation of the artistic process that does not include artistic motivation—as long as the computer system is capable of making objects that other people can respond to as art then one has indeed succeeded in producing bona fide artworks. Supposedly no one would need to know why or even how they had been made. But to concentrate attention on the art object in its final state without regard to the context in which it was made would be to neglect the function of artistic endeavours. Normally it is difficult to see how it can make sense to talk of 'simulating' or 'modelling' art, because the model always tends to become part of the artwork itself. If we see a computer-simulated Mondrian next to a 'real' Mondrian, for instance, then obviously much of the meaningfulness of that comparison is generated by the knowledge that one was created by a human and the other by a machine. To take this one stage further, if the spectator is deliberately prevented from gaining knowledge of how the work was created, or given false information regarding this, then it would seem wise to regard part of the content of the resulting artwork as being determined by the motive behind this act of deception. To doom the spectator to perpetual ignorance concerning the true origins of what is being presented as art is to deny one of the great objectives of art: a means of gaining self-knowledge. How much of ourselves would we see reflected in an 'autonomous' computer's art? Would we feel sympathy with it or alienation?

A mind is a bit like a stone falling into a pond and sending ripples travelling out all over the surface and bouncing back again from the banks. We might point to the center of the ripples where the stone first struck and say 'Here is a mind', but we must also look beyond this to the undulating surface where the interference of many drops is apparent. A computer is then like a plastic beaker half filled with water; it can gently bob up and down to the rhythm of the waves and its contents are also the constituents of the pond water, but it is essentially sealed from its environment. To accurately model the complex dynamics of turbulent flow, research suggests we need an explicit simulation rather than to study particles in isolation [9]; perhaps to build a really human-like mind it would be necessary to model a whole society of minds. But the computer-mind, of course, is already functioning in a society of minds—the human society that spawned it—and it can be semantically grasped only with respect to that social context.

It has been suggested that we can either use the computer in a premeditated way for a particular end like any other medium or tool, or else leave it to operate without human interference as much as possible, presenting the results later, for the viewer to provide semantic content [10]. But we cannot unload our artistic responsibilities onto the computer quite so easily as this. If we agree that art is a language and that its functioning depends on our sharing a common cultural context, then we must concede that an artist and his or her public do not operate in isolation from one another. To function as an artist, an artificially intelligent machine would have to be aware of the world of social intercourse, but this does not mean that it cannot produce art, as long as we recognise the wider significance of the computer in human affairs as part of the context in which the artwork is understood.

The use of computer-generated art as a way of revealing and exploring some intrinsic language of the machine itself is to suggest a rather more independent and objective relationship between human and machine than seems justified. But this idea that mathematical systems have a 'life of their own' is something that we shall return to later. We now turn our attention from the computer as artist to the mathematician as artist, to see if an examination of mathematical research can tell us a little more about the mathematical models that are implemented on and that define the operation and nature of the computer.

Platonism and Formalism in Mathematics and Art

Most mathematicians feel themselves to be discovering true and objective facts about mathematical objects (i.e. Platonism [11]), while artists have always been seen as the individual creators of what they produce. If we accept this view of mathematical activity, then artists working with mathematics (presenting mathematical objects as art) are put in the position of appropriating a kind of mathematical 'readymade' by placing it in an artistic context [12]. But can artists legitimately feel they are able to create their 'own' mathematical objects? Are they not rather in the position of selecting certain structures that already exist conceptually in an external mathematical world?

Probably the most successful recent exhibition of mathematical art was 'Map Art', images of iterative mappings in the complex plane, produced by a team of mathematicians and physicists at the University of Bremen in West Germany [13]. These images were colour plots of the parameter spaces and dynamics of some non-linear functions, particularly of the simplest one called the Mandlebrot set. They were created not with artistic issues in mind but for mathematical research and for their interest as mathematical objects. (It is still a common presumption that geometric complexity is equivalent to semantic complexity; this tends to promote the view that pictures of dynamic systems are more 'artistic' because of their visual irregularities. This idea, however, is misleading. Islamic art, for instance, is an expression of a vast religious and cultural belief system, but when taken out of context it appears to many Western eyes as wallpaper patterns.) Visually the images are striking; they seem to exhibit a fairly ordered nesting of catherine wheel spirals and paisley patterns but with an infinite degree of detail that one would not normally associate with regular forms. They do not appear 'mechanical', but are still too precise to be manufactured by human hands. When we come to confront them as art, how are we to come to terms with their existence as mathematical phenomena with objective properties, seemingly independent of their discoverers, almost like the products of the artificially intelligent art machines discussed above?

Variations of this impersonal aspect of mathematical art emerge when we consider the question of authenticity. When a mathematician or scientist has published the results of his research then that work seems to become the common property of the scientific community. It is not appropriate to try to pursue ownership rights over a law of nature. Mandelbrot did not copyright his set of points so that artists would not be able to use them. It might be argued that although no individual can claim exclusive right to a scientific theory that is part of the general intellectual achievements of humankind, he or she could take out a patent on a particular *application* of that knowledge. Likewise an artist might share his ideas about art with his fellows and examine the work of others, but any particular painting or sculpture that he executes is his and his alone. But the situation is not always this straightforward. Consider an artist (or mathematician) using a mathematical function to generate images that he intends to exhibit as art. While he is at lunch another 'artist' comes into his studio/laboratory and generates a completely different image just by tweaking one of the parameters of the function. Is this small act enough to warrant the intruder as the creator of a new work? And in any case does the original artist have any more right to a mathematical object whose existence might seem as objective as the sun in the sky? In addition, due to the mechanical or electronic means of production, no appeal to individuality can be made by emphasising any stylistic attributes caused by a traditional manual execution of the picture. If an artist engages in mathematical research, can this in any sense be an artistic activity? If the artistic act lies mainly in the appropriation of a particular mathematical object into an artistic context, we are close to saying that mathematics cannot in itself be used as a language for art and that the artist's role is little more than that of a selector.

It is difficult to explain the power of mathematics when applied to the external world except by an appeal to some kind of objective existence. For example, before the First World War David Hilbert had developed a generalaistion of Euclidean geometry which involved a space of infinitely many dimensions. Later John Von Neumann used these 'Hilbert spaces' to make precise the idea of the state of a quantum-mechanical system like an electron in a hydrogen atom. Likewise in 1932 physicists discovered the positron, whose existence had been predicted some years before by P.M. Dirac on the basis of an abstract mathematical theory. The expansion of pure mathematics for its own sake has often borne unexpected fruit in science [14].

No one today would try to demand the empirical justification of different mathematical systems such as the 'truth' of Euclidean or non-Euclidean geometry, and mathematicians are free to choose between the two. Since the nineteenth century, mathematics has come to be seen more and more as a creation of the human mind, and Platonism as a philosophy has declined. Platonism had originally been a belief in the intuitive truths of the axioms of Euclidean geometry, but after the discovery of non-Euclidean geometry and the existence of counter-intuitive objects such as in Cantor's theory of infinite sets, there arose a concern that intuition could not be trusted [15]. Mathematical objects were to be considered valid only if they could be derived rigourously by logical deduction from a set of axioms. Perhaps the logical basis of mathematics guaranteed its correspondence with the orderly laws of nature.

At first there was an attempt to reduce the foundations of mathematics to set-theoretical logic (e.g. Frege, Russell et al.), but when that proved too problematic mathematicians turned to place their faith in the logical consistency of language itself. The resulting philosophy formulated by David Hilbert was called Formalism, and although his ultimate goal of proving the consistency and completeness of mathematics as a formal system was shown by Kurt Gödel not to be possible, it became the dominant foundationist dogma. Formalism avoided the Platonic absolute character of mathematical existence and gave mathematicians the freedom to explore alternative axiomatic systems, but by concentrating on the logical syntax of the language it denied that mathematics was 'about' anything and tended to empty mathematics of meaning [16]. This century many Constructivist artists have pursued 'formal relationships' [17], but this has led to the appearance of a certain sterility in their work and an aversion to mathematics by many other artists.

The formal analysis of mathematical language led to the idea that if mathematical propositions were derived logically and consistently from the axioms in a mechanical fashion, then maybe the process could be completely automated. This resulted in the 1930s in the beginnings of computer science in the form of the Turing machine, the only machine conceivably powerful or general enough possibly to be able to solve any mathematical problem put to it. But rather than reach any final conclusion on the limits of mathematics, the project launched a whole new field of study in mathematical logic and the theory of automata, emphasising the open-ended nature of the issues it was developed to settle once and for all.

It can be a source of amusement to ponder the total number of images that, theoretically, could be produced on a digital framestore. As a problem in combinatorics it is easily solved by raising the total number of colours available in one pixel by the total number of pixels addressable. Even for a framestore of moderate capacity this number is immense (16 million raised to the half million would be fairly common), and this number is usually very much larger than the total number of particles in the known universe (about 10 to the 80). It is interesting to speculate on the advantages of working through and classifying this set of all possible images—it would include the faces of everyone who ever lived, a page or two of text from every book ever written, a copy of every painting executed and all possible variations of each, as well as all sorts of mathematical graphics and diagrams. But supposing the number of all possible pictures in digital form was much smaller than this, only about a thousand, say, and supposing someone generated all these pictures and exhibited them in a large gallery. What would this mean? Would it mean that they had solved all problems of the plastic arts? No, because it makes no sense to talk of solutions without a clear understanding of the problems. It is rather like an ultra-Formalist philosopher of mathematics who believes that all mathematical theorems are just combinations and permutations of symbols, or that painting is merely the business of placing marks on a canvas.

Turing was a Formalist and tended to treat mathematics as a game without connection to the outside world. He avoided explicitly defining what intelligence really was, just as Formalism avoided asking what mathematics really was by reducing it to a system of formal rules. In the Turing model, thinking became the activity of shuffling abstract symbols; this might be described as not so much the ability to think as the ability to dream [18].

By the mid-twentieth century Formalism had become the official philosophy of mathematics, although most practicing mathematicians were still Platonists in that they believed they were discovering true facts about real mathematical objects. Formalism was linked to Logical Positivism, the philosophy of science that rose to dominance in the 1940s and 1950s, and which has lingered on in the absence of anything definite to replace it. Its goal was a unified science expressed in a formal logical language and with a single deductive method. In order to relate theory to experiment, rules were devised for the interpretation of results, rules of physical measurement, mass, length and time. Mathematics is viewed as the language in which scientific theory is formulated and enveloped, with no independent subject matter of its own.

The heritage of Frege, Russell and early Wittgenstein left a school of Analytical Philosophy in which the central problem is the analysis of meaning using the logical syntax of language. The philosophy of mathematics was identified with the study of logic and formal systems, making an account of its historical and pre-formal development an irrelevance [19].

In 1934 there was a revolution in the philosophy of science when Karl Popper proposed that scientific theories are not derived simply by inductive logic from experimental observations, but are invented hypotheses which are then subjected to critical analysis. A theory is scientific if it is capable of being tested and refuted—if it survives it attains some degree of credibility but can never be proved. In the 1960s Imre Lakatos decided to apply this approach to the philosophy of mathematics.

MATHEMATICS AS CULTURE

Lakatos' major work, *Proofs and Refutations,* describes a classroom dialogue [20]. The students are made to take the parts of various historical figures in mathematics as they try to find a final version of Euler's law $V - E + F = 2$ for solid polyhedra. During the resulting discussion, different pupils put forward different theories that they attempt to prove and disprove by argument and counter-examples. At the same time Lakatos details the corresponding historical events in a series of footnotes, showing the role that proof plays in the development of mathematics and the formation of concepts. Lakatos uses this representation of history to show that mathematical knowledge grows like natural science, by the continual criticism and correction of its theories. 'Proof' in this context does not mean the mechanical process by which theorems are derived from axioms; it is a method of explaining new ideas more fully, of justifying and elaborating them. Lakatos describes the use of proof and logical deduction in mathematical research as it is practiced every day by mathematicians. He uses this to show that the Formalist view of mathematics is an abstraction that is hardly to be found anywhere outside textbooks on symbolic logic. Lakatos argues that the dogmatic foundationist philosophies of mathematics are untenable because of their inability to accept the informal growth of mathematics as the basis of mathematical knowledge.

What gives mathematics its descriptive power is its close relationship to other areas of human thought—because it is consistent with our culturally defined beliefs [21]. Similarly, empirical science is seen to be successful simply because we are in a society which places high value on the areas in which the scientific method is appropriate. The search for solid foundations for mathematics in logic was like the need of a subculture to strengthen its own identity. After it was discovered that logic was not a unique theory, it became another branch of mathematics. Mathematical concepts are like cultural artifacts, continually expanding in a way that prevents any final definition or perfect rigour. The meaning of mathematical objects lies in the shared understanding of human beings, not in external reality. In this respect it is similar to an ideology, religion or art form; it is intelligible only in the context of human culture. Having said this, can we get an idea of what cultural or artistic values could be identified in a mathematical art?

MATHEMATICS AS COMPUTER ART

The only objects that can be studied visually are ones that can be 'constructed', that is, classes of mathematical objects of which an actual example can be constructed (in contrast to objects whose only reason for being is that it would be logically contradictory for them not to exist). Here then is a movement away from dialectical and existential mathematics, towards the concrete and algorithmic. Indeed, Lakatos describes his philosophy as 'quasi-empiricist' [22].

In mathematical research, graphics generally are used to explore the structure of an object and to reveal properties not so immediately apparent using other means. Any visually perceived regularities can then be followed up by more rigourous methods of study. One example of this is in the field of research into cellular automata [23]. To some mathematicians it seems inappropriate to make mathematical judgments based on graphical representations ('Pictures don't prove anything'). But it is strange to think that the very first proofs were prompted by geometric forms—Thales' theorem that a circle is bisected by its diameter is the first recorded, in about 600 BC, and it is difficult to see how he would have been inspired to form this concept without the stimulus of his diagrams. This intuitive certainty of the properties of the visual world seemed to justify the construction of the axiomatic system and the deductive method itself. It was appreciated by the ancient Greeks that some facts of number theory could be more easily proved by representation as geometrical figures [24]. Since then the reverse has tended to be the norm. Geometrical intuition came to be distrusted in the nineteenth century, partly due to the discovery of fractal 'monster' curves whose analytical properties seemed to defy geometrical sense [25]. These contentions were resolved by the re-definition of geometry using point sets in the 1930s, but by then the search for foundations in mathematics had shifted focus. It would be unfair, however, to blame this episode on any supposed inadequacies of perception rather than on the inability of analysis to model the human visual system.

Proof is only one tool whereby mathematicians progress in their understanding of the objects they study, and it is meaningless without regard to the current state of mathematical consciousness. There is no reason to devalue properties as being irrelevant to the aims of mathematics. This is to say that both mathematicians and artists have cause to be interested in graphical representations of the conceptual forms of mathematics. Graphics are used as a method of visual thinking similar to a designer sketching out his or her ideas; they are not just to communicate information.

There is now a tendency to view mathematical formulae as processes to simulate phenomena rather than to describe their structure explicitly. It is becoming clear that general laws to

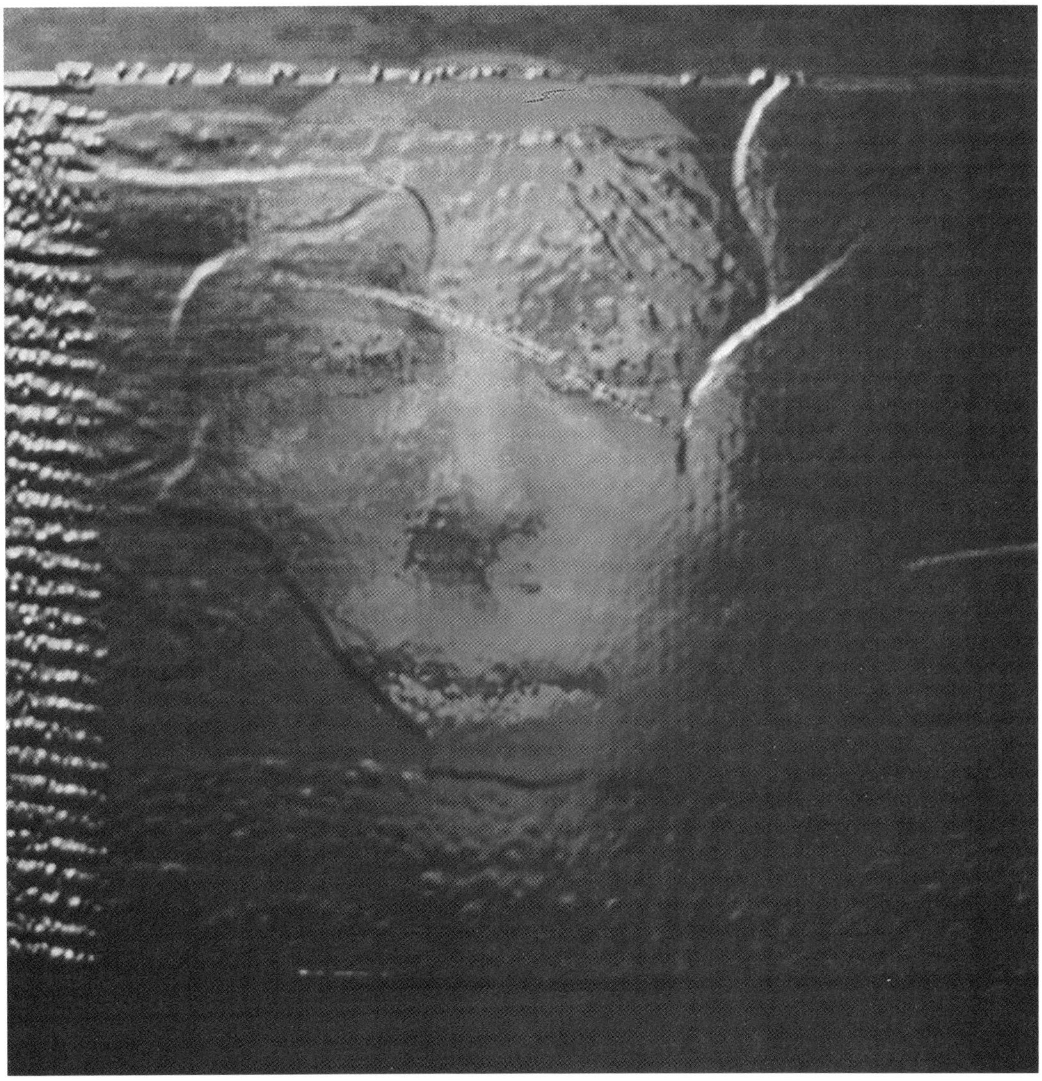

Fig. 5. Richard Wright, *Medusa.* Face Model by Keith Waters. Software: artist's own software in 'C'. Hardware: VAX 11/785, Ikon Framestore. Format: 35mm slide of computer-generated image, 1988. A nude from a pin-up magazine has been digitised and converted into a bump-map. It forms a stony relief over the plane of the screen in which there is seen the dispassionate reflection of a mask. This image might be the face of a spectator being confronted with the surface as a barrier, or an attempt by the computer to represent the environment external to the picture and build a more direct relationship with the world of humans.

describe the behaviour of many natural systems may not exist, and that they can only be studied by direct simulation [26]. Once the system has been constructed it can be studied as an object in its own right. This stresses the creative aspects of mathematics and the importance of using all humanity's perceptive faculties; it is a move away from analysis to synthesis. Systems with an unpredictable character might find more personal resonance in a spectator. But even with unpredictable dynamics, it would still take an act of creative perception to recognise their characteristics as significant or meaningful, rather than just autonomous facts. Fractal curves were around for over a century before their relevance was discovered (or created). It has been said that mathematics can generate 'unimaginable' forms, but these forms must be imbued with some personal relevance by their instigators in order to merit any attention at all.

There is no mathematics of art, only mathematics as art. Any mathematical model becomes the content of the artwork. It is used to create, and mathematics can form the subject of art by virtue of its function as an expression of human sensibilities. Mathematicians are free to build theories and to make pronouncements about them, but this activity is not arbitrary. Their development must satisfy some cognitive need, and it is in the wider context of such needs that the artist operates. Our humanistic definition of mathematics allows a more artistic evaluation of mathematical concerns—the quality of the existence of mathematical objects like numbers, the nature of mathematical truth.

Issues in the philosophy of mathematics can be generalised to the artistic arena. It is appropriate to subject the products of mathematical research to all the methods that are usually applied in order to come to terms with cultural artifacts like art, the tension between objectivity and subjectivity, their metaphorical meanings and the character of representational systems.

References

1. B. Russell, *The Principles of Mathematics* (Cambridge: Cambridge University Press, 1903).

2. J. Gips and G. Stiny, "An Investigation of Algorithmic Aesthetics", *Leonardo* **8**, 213–220 (1975).

3. C. Bouleau, *The Painter's Secret Geometry* (London: Thames and Hudson, 1963).

4. M. Baxandall, *Painting and Experience in Fifteenth Century Italy* (Oxford: Clarendon Press, 1972).

5. A.M. Noll, "The Digital Computer as a Creative Medium", *Bit International* **2**, 61 (1968).

6. H. Cohen, "Off the Shelf", *The Visual Computer* **2**, 191–194 (1988).

7. S.B. Torrance, "Philosophy and A.I.: Some Issues", in *The Mind and the Machine*, S.B. Torrance, ed. (Chichester: John Wiley and Sons) p. 16.

8. A.M. Turing, "Computing Machinery and Intelligence", *Mind* **59** (1950). Reprinted in *Minds and Machines*, A.R. Anderson, ed. (New Jersey: Prentice Hall, 1964).

9. J.P. Crutchfield, J.D. Farmer, N.H. Packard and R. Shaw, "Chaos", *Scientific American* (December 1986) pp. 38–49.

10. F. Dietrich, "The Computer: A Tool for Thought Experiments", *Leonardo* **20**, No. 4, 315–325 (1987).

11. J. Dieudonne, "The Work of Nicholas Bourbaki", *American Mathematical Monthly* **77**, 134–145 (1970).

12. A. Hill, "A View of Non-Figurative Art and Mathematics and an Analysis of a Structural Relief", *Leonardo* **10**, 7–12 (1977).

13. H.O. Peitgen and P.H. Richter, *Frontiers of Chaos*. Exh. Cat. (Bremen: University of Bremen, 1985).

14. P.M. Dirac, "The Evolution of the Physicist's Picture of Nature", in *Mathematics in the Modern World*, M. Kline, ed. (San Francisco: W.H. Freeman, 1968).

15. H. Hahn, "The Crisis in Intuition", in Kline, ed. [14].

16. P.J. Davis and R. Hersh, *The Mathematical Experience* (London: Penguin Books, 1983) pp. 330–338.

17. G. Rickey, *Constructivism: Origins and Evolution* (London: George Braziller, 1967).

18. A. Hodges, *Alan Turing: The Enigma* (London: Burnet Books, 1983) p. 425.

19. Davis and Hersh [16] p. 342.

20. I. Lakatos, *Proofs and Refutations*, J. Worral and E. Zahar, eds. (Cambridge: Cambridge University Press, 1976).

21. R.L. Wilder, *The Evolution of Mathematical Concepts* (Great Britain: Open University Press, 1978) p. 185.

22. I. Lakatos, "A Renaissance of Empiricism in the Philosophy of Mathematics?" in *Problems in the Philosophy of Mathematics*, I. Lakatos, ed. (Amsterdam: North-Holland, 1969) pp. 199–203.

23. T. Toffoli and N. Margolus, *Cellular Automata Machines* (London: MIT Press, 1987).

24. Wilder [21] p. 87.

25. Hahn [15].

26. S. Wolfram, "Computer Software in Science and Mathematics", *Scientific American* **251**, No. 3, 188-192 (September 1984).

Editor's Note: The reader is referred to Color Plate A No. 3 for an illustration by Richard Wright.

Orphics: Computer Graphics and the Shaping of Time with Color

Edward Zajec

ABSTRACT

In view of the unprecedented control and flexibility now offered by computers, the author discusses ideas and techniques for the fluid articulation of color in time and illustrates his concepts with recent work. Parallels with music and mathematics (fractals) are discussed concerning such musical practices as modulation and thematic transformation. The nature of dividual as opposed to individual forms is considered from the point of view of color dynamics and dimensional upgrades. Parallels with music and film are made concerning the nature of thematic dissolves. The emergence of a hypothetical language of light and sound (Orphics) is envisioned.

This paper is mainly about asking questions, not only in the narrower sense of exploring the computer as an image generator, but also in a wider context concerning the art-technology intersection seen as a field open to experiment for new codes of communication. I present some workable ideas and techniques for the fluid articulation of color and form in time. The focus is not on the choreography of objects in motion (animation), but rather on those as yet ambiguous transitional states where the individual becomes dividual, dimensions interpenetrate, motives dissolve into patterns, and the geometric blends with the organic. Some of these techniques, such as the idea of dimensional upgrades, relate to the visual fine arts and mathematics; others, like the ideas of thematic dissolves and transformations, straddle the media of music and film. The various subjects are illustrated by my discussion of a completed work titled *Chromas* and some newer developments. Overall, the main intention behind this work was to outline and perhaps formulate some codes for a hypothetical language of light and sound (Orphics).

THEMATIC TRANSFORMATION

The actual unfolding of the images in *Chromas* is based on the rhythms and sounds of *Seconda Sonata,* a composition for piano by Giampaolo Coral [1]. Coral is one of the few contemporary Italian composers who looked to the Vienna Schooi as a model, rather than upon the Italian or French musical traditions. However, as he is also an admirer of Pierre Boulez [2], one could say that at least in part Coral's music takes sight of Vienna through French eyes.

The structure of *Seconda Sonata* is summarized briefly as follows. The first part, which has an indication of "Mosso Nervoso", besides being a complete exposition of the serial space in its sequential and textural extensions, also embodies the rhythmic and thematic blueprint for the remaining three parts of the sonata. The second part, with a "Con Grande Liberta" indication, initially comes very close to tonality in its sonorities. It starts out softly while simultaneously building a tension which climaxes several times in a very dramatic conflagration of iterative chords. The third part, which has the indication of "Vivacissimo, Scherzando", is again an outline of the serial material, but this time given in a relentless succession of rising and descending contrapuntal arpeggios. The indication of "Mosso Frenetico" already hints at the character of the fourth part, which manages to retain a crisp exactness of pitch in spite of its extreme rhythmic complexity. Complexively, Coral's *Seconda Sonata* amply fulfills Schoenberg's [3] and Webern's [4] principal concern of deriving a whole composition from one central unifying idea.

This power to develop and manipulate a theme in time has no parallel in the visual arts. *Chromas* is an attempt to tackle this problem in terms of color and form. It opens with a simple motive, a set of crossed rays (Fig. 1, top row)—this motive is a variation of a Paul Klee watercolor titled *Eros* (1923)—and develops through a continuous thematic, chromatic and rhythmic reinterpretation of this central idea. The forming principle behind this development is not shape animation but thematic transformation. This approach is radically different from traditional animation—first, because the action is shaped in real time and, second, because the action no longer consists of figures moving on a background but of color motives fluidly dissolving into their constituent components and reappearing in different configurations. In this context, to animate means to orchestrate the flow of color passages in time, rather than to choreograph the motions of objects in space.

IMAGE FORMATION

The system underlying *Chromas* consists of two parts: a drawing part in which a static composition (plate) is organized and displayed on the screen, and a dynamic part in which a composition is performed in a complex of color changes.

The important features regarding the drawing part relate to the nature of the plates, which are composite and organized by level. They are composite in the sense that each plate consists of two juxtaposed images (transparencies). It is possible to display two transparencies concurrently on the screen and to layer and unlayer them in different modes (and, or, xor). They are organized by level, in the sense that the color coding of each transparency allows two levels of control. On the micro level, the elements are recursively configured on a diamond lattice according to a given series of 16 colors. On the macro level the elements are organized to display either the main theme or two variations: a moebius strip and a diamond (Fig. 1, top row). Changing the

Edward Zajec, Department of Art Media Studies, College of Visual and Performing Arts, Syracuse University, Syracuse, NY 13210, U.S.A.

Received 29 April 1988.

0024-094X/88 $3.00+0.00

series provides different chromatic or intervallic interpretations of the same transparency on a micro level (Fig. 1, columns 1 and 3), just as the overlay of different pairs of transparencies, for instance, the rays with the moebius or the moebius with the diamonds, provides thematic variations on a macro level (Fig. 2).

In more recent work I have been experimenting by juxtaposing fractal [5] configurations on the uniform lattice transparencies. By way of the midpoint displacement algorithm [6] it is possible to calculate a random fractal surface [7] with a relatively small amount of computation. The method consists of recursive subdivisions of a given surface, adding random irregularities at smaller and smaller scales. The resulting surface can be presented in a volumetric projection and shaded using the 16 colors of the aforementioned series (Fig. 3), or it can be flattened to the plane by viewing it from a zenith position, in which case it can function as a transparency, featuring a distinctly unique micro element configuration. (Fig. 4)

The introduction of random fractal surfaces opens up a new domain and a rich source of thematic variation possibilities. A point of note here is that the fractal midpoint displacement method causes artifacts in the form of creases along grid lines. These defects are particularly noticeable in Fig. 4, where they appear in the form of marked vertical and horizontal discontinuities in texture and gradient. Artifacts are probably most annoying to someone striving for a naturalistic surface effect, but they are a welcome feature in my work. Their gridlike character provides a common link between the fractal and Euclidean geometries, as can be seen from the overlay in Fig. 5.

There are prominent examples in twentieth-century art of such attempts at bridging the natural with the geometric. A few painters in particular made a concentrated effort towards resolving this dichotomy. Paul Klee's entire pictorial opus as well as his theoretical writings [8] testify to this concern. M. C. Escher's mastery of molding what are otherwise organic forms into subtle geometric tessellations is well known [9]. Perhaps less known, but becoming increasingly more relevant, are Pavel Filonov's dense, magmatic compositions, where the larger, naturalistic forms are simultaneously structured and atomized by a relentless swirl of suprematist-inspired microforms [10, 11].

Similarly, with fractals we now have a means of visualizing nature's more complex phenomena and, more importantly, the possibility of visualizing the morphological rules shaping these phenomena. By choice, we can visualize just these rules in themselves without necessarily intending to simulate or emulate a natural object. This is the point where the two geometries meet and can interplay with the greatest freedom. Furthermore, by blurring the distinction between figure and background and by opting for color

Fig. 1. Nine plates are shown from a computer-generated work titled *Chromas*. The whole composition, lasting 20 minutes, is derived from one central theme: a set of crossed rays and two variations (top row). The individual form (theme) is shown in different chromatic and intervallic arrangements in the first and third columns. The upgrade of elementary units into larger units is shown in the central column. The theme can be seen as an individual form if taken as a composition of shapes, or as a dividual, variable entity if considered in its color breakdown (any of the nine plates).

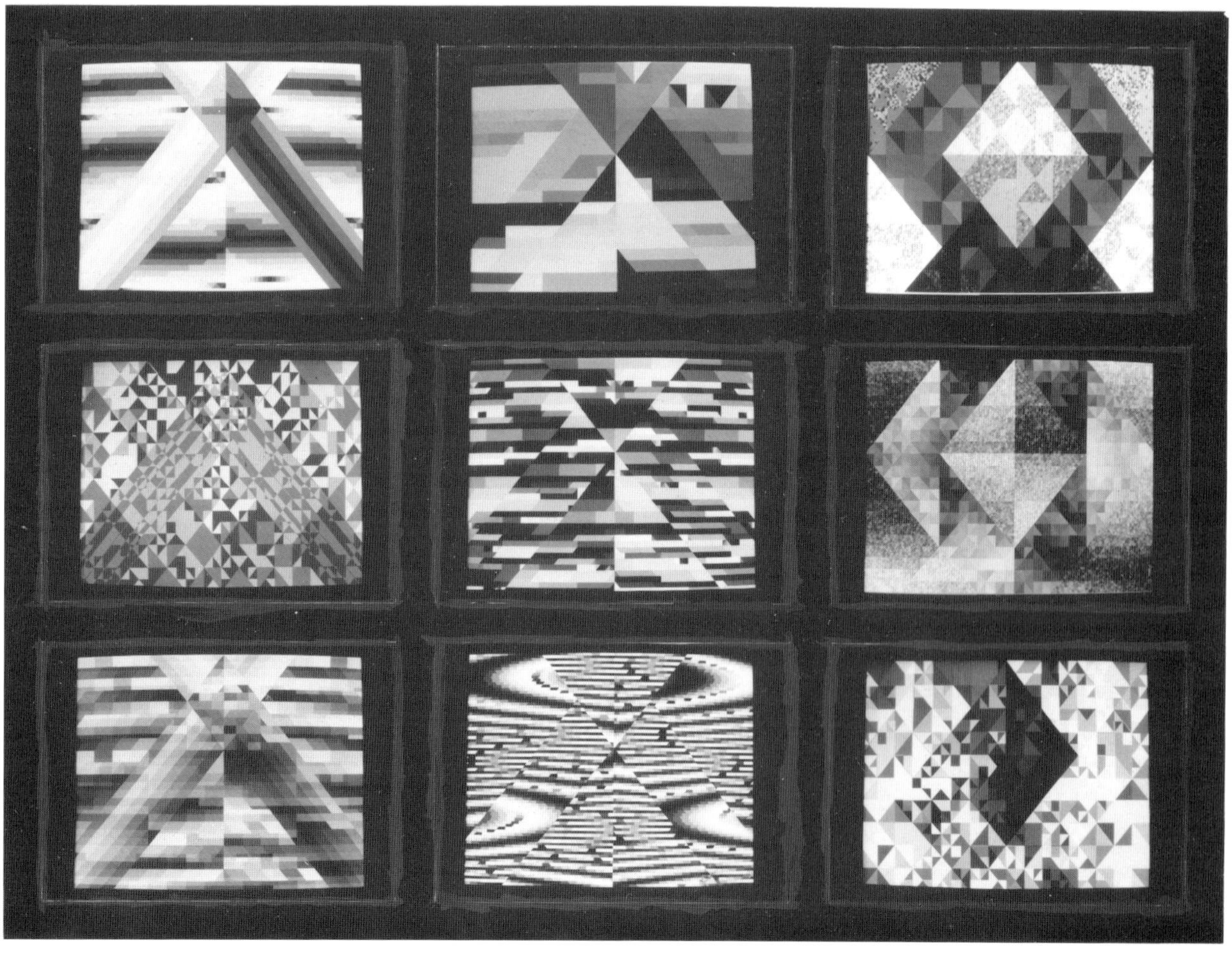

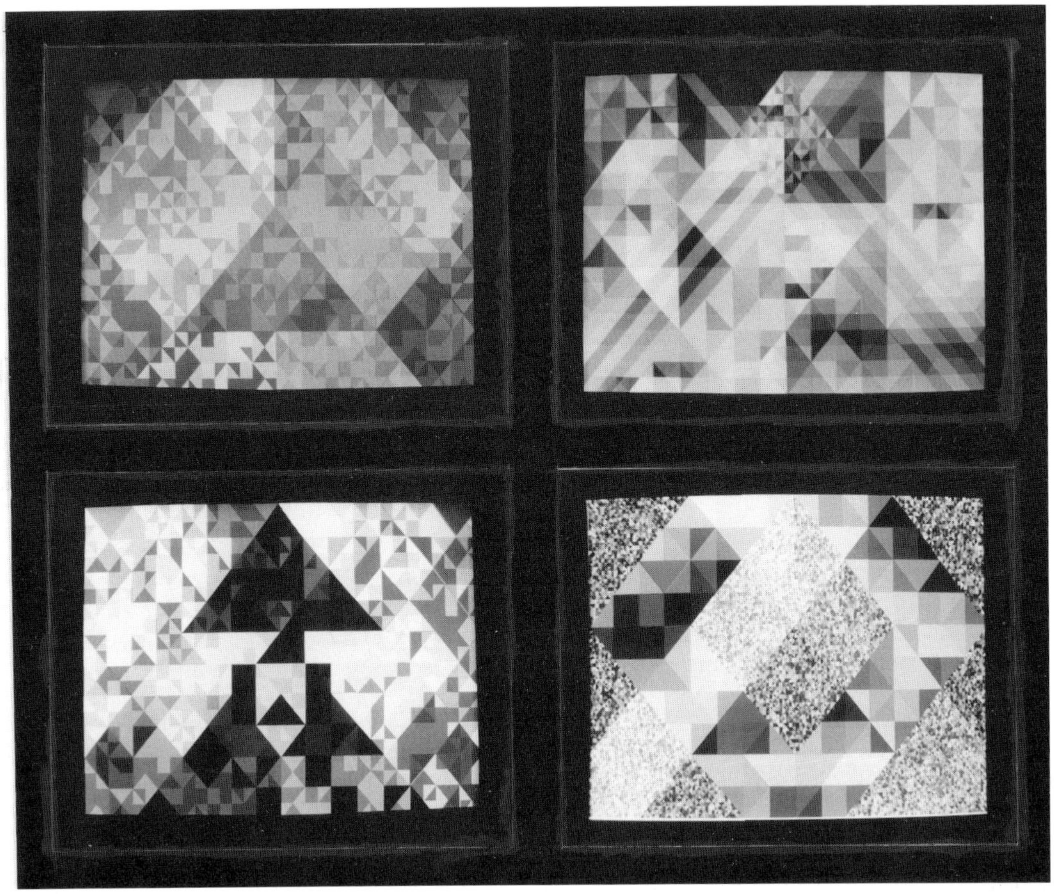

Fig. 2. Variations on an individual (theme) level are illustrated. Each of the four plates consists of a juxtaposition of two different transparencies. The transparencies can be intertwined in theme and in color, providing unlimited variation and development possibilities.

progression as a forming principle, it becomes possible to orchestrate large numbers of elements, each of which can be individually controlled like the notes in a musical composition. This is where the computer becomes essential by providing the speed and control needed to process and interrelate very large quantities of information.

DIMENSIONAL UPGRADES

The concept of dimensional upgrade bears some analogy to polyphony in music. It implies a transition from one voice, for instance a linear entity such as a series of colors, to many voices—that is, the extension of the series to the visual plane. What matters is having some rules to ensure that a particular series retains its signature, its unique progression of colors, not only in linear form but in a planar setting as well [12]. By using these rules in a recursive fashion it is possible to project a particular series on the plane at any desired upgrade level. Thus a dimensional upgrade does not involve spatial transformations such as the projection of an object from a planar to a volumetric dimension, but provides a structural framework for related changes in magnitude as well as in organization.

Contemplating such possibilities of controlled action and duration on the plane is evidence of the meagerness of our color-structuring principles in comparison to music. While the spatial aspects of color dimensionality have been codified systematically, the temporal aspects of color remain almost completely uncharted. In traditional animation, for instance, synchrony of action is determined by the unfolding story line. Beyond this, the objects follow their individual trajectories, bound in color and shape only by the constraints of naturalistic representation. In other art forms such as dance or ballet, synchronized movement does assume a prominent role. Nevertheless, color remains of marginal importance and it is not intrinsic to the action. Only in some festive or ceremonial situations, when huge crowds are gathered, can we see synchrony of action unfolding in terms of color, for instance, when one section of the performing ensemble in a stadium simultaneously displays one or another side of its multi-color uniforms. Note that each of the cited examples involves the human figure in action. It should be clear by now that the dichotomy here is not abstract versus realistic, or even two-dimensional versus three-dimensional, but dividual versus individual forms. This central antithesis starts with Cézanne, but it was systematically (and yet poetically) outlined for the first time by Klee in his theoretical writings:

> The question as to whether a thing is dividual or individual is decided by the criterion of indefinite extension or definite measure. For where there is indefinite extension, arbitrary division can be made without changing the structural style. But where an individual has definite measure, nothing can be added or subtracted without changing it into another individual [13].

He follows with a concrete example:

> For example, the fish seen as an individual, breaks down into head, body, tail, and fins. Seen dividually it breaks down into scales and the structure of the fins. The individual proportion is determined by the relation between head, body, tail and fins and can not be essentially changed; in any case, nothing can be omitted. A few scales may be missing from the body, but we cannot do without the head, the eye, or any of the fins. The dividual structure of this fish is variable in so far as it matters much less whether it has 330 or 350 scales than whether or not it has a head. Thus the distinction between dividual and individual involves a value judgment. But is the

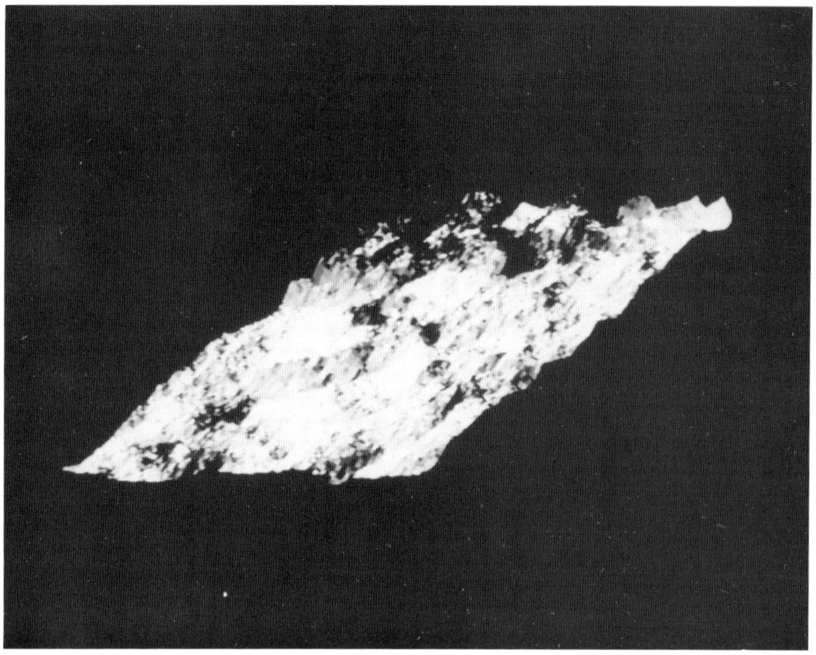

Fig. 3. Computer-generated image showing a volumetric projection of a shaded random fractal surface.

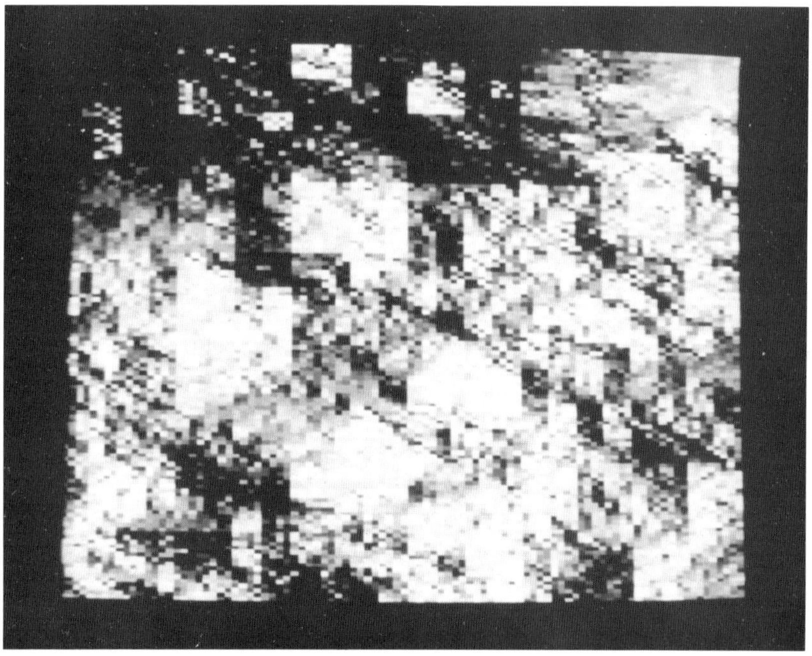

Fig. 4. The same surface used in Fig. 3, flattened to the plane and seen as a transparency featuring a unique microcomponent configuration.

fish always an individual? No, not when it occurs in large numbers, not when "it's teeming with fish", as the saying goes. The concepts lower (or dividual) and higher (or individual) are not absolute but mutually dependent; when I broaden the conceptual field, I create a higher perceptible whole. It is good that in the course of time a certain elasticity has been achieved in regards to limits [14].

The beauty of the above passage lies in Klee's depth of insight for having resolved and unified such disparate and, in many ways, mutually exclusive concepts as measure, proportion and dimension, as well as the broader dichotomies of representation and non-representation under the wider concept of limit. When it comes to establishing limits, be it in art or science, it becomes a matter of choice, of 'value judgment' as Klee says, on how we look upon the world. These then are matters that go beyond mere perceptual or formal issues but involve a definite conceptual stance.

Dimensional upgrades fit into this picture as structuring devices determining the arrangement of elements in the formation of intermediate or higher dividual units (Fig. 1, column 2). For instance, expanding a musical motive consisting of a few notes into a phrase is a well-defined process in music. Nothing similar exists in a visual context. Besides, the very idea of a musical motive as a dynamic (dividual) nucleus charged with developmental potential stands sharply in contrast to a visual motive, which has been traditionally perceived as a fixed ornamental unit recurring at given intervals. In *Chromas,* dimensional upgrades are instrumental in the organization of the primary color constituents, the basic motive being a series of 16 colors. The main theme (Fig. 1, top row) can then be seen either as an individual form if taken as a composition of shapes, or as a dividual, variable entity if considered in its color breakdown.

I hope that the above discussion may contribute to clearing up some long-standing ambiguities regarding the role of color in some of the more established time-based art forms such as film, video and animation, as compared to the role of color in what I here call Orphics. In view of this and in light of the dividual-individual antithesis discussed above, I would venture to say that if color can assume the emotional-expressive prominence that sound has for music, we will have to learn how to shape time in terms of dividual rather than individual forms.

THEMATIC DISSOLVES

Thematic dissolves are based on the possibility of displaying two transparencies concurrently on the screen and of layering and unlayering them at will. Technically, a dissolve is an operation that allows a smooth transition from one digital image to another. The action proper is given by color mapping, a technique that allows altering the color of an image rather than the image itself [15]. For now, the advantage of color mapping is in the high speed of the action, which occurs in real time, meaning that the color changes can be seen immediately, at the same time the program is run.

The key to this layered ensemble in *Chromas* is the color climate (which is predominantly blue) and four sets of plates (six to twelve plates per set) to fit the parts of *Seconda Sonata*. Each set is matched with a distinct color atmosphere and has a unique visual texture congruent to the musical character of the part in question. The color vicissitudes for each part are played out in a basic juxtaposition of two 16-color series, one for each transparency forming a plate. The two series, in combination, group the microcomponents into various flow patterns and create rising or descending color sequences in different sections of the plate. Sometimes the microcomponents are grouped carefully and synchronized to highlight a particular section of a theme or to blur the same section into a shimmering textural mass, as is the case for certain passages in the first and second part of the sonata. At other times, the microcomponents are arranged so as to activate the whole screen, a situation that matches the relentless succession of arpeggios in the third part. Within this part the dissolves from one transparency to the other are not arrived at directly, but in a way that creates a tension between partial advances and partial recessions from each of the two transparencies. The frantic rhythm of the fourth part is visually reflected in a contrasted distribution of the microcomponents, which produces ascending sequences and immediate shifts in the opposite direction, changing intermittently from a rising to a falling motion.

The thematic character of the dissolves discussed above comes to light through the action of the underlying transparency weaving itself into the upper transparency's action (Color Plate B No. 2). The first transparency demands that the second be adjusted to suit it in color and design, and vice versa. Within this framework it is then possible to intertwine and unify different interlocking shapes that reveal hidden patterns as well as unexpected color harmonies that are not part of either transparency but surface only for the duration of a thematic dissolve (see Fig. 2)

The result of all this has similar although distinct precedents in two well-established art forms. The action of a thematic dissolve is in certain ways equivalent to the effect of a filmic dissolve where, given two scenes, we see one blending into the other. The same action is also a close visual parallel to the musical practice of modulation, where changes from key to key are accomplished smoothly, as a continuous process.

What distinguishes a thematic dissolve from both precedents is the nature of the visual flow and the duration of its enactment. Given the composite nature of the image and the separate micro-macro levels of control, it is possible, as shown above, to plan the two images in such a way that they intertwine in color and design to form a third image, visible only for the duration of the dissolve (see Fig. 2).

Furthermore, when one of the transparencies is a random fractal surface (see Fig. 5) the thematic interplay takes on completely novel dimensions that are particularly promising in a temporal context. The stochastic distribution of tones in a random surface creates a unique rhythmic entity, which is in subtle contrast to the rhythms of the more linear geometric progressions.

Thus the effect of a thematic dissolve merges both the filmic and the musical aspects into a single action, since the transition from one transparency to another involves structural changes that closely interrelate motive development with color modulation. In this sense, a thematic dissolve transcends the level of being a mere technique and becomes a new mode of visual communication, one that intrinsically merges the fluid qualities of sound with the radiant nature of light.

Discussion and Conclusion

Chromas' complexive duration is 20 minutes. It took 3 years to complete, from 1984 to 1987. Its present form leaves room for much improvement, partially because of the color distortion and the loss of resolution that occurs in transferring the images to videotape. Metaphorically, as it stands, *Chromas* is an elaborate study of an idea but not yet a finished picture. Nevertheless, I hope its worth will be judged not in terms of broadcast quality, but rather by the extent to which it might stand as a possible, even if archaic, model for the embodiment of a sound experience in visual terms.

Coral's *Seconda Sonata,* with its brilliant score, provided an excellent lead and at the same time a formidable challenge. By this I mean that the most difficult obstacle in shaping a color counterpart to *Seconda Sonata* was the disorienting lack of any frame of reference. Clearly, my intent was not to mimic the sound impulses one on one or to design a visual choreography to underscore the musical developments. I was looking for some kind of focus, a guiding principle on which to base an active autonomous visual line of development. I found it in the con-

Fig. 5. A plate showing an overlay of the random surface transparency (Fig. 4) with a regular, geometric transparency. The thematic interplay between the two images reveals new possibilities that are particularly promising in a temporal context.

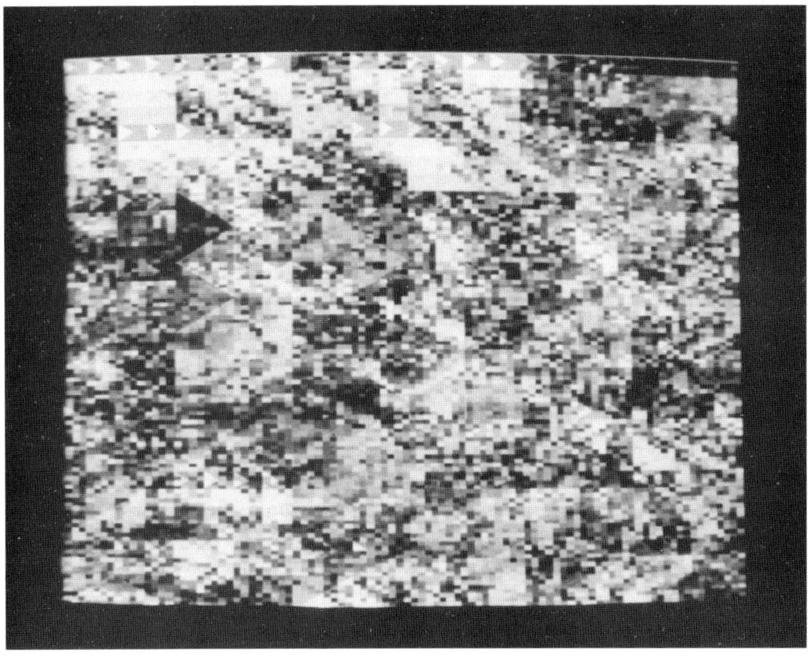

cept-practice of thematic transformation. A central theme—being dividual—is built from the same color material as the smallest detail and set off in time and space in such a way that this kinship is immediately visible, closely relating the parts to the larger plan. Dimensional upgrades and thematic dissolves make sense only within this thematic perspective; indeed, they are ramifications of this basic idea. Furthermore, I strongly suspect that this type of composition is only possible in terms of dividual forms. My feeling is that a theory of dividual color-time articulation might prove to be that long-sought common ground bridging the two art forms and might provide the right focus in the ongoing search for new codes of visual communication.

This is implicitly a long-term development. We have much to learn from music, from the works of Klee, Filonov and others, and from some recent mathematical inventions, fractals in particular, but also from cellular automata and formal grammars. Obviously, this development is beyond the reach of any individual artist, and one that does not bear an immediate impact on the cultural and sociopolitical spheres, but only filters gradually into the information mainstream as new attitudes change existing conventions. With the computer we now have acquired the technical means to control time and light as music controls time and sound. In contrast to music, however, we do not have a theoretical body of rules and conventions that would allow us to communicate visual ideas unrelated to narrative and figurative representations within a temporal framework. What we do have, however, is a huge amount of experimental work attempting to bridge the sound-image-time relation [16], going back at least a few centuries, and which seems presently to be on the verge of reaching critical mass [17].

Clearly, a new art category is emerging. Efforts to name it or just to distinguish it from both traditional and computer animation have resulted in various names: abstract film [18, 19], vision in motion [20], audio-kinetic art [21], graphic music [22], color music [23], visual music [24], digital harmony [25] and, more recently, abstract dynamic visual art [26]. In seeking vividness of expression, musicians of all ages have alluded to the color of sound, as painters have told of the sound of color. Glancing backwards, I find that, for some reason or another, the name of Orpheus has been a frequent choice in indicating works tinged by metaphors of this kind. A good example, coming from the music side, is Stravinsky's and Balanchine's ballet *Orpheus*. On the opposite side, the French poet Apollinaire coined the term "Orphism" to celebrate the reappearance of color in a new art movement and in homage to Robert and Sonya Delaunay's pure color explosions in the otherwise-monochrome realm of abstract cubism. Following this tradition and in renewed homage to the ancient bard for having stolen the secrets of the gods, I here propose the appellation: Orphics [27].

References and Notes

1. G. Coral, *Seconda Sonata per Pianoforte* (Milan: Edizioni Curci, 1980).

2. P. Boulez, "Technology and the Composer", *Leonardo* **11**, 59–62 (1978).

3. A. Schoenberg, *Analisi e Pratica Musicale* (Turin: Einaudi Editore, 1974).

4. A. Webern, *Verso la Nuovo Musica* (Milan: Edizioni Bompiani, 1963).

5. B. Mandelbrot, *The Fractal Geometry of Nature* (New York: Freeman, 1982).

6. Alain Fournier, D. Fussel and L. Carpenter, "Computer Renderings of Stochastic Models", *Communications of the ACM* **25**, 371–384 (1982).

7. G. Miller, "The Definition and Rendering of Terrain Maps", SIGGRAPH 86, *Computer Graphics* **16**, 39–48 (1986).

8. P. Klee, *The Thinking Eye*, J. Spiller, ed. (New York: Wittenborn, 1964).

9. *M.C. Escher, Art and Science*, H.S.M. Coxeter et al., eds. (Amsterdam: North Holland, 1986).

10. P. Filonov, "The Ideology of Analytical Art and the Principle of Craftedness", *Leonardo* **10**, 227–232 (1977).

11. J. Bowlt, "Pavel Filonov", *Studio International* **186**, 30–36 (1973).

12. E. Zajec, "Computer Imaging and the Musicality of Dimensional Upgrades on the 2D Plane", *Proceedings of the 6th International Conference on Computers and Humanities* (1983) pp. 763–771.

13. Klee [8] p. 237.

14. Klee [8] p. 264.

15. E. Zajec, "Computer Graphics: Color Based Time", *Leonardo* **19**, 39–43 (1986).

16. *Leonardo* **20**, No. 2, Special Issue (1987). This special issue dedicated to visual art, sound, music and technology carries a wealth of information and a complete bibliography of articles published to date in *Leonardo* on this subject.

17. G. Youngblood, *Expanded Cinema* (New York: Dutton, 1970).

18. D. Curtis, *Experimental Cinema* (New York: Dell, 1971).

19. M. Le Grice, *Abstract Film and Beyond* (Cambridge, MA: MIT Press, 1981).

20. L. Moholy-Nagy, *Vision in Motion* (Chicago: Theobald, 1946).

21. F. Malina and P. Schaeffer, "A Conversation on Concrete Music and Kinetic Art", *Leonardo* **5**, 255–260 (1972).

22. H. Franke, "Graphic Music", in *Artist and Computer*, R. Leavitt, ed. (Morristown, NJ: Creative Computing, Harmony Press, 1976.)

23. E.H. Gombrich, *The Sense of Order* (Ithaca, NY: Cornell University Press, 1979) pp. 285–305.

24. Title of "The International Visual Music Festival" held at the University of California at Los Angeles (UCLA), June 1982.

25. J. Whitney, *Digital Harmony* (New York: Byte Books, McGraw Hill, 1980).

26. H. Clauser, "Towards a Dynamic Generative Computer Art", *Leonardo* **21**, No. 2, 115–122 (1988).

27. This proposition is a spin-off from discussions held at an ad hoc meeting on "Abstract Dynamic Art" held at the Industrial Research Institute in New York City on 20 November 1987. The meeting was organized by Hank Clauser in an attempt to bring together a number of interested people to confront and define the issues regarding a new visual art form variously indicated during the meeting as Visual Harmony, Motion Graphics, Abstract Dynamic Visual Art (ADVA), Dynamics Visual Music and Systematic Synthetic Moving Imagery. It was a useful beginning although no agreement was reached. The participants were musicians Warren Lehr and Reynold Weidenaar; computer scientists Ken Knowlton (also artist) and Herbert Maisel; visual artists Hank Clauser (also engineer), Larry Cuba, Jeffrey Horowitz, Margot Lovejoy, George Shortess (also psychologist), Bill Yarrington and Edward Zajec.

MIXED MEDIA STUDIES IN TACTILITY: AN ALTERNATIVE TO 'COMPUTER ART'

Anna Campbell Bliss, 27 University Street, Salt Lake City, Utah 84102, U.S.A.

Not all of us are to the computer born but some look to it as an important area of technology to explore in relation to our own direction in art.

Early work on the computer came at a time when I was examining color in its smallest visible dimension [1]. I created a triangular grid with intersections omitted to study form and develop it by the optical mixing of colors. It was very much related to what takes place with the mixing of threads in weaving. I used layers of the grid in different colors. I edited each one to omit portions of the grid, gradually developing an image by the changes in color. Serigraphy was the printing medium.

It became apparent that this was an area for which the computer was ideally suited. One could draw repetitive units quickly and visualize composite layers before printing. One can be certain of the artistic impact of an experimental serigraph only after the last printing.

Comparisons of hand-drawn positives with the computer-generated drawings did reveal one disturbing quality. The computer images are so perfect that they appear 'dry' or sterile. They lack the tactile qualities of hand drawing, those subtle inflections that appear even when work is geometric.

Generating textures by combinations of lines and simple forms can be endlessly fascinating on the computer but I found it difficult to prevent patterns from forming until I introduced a random number generator. This is an area that can be explored much further. Printing on handmade Japanese paper, Inomachi Nacre, added another dimension of tactility.

One limitation occurs in the printing medium itself. As one prints each layer of color in serigraphy the areas tend to be flat and frontal although one can modify the tonal quality and the density of paint to some extent. Etching and lithography are more flexible media for a softer quality of color.

In more recent studies, airbrush applied in several layers provided a balance to the computer drawings in small editions. For larger editions it would be more practical to modify the screen. Further experimentation with the computer may provide the solution.

Reference

1. Equipment used: Interdata 70 mainframe with DOS operating system and Calcomp 936 plotter. The program was lost when the university updated equipment; it is continuing now on an Amiga 2000 personal computer.

Fig. 1. Anna Campbell Bliss. (top) *Mirage*, screenprint and airbrush, 22 × 30 in, using computer-generated screen, 1985. Printed on Mangani Incisioni paper. (bottom) *Chan Chan*, screenprint, 18 × 26 in, 1981. The hand-drawn positive suggested a computer solution. Printed on Vicksburg Vellum cover stock.

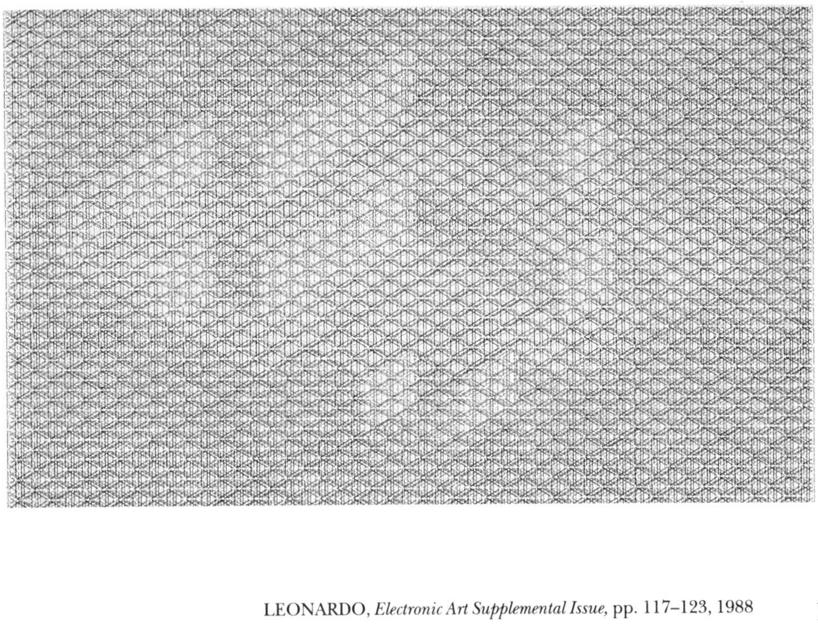

Pergamon Press plc. Printed in Great Britain.
0024-094X/88 $3.00+0.00

Art Communication and the WELL

John Coate, Whole Earth Lectronic Link (WELL), 27 Gate Five Road, Sausalito, CA 94965, U.S.A.

A computer conference network is more than a bundle of online utilities. It is a place where people meet. Because the connections are through the phone lines, it no longer matters where in the world the users are. There does not have to be any one 'art capital', because art can exist 'virtually' everyplace.

There has always been and there will always be the need for artists to talk. Art is about communication and relationships. As more artists use computers to make art, so will the art community of the world use computers to communicate about art. The computer is an amazingly obliging communications tool.

There are several reasons why computer conferencing makes sense for artists' communication. The cost of computers falls every year. Individuals are more able to work on and complete projects on their own. Each year there is more computing power in the hands of the individual artist. This means there are more possibilities, more variations, more methods, more ways to do things. As computer and other media technology rapidly change, the need is strong to keep up with developments. A computer network is a place where artists can talk with programmers who make the computer tools.

The discussions are ongoing. They are there for whoever wants to read or contribute. In that way they have a life of their own. Developments in technologies spawn new ideas that in turn stimulate and feed the discussion. Relationships form. Collaborations result. Growth happens.

Public discussions are non-elitist. A person's words are what count—not one's title or resume. Ideas stand on their own. Computer conferencing is fast. The message is available right now. When a number of colleagues or acquaintances are logged in at the same time it becomes a comfortable 'hangout'. Users throw out ideas, argue, talk shop, get funny. I agree that artists should write about their work, but I also think conferencing on a computer network makes it possible for ideas to move quickly between people. It provides a readily available brain trust that helps the more formal processes of writing.

If there is a need for "an organization to coordinate events, establish standard groups . . . connecting workers in the electronic arts who have shared concerns", as stated by *Leonardo* editor Roger Malina, then there is a need for that organization to meet regularly online.

The online meeting place has to be accessible from anywhere. It has to handle several users at once. There need to be public discussion areas and private exchange. The cost has to be low so that participation is possible by a wide range of groups and individuals. File transfer facilities are essential and there ought to be access to USENET and UUCP.

Besides being efficient, the network must have a comfortable 'atmosphere' that encourages participation. Atmosphere in that sense is very important. The right ambience online has a strong leavening effect on the thinking of the group.

I submit that the WELL is exemplary of the kind of online network that should be home to such a diverse and far-flung group because it fits all the criteria listed above [1].

Reference

1. The WELL is a computer conferencing system that can be reached anywhere around the world. The ACEN Bulletin Boards are accessible on the WELL and are addressed to artists; they provide a number of resources, discussion boards as well as on-line art-making. Contact Whole Earth Lectronic Link, 27 Gate Five Road, Sausalito, CA 94965, U.S.A.

New Art Online

Carl Loeffler, Executive Director, Art Com, P.O. Box 3123 Rincon Annex, San Francisco, CA 94119-3123, U.S.A.

Imagine an artist-run organization that ran the programming gamut from maintaining a magazine and gallery for video and performance art, to international distribution of art books and video, to broadcast TV, distribution of video art on VHS cassettes and laserdiscs, and pioneering of artist-based computer software, electronic publishing and electronic exhibition spaces in art. Such an organization is Art Com/La Mamelle, Inc.

Founded in 1975 under the name of La Mamelle, Inc., this organization has contributed to the seminal basis of artists' publications, computer art, conceptual art, correspondence art, performance art, television art, video art and more. In 1980 the name Art Com, which stands for art and communication, was adopted by the organization. Art Com is oriented toward the growing information and telecommunication environment.

In 1986 Art Com launched its latest pioneering effort, the Art Com Electronic Network (ACEN) [1]. The project offers three tiers of operation: the electronic publishing of *Art Com* and *Parallelogramme* magazines; electronic bulletin boards and mail systems; and an 'electronic exhibition space'. ACEN also features the release of special creative online projects such as 'The First Meeting of the Satie Society', authored by John Cage, and a host of other works written by artists.

Why ACEN?

The ACEN project is sponsored by Art Com/La Mamelle, Inc., a first-generation artist-run organization in the United States. It remains important to indicate that the seminal artist-run organizations were once called 'alternative spaces' and that many of them, especially in Canada, were started by visual artists who came into contact with one another through the medium of correspondence art, the sending of artworks through the postal system to create an international community or 'network', as it once was called. The early alternative spaces were true alternatives in terms of attitude and the programming presented. In those days performance and video, for example, had not yet made their way into the mainstream as they have today. Communication among artists served an important purpose in terms of the formation of contemporary art movements and artist-run organizations.

ACEN supports a new form of correspondence art called electronic mail. And just as correspondence art served to launch the alternative spaces, so too is electronic mail serving to launch new spaces for the continuation of experimental art and ways to present it.

ACEN staff members and participating artists exchange electronic communications on a regular basis, consisting of feedback and criticism of their creative projects, assistance with project programming, online theater works and good solid fun.

ACEN has created the atmosphere of an online 'media lab'. As in the case of experimental labs, ideas are tested, projects developed, and the best are brought out into the world. In this case another division of the Art Com organization has been founded, Art Com Software, which is dedicated to the creation and distribution of software by artists for personal and mainframe computer applications.

So as in the 1970s, when the 'best' of the efforts of artist-run organizations served to inspire and propel experimentation in art, the Art Com Electronic Network is oriented toward these means. Where the new art experimentation is headed and what the end conclusions will be remain to be discovered, but they are limited only by the imaginations of artists.

Reference

1. ACEN is carried by the Whole Earth Lectronic Link (WELL) and can be reached at (415) 332-6106 (modem); for long-range access in the U.S. contact PC Pursuit (800) 336-0437 (voice); international access to 70 countries is available via Tymnet (800) 336-0149 (voice). For further information contact Art Com (415) 431-7524 (voice).

Image Processing: An Under-Utilized Resource for Computer Art

Robert Mallary, University of Massachusetts, Amherst, MA 01003, U.S.A.

The image-capture and transformational techniques associated with current image processing, developed primarily for scientific and technical applications, have important implications for raster-graphic and other kinds of computer art. Existing paint systems, in focusing on the emulation of painting and other traditional media, largely neglect these and other computer-specific capabilities. Standard image processing operations are identified and related to existing and potential applications in computer art, while the concept of image processing is expanded to include transformational operations specific to art. A unique 'vernacular' approach to image processing for art is illustrated by examples of the author's recent work with the Atari 1040 ST personal computer and its inexpensive low-resolution graphics package called Degas-Elite.

Image Processing

Harold J. McWhinnie, Department of Design, Department of Curriculum and Instruction, University of Maryland, College Park, MD, U.S.A.

Like many artists and designers, I, too, had for a long time resisted involvement with the personal computer. I had conceived of the microcomputer as being too impersonal, remote, non-creative and certainly less than 'user-friendly'. I did not view it as a possible design tool.

In the summer of 1985, due to an IBM project, my own attitude towards the computer took a dramatic change. I became fascinated with this new technology. I began to face the 'green screen' with a new openness and with a spirit of adventure. The IBM project was called HANDY, and it involved the use of a new authoring language for the development of interactive teaching lessons for use with adults as well as children. I began to create a series of lessons exploring various aspects of color and motion in relation to general principles of basic design. This new IBM language will soon be on the educational market. It will be called 'experimental playmaker language' and, as the title implies, it is designed so that the teacher can write a script, create graphic images and call upon video disk, audio tapes and music to create a drama or event upon the screen.

As my own design work with this new language began to evolve, I saw almost unlimited possibilities for the artist and designer. The computer became my electronic sketchbook. It became an essential artistic vehicle in which I could state an idea, vary the idea, try all possible combinations of color, texture, and movement and finally produce an almost endless series of variations upon the basic theme. The output has assumed many forms: a series of slides that can be used as the basis for paintings or design; a sequence of images that, when combined with text, can serve as the basis for book and story illustrations; films or video tapes that can exist as their own creative statements. Output can be stored on hard or soft disk files. With a color printer one can produce output as hard copy. For some the computer has become an image processor.

Has the machine taken away my personal and creative vision? Has the 'life of the studio' with the smell of the paint, the taste of the clay and plaster dust come to be replaced by the blinks, beeps and shakes of my electronic images? Am I a slave of the machine? I think not. For me, the personal computer has become yet another tool. It, like the camera, can extend the perceptual limits of the artistic imagination. With it the artist can function at yet another level of reality and awareness.

The Department of Housing and Design at the University of Maryland as a part of the general university FULCRUM grant has opened a laboratory for computer-assisted design. Since the fall of 1985 I have completed three basic projects using the IBM HANDY software:

1. *Adventures in Color.* My first project was an exploration of the use of color in design. This is a sequence of four interactive lessons on color that are designed to be used with young children. These units introduce the child to the general world of color and to what can be done with the limited range of colors in my program. HANDY provides 16 colors that can be combined in foreground as well as background sequences. Those 16 colors can provide an almost endless set of color variations.

The children can watch the entire sequence at the micro-computer, and instructional programs can be developed as questions and answers about color are recorded. In this mode, the micro-computer can function much like the teaching machine of the 1960s. A unit using computer color images will be incorporated into the department's core course on the subject of color in the summer of 1986.

2. *Totem Figures Dance.* This sequence of lessons explores movement in design and how an almost unlimited set of variations on figure and ground relationships might be created. Slides are now being used for a series of colored pencil drawings that will be exhibited in 1986-87 in a one-person show.

3. *Garden of the Golden Section.* In this series of 10 sequences both color and motion are used. These sequences, which include poetry and music, construct a series of stories about the adventures of color in the Garden. The Garden of the Golden Section is a program that creates a

series of images that are varied according to design principles and elements.

Theoretical Statement Concerning Computer/Robotic Paintings

Joseph Nechvatal, 143 Ludlow Street #14, New York, NY 10002, U.S.A.

Electronic overload has smashed the narrow limits of assigned meaning. A doorway has opened. We have the power to shape our own meaning. We have the tools and the weapons for our own personal, magical transformation. With deconstruction, re-contextualization, non-conformity and destruction we take symbolic control over given hierarchical systems. This allows us some simulated personal dignity in light of our actual relative helplessness. The resilience of the human spirit is at stake. It is not a question of demystification. It is the task of absorbing, annihilating and desublimating. We turn it around and in effect reject the dialectic of the herd's mass meaning. We take control. We take the power as social conditioning is liquidated, and we are liberated from the constraints imposed upon us by mass/pop cultural patterns. We destroy and return the tired concepts of the dominant culture in the creation of freer thought. We are the autonomous subject making free choices.

The computer is the social organizer of production in the 1980s. It frees us from the psychic condition of the nineteenth-century factory worker, which has been the universal condition of the twentieth century. The computer's work is free from sweaty compromise, self-doubt and human fallibility. Computer/robotic paintings address this faith in the infallibility of the computer technology that is rapidly changing all society. Through the theme of control and release, they confront the potentially totalitarian technology of the digital society which symbolizes and appeals to both external order (efficiency, hierarchy, security) and internal order (tidy compartmentalization, strict logic). Information technology is meant to make all of society run on time through control under the guise of benevolent connectedness. The mode and manifestation of this control is the fragmentation of collectivity and the isolation of the individual, the tendency to identify people with machines, and the parallel tendency of individuals to internalize this implicit description of themselves and therefore behave as machines. Computers are compulsive to people in that they offer a form of apparently total control, yet the user is also compelled into a form of submission to the limitations and constraints that the computer's design imposes. The user willingly accepts the tyrannies of the computer because computers traditionally provide a model of clarity. However, they also traditionally limit what can be expressed and transmitted, thereby standardizing knowledge and inference through efficiency, planning, rationalization and managerialism. The great problem of today is to attain a balance and wholeness in our civilization so we can command the machine we have created instead of becoming its helpless accomplice and passive victim. We must leave room for an answering response, of an indeterminable kind, in order to allow for participation in the creative act. We must avoid a world in which whatever seems obscure and inward, whatever cannot be reduced to a quantity, is thereby treated as unreal—a world that is impersonal.

Creators must place themselves above the level of the mechanical through the integration of art and technique. They must resist the quantifying of life in the interests of power, prestige and profit and resist the fashion of idealizing mechanical forces. Computer/robotic paintings symbolize a society that has freed itself from total rational utilitarianism through the symbolism of poetry in technology and by linking the primordial horrors to the technology of today. They are in great measure a reaction against the organizational harness of the post-industrial society, the technocratic mind view. By detaching the signifier from the signified, the subjective spectacle of ecstatic spirituality is simulated. Since spirituality cannot be signified (no signifying unit refers to spirituality, which is a mode of being, of feeling), the images of authority in the technetronic society can be used against themselves and thereby keep us from the curse of single vision/new sleep. Western cultures' privileged reason has divided the world into the rational, calculating 'objective' and the intuitive 'subjective'. A holistic culture would balance reason and intuition and challenge the dualism of science and art at the level of production. The potential impact of computer technology as an integrator of art and science is well known. Yet if we contrast the computer's compulsion for order with the primal retentions in the social unconscious, a dreamier, more subjective use of the computer revolution becomes obviously needed. Today everything is spread over, blown apart, simultaneously known, shared and forgotten. No media mysticism can relieve our bloated media millennium. Inner lives have become impoverished through the mechanization of the overdisciplined orbital society due to lack of spontaneity. The trend to an information-centered society threatens to collapse the categorical mind of fixed images into a monoworld of abstract, overloaded imagery spread. This unconscious conspiracy of heady technological freedom promises to transform human-machine relationships for better or worse.

Appendix: Technical Information

Four consecutive processes are at work in the production of computer/robotic-assisted acrylic-on-canvas paintings:

1. An electronic laser scans and digitizes 2D information (drawing and/or photograph).
2. The information is computerized.
3. The computer magnifies information to project the imagery out into a larger distance for perceptual reading, thereby publicizing the inner workings (the inner space) of the work of art. This creates a long-range painting for public consumption.
4. Robotic arms carry out the orders of the computer, applying the acrylic pigment to canvas with computer precision.

Cybernetic Jewelry

Vernon Reed, 4407 Sinclair Avenue, Austin, TX 78756, U.S.A.

Historically, jewelry has been a form of adornment and expression existing in the three dimensions of space and defined by configurations of some kind of hardware, whether gold, plastic or, more recently, integrated circuits. The advent of the single chip CMOS microcomputer allows for a radical new possibility: cybernetic jewelry, in which the esthetic entity is defined largely in terms of software instructions executing in real time and controlling an appropriate output device.

I originally conceived of this new kind of jewelry in 1974. At that time the requisite microcomputer technology was not available, but I was immediately fascinated by the then-emerging liquid crystal display (LCD) technology, which I saw as the perfect output device. I learned to make LCDs, and until 1985 created jewels incorporating them along with pattern-generating drivers made with integrated circuits. This series of jewels made extensive use of the dimension of time, but was still totally defined by the physical configuration of the hardware.

The jewelry I have been creating since 1985 is truly cybernetic, in the sense that it makes use of on-board computer intelligence to create the timing and patterns in the LCD output panels. Each piece contains a Motorola 1468705G2 or 68HC805 CMOS microcomputer, which runs a program contained in internal read-only memory. These programs are written in a proprietary language optimized for controlling LCDs and allow patterns to be computed and displayed or simply pulled from memory as existing patterns. The on-chip memory of these micros is exceedingly tiny, so the code must be very compact.

The application of computer technology to jewelry allows us to make some very interesting observations about the esthetic entity which comprises the jewel. Most of the visual weight of the jewel is carried by the time-dependent changes in the LCD panel, and these changes are in turn controlled by the program running on the internal microcomputer. This means that the appearance of the piece can be rapidly and extensively modified without altering the hardware in any way, simply by changing the software instructions which are controlling the output. Conversely, the same software could be run on a different computer without that being evident in any way from observing the movement in the LCD. This divorcing of the jewelry entity from its hardware base is the essence of cybernetic jewelry and provides the basis for an entirely new jewelry esthetic appropriate for the dawning information age. The cybernetic feedback and control mechanisms that characterize all computer systems can be used to create jewelry objects that become bionic coding devices uniquely responsive to a multi-dimensional information environment.

Extended Musical Interface with the Human Nervous System: Assessment and Prospectus

David Rosenboom, Center for Contemporary Music, Mills College, Oakland, CA 94613, U.S.A.

Many decades ago American composer Charles Ives speculated that eventually music would be made through a direct connection of the human brain to devices for sound production. Subsequently, the pioneering physiologist Adrian reported on experiencing a translation of the human electroencephalogram (EEG) into audio signals. Decades later, composers Lucier, Teitelbaum, Rosenboom and others produced major works of music with EEG and other bioelectronic signals. Since then many have expanded these applications into the kinetic arts as well. The author's work in biofeedback and the arts, begun 20 years ago, is experiencing a revival due to the fact that advances in technology now permit realization of musical concepts in performance which depend on complex real-time analysis of EEG signals, previously achievable only with cumbersome, non-real-time, laboratory-bound methods.

In this paper the author provides an assessment of current techniques and prospects for further development of extended musical interface with the human nervous system. Topics discussed include the following:

- the musical cognitive significance of stimulus-bound EEG events measurable in real-time
- the relationship of these events to aspects of musical formal perception, such as feature extraction and temporal gestalt (TG) boundary detection in musical holarchic structures
- methods of circumventing inherent limitations on the information bandwidth of EEG signals
- application of event-related potentials (ERPs) to the building of formal musical holarchies in real-time
- paradigms for algorithmic improvisation using these signals
- traversing a musical knowledge base by driving an inference engine with cognitively significant ERPs
- the EEG analysis expert system—application of AI techniques
- comparison of the uses of EEG information in making decisions on relatively high levels of musical structure versus direct, low-level event feedback in musical textures—the applications of each approach
- techniques from the study of chaos dynamics applied to analysis of long-term EEG waveform patterns—their significance for music
- applications of recent advances in measurement technology, such as use of the SQUID (Super-cooled QUantum Interference Device) enabling EEG detection without direct electrical contact with the subject, super-conducting electrodes, etc.
- speculations on possible extensions of these ideas in the conception of musical instruments, performance and education
- EEG-to-MIDI—some direct mapping ideas for an input device.

Finally, a configuration of hardware and software currently being used to develop the author's work-in-progress, *On Being Invisible II*, will be described. This includes use of a composition and performance language, HMSL (Hierarchical Music Specification Language), to implement real-time composition strategies in response to EEG analyses; a software synthesis and signal processing environment, Cmix, for non-real-time mapping of these events to precomposed sound tracks; and EEG analysis software—all running on a Macintosh II outfitted with data acquisition and MIDI interface hardware and a NuBuss interface to the Digisound-16 audio conversion system.

DYNAMIC ON-LINE ARCHITECTURE

Frederick John Truck, The Electric Bank, 4225 University, Des Moines, IA 50311, U.S.A.

The Present Direction

On-line publishing is a format resembling traditional print media in its intent to achieve wide-spread accessibility and distribution. In the print medium, writers and editors generate textual content, which is then processed by a technical staff. The finished product is then distributed via the post or other shipping channels. On-line publishing makes use of writers, editors and artists, but there the similarities end, because this dynamic medium also incorporates environmental tools for generating and distributing information.

An environmental tool is a feature built into the telecommunications software that encourages users to participate in a certain way. Here is a list of typical environmental tools found in on-line services: the user's personal area or home directory; the bulletin board service, where topics are discussed or debated; conferencing areas where groups can converse simultaneously; electronic mail for private communication; electronic malls and financial services, for commercial transactions; file and language libraries, for those who program and those interested in public domain software; and databases and reference, for those who need to know.

Typically, on-line services isolate these environments from each other. For example, there is no channel for information to flow from the bulletin board service to the database. By forcing normally separate on-line tools to collide, artists can create an electronic publishing format in which material furnished by writers and editors in the database can be supplemented or contrasted with texts and artwork from bulletin board service users on a daily, or even hourly, basis.

Future Directions

Two environmental tools offered by most on-line services offer intriguing possibilities for artists involved in electronic publishing: integration of (1) file and language libraries and (2) electronic malls:

1. The following aspects of file and language libraries are germane to artists' concerns: (a) Increasingly, artists are not content to use commercially available software, but are programming it themselves. Offering languages on-line encourages artists to experiment, without investing in a language first. (b) Software that is of value to artists, but may be expensive to purchase, can be distributed on-line. Artificial intelligence programs for artists, such as retrieval applications for on-line use or expert systems that aid artists in design choices, can be used to make on-line artworks.

2. The electronic mall provides a place for artists to sell their work and a place for users to buy it, within a single information package. It extends the power of the on-line medium and gives the artist economic clout.

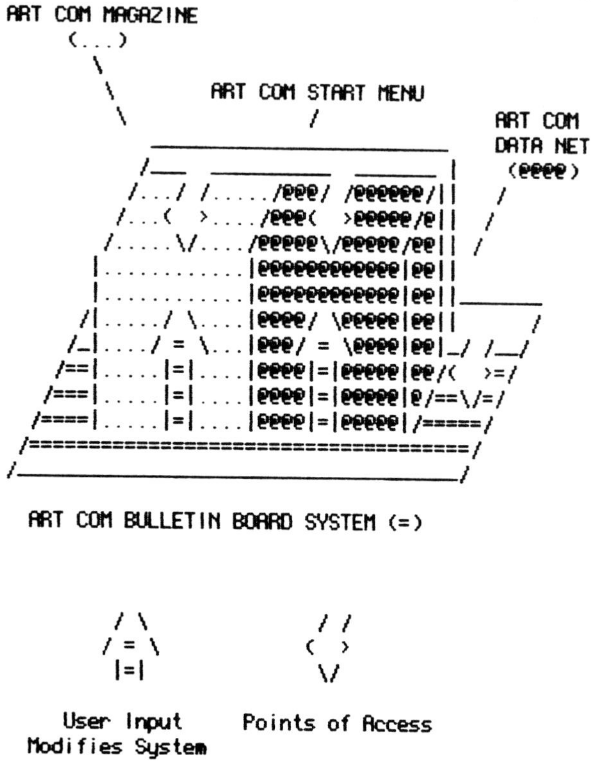

Fig. 2. Fred Truck, bulletin board system (BBS) used in designing Art Com Electronic Network (ACEN).

Conclusion

Emphasis here has been on making use of existing, and currently in place, telecommunications software rather than setting up one's own on-line service. This approach not only saves the expense of investing in equipment and software development, but allows artists to exploit this unique advantage: once the file is uploaded, or the word is typed, distribution is instantaneous—publication and distribution are likewise.

PATT_PROC1: A COMPUTER-ASSISTED COMPOSITION PROGRAM

Phil Winsor, Center for Experimental Music and Intermedia (CEMI), North Texas State University, Denton, TX 76203, U.S.A.

Overview

Patt_Proc1, in use at North Texas State University (NTSU) Center for Experimental Music and Intermedia since 1985, is an interactive pattern/process-oriented composition program originally written in BASIC and subsequently translated into C. At its inception, the program was designed to output scores (from 1 to 20 voices) exhibiting characteristics commonly found in so-called minimal music: the application of conceptual, operational and physical loop processes to user-input or algorithmically composed melodic material. As the program evolved, however, it became clear that the constituent routines could be used to produce compositions that were anything but minimal in effect by allowing maximum flexibility in relation to input data and internal parameter limits.

Presently, the program has grown large enough to require interactive execution in two segments: Part 1, the generation and storage of a chordal, scalar or synthetic pitch gamut file for

```
100 NOTELIST FLUTE
110 P  D#0   B3   C#4   A2  G#3  C1   F0  D5  A#4  C2   F#4  G3
120 P  G3    F#4  C2    A#4 D5   F0   C1  G#3 A2   C#4  B3   D0
130 R  1/2   3/16 1/16  1/5 1/5  1/5  2/7 2/7 1/4  1/8  1/3  1/3
140 R  3/16  1/16 1/5   1/5 1/5  2/7  2/7 1/4 1/8  1/3  1/3  3/8
150 A  10    40   22    94  66   12   19  82  54   52   50   19
160 A  66    12   19    82  54   52   50  19  66   12   19   82
170 V  94    66   12    19  82   54   52  50  19   66   12   19
180 V  82    54   52    50  19   66   12  19  82   94   66   12
190 T  23    98   55    21  12   45   45  65  75   87   98   12
200 T  21    12   45    45  65   75   87  98  12   21   12   45
210 END /*FLUTE*/
```

Fig. 3. Phil Winsor, sample Patt_Proc1 program output.

later retrieval by the score generation routines; and Part 2, the melody-writing, embellishment and loop-processing segment that controls the note derivation, element cycling and parameter coordination of the resultant instrumental voices. In broad terms, Patt_Proc1 now functions as a general compositional utility program with a pattern-processing bias—that is, features have been added that allow the user wide latitude in terms of musical style and the transformation of motivic material.

Program Function

Part 1 of the program offers three methods of generating a background chord/scale/gamut file: manual input of a series of articulated aggregates that may be retrieved individually; application by the computer of a user-determined interval-class sieve to generate gamut pitch elements; and octave-repeating or non-octave-repeating pitch scales/gamuts built (low to high registers over the total chromatic) from a user-input interval set. Thus, an entire set of registrated background materials for melody derivation and elaboration in program Part 2 may be generated in a single execution of Part 1. Naturally, such usage requires a degree of planning prior to the interactive computer session; in practice, some composers choose to build their source file by concatenating shorter program runs or by alternating runs of Part 1 and Part 2.

Part 2 of the program retrieves the chords/scales/gamuts filed in Part 1, then prompts the user to enter the number of coordinated score voices and the preferred method of assigning part pitch ranges (which may overlap, interlock or share a common range). At this juncture the program invokes the melody writing routine once for each constituent voice and once for each component chord/scale/gamut of the piece. During execution of the routine the user enters formative specifications chosen from the following procedures:

- method of melodic derivation from chordfile: serial, random-order distribution of available pitches, or minimum/maximum interval choice sieve applied to pitches in current chord/gamut
- occurrence probability weights for rests, number of notes to be embellished and type of embellishment to be selected from four available ornaments
- rhythmic complexity level (ranging from uniform pulse to multiple beat-subdivision/micropulse regrouping) assigned to the derived pitch sequence
- type of loop process to be applied (there are three choices: accretions to a melodic nucleus; subtractions from the total sequence; and constant length, metrically justified, element rotation (prime or retrograde order)
- specific parameters to be affected by selected loop process: pitch, rhythm, articulation, volume and/or timbre
- number of iterations over which the selected loop process is to take place.

Program Output Form

After all orchestral voices have been composed, Patt_Proc1 compiles a defined (five parameters) alphanumeric notelist score in Script Music Language, a standard text file format that may be read by micros or ported for performance to synthesizers such as the Synclavier digital instrument. For each notelist (voice), data for five parameters are written in block form as in Fig. 3.

Previous Compositional Uses

The author has composed several pieces using Patt_Proc1, including *Dulcimer Dream* for amplified piano (presented at the 1987 ICMC in Urbana, Illinois), *Dervish #2* for Synclavier, and *Les Chemins des Nuages* for dancer, projections and Synclavier. A number of NTSU graduate students in computer music have also produced stylistically diverse works with the program.

Headquarters
Theodosia Ferguson
Executive Director
I.S.A.S.T.
2020 Milvia Street
Berkeley, CA 94704
U.S.A.
Phone: 415-845-8306

Secretariat
Heide Scheiter-Rohland
Membership Manager
I.S.A.S.T.
8000 Westpark Drive, Suite 400
McLean, VA 22102
U.S.A.
Phone: 703-790-1745

European Office
c/o Mrs. Marjorie Malina
Leonardo
8 rue Émile Dunois
92100 Boulogne-sur-Seine
France

I.S.A.S.T.

The International Society for the Arts, Sciences and Technology is a non-profit organization founded in 1981 for professional artists, scientists, engineers and others interested in the contemporary arts. The Society, through its projects and services, seeks to encourage the interaction of art, science and technology. The Society's activities include the following:

Publication of Educational and Scholarly Materials

The International Journal *Leonardo* is the Society's official journal. Published quarterly, *Leonardo* is the leading international forum on the interaction of art, science and technology.

The Society's *Bulletin,* published as the International News and Opportunities section of *Leonardo,* provides a survey of services and resources of potential interest to members. An annual Directory of Members and Resources is also published.

The Society's electronic bulletin boards, FINEART Forum and F.A.S.T., provide rapid dissemination of timely information.

Awards and Other Assistance

The Society awards medals and prizes to honor those encouraging the synthesis of the contemporary arts, science and technology.

Frank J. Malina–*Leonardo* Prize
1985 Gyorgy Kepes
1986 Nicolas Schöffer
1987 Max Bill

Coler-Maxwell Medal for Excellence
1987 Rudolf Arnheim
Otto Piene

New Horizons Award for Innovation
1986 Evelyn Edelson-Rosenberg
1987 Jean-Marc Philippe

Sponsorship of Competitions

I.S.A.S.T. sponsored a Computer Art Competition for the cover of the International Journal *Mathematics and Computers with Applications.*

I.S.A.S.T is co-sponsoring Project 2001 for a monument to celebrate the start of the third millennium.

Collaboration with other Organizations

The Society publishes Special Issues and Supplements in collaboration with other organizations:

Special Issue 16–3, 1983 Psychology and the Arts
Special Issue 18–4, 1985 Jacob Bronowski: A Retrospective
Special Issue 20–2, 1987 Visual Art, Sound, Music and Technology
Special Issue 20–4, 1988 Art of the Future—The Future of Art. In Commemoration of Frank J. Malina

Forthcoming

Special Issues: Holography and Art, Biology and Art, Art and Telecommunications, Art and Technology Lessons for the Classroom.

Associate Membership in I.S.A.S.T.

Associate membership in I.S.A.S.T. costs $35.00 and is open to professionals in the arts, sciences and technology. To apply for associate membership send a check for $35.00 to: I.S.A.S.T., 8000 Westpark Drive, Suite 400, McLean, VA 22102, U.S.A.

Membership benefits include: subscription to *Leonardo;* participation in competitions sponsored by I.S.A.S.T.; reduced-rate advertising in *Leonardo*; activity reports published in the I.S.A.S.T. Bulletin; and access to the Society's Newsletter.

I.S.A.S.T. Board of Directors

LEONARDO

SUPPLEMENTAL ISSUE

ELECTRONIC ART

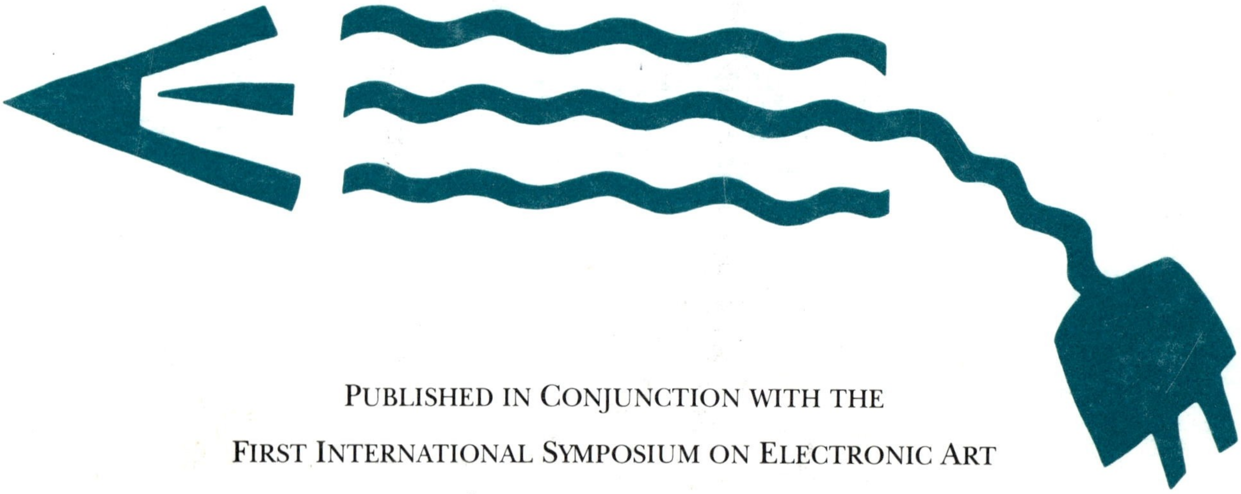

PUBLISHED IN CONJUNCTION WITH THE

FIRST INTERNATIONAL SYMPOSIUM ON ELECTRONIC ART

27–30 SEPTEMBER 1988

THE NETHERLANDS

ORGANIZED BY THE FOUNDATION FOR CREATIVE COMPUTER APPLICATIONS (SCCA)

AND

THE CENTER FOR ART, MEDIA & TECHNOLOGY OF THE

UTRECHT ACADEMY OF ARTS